Low-Intensity Practice with Children, Young People and Families

Low-Intensity Practice with Children, Young People and Families

Edited by
Catherine Gallop, Peter Fonagy & Rob Kidney

§ Sage

1 Oliver's Yard
55 City Road
London EC1Y 1SP

2455 Teller Road
Thousand Oaks, California 91320

Unit No 323-333, Third Floor, F-Block
International Trade Tower Nehru Place
New Delhi – 110 019

8 Marina View Suite 43-053
Asia Square Tower 1
Singapore 018960

Editor: Susannah Trefgarne
Editorial Assistant: Esmé Sawyer
Production Editor: Gourav Kumar
Copyeditor: Mary Dalton
Proofreader: Derek Markham
Indexer: KnowledgeWorks Global Ltd
Marketing Manager: Anca Dunavete
Cover Design: Wendy Scott
Typeset by KnowledgeWorks Global Ltd
Printed in the UK

© Editorial arrangement Catherine Gallop, Peter Fonagy and Rob Kidney 2023
Chapter 1 © Catherine Gallop and Peter Fonagy 2023
Chapter 2 © Jonathan Parker and Helen Barker 2023
Chapter 3 © Laura Raymen 2023
Chapter 4 © Hannah Vickery 2023
Chapter 5 © Markku Wood and Mike Turnbull 2023
Chapter 6 © Alex Boyd 2023
Chapter 7 © Kirsty Roberts and Annette MacKinley 2023
Chapter 8 © Laura Pass and Shirley Reynolds 2023
Chapter 9 © Sarah Holland 2023
Chapter 10 © Chelsie Smith and Rosie Jones 2023
Chapter 11 © Rob Kidney 2023
Chapter 12 © Kate Phillips and Philip C. Kendall 2023
Chapter 13 © Gary O'Reilly 2023
Chapter 14 © Julia Butler 2023
Chapter 15 © Mark Kime 2023
Chapter 16 © Chloe Chessell, Gemma Halliday and Cathy Creswell 2023
Chapter 17 © Jonathan Parker and Hollie Gay 2023
Chapter 18 © Kirsty Roberts and Jonathan Parker 2023
Chapter 19 © Lealah Hewitt-Johns 2023
Chapter 20 © Indiana Montaque 2023
Chapter 21 © Sadie Williams, Susanna Payne, Carolyn Edwards and Jessica Richardson 2023

Apart from any fair dealing for the purposes of research, private study, or criticism or review, as permitted under the Copyright, Designs and Patents Act, 1988, this publication may not be reproduced, stored or transmitted in any form, or by any means, without the prior permission in writing of the publisher, or in the case of reprographic reproduction, in accordance with the terms of licences issued by the Copyright Licensing Agency. Enquiries concerning reproduction outside those terms should be sent to the publisher.

Library of Congress Control Number: 2023932841

British Library Cataloguing in Publication data

A catalogue record for this book is available from the British Library

ISBN 978-1-5297-9296-6
ISBN 978-1-5297-9295-9 (pbk)

At Sage we take sustainability seriously. Most of our products are printed in the UK using responsibly sourced papers and boards. When we print overseas we ensure sustainable papers are used as measured by the Paper Chain Project grading system. We undertake an annual audit to monitor our sustainability.

Contents

List of Figures and Tables	*viii*
About the Editors	*xi*
About the Authors	*xii*
Preface	*xviii*
Acknowledgements	*xxi*

PART 1: CONTEXT AND VALUES | **1**

1. Context and Development | 2
    Catherine Gallop and Peter Fonagy

2. Values and Practice | 14
    Jonathan Parker and Helen Barker

PART 2: LOW-INTENSITY CYP ASSESSMENT AND KEY PRACTICE CONSIDERATIONS | **29**

3. Assessment in Low-Intensity Practice | 30
    Laura Raymen

4. Risk Assessment and Management | 53
    Hannah Vickery (née Whitney)

5. Overview of Low-Intensity Interventions, the Evidence Base and Treatment Planning | 66
    Markku Wood and Mike Turnbull

vi | LOW-INTENSITY PRACTICE WITH CYP AND FAMILIES

6. Creativity and Adaptation within CYP Low-Intensity Practice 81
Alex Boyd

7. Key Tips and Working with Common Difficulties 93
Kirsty Roberts and Annette MacKinley

PART 3: LOW-INTENSITY CYP INTERVENTIONS **103**

8. Brief Behavioural Activation (Brief BA) 104
Laura Pass and Shirley Reynolds

9. Exposure and Habituation 117
Sarah Holland

10. Cognitive Restructuring 130
Chelsie Smith and Rosie Jones

11. Behavioural Experiments 144
Rob Kidney

12. Brief Coping Cat 162
Kate Phillips and Philip C. Kendall

13. Pesky gNATs: A CBT Computer Game for Young People 175
Gary O'Reilly

14. Lifestyle Management Intervention 191
Julia Butler

15. Behavioural Problems and Parenting 207
Mark Kime

16. Brief Guided Parent-Delivered CBT for Child Anxiety 223
Chloe Chessell, Gemma Halliday, and Cathy Creswell

PART 4: PROFESSIONAL ISSUES AND SERVICE IMPLICATIONS **239**

17. Service Implementation and Evaluation 240
Jonathan Parker and Hollie Gay

18. Supervision of Low-Intensity Practice with Children and Young People 251
Kirsty Roberts and Jonathan Parker

19.	Adaptations to working with Children and Young People with Neurodiversity *Lealah Hewitt-Johns*	261
20.	Inclusive Practice *Indiana Montaque*	272
21.	Developing Meta-Competencies in Low-Intensity Practice *Sadie Williams, Susanna Payne, Carolyn Edwards and Jessica Richardson*	281
Index		291

List of Figures and Tables

Figures

Figure 2.1	The Ingredients of Evidence-Based Practice	16
Figure 3.1	Structure of a low-intensity assessment session	32
Figure 3.2	Theo's presenting Descriptive Formulation	39
Figure 3.3	The COM-B model of Behaviour	49
Figure 5.1	Low-intensity intervention map	69
Figure 5.2	Summary of Theo's RCADS scores	75
Figure 6.0	Example Crib Sheet	83
Figure 6.1	An example of a body map	85
Figure 6.2	Using thought bubbles and simple drawings can help elicit thoughts	86
Figure 8.1	The Brief BA cycle (Pass & Reynolds, 2020)	105
Figure 9.1	Descriptive formulation diagram of Elna's anxiety	120
Figure 9.2	Elna's exposure hierarchy, known as her 'fear ladder'	121
Figure 9.3	An illustration of a CYP's anxiety levels associated with repeated avoidance and a prolonged exposure task	122
Figure 9.4	Habituation of anxiety over time during three repeated exposure exercises	123
Figure 9.5	Elna's exposure exercise. Anxiety level is recorded at three time periods on a scale of 0–10	125
Figure 10.1	Theo's Descriptive Formulation Diagram	133
Figure 10.2	Three-part thought record	135

LIST OF FIGURES AND TABLES | ix

Figure 10.3	Chris's completed three-part thought record	136
Figure 10.4	Example of thought challenging using the five-part thought record with Chris	140
Figure 11.1	Characters Zee and Tao, who illustrate the stages of Behavioural Experiments	149
Figure 11.2	Diagram to show the therapeutic model	151
Figure 11.3	Zee's concerns	152
Figure 11.4	Tao's concerns	153
Figure 11.5	Tao and Zee considering their step 1 thoughts	154
Figure 11.6	Zee and Tao identify their step 3 predictions	157
Figure 13.1	Level structure	177
Figure 13.2	Elna (left) and Theo's (right) in game completion of the revised children's anxiety and depression scale game level one	179
Figure 13.3	Example from gNAT gallery	183
Figure 13.4	Example gNAT Trap	184
Figure 13.5	gNAT Swatting example	186
Figure 14.1	Elna's descriptive formulation diagram	195
Figure 14.2	Elna's mum's descriptive formulation diagram	196
Figure 14.3	Elna's sleep diary extract week 1	198
Figure 14.4	Theo's descriptive formulation diagram	201
Figure 15.1	The Thoughts, Feelings and Behaviour Cycle	212
Figure 15.2	The 'What about behaviours' activity Session 1	213
Figure 15.3	Home practice feedback review from the LI CBT parenting workbook	213
Figure 15.4	Example of time-out to calm down routine	220
Figure 16.1	Handout 2, part 1: Tigger or situation for Elna's anxiety	229
Figure 16.2	Handout 2, part 2: Elna's anxiety cycle	230
Figure 16.3	Handout 2, Full Version, Elna's anxiety cycle	231
Figure 16.4	Handout 8: Elna's Step-By-Step Plan	234
Figure 17.1	Regional CWP Evaluation Summary (2017 – 2021)	248
Figure 18.1	Typical Inclusions within a Low-Intensity Supervision Contract	254

Tables

| Table 2.1 | Examples of Referral Suitability for Low-Intensity Practice with CYP and Families | 21 |
| Table 3.1 | Routine Outcome Measures (ROMs): Minimum data set for low-intensity assessment | 42 |

Table 4.1	Areas and example questions covered in risk assessments	58
Table 4.2	Clinical example of FINDIE areas and answers	60
Table 4.3	Clinical example of an ABC chart to explore the function of Lina's self-harm punching objects behaviour	61
Table 11.1	The steps to complete a behavioural experiment	150
Table 11.2	Worksheet part 1 applied to Zee	153
Table 11.3	Worksheet part 1 applied to Chris	154
Table 11.4	Worksheet part 2 applied to Zee	155
Table 11.5	Worksheet part 2 applied to Chris	155
Table 11.6	Illustration of Zee's step 3 predictions completed on the worksheet	157
Table 11.7	Illustration of Chris's step 3 predictions completed on the worksheet	158
Table 11.8	Illustration of Zee's step 5 learning completed on the worksheet	159
Table 11.9	Illustration of Chris' step 5 learning completed on the worksheet	160
Table 12.1	Illustration of an initial hierarchy with Elna	167
Table 16.1	Table to show the overview of session content	227
Table 16.2	What does my child need to learn?	233
Table 17.1	Example Implementation Checklist	243
Table 17.2	Benefits of Routine Outcome Monitoring	246
Table 18.1	Information for Cases Required in Case Management Supervision	255

About the Editors

Catherine Gallop is a Clinical Psychologist and accredited CBT therapist. She is the Co-Chair of Psychological Professions Network in the South West, Chair of the British Psychological Society Children and Young Peoples' Training Committee and an Associate Professor at the University of Exeter where she is Director of CEDAR (Clinical Education Development and Research) Applied Psychological Centre of Excellence and Clinical Training (PGT). She leads on the development and delivery of Psychological Professions training programmes and post-qualifying practice training and works nationally supporting Children and Young People's workforce strategy, training and implementation, including the low-intensity curriculum and implementation groups.

Peter Fonagy OBE, FMedSci, FBA, FAcSS is Chief Executive of the Anna Freud National Centre for Children and Families; Director of the Division of Psychology and Language Sciences at UCL; and, National Clinical Advisor in NHS England on Children and Young People's Mental Health. His research interests are: early attachment relationships; social cognition; conduct problems; violence; personality disorder; treatment evaluation; and, improving mental health services. Peter has published over 650 scientific papers, 280 chapters, and authored/co-authored 21 books. He has received Lifetime Achievement Awards from several professional associations and is first UK recipient of the British Academy's Wiley Prize for Outstanding Achievements in Psychology.

Rob Kidney is Program Lead for CWP and EMHP practitioner training at the University of Exeter. Rob is a Consultant Clinical Psychologist and BABCP accredited practitioner. He was Lead Clinical Psychologist for South Devon CAMHS and retains clinical time with young people working with common mental health difficulties. He worked on the CoBalT treatment trial for depression and formerly worked to set up IAPT services within the South West. He is the author of the Mind and Mood transdiagnostic treatment and has developed LI workbooks and apps for children and young people.

About the Authors

Helen Barker is a consultant clinical psychologist with over 15 years of experience working within child and adolescent mental health services within the NHS. She is the Co-Module Lead for the PG Certificate in CYP Psychological Wellbeing Practice (CWP) at Kings College London (KCL) where she has acted as an external site link supporting sites in the development and implementation of CYP low-intensity mental health services. She is also the clinical team lead for Luton Specialist CAMHS emotional and behavioural pathway where she provides clinical leadership to a team of multi-disciplinary professionals and has a lead role in supporting the implementation of new workforce developments within the service utilising low-intensity practitioner training programmes.

Alex Boyd is a Chartered Clinical Psychologist and BABCP accredited Cognitive Behavioural Therapist, she is the Co-Director of the portfolio of Children and Young People's Mental Health Training within Clinical Education Development and Research (CEDAR) at the University of Exeter. After many years in the NHS she now combines this role with independent practice and is passionate about bringing psychological therapy to life through creative approaches to meet the needs of young people and families.

Julia Butler is a Lecturer and academic tutor on the Education Mental Health Practitioner (EMHP) and Children's Wellbeing Practitioner (CWP) programmes at the University of Exeter. She completed the EMHP training at Exeter and worked within a Mental Health Support Team for a third sector organisation delivering low-intensity CBT to children and young people. Julia previously worked in education in various roles, including as a forest school and outdoor learning practitioner and trainer, and as a visiting lecturer at Bath Spa University.

ABOUT THE AUTHORS | xiii

Chloe Chessell is a Psychological Wellbeing Practitioner, PhD candidate (University of Reading) and post-doctoral researcher (University of Oxford). Chloe has extensive experience in delivering therapist guided, parent-led CBT to parents of children with anxiety disorders, as well as training CWPs and Educational Mental Health Practitioners (EMHPs) to deliver this treatment approach. Chloe's current research involves adapting therapist guided, parent-led CBT so that it is suitable for parents of pre-adolescent children with Obsessive Compulsive Disorder (OCD).

Cathy Creswell is a Professor of Developmental Clinical Psychology who leads The Oxford Psychological Interventions in Children and adolescents (TOPIC) research group at the University of Oxford. Cathy qualified as a clinical psychologist at UCL before also completing a PhD there. Cathy's research particularly focuses on the development, maintenance, and treatment of child and adolescent anxiety disorders. With Lucy Willetts, she developed the parent-led CBT programme 'Helping Your Child with Fears and Worries' which is widely used as a means to increase access to CBT for children with anxiety problems.

Carolyn Edwards is a clinical psychologist with over 20 years of CAMHS experience working directly with CYP and their families and supervising mental health professionals. In 2017 Carolyn set up of one of the first CWP services. Carolyn has been the Module Lead for the PG Certificate in Supervision (CWPs and EMHPs) at King's College London (KCL) and teaches on the CWP and EMHP practitioner, and Leadership programmes. Carolyn is currently the Module Lead for the Senior Wellbeing Practitioner Diploma at KCL.

Hollie Gay is a Postdoctoral Research Fellow and leads a team of researchers evaluating the low-intensity mental health training programmes for children and young people in the South West: Hollie has presented CWP and EMHP outcomes at national and international conferences to demonstrate the impact of routine outcome monitoring and promote the low-intensity workforce. Hollie also leads on several research projects including an externally funded collaboration with Sidmouth College. The cluster RCT explores wellbeing and resilience across 22 secondary schools using a licensed CBT-based life skills course.

Gemma Halliday is a Research Clinical Psychologist in the TOPIC research group (University of Oxford). Gemma has extensive experience in delivering, supervising, and training CWPs and EMHPs in delivering this approach in both face-to-face and online formats. She is currently working on child anxiety early intervention and prevention research involving the online delivery of parent-led CBT to primary school-aged children. Gemma previously worked with children, young people, and their families in CAMHS, paediatrics and the care system.

Lealah Hewitt-Johns is a clinical psychologist specialising in working with people with Autism and Intellectual Disabilities. She works as one of the Clinical Leads for Plymouth's Autism Spectrum Service, for the University of Plymouth as Clinical Lead for the MSc Clinical Associate in Psychology programme and for The Kintsugi Project CIC as Co-Director. She is a visiting lecturer for both Plymouth and Exeter Universities on disability, mental health and community psychology approaches to wellbeing.

Sarah E. Holland is a Lecturer within CEDAR at the University of Exeter. She teaches on courses covering low-intensity interventions for children and young people (CYP), including the CWP and EMHP programmes. Sarah has worked clinically in CYP services for over 10 years, including supporting CYP with common mental health problems, autism spectrum disorder, and learning disabilities. In her most recent clinical role, she worked as a CWP and clinical supervisor at the University of Exeter.

Rosie Jones is a Lecturer on the PGCert Psychological Therapies Practice (Low-Intensity Cognitive Behavioural Therapy for Children, Young People and Families) and the PGDip Mental Health Practice in Education Settings training at the University of Exeter. She is a practising CWP and completed her Masters in Clinical Psychology at the University of Leiden. Her thesis used network analysis to consider and compare symptoms of depression and anxiety, with a particular focus on rumination.

Philip Kendall is Distinguished University Professor at Temple University (H Index =145). He was twice a Fellow at the Center for Advanced Study in the Behavioral Science, was awarded the Aaron T. Beck Award for 'Significant and Enduring Contributions', and was honoured by ABCT with their Career/Lifetime Achievement Award. In 2022 he won the APF Gold Medal Award for impact in psychology. His treatment for anxiety (Coping cat) has been evaluated in randomised clinical trials, reviewed, and designated as an 'empirically supported treatment'. Dr. Kendall is known for methodology, creativity, and commitment to mentoring. He enjoys basketball, tennis, and spending time with his family.

Mark Kime is a qualified High Intensity Parenting Therapist and CWP with 20 years' experience of working alongside parents, children, and families. Mark has worked across a range of community and clinical contexts including children's social care, education, community CAMHS services, third sector non-governmental organisations (NGOs) both in the UK and Romania, and community CAMHS services. Mark is accredited to deliver evidence-based Parenting Interventions to group and individual families in clinical and community settings. Mark is a Lecturer at Exeter University and is part of CWP teaching team, and has an interest in the delivery of Low-Intensity Parenting Intervention.

Annette MacKinley joined Exeter University in 2015 after working as a CBT therapist for 10 years. Annette has worked for the CWP and EMHP programmes at the

ABOUT THE AUTHORS | xv

Universities of Exeter, Reading, and East Anglia, as well as the CBT and Supervisor training courses at the University of Reading. Annette is currently a children's service manager across two trauma therapeutic services working with looked-after children across North, and North-East Lincolnshire.

Indiana Montaque is a Trainee Clinical Psychologist and a qualified CWP and CWP Supervisor. She has worked in these roles across a variety of services for several years, collaborating with young people and their families using Low-Intensity Cognitive Behavioural Therapy. Indiana has an interest in participatory approaches and in her capacity as a CWP Supervisor she has advocated for inclusive, collaborative methods of working. At present, Indiana has an interest in trauma-informed approaches and community psychology and is completing her doctoral research in this area.

Gary O'Reilly is Professor of Clinical Psychology at University College Dublin where he is the Director of the Doctoral Training Programme in Clinical Psychology. He is also a practising Principal Clinical Psychologists at Children's Health Ireland, which is part of Ireland's public health care system. He is the co-developer of *Pesky gNATs* which is a therapist assisted CBT computer game for children aged 9–12 with anxiety or low mood and *The Feel Good Island* which is a therapist assisted CBT computer game for adults with an Intellectual Disability who experience anxiety or low mood.

Laura Pass is a Clinical Associate Professor at the University of East Anglia (UEA), where she is Programme Director for the EMHP Trainee and Supervisor programmes. She previously worked as a Research Clinical Psychologist at the Charlie Waller Institute, University of Reading with Professor Shirley Reynolds, where they co-developed Brief Behavioural Activation for adolescent depression (Brief BA). Laura has a particular interest in adolescent depression and brief interventions for youth mental health, especially in education settings. She is a regular external trainer for new mental health practitioners.

Jonathan Parker is a Director within the CEDAR clinical training department at the University of Exeter, a Clinical Advisor for NHS England and is a qualified CBT practitioner, psychotherapist, and clinical supervisor. He has specialist interest in clinical leadership, implementation, and organisational development and provides support, guidance, and challenge to a range of NHS, Local Authority, and community sector organisations delivering children and young people's mental health services. He works closely with regional, national, and international partners in support of the development and implementation of key mental health initiatives.

Susanna Payne is Co-Director of CYP-MH Trainings at King's College London. She is experienced in delivering, supervising, and training high- and low-intensity evidence-based therapies for children and young people and their families, and translating national curricula for training practitioners. She has clinical experience in complex and severe presentations and acute settings, and research experience in anxiety disorders and mindfulness, including as a trial therapist. She has a special interest in widening access to clinical trainings and clinician and training practitioner wellbeing.

Kate Phillips is a doctoral candidate in Clinical Psychology at Temple University. Her research involves evidence-based interventions for youth anxiety. She has experience treating many anxious youths using the Coping Cat. Additionally, she has provided training and consultation in evidence-based interventions for youth anxiety in schools. She is currently completing her clinical internship at Zucker Hillside Hospital where she works in the comprehensive DBT program, eating disorders program, and anxiety and OCD clinic.

Laura Raymen is a Senior Lecturer and Academic Lead on the University of Exeter's CWP and EMHP training programmes. Laura holds a BSc in Applied Psychology (Clinical) and an MSc in Psychological Research Methods and has worked on the KARE clinical trial, where psychopharmacological treatments for addiction were researched. Laura has also trained as a Psychological Wellbeing Practitioner (PWP) and worked for an NHS IAPT service, delivering evidence-based, low-intensity CBT interventions to support individuals with symptoms of low mood and anxiety.

Shirley Reynolds is Director of CBTReach and Senior Clinical Advisor for the BABCP (British Association of Behavioural and Cognitive Psychotherapies). She has a clinical research background in evidence-based psychological treatments, with a specific focus on treatments for children and young people with anxiety and depression. Shirley developed Brief Behavioural Activation for adolescent depression with Dr Laura Pass during her time as Director of the Charlie Waller Institute at the University of Reading. Together, Shirley and Laura have delivered Brief Behavioural Activation in schools and NHS clinics and disseminated the method through research publications, training, and publishing a treatment manual.

Jess Richardson is a Consultant Clinical Psychologist working in the Trauma, Anxiety and Depression Clinic of National and Specialist CAMHS at South London and Maudsley NHS Trust. She is also the Co-Director of CYP-MH Trainings at King's College London and in this role has been developing and delivering high-quality CYP-MH training courses for over 10 years. She is particularly passionate about the significant role of supervisors in supporting the low-intensity workforce.

Kirsty Roberts joined Exeter University in 2015, having previously worked as a Psychological Wellbeing Practitioner within IAPT services. Completing an MSc in Health Psychology helped to further focus on behaviour change and models used within LICBT, furthering her interest in this area. Kirsty has previously taught on PWP training courses, moving to work on the CWP in 2017, alongside the EMHP Programmes in 2018 as Academic Lead on both courses. Kirsty is currently Programme Lead on the CWP and EMHP Supervisor training courses at Exeter University.

Chelsie Smith is a Lecturer on the PGCert Psychological Therapies Practice (Low-Intensity Cognitive Behavioural Therapy for Children, Young People and Families) and the PGDip Mental Health Practice in Education Settings training at Exeter University. Chelsie is also a qualified CWP and currently working as an Assistant Clinical Psychologist, involved in research trials focusing on the delivery of CBT for children via text messaging, as well as supporting adults with epilepsy.

Mike Turnbull is a Chartered Occupational and Clinical Psychologist and a BABCP Accredited Behavioural and Cognitive Psychotherapist, Supervisor and Trainer. With over 20 years' experience of practice within Psychology, he has developed multiple services and most recently set up and led Children Young Peoples-IAPT low-intensity services within his local NHS Trust. Mike is currently the BABCP accreditation pathway lead at Newcastle University and was until recently the programme lead for the PG Diploma in Low-Intensity Psychological Therapy at Northumbria University.

Hannah Vickery (*née Whitney*) is Associate Professor and Director of Training at the Charlie Waller Institute, University of Reading. She leads the delivery of a range of clinical programmes and contributes regionally/nationally in relation to Children and Young People's workforce strategy. Hannah is passionate about centring equity, diversity, and inclusion within the recruitment and training of different psychological professions. She is committed to decolonising the curricula and ensuring that marginalised groups are not only represented, but that all mental health practitioners adopt an intersectional approach. As a practising clinical psychologist, Hannah's areas of special interest include post-traumatic stress disorder and adolescent depression.

Sadie Williams is a Consultant & Lead Clinical Psychologist for an NHS CAMHS service. Sadie is passionate about early intervention and prevention for children, young people, and families and has developed both CWP and MHST services within the local borough. Sadie is currently co-module lead for the Child Well Being Practitioner module at Kings College London (KCL) where she has been part of the CWP programme since its inception.

Markku Wood is Clinical Director for the CYP IAPT programmes at Northumbria University and a practising (NHS CAMHS) Consultant Clinical Psychologist. He is accredited with the HCPC, BPS, BABCP and a Fellow of the HEA. Markku leads a research team with regional and national projects, focused on improving psychological therapies for YP and their families. Markku is a board member of the NE PPN and regularly contributes to the development of projects with NHSE/I and HEE. Markku's specialist clinical interests lie in Trauma, ASC, and psychosis however, he has focused his recent attention on the development of the LICBT workforce.

Preface

Children's mental health is now, perhaps for the first time ever, clearly a significant public and political concern which frequently finds its way into media headlines. And this is how it should be. Young people, by which we mean from school age to 24 years, represent a quarter of the world's population and mental ill-health represents the number one threat to their health. The oft quoted figures in relation to the first appearance of sometimes lifelong mental health problems (50 percent before age 14 and 75 percent by age 25) fail to reflect the gravity of the difficulty young people face in relation to their wellbeing. Half of them are likely to be impacted by mental ill health before they reach the age of 25 and mental ill health between 10–24 years. It accounts for 45 percent of the overall burden of disease for children and young people. Suicide remains the second most common cause of death in this age group. Numerous studies which we will review in this book have documented the rising prevalence of mental ill-health (anxiety, depression, eating disorder and suicide, especially among girls). Self-harm tripled in prevalence between 2000 and 2014, long before the pandemic, which as we know presented a greater wellbeing challenge to young people than other age groups. Figures which we will later review in detail suggest that the trend for increasing prevalence of mental disorder is accelerating. The surveys conducted in England by NHS Digital suggest that the prevalence of probable disorder increased by 50 percent between 2017 and 2021 compared with a rather gentler increase of 10 percent in the 13 years from 2004 to 2017. The referrals to mental health services are increasing at an even faster rate – 60 percent increase between 2021 and 2022.

To meet the demand our pattern of working needs to change. We need more clinicians on the frontlines dealing with problems as these emerge. Early intervention based in the setting where children first manifest mental health problems is key to avoid demands that will be impossible to meet. The intervention has to focus on mild and moderate problems even if these do not meet the threshold for a clinical diagnosis. We cannot afford to wait the many years while a psychologist or nurse or other professional is trained to be able to offer comprehensive interventions. The solution is needed now. And it is this solution which the book is aiming to support. We need many effective interventions in which low-intensity practitioners need to be rapidly trained, practitioners who can be deployed in schools and other community settings. We have the potential workforce who would like to spend many years offering emotional support and therapeutic help to children and young people. They just need to be empowered to deliver care that is practical, brief, evidence-based, and effective in the contexts where it is needed.

The book was written to support the training of this new workforce of low-intensity practitioners who can deliver help where it is needed most – where most refers to the number in need and the number potentially available to be helped by short-term well-structured and clearly described interventions. Contributors to this book are leading national and international authors and trainers, offering expertise in low-intensity interventions and practice, clinical training, and service implementation. This is the essential 'how to' guide for low-intensity practitioners and those that support them. It provides a manual for practice covering assessment, decision-making and key interventions, with step-by-step guidance, case vignettes and accompanying worksheets to support each evidence-based intervention. It also offers guidance on key service implementation principles, supervision and adaptations to practice. It is an ideal resource for those in low-intensity training, practitioner, or leadership roles, looking to develop competency in the low-intensity cognitive behavioural clinical method.

This book is divided into four sections. In Part 1 (Context and Values) we set out the context and development (Chapter 1) of low-intensity practice with children and young people (CYP) and the low-intensity CYP psychological practitioner roles (Children's Wellbeing Practitioner (CWP) and Education Mental Health Practitioner (EMHP). Foundational principles and core values are then outlined and explored utilising real-world examples that help translate these into practice (Chapter 2).

In Part 2 (Low-Intensity CYP Assessment and Key Practice Considerations) we take the reader through the structure of a low-intensity cognitive behavioural assessment (Chapter 3) with CYP, exploring how to gather client-centred information and create collaborative problem statements and goals to support treatment planning. The process of risk assessment (Chapter 4) within the low-intensity framework is then being outlined, with consideration of how risk information can be gathered in a culturally competent and client-centred way. Chapter 5 provides an overview of the current evidence base for low-intensity interventions with CYP and presents an intervention mapping tool to guide intervention planning, alongside CYP preferences. This section finishes with a consideration of how practitioners can adapt low-intensity practice in creative and child-focused ways (Chapter 6) and explores some of the difficulties (Chapter 7) that can arise, offering key tips and possible solutions to enhance low-intensity practice and overcome potential barriers.

Part 3 (Low-intensity CYP Interventions) outlines the commonly used low-intensity interventions with CYP experiencing anxiety, low mood, and behavioural difficulties. These include: Brief Behavioural Activation (Chapter 8), exposure and habituation (Chapter 9), cognitive restructuring (Chapter 10), and behavioural experiments (Chapter 11). Further chapters in this section outline specific packages including Brief Coping Cat (Chapter 12), Pesky Gnats (Chapter 13), Lifestyle Management (Chapter 14), Behavioural Problems and Parenting (Chapter 15) and finally Brief Guided Parent-Delivered CBT for child anxiety (Chapter 16).

In the final section, Part 4 (Professional Issues and Service Implications), key considerations to support the implementation of low-intensity practice within CYP mental health, education, and community settings are outlined. This includes a consideration of the principles and practicalities associated with successful implementation of low-intensity practice (Chapter 17), the purpose and requirements of supervision (Chapter 18), adaptations to practice for CYP with neurodiversity (Chapter 19), and the foundations of inclusive practice within the low-intensity framework (Chapter 20). The final chapter (Chapter 21) of the book explores the development of meta-competencies within low-intensity practice, outlining a pragmatic approach to supporting the development and sustainability of the low-intensity CYP workforce.

Acknowledgements

We would like to thank Laura Hitt (Project Co-Ordinator) and Sarah Dobson (Project Manager) for supporting us as Editors in compiling this text.

Part 1
Context and Values

1

Context and Development

Catherine Gallop and Peter Fonagy

Introduction

This chapter will outline the context of mental health need within children and young people (CYP) in relation to rising prevalence of common mental health difficulties and the widening treatment gap. The CYP mental health political context and ambitions will be summarised and consideration of how these relate to low-intensity practice will be explored. The key CYP low-intensity workforce initiatives and roles will then be described with consideration given to their scope of practice, service contexts and the training models that underpin the new workforce.

The Context of Need for Low-Intensity Practice with Children and Young People

Prevalence and Impact of Mental Health Issues in Children and Young People?

Mental health problems affect a significant number of adults, young people and children. This means that individuals have problems with aspects of their mental health to such an extent that it impacts on their daily lives. There is strong indication that 50 per cent of mental health problems are established by age 14 and 75 per cent by age 24 (Kessler et al., 2007; Meltzer et al., 2003; World Health Organization, 2022). In 1999 and 2004, the Office for National Statistics (ONS) carried out two large surveys of young people aged 5–15 years living in England, Scotland and Wales (Green et al., 2004; Macmillan et al., 2005) but more recent comparable figures are available for England only: a survey of a cohort of 5–19-year-olds carried out by NHS England in 2017 (NHS Digital, 2018; Sadler et al., 2017). This sample was followed up during the COVID-19 pandemic in 2020 and 2021 (NHS Digital, 2021; Vizard et al., 2020). The ONS estimated that one in six children aged 5–19 have a probable mental disorder which increases to one in five for those aged 20–22. Since 2017 the prevalence of probable mental health diagnoses in CYP increased 73 per cent for 6–10-year-olds (NHS Digital, 2018; Peytrignet et al., 2022). The increases in prevalence are particularly marked in young women under 25 with more than one in four experiencing a common mental disorder compared to less than one in five adults (Deighton et al., 2019; Patalay & Gage, 2019). Furthermore, there has been a sharp rise in self-harm in adolescent girls since 2010 with an associated increased risk of suicide (Morgan et al., 2017). Although prevalence estimates are not directly comparable over time due to changes in methodology, the indications are that the prevalence of mental health conditions among CYP in the UK has significantly increased over the past two decades (Angel et al., 2021; Patalay & Gage, 2019). There is little doubt that the pandemic has contributed to this trend, with the mental health effects of pandemic restrictions greatest for children and young adults (McGinty et al., 2020; NHS Digital, 2021; Pierce et al., 2020; Davis et al., 2021; Vizard et al., 2020).

There is strong evidence that adolescent mental health problems can have a significant impact and CYP with persistent mental health problems face unequal chances in life. Common challenges that CYP with mental health problems experience include being more likely to experience time off school and exclusions; more likely to experience problems in future employment and certain groups, e.g., young people with conduct disorder, are more likely to engage in criminal activity (Clayborne et al., 2019). The impact of untreated mental health problems is therefore large including substantial harm to physical health, premature mortality (including increased death by suicide), impact on educational, social and occupational functioning, reduced life income and limited interpersonal relationships, and costs the UK £118 billion a year (5 per cent of GDP in 2019) including increased costly contact with the criminal justice system (McDaid & Park, 2022; Royal College of Psychiatrists, 2022).

Successive UK Governments since the turn of the century have watched with growing concern the rising prevalence of mental health problems among CYP (House of Commons Health and Social Care Committee, 2021a; Ward et al., 2021). More recently, national lockdowns, disruptions to schooling and social life, and an increasing number of families in financial distress have exacerbated mental health struggles among CYP (Office for Health Improvement and Disparities, 2021). The one in six young people aged 6–16 years in England with probable mental health disorder referred to above is equivalent to 1.3 million individuals who might benefit from support (Peytrignet et al., 2022). It seems unlikely that existing plans to increase the availability of services across the UK will be sufficient to provide support for all young people who need it.

Increase in Referrals, Access, and the Widening Treatment Gap

The number of CYP and their families accessing mental health services has increased. In England, the number of CYP in contact with Child and adolescent mental health services (CAMHS) rose by 46.6 per cent between 2019 and 2021 (Peytrignet et al., 2022). Over 420,000 children and young people were treated through NHS-commissioned community services in 2020/21. This is approximately 39.6 per cent of children and young people with a diagnosable mental health condition, exceeding the target of 35 per cent (based on the 2004 prevalence estimates that applied when the target was set). However, there is still much progress to be made to ensure access for CYP who need mental health services and due to the rising prevalence of mental health disorders, overall access to support remains low (27 per cent of CYP who needed support were receiving it, compared to 25 per cent in 2017; Peytrignet et al., 2022). Mental health services across the UK were struggling to meet demand even before the COVID-19 pandemic (Children's Commissioner for England, 2022) but the pandemic has already, and will continue to have a significant impact on the health and social care workforce which will challenge the capacity of services to respond.

In addition to the widening treatment gap, the quality of existing services for CYP with mental health problems is variable and some care is of poor quality especially where different organisations that support CYP are not joined up. This can result in long waits for support and there is a need for CYP to be able to access services more quickly so that they can get the support they need. In England, the average waiting time for those accepted into services was reduced by 25 per cent to 32 days between 2019/20 and 2020/21 (Children's Commissioner for England, 2021) but there is substantial variation between geographical areas with some with unacceptably long waiting times. Furthermore, we do not know what happens to CYP who are referred but not accepted for treatment in CYP-MH services, whose unmet need is likely to be significant given the large gap between prevalence and CAMHS treatment rates.

CYP Political Context and Mental Health Ambitions

Since 2015, the NHS has been undergoing the most significant transformation since its foundation in 1948. Governments in England, Scotland, and Wales have published strategies to improve support and services in the NHS, schools and colleges, and the wider community (National Health Service, 2019; Welsh Government, 2012; Scottish Government, 2017).

The *Five Year Forward View* (FYFV) described a vision for the future of the NHS setting out the principles and ambitions that have guided how mental health services for CYP could be transformed in the ensuing period taking us up to 2021. It focused on new ways of working to improve quality of care. It stressed the needs of service users, rather than organising services around institutions and structures. The new approach placed more emphasis on how services collaborated, and how care could be integrated. The central theme was the breaking down of traditional barriers between health, social care, education and voluntary sectors. The goal was the creation of a 'whole system-based' approach to service delivery organised around networks of care. The intention was to create shared responsibility for outcomes between services organised around specific population groups, not individual encounters with specific patients. This welcome integration of care and joint accountability (Kossarova et al., 2016; NHS England, 2016) was underpinned by funded service development at all levels as the programmes received substantial investment between 2015 and 2020. CAMHS specifically received £1.25 billion between 2016 and 2021. This is likely to be the most significant funding injection that Child and Adolescent Mental Health services ever received in the history of the NHS. The goals linked to the investment were the beginning of a fundamental reform addressing serious concerns surrounding the accessibility and quality of care in CAMHS (Kossarova et al., 2016).

The Children and Young People's Improved Access to Psychological Therapies (CYP-IAPT) programme benefited, as its key principles were well aligned with the FYFV (NHS England, 2016). It also targeted the sustainable transformation of CAMHS across England (Fonagy & Clark, 2015). At the core of the CYP-IAPT Programme was the commitment to train existing and new psychological staff in evidence-based practice approaches. In 2019, with the CYP-IAPT initiative approaching 100 per cent national coverage, it transitioned into expected standards of delivery of CYP mental health services.

In 2017, the Government published its Green Paper for Transforming Children and Young People's Mental Health (Department for Health and Social Care and Department for Education, 2017). This set out detailed proposals for expanding access to mental health care for CYP through schools and colleges, aiming to reduce waiting times for treatment. The Green Paper built on proposals incorporated in Future in Mind (Children and Young People's Mental Health Taskforce, 2016) and the Five Year Forward View (NHS England, 2014), but also activity that schools and colleges undertake to promote positive mental health. It set out additional action to promote good mental health for CYP, to provide effective early support and to continue to improve access to specialist services. In doing so it aimed to improve the links between NHS mental health services and schools/colleges and better meet the mental health needs of CYP in these settings. It proposed three pillars to the approach: designated Senior Leads for Mental Health, Mental Health Support Teams, and reducing waiting times, be rolled out to at least a fifth of the country by the end of 2022/23. A robust evaluation has been commissioned to build understanding on the costs, benefits, and implementation challenges as well as gathering best practice to feed back into services.

The launch of the NHS Long Term Plan (NHS, 2019) had considerable ambition for the further expansion of mental health services. The plan for MH proposed a significant expansion of the mental health workforce with a strong emphasis on the psychological professions, recommending expansion in these groups typically ranging from 25 to 50 per cent. The emphasis on psychological interventions arose from the recognition that for a significant number of common mental health disorders, evidence-based, structured, collaboratively conducted psychological interventions are the first line treatment of choice. Specific to CYP, the LTP made several recommendations: (1) At least an additional 345,000 children and young people aged 0–25 will be able to access support via NHS funded mental health services and school or college-based Mental Health Support Teams by 2023/24. This was on top of the Five Year Forward View for Mental Health promise of 70,000 additional children and young people to access NHS mental health services each year by 2020/21 (35 per cent of those with mental health needs based on 2004 prevalence data). (2) Over the next five years new Mental Health Support Teams working in schools and colleges will be rolled out to between one-fifth and a quarter of the country by the end of 2023. (3) By 2028/29 it is anticipated that over 1 million CYP will receive an evidence-based intervention by a MHST practitioner. (4) Over the coming decade the goal is to ensure that 100 per cent of children and young people who need specialist care can access it. (5) A four-week waiting time target has since been proposed for CAMHS, from referral to receiving 'help', ranging from an assessment for specialist help to redirection to another service (Powis, 2019).

More recently, the 2021 report from the Health and Social Care Committee recognised that whilst progress had been made in expanding both CAMHS and NHS services in schools and the community, it viewed current plans as insufficiently ambitious (House of Commons Health and Social Care Committee, 2021a). It pointed out that more than half of young people were without the support that they needed and 'the proportion accessing adequate care has gone into reverse because of the pandemic'. The current estimates are that 60–70 per cent of children and young people with probable diagnosable mental health condition do not receive any NHS care and it has issued a call for evidence to create a new 10-year cross-government mental health strategy (Department for Health and Social Care, 2022). This seems timely as the last strategy was published over a decade ago.

The Psychological Professions Workforce

We have been involved on behalf of the Health Select Committee in an expert review of selective government undertakings in relation to mental health which found that workforce, CYP Mental Health services and the treatment of common mental health conditions all required improvement (House of Commons Health and Social Care Committee, 2021b). The report concluded that 'workforce shortages represent the single biggest threat to national ambitions to improve mental healthcare, impacting delivery across all mental health services'. The report recognised that 'funding has been allocated to train new staff' but qualified its conclusions saying: 'the increase in

CONTEXT AND DEVELOPMENT | 7

numbers is only meaningful if they represent appropriately trained and profession-ally governed individuals'.

This report appeared on the same day (9 December 2021) as the Select Committee's Eighth Report of Session 2021–22 on Children and Young People's mental health which concluded: 'One of the largest barriers to increasing access to mental health provision for children and young people remains the size of the mental health work-force.' This conclusion was based on access numbers to professional help of about 33 per cent (of 2017 prevalence). Elsewhere in the Report the Select Committee said:

> We recommend that NHS England & Improvement set out a clear action plan including key milestones, deadlines, and funding for how they will meet their target set out in the NHS Long Term Plan of 100% access to specialist support for all children and young people aged 0–25 by 2029, without raising the already high thresholds for accessing support. (Paragraph 56)

If meeting a 33 per cent target created workforce shortages in 2020–21, one can only imagine the workforce gap when the full ambitions of 100 per cent access set out in the Long Term Plan are mapped over the coming years.

The Psychological Professions Workforce Plan for England with a Priority Action Annexe was released by HEE in December (Health Education England, 2021) and unsurprisingly shows the need for a planned expansion of the psychological profes-sions workforce at an unprecedented rate, by approximately 10,500 posts by 2024 (60 per cent growth) to meet the psychological needs of service users, carers, and families. This national initiative finally comes close(er) to closing, the 'treatment gap' whereby it appears 'acceptable' that the vast majority of those with MH prob-lems receive no expert help from the NHS. It would not be an exaggeration to say, that after 25 years of solid research and campaigning, psychological interventions are now, for the first time, represented in the NHS offer to MH patients in the way that this modality had always deserved.

The Psychological Professions Workforce currently comprises three main groups: (a) practitioner psychologists with the large majority being clinical psychologists, (b) psychological therapists with a largest group being CBT therapists and (c) psycho-logical practitioners, predominantly staff in paraprofessional roles such as Psycho-logical Wellbeing Practitioners, Child Wellbeing Practitioners and Education Mental Health Practitioners. All these groups have already seen significant expansion over the past ten years, with the exception of psychologists. Current plans, as set out in the Psy-chological Professions Workforce Plan for England (December 2021) include ambitious plans for the expansion of all three groups: these include a 25 per cent increase in the number of clinical psychologists, a 25 per cent increase in the number of psychologi-cal therapists, and a 25 per cent increase in the number of psychological practitioners.

Psychological Practitioners and Low-Intensity Practice with Children and Young People

It is clear that much will have to happen in terms of service re-design and workforce training for the access gap to be closed and parity for MH to be achieved. The evidence-based management of childhood mental health difficulties within a comprehensive, integrated and responsive mental health services in community-based settings enabling early recognition of developmental difficulties is internationally acknowledged (World Health Organization, 2022). The increasing prevalence of young people's mental health difficulties has made the issue of appropriate workforce the key NHSE priority. It was recognised that tackling CAMHS waiting times required three fundamental changes in practice: (1) tailoring interventions and therapies to fit clinical practice better (Weisz et al., 2012; Weisz et al., 2015), (2) tailoring interventions and therapies to fit CYP's needs and preferences (Weisz et al., 2015), and (3) building and tailoring interventions and therapies to fit non-clinical (non-NHS) contexts (Chorpita et al., 2014). In addition, building on this evidence, care delivered through goal-focused approaches has been shown to improve patient flow through the service, reducing waiting times, and improving service accessibility (Clark et al., 2018; Nooteboom et al., 2021).

While consecutive governments have committed to expand preventative services, particularly outside traditional NHS services, there is a need to target resources more deliberately at the early appearance of mental health problems and at those most at risk of future difficulties (Grimm et al., 2022). The need for brief, low-intensity, cost effective interventions from well-trained staff became a key consideration for policy makers (Fonagy et al., 2016). However, Health Education England, since 2012 responsible for training the NHS workforce, acknowledged that for CYP there was insufficient provision for brief, evidence-based early intervention (Health Education England, 2017). This realisation led to the development of two low-intensity psychological practitioner workforce roles for the CYP-MH service: Children's Wellbeing Practitioners (CWPs) and Education Mental Health Practitioners (EMHPs).

The CWP and EMHP Psychological Practitioner Roles and Scope of Practice

The CWP role was developed in 2017 (Health Education England, 2017) to provide additional, accessible mental health provision to CYP via evidence-based interventions as part of a wider team in community settings (i.e., community mental health, CAMHS, primary care, local authority, or voluntary sector organisations). In 2019, the EMHP role emerged via a collaboration between NHS England, the Department for Education, and Health Education England and as a result of the *Transforming*

Children and Young People's Mental Health: A Green Paper (Department of Health and Social Care & Department for Education, 2017). Similar to CWPs, the EMHP role aims to support early intervention, but its focus is to ensure CYP have access to evidence-based mental health support in *educational* rather than community settings. EMHPs are based in Mental Health Support Teams (MHSTs), made up of senior clinicians and specialist CAMHS practitioners that work across local mental health support systems to ensure that the needs of both the CYP and the education settings are met.

CWPs and EMHPs provide interventions, under supervision, at an early stage to CYP and their families with common mild-to-moderate mental health difficulties (anxiety, low mood, and behavioural difficulties) including guided self-help, psycho education and brief LI cognitive behavioural interventions. In addition, EMHPs support schools and colleges on whole system initiatives aimed at preventing mental health difficulties and improving mental wellbeing of students. Both roles aim to improve outcomes and reduce the requirement for future/specialist interventions; however, they develop relationships across the wider CYP mental health care system and can therefore facilitate effective signposting where appropriate.

Training the CYP Low-Intensity Workforce

CWPs and EMHPs must complete a nationally designed and funded 12-month Graduate or Post Graduate Diploma via applying for a position as a trainee in a CYP mental health service or MHST. Since the commencement of the training programmes, more than 1,900 CWPS and 1,600 EMHPs have been trained or are currently in training at universities across the country, and a further 387 CWPs and 456 EMHPs starting in 2022/23. The training programmes are open to applicants with a range of experience of working with CYP and who can demonstrate the ability to study at degree or post graduate levels. The editors and many of the authors of this text have been involved in designing and developing the curricula and accreditation standards to enable CWPs and EMHP to gain the skills and knowledge in delivering brief, CBT-informed low-intensity interventions. This text aims to be a useful adjunct to these national training curricula and programmes, containing core elements relating to LI assessments, interventions, practice considerations, and role implementation.

Both training programmes share three foundational modules, the first of which aims to build trainee understanding of the CYP psychological practitioner roles within their respective contexts and includes service principles, legal and professional issues, and an overview of the low-intensity evidence base. The second module develops effective engagement and low-intensity CYP-centred assessment skills (see Chapter 3) across relevant CYP mental health difficulties. Trainees are required to be able to collaboratively develop a shared understanding of difficulties, identify goals, and potential risk factors (see Chapter 4) and consider appropriate evidence-based interventions (see Chapter 5 for an overview). The final shared module focuses on a range of LI interventions for mild-to-moderate anxiety, low mood, and behavioural difficulties (see Chapters 8–16), optimising the use of self-management techniques. CWPs and EMHPs then undertake additional specialist training modules in whole-school approaches to wellbeing and education-specific support, liaison, and consultation (EMHPs) and community engagement and approaches (CWPs).

CWPs and EMHPs must evidence 80 hours of clinical practice during their training, across a spread of mental health difficulties and approaches and work with CYP, their families and other professionals. They must also undertake regular (a minimum of 40 hours) clinical supervision appropriate to their Psychological Practitioner role (see Chapter 18 for further details). Both trainings require rigorous assessment of both low-intensity knowledge and skills in their applied context, including the assessment of live clinical practice (assessment and intervention sessions).

Summary

This chapter has outlined the rising prevalence and impact of common mental health difficulties experienced by CYP and the widening treatment gap. Key CYP mental health policies and ambitions have been summarised and the need for the expansion of low-intensity CYP psychological practitioner roles identified. The key CYP low-intensity workforce initiatives (CWP and EMHP) have been outlined with consideration given to their scope of practice and the nationally prescribed training models.

References

Angel, L., Anthony, R., Buckley, K., Copeland, L., Edwards, A., Hawkins, J., Moore, G., Morgan, K., Murphy, S., Ouerghi, S., Pell, B., Roberts, J., & van Godwin, J. (2021). *Student health and wellbeing in Wales: Key findings from the 2021 school health research network primary school student health and wellbeing survey.* School Health Research Network. www.shrn.org.uk/wp-content/uploads/2021/11/PriSHRN-Key-Findings-Summary-1.pdf

Children and Young People's Mental Health Taskforce. (2016). *Future in mind: Promoting, protecting and improving our children and young people's mental health and wellbeing.* Department of Health. https://assets.publishing.service.gov.uk/government/uploads/system/uploads/attachment_data/file/414024/Childrens_Mental_Health.pdf

Children's Commissioner for England. (2021). *The state of children's mental health services 2020/21.* www.childrenscommissioner.gov.uk/wp-content/uploads/2020/01/cco-the-state-of-childrens-mental-health-services.pdf

Children's Commissioner for England. (2022). *Briefing on children's mental health services – 2020/2021.* www.childrenscommissioner.gov.uk/report/briefing-on-childrens-mental-health-services-2020-2021/

Clark, S., Emberly, D., Pajer, K., Delong, E., McWilliam, S., Bagnell, A., Abidi, S., Casey, B., & Gardner, W. (2018). Improving access to child and adolescent mental health care: The choice and partnership approach. *Journal of the Canadian Academy of Child and Adolescent Psychiatry, 27*(1), 5–14.

Clayborne, Z.M., Varin, M., & Colman, I. (2019). Systematic review and meta-analysis: Adolescent depression and long-term psychosocial outcomes. *Journal of the American Academy of Child and Adolescent Psychiatry, 58*(1), 72–79. https://doi.org/10.1016/j.jaac.2018.07.896

Chorpita, B.F., & Daleiden, E.L. (2014). Structuring the collaboration of science and service in pursuit of a shared vision. *Journal of Clinical Child and Adolescent Psychology, 43*(2), 323–338. https://doi.org/10.1080/15374416.2013.828297

Davies, A.R., Song, J., Bentley, L., Akbari, A., Smith, T., Carter, B., John, G., Trigg, L., Parry, G., Dundon, J., & Cross, L. (2021). COVID-19 in Wales: The impact on levels of health care use and mental health of the clinically extremely vulnerable. Cardiff: Public Health Wales.

Deighton, J., Lereya, S.T., Casey, P., Patalay, P., Humphrey, N., & Wolpert, M. (2019). Prevalence of mental health problems in schools: Poverty and other risk factors among 28,000 adolescents in England. *The British Journal of Psychiatry, 215*(3), 1–3. https://doi.org/10.1192/bjp.2019.19

Department for Health and Social Care and Department for Education. (2017). *Transforming children and young people's mental health provision: A green paper.* https://assets.publishing. service.gov.uk/government/uploads/system/uploads/attachment_data/file/664855/ Transforming_ children_and_young_people_s_mental_health_provision.pdf

Department for Health and Social Care. (2022). *Mental health and wellbeing plan: Discussion paper; 2022.* www.gov.uk/government/consultations/mental-health-and-wellbeing-plan-discussion-paper-and-call-for-evidence/mental-health-and-wellbeing-plan-discussion-paper

Fonagy, P., & Clark, D.M. (2015). Update on the Improving Access to Psychological Therapies programme in England: Commentary on … Children and Young People's Improving Access to Psychological Therapies. *British Journal of Psychiatry, 39*(5), 248–251. https://doi.org/ 10.1192/pb.bp.115.052282

Fonagy, P., Cottrell, D., Phillips, J., Bevington, D., Glaser, D., & Allison, E. (2016). *What works for whom: A critical review of treatments for children and adolescents* (2nd ed.). Guilford Press. http://dx.doi.org/10.1080/07317107.2016.1203157

Green, H., McGinnity, A., Meltzer, H., Ford, T., & Goodman, R. (2004). *Mental health of children and young people in Great Britain.* https://digital.nhs.uk/data-and-information/publications/ statistical/mental-health-of-children-and-young-people-in-england/mental-health-of-children-and-young-people-in-great-britain-2004

Grimm, F., Alcock, B., Butler, J.E., Fernandez Crespo, R., Davies, A., Peytrignet, S., Piroddi, R., Thorlby, R., & Tallack, C. (2022). *Improving children and young people's mental health services: Local data insights from England, Scotland and Wales.* The Health Foundation. https://doi. org/10.37829/HF-2022-NDL1

Health Education England. (2017). *Headline plan and process for the establishment of the CYP PWP role.* London: Health Education England.

Health Education England. (2021). *Psychological professions workforce plan for England.* https:// ppn.nhs.uk/north-west/resources/news/item/hee-launch-psychological-professions-workforce-plan-for-england

House of Commons Health and Social Care Committee. (2021a). *Eighth report - Children and young people's mental health.* https://publications.parliament.uk/pa/cm5802/cmselect/ cmhealth/17/report.html

House of Commons Health and Social Care Committee. (2021b). The health and social care committee's expert panel: Evaluation of the government's progress against its policy commitments in the area of mental health services in England. https://committees. parliament.uk/publications/8156/documents/83466/default/

Kessler, R.C., Amminger, G.P., Aguilar-Gaxiola, S., Alonso, J., Lee, S., & Ustün, T.B. (2007). Age of onset of mental disorders: A review of recent literature. *Current opinion in psychiatry, 20*(4), 359–364. https://doi.org/10.1097/YCO.0b013e32816ebc8c

Kossarova, L., Devakumar, D., & Edwards, N. (2016). *The future of child health services: New models of care.* Nuffield Trust.

Macmillan, H.L., Patterson, C.J., & Wathen, C.N. (2005). Screening for depression in primary care: Recommendation statement from the Canadian Task Force on Preventive Health Care. *Canadian Medical Association Journal, 172*(1), 33–35. https://doi.org/10.1503/cmaj.1030823

McDaid, D., & Park, A. (2022). *The economic case for investing in the prevention of mental health conditions in the UK.* Mental Health Foundation. www.mentalhealth.org.uk/explore-mental-health/publications/economic-case-investing-prevention-mental-health-conditions-UK

McGinty, E.E., Presskreischer, R., Han, H., & Barry, C.L. (2020). Psychological distress and loneliness reported by US adults in 2018 and April 2020. *JAMA, 324*(1), 93–94. https://doi.org/10.1001/jama.2020.9740

Meltzer, H., Gatward, R., Corbin, T., Goodman, R., & Ford, T. (2003). *Persistence, onset, risk factors and outcomes of childhood mental disorders.* Office for National Statistics. www.dawba.info/abstracts/B-CAMHS99+3_followup_report.pdf

Mental Health Taskforce. (2016). *The five year forward view for mental health. A report from the independent Mental Health Taskforce to the NHS in England.* NHS England. www.england.nhs.uk/wp-content/uploads/2016/02/Mental-Health-Taskforce-FYFV-final.pdf

Morgan, C., Webb, R., Carr, M., Kontopantelis, E., Green, J., Chew Graham, C., Kapur, N., & Ashcroft, M. (2017). Incidence, clinical management, and mortality risk following self harm among children and adolescents: Cohort study in primary care. *British Medical Journal, 359*:j4351. https://doi.org/10.1136/bmj.j4351

NHS England. (2014). *Five Year Forward View.* www.england.nhs.uk/wp-content/uploads/2014/10/5yfv-web.pdf

NHS England. (2016). Implementing the Five Year Forward View for Mental Health. www.england.nhs.uk/wp-content/uploads/2016/07/fyfv-mh.pdf

National Health Service. (2019). *The NHS Long Term Plan.* www.longtermplan.nhs.uk/publication/nhs-long-term-plan/

NHS Digital. (2018). *Mental health of children and young people in England, 2017.* https://files.digital.nhs.uk/A6/EA7D58/MHCYP%202017%20Summary.pdf

NHS Digital. (2021). *Mental health of children and young people in England, 2021.* digital.nhs.uk/data-andinformation/publications/statistical/mental-health-of-children-and-young-people-in-england/2021-follow-up-to-the2017-survey

Nooteboom, L.A., Mulder, E.A., Kuiper, C., Colins, O.F., & Vermeiren, R. (2021). Towards integrated youth care: A systematic review of facilitators and barriers for professionals. *Administration and Policy in Mental Health, 48*(1), 88–105. https://doi.org/10.1007/s10488-020-01049-8

Office for Health Improvement and Disparities. (2021). *COVID-19 mental health and wellbeing surveillance report – 4. Children and young people; 2021.* www.gov.uk/government/publications/covid-19-mental-health-and-wellbeing-surveillance-report/7-children-and-young-people

Patalay, P., & Gage, S.H. (2019). Changes in millennial adolescent mental health and health-related behaviours over 10 years: A population cohort comparison study. *International Journal of Epidemiology, 48*(5), 1650–1664. https://doi.org/10.1093/ije/dyz006

Peytrignet, S., Marszalek, K., Grimm, F., Thorlby, R., & Wagstaff, T. (2022). *Children and young people's mental health: COVID-19 and the road ahead.* The Health Foundation. www.health.org.uk/news-and-comment/charts-and-infographics/children-and-young-people-s-mental-health

Pierce, M., Hope, H., Ford, T., Hatch, S., Hotopf, M., John, A., Kontopantelis, E., Webb, R., Wessely, S., McManus, S., & Abel, K.M. (2020). Mental health before and during the

COVID-19 pandemic: A longitudinal probability sample survey of the UK population. *The Lancet Psychiatry, 7*(10), 883–892. https://doi.org/10.1016/S2215-0366(20)30308-4

Powis, S. (2019). Clinically-led review of NHS access standards: Interim report from the NHS national medical director. NHS England. www.england.nhs.uk/publication/clinical-review-nhs-access-standards/

Royal College of Psychiatrists. (2022). *Public mental health implementation: A new centre and new opportunities*. Royal College of Psychiatrists. www.rcpsych.ac.uk/improving-care/public-mental-health-implementation-centre#:~:text=The%20College%20has%20launched%20%20the,promote%20mental%20wellbeing%20and%20resilience

Sadler, K., Vizard, T., Ford, T., Goodman, A., Goodman, R., & McManus, S. (2017). *Mental health of children and young people in England*. NHS Digital. https://openaccess.city.ac.uk/id/eprint/23650/

Scottish Government. (2017). *Mental health strategy: 2017–2027*. https://www.gov.scot/binaries/content/documents/govscot/publications/strategy-plan/2017/03/mental-health-strategy-2017-2027/documents/00516047-pdf/00516047-pdf/govscot%3Adocument/00516047.pdf

Vizard, T., Sadler, K., Ford, T., Newlove-Delgado, T., McManus, S., Marcheselli, F., Davis, J., Williams, T., Leach, C., Mandalia, D., & Cartwright, C. (2020). Mental health of children and young people in England. *Health and Social Care Information Centre*. www.infocoponline.es/pdf/mhcyp_2020_rep.pdf

Ward, J., Hargreaves, D., Turner, S., & Viner, R. (2021). Change in burden of disease in UK children and young people (0–24 years) over the past 20 years and estimation of potential burden in 2040: Analysis using Global Burden of Disease (GBD) data. *MedRvix*. https://doi.org/10.1101/2021.02.20.21252130

Weisz, J.R., Chorpita, B.F., Palinkas, L.A., Schoenwald, S.K., Miranda, J., Bearman, S.K., Daleiden, E L., Ugueto, A.M., Ho, A., Martin, J., Gray, J., Alleyne, A., Langer, D.A., Southam-Gerow, M.A., Gibbons, R.D., & Research Network on Youth Mental Health (2012). Testing standard and modular designs for psychotherapy treating depression, anxiety, and conduct problems in youth: A randomized effectiveness trial. *Archives of General Psychiatry, 69*(3), 274–282. https://doi.org/10.1001/archgenpsychiatry.2011.147

Weisz, J.R., Krumholz, L.S., Santucci, L., Thomassin, K., & Ng, M.Y. (2015). Shrinking the gap between research and practice: Tailoring and testing youth psychotherapies in clinical care contexts. *Annual Review of Clinical Psychology, 11*, 139–163. https://doi.org/10.1146/annurev-clinpsy-032814-112820

Welsh Government. (2012). *Together for mental health: A strategy for mental health and wellbeing in Wales*. www.gov.wales/sites/default/files/publications/2019-04/together-for-mental-health-summary.pdf

World Health Organisation. (2022). *World mental health report: Transforming mental health for all*. WHO. www.who.int/publications/i/item/9789240049338

2

Values and Practice

Jonathan Parker and Helen Barker

Introduction

This chapter will outline the foundational principles of low-intensity (LI) practice. Beginning with a working definition of LI practice for children, young people (CYP) and families, the chapter will then present a summary of the core values of evidence-based practice, outcome informed practice, participation, and collaborative practice. Latterly, and utilising real-world examples, it will consider how these principles and values translate into practice to help shape the delivery of effective LI support. This chapter will introduce and discuss several key elements of delivery, including the wider family and systemic context and essential considerations when providing low-intensity support, from assessment to case closure.

Values

What is Low-Intensity Practice with Children, Young People and Families?

To help understand the values and principles of LI practice for CYP and families, it is important to first clarify and attempt to define what it is. It has been widely acknowledged that the CYP LI initiative in England was inspired by the accomplishments of the adult Improving Access to Psychological Therapies (IAPT) LI Psychological Well-being Practitioner (PWP) programme (Clark, 2018), with a consequent commonality of core practice components. However, there is contnued deliberation in respect to an exact definition of LI practice for CYP (Shafran et al., 2021), with elements of commonality with longer-term Cognitive Behavioral Therapy (CBT) as well as brief, blended or intensive CBT approaches. Despite these overlaps, several key practice principles are acknowledged as fundamental characteristics of LI practice with CYP and families.

Low-Intensity Practice Principles for Children, Young People and Families

- Inclusion of guided self-help resources, worksheets and/or manualised interventions
- Predominantly draws on cognitive behavioural theory/approaches
- These may be delivered face-to-face, remotely or through an evidence-based/approved technological medium e.g., mobile phone application
- Brief course of intervention of between four to eight sessions
- Shorter duration of intervention sessions of 30 to 45 minutes
- Interventions are informed by evidence-based practice principles and delivered by correspondingly trained LI practitioners

Whilst there are benefits to a precise definition of LI practice, particularly for research purposes, it is critical to consider the developmental diversity of CYP and the subsequent variability of real-world practice. In addition, compared to the more established adult provision in England (Farrand, 2020) the CYP LI offer is relatively novel and emergent. Consequently, the design, development and implementation of LI clinical materials reflect this, with evidence-based treatment protocols, guided self-help materials and online resources likely to expand and diversify over time to reflect the broad range of factors and considerations of mental health support for CYP.

Evidence-Based Practice

Within CYP mental health care, evidence-based practice (EBP) can be defined as combining research-based data with practitioner expertise and, critically, the choice and values of those receiving support (Fonagy et al., 2016). Interventions informed by the best available evidence are a core value of LI support for CYP with EBP shown to largely outperform usual care in direct, randomised comparisons (Weisz et al., 2006).

Cognitive- and behavioural-informed interventions, that underpin the majority of LI practice, have demonstrable efficacy for the treatment of two of the most prevalent mental health difficulties experienced by CYP; anxiety (James et al., 2020) and low mood / depression (Oud et al., 2019). Within this, the evidence base for brief, LI interventions for children, young people and families, is evolving (Bennett et al., 2019) and CBT-informed group work for anxiety is yielding comparable results to individual CBT treatments or wait list controls (Flannery et al., 2000 as cited in Fonagy et al., 2016; Lau et al., 2010; Muris et al., 2002; Silverman et al., 1999). Although the evidence base for remote and technologically delivered interventions is evolving, these approaches are likely to increasingly inform brief, LI interventions for CYP. A 2019 systemic review of technology delivered interventions for depression and anxiety in children and adolescents (Grist et al., 2019) reported innovations based on CBT produced a medium post-intervention effect compared to waiting list control groups.

Figure 2.1 The Ingredients of Evidence-Based Practice

It is contended that intervention founded principally on trial-based protocols may encounter significant procedural limitations that undermine real-world effectiveness (Weisz et al., 2006). Consequently, there is recognition of a need to pragmatically understand and evaluate interventions for CYP within community settings (Fonagy et al., 2016). Several well established, community delivered LI treatment protocols from the adult IAPT LI programme (Clark, 2018) have contributed to the clinical architecture of CYP LI training curricula in England. There are growing indications of the effectiveness of these interventions, informed by the evaluation of real-world outcomes when delivered by practitioners who have undertaken these training programmes (Fuggle and Hepburn, 2019; Lockhart et al., 2021).

Outcome Informed Practice

Establishing itself as a core value of CYP mental health delivery in England (NHS England, 2014), the principle of outcome informed practice is central to guiding good clinical practice and improving our understanding of the real-world impact of clinical interventions. Outcome informed practice is largely directed by the application of routine outcome measurement (ROM) and feedback tools within clinical practice. The appropriate and collaborative use of ROM with CYP and families can inform and guide good practice and clinical decision making (Gondek et al., 2016; Law & Wolpert, 2014). Outcome informed practice should guide the course of LI support from initial assessment into the direction and application of intervention and support planning and instigating the completion of treatment. Outcome and feedback tools should be used collaboratively with the CYP and family as well as

Collaborative Practice

Working collaboratively with CYP and their families is a core value in LI work; gathering the views of CYP and supporting them to make decisions about their care should permeate through all areas of practice (Department of Health, 2015). Low-intensity practitioners should utilise a shared decision-making model when working with children and families which may improve the outcome of interventions and has been shown to facilitate engagement and satisfaction with care (Da Silva, 2012).

The CYP IAPT Principles in Child and Adolescent Mental Health Services; Values and Standards: 'Delivering with and delivering well' (NHS England, 2014) outlines some of the key principles of collaborative practice and the importance of listening to the voice of the child and young person throughout service development and provision. Working 'with' children and families should be considered at all stages of care. CYP and families should be informed about how to access support, what to expect from services and about the different types of interventions available. CYP and families should be given opportunities to make informed decisions about the interventions they receive and supported through any transitions or change in care provision. In addition, feedback should be sought from children and families throughout their care and used to inform service improvement and development.

Setting clear, collaborative goals with CYP is key to the process (Jacob et al., 2017) and LI practitioners should seek to understand what young people hope to gain from any support offered and how they would know if the intervention has been effective. Goals should be reviewed regularly and used to inform the practitioners' understanding of the progress of the intervention. In addition, utilising routine outcome measures collaboratively to track and monitor change throughout the intervention has been shown to improve collaboration by increasing satisfaction with treatment and motivation (Godenk et al., 2016). Several LI interventions rely on the active engagement of parents and CYP to read and discuss information, try out strategies and work out what fits for them as individuals. The skill of the LI practitioner is to guide CYP through this process using collaborative empiricism.

Service User Involvement and Participation

In England, The Five Year Forward View for Mental Health (Department of Health, 2014) emphasises that all service users should have confidence that services have been designed in partnership with people with lived experience of mental health problems.

The development of a new, LI workforce offers the opportunity to ensure participation is central to service implementation across all levels of development. Utilising frameworks such as the 4Pi Standards for Involvement (Department of Health, 4Pi Involvement for Influence, 2015) can be a useful implementation tool for services, providing key standards for principles, purpose, presence, process, and impact.

4Pi Principles for Effective Service User Engagement

- Service-users' views being valued equally to those of professionals
- Ensuring the purpose of their involvement is clear
- That their presence should be evident at all levels of the organisation and project
- That representation should reflect the diversity of the community
- The process of involvement should be inclusive, transparent, and well supported
- That impact should be clearly evaluated, and outcomes shared

In practice, this may include gathering community and service user views on local need and gaps in service provision, engaging local and hard-to-reach communities in these discussions and considering where services should be placed to best meet the needs of these communities. The views of CYP and families can be included at all levels of service delivery, including supporting poster/leaflet design, shaping the environment that children and families are seen in and being involved in recruitment of staff. Feedback from CYP and families should be gathered routinely and used to improve practice and service provision.

Experience of CYP Participation

'I got the amazing opportunity to be a panelist representing service user participation while hosting the interviews for the school Mental Health Support Team. It was such an eye-opening experience seeing how many people have such pure intentions for children and their mental health. It felt so empowering to be able to share my own experiences with the applicants, helping them understand what would be required of them in the role, all the different things they can do and ways they can help. It felt like such a game changer to be able to pinpoint the exact people we knew would have helped me when I was in the position of the children they will work with.' – Molly, 18 from Luton

Working with Families and Systems

CYP are best considered part of a wider system, their development and wellbeing being fostered by their environment and interactions with others (Bronfenbrenner & Morris, 2006). Viewing CYP in isolation would fail to recognise the significant impact that family, peers and the wider community have on their lives. These are central considerations for practitioners in terms of understanding the development and maintenance of presenting difficulties and, importantly, in respect to opportunities to build coping strategies, resilience and supportive networks.

A key aspect of providing LI intervention for CYP is working alongside the family and community supporting the CYP at a preventative level, to increase awareness of risk factors and promote positive psychological development (Law et al., 2015). Preventative family support programmes have been found to be effective in improving adolescent behavioural and mental health problems, particularly when targeting individuals at higher risk (Kuhn & Laird, 2014).

Where appropriate, and with the required consent, inclusion of parents/carers, school staff or other key adults at the point of assessment and throughout intervention is integral and assists the practitioner in developing a comprehensive understanding of key relationships and systemic factors influencing the young persons' experience (Faulconbridge et al., 2015). Intervening to support CYP to strengthen positive relationships within their family and wider community is key. This may involve working directly with parents/carers or other adults in the young person's life to support changes to factors that are contributing to the maintenance of the CYP's difficulties. In some cases, parent or carer participation is fundamental and interventions are delivered directly through them, such as within parent-led CBT for child anxiety (Chapter 16) and common child behaviour problem interventions (Chapter 15). Practitioners should also consider how families and systems can support strengths in the CYP, encouraging them to identify key people in their life that can provide support and encouragement and help them to build resilience at an individual and family level as well as in their social environment, such as school (Zolkoski & Bullock, 2012).

Another important part of systemic work for LI practitioners is liaising with the network supporting the child, young person and family. This may include attending joint meetings and offering advice or gathering information from other agencies, such as social care services, schools and youth centers. A key role for practitioners during any liaison or network support should be to advocate and provide a space for the views of the child or young person. Multi-agency working has been found to improve access to services and outcomes for CYP and families (Atkinson et al., 2002).

Practice

Overview

On a day-to-day basis, a CYP LI practitioner will deliver assessments and interventions face-to-face, by phone or online, working either 1:1, with the wider family and/or through the facilitation of group work sessions or psychoeducation workshops. When part of a service delivery model, it will be important for the practitioner, under guidance from the supervisor and line manager, to develop and implement a realistic but optimum workplan. This process would need to consider how best to maximise clinical delivery, whilst offering the required level of supervision and management support for the practitioner to experience being upheld, encouraged and sustained in their role. The workplan may also consider variation in working pattern; mixing group work, remote delivery and in-person support across different weekly schedules. Creating a variability of practice and changing experiences of workflow patterns may contribute to supporting practitioner engagement, motivation, and sustainability of role, but these would need to be agreed locally and based on service needs and operational requirements.

Access, Referral and Assessment

In line with values of the LI roles, the emphasis of LI services should be on ease of access. In England, the publication of *Future in Mind* (Department of Health, 2015) highlighted the importance of children, young people and parents/carers being able to access support for their mental wellbeing easily and in a timely manner. In practice, consideration needs to be given to how people are made aware of LI services, where services are based to promote ease of access, reducing stigma and engaging local communities and young people who may otherwise not seek or access support. Creating self-referral routes and/or linking services into a single point of entry referral system has been shown to improve access (Rocks et al., 2020) and should be a key consideration when setting up LI services.

It is critical that CYP, families and other professionals understand the types of support on offer through LI services and the types of mental health difficulties practitioners can offer support for. Services are encouraged to define local referral criteria and ensure this is communicated in an accessible way. The LI role is designed to support CYP with common mild to moderate mental health difficulties between the ages of five and 18. Possible presentations and referral criteria, as well as possible service exclusions, are summarised in Table 2.1.

All children, young people and families should be offered an assessment at the start of intervention. One of the key purposes of the assessment should be to listen to the views of the young person, understand what they are seeking support for and establish whether LI intervention is appropriate. Assessments should be holistic and collaborative, involving and gathering information from the child/young person/family and wider system supporting the child. Outcome measures should be used routinely as part of the assessment process to inform understanding of the presenting difficulties and impact on the child or young person's life. Children/young people and families should also be given the opportunity to discuss and set goals for any intervention offered. Chapter 3 describes and discusses the LI assessment process in further detail.

VALUES AND PRACTICE

Table 2.1 Examples of Referral Suitability for Low-Intensity Practice with CYP and Families

DO	MAY DO	SHOULD NOT DO
Common mental health difficulties that should respond well to low-intensity intervention	**Conditions which may respond to low-intensity intervention but require clinical discretion**	**Significant levels of need / complex conditions which are not suitable for brief or low-intensity intervention**
Low Mood / Mild to Moderate Depression	Anger difficulties	Pain management
	Low self-esteem	PTSD
Panic Disorder	Mild social anxiety disorder	Bipolar Disorder
Panic Disorder & Agoraphobia Generalised Anxiety Disorder / Worry	Some compulsive behaviours or emergent OCD	Psychosis
		Personality Disorders
Simple Phobia	Mild health anxiety	Eating Disorders
Sleep problems	Assertiveness/interpersonal challenges (e.g., with peers)	Chronic depression/anxiety
Stress management	Self-harm is disclosed but is assessed as linked to low-mood but is not assessed as enduring and high risk in nature	Established health anxiety
Behavioural Difficulties		Historical or current experiences of abuse or violence
		Complex interpersonal challenges
		Bereavement
		Enduring significant self-harm
		Relationship problems

Signposting and Liaison Work

Advising young people and families where they can access the right sort of early support is an important element of the LI role. When working with CYP, it is important to take a holistic approach to their care and consider what is needed to support their overall wellbeing and development in order to enable them to cope and thrive. The importance of signposting, and its role in supporting overall wellbeing, is increasingly recognised in mental health service provision (Health and Social Care Alliance Scotland, 2017). As a result, it is important for the practitioner to have an up-to-date awareness of the range of services available locally; this may include local youth centres or groups, leisure and sports facilities and financial/housing or legal support for families. In addition, LI practitioners will need to ensure that local services and teams develop a good understanding of their role and how it fits into the network of mental health support and services available to children, young people and their families.

Liaison and consultation should also be seen as an integral part of LI practice and may serve as an intervention in its own right. Supporting other professionals, such as teachers, youth workers or healthcare workers, to develop an increased awareness of mental health difficulties affecting CYP can be a key function of the role. In practice, this can be considered both at an individual and universal level. At an individual level, LI practitioners should support CYP to share their views with other professionals involved in their care and help the systems around the CYP to understand the factors maintaining the child or young person's difficulties and how best to intervene to support change. At a universal level, LI practitioners have a role in health promotion and training, increasing awareness of mental health and wellbeing and reducing stigmatisation of mental health problems (Law et al., 2015).

Case Management, Interventions and Case Closure

A qualified LI practitioner would typically work with a higher number of children, young people and families than other, more intensive, longer-term psychological therapies. This echoes the expected lower level of mental health difficulty that should be engaged with and the comparatively brief nature of the work that is intended. The proficient and professional management of the LI practitioner's caseload is a vital component of the role and one largely facilitated through the process of case management supervision (see Chapter 18). It is acknowledged that different localities will have discrete and variable service requirements leading to degrees of adaptation in how LI roles might be utilised. As a result, each service will need to establish its own caseload expectation and operating remit whilst maintaining fidelity to the LI caseload practice principles and the values of evidence-based, collaborative practice.

Where intervention is required, CYP and their families would usually be seen/ contacted on a weekly or fortnightly basis depending on the agreed optimum frequency of support. A course of intervention would normally be expected to be completed within four to eight contacts, with a degree of flexibility in contact type and frequency (rather than the uniformity of the standard 'same time, same place' approach) – an important consideration of the CYP's low-intensity role. Caseload supervision will be a helpful arena for a practitioner to discuss flexibility of approach but will also be an element of the role that will develop with experience. As previously outlined, the expectation is that, where appropriate and safe to do so, all LI practice is undertaken in full partnership with the family informing a shared decision-making approach and agreeing goals for the work to be carried out together. The child, young person and family should have a clear understanding of the rationale for the course of intervention proposed in line with the assessment undertaken, with the key components and expectations of the support offered, discussed, and jointly understood. Risk to the young person should be appropriately and sensitively monitored during intervention. Should needs or complexity escalate, or unforeseen risk or safeguarding concerns emerge during the work (see Chapter 4), it will be appropriate to seek guidance from senior professionals and in line with local policy and procedures. Where necessary, and under supervision/guidance from senior colleagues, it may be appropriate to support access or referral to a more suitable provision.

Case Closure Reasons

Cases will usually be closed in line with local policies and protocols but may include:

- The intervention has been completed with goals met and/or agreed completion
- During the course of assessment or intervention, an alternative service is deemed appropriate
- A young person and/or family consistently fail to attend agreed sessions

Professional Practice and Ethical Frameworks

LI practitioners should practice within the professional and ethical frameworks outlined by their service and in accordance with legal requirements and local policies. If accredited or registered with a particular governing body, such as the British Psychological Society (BPS, 2018) or the British Association for Behavioural and Cognitive Psychotherapies (BABCP, 2021), then practitioners will be bound by the relevant codes of conduct and standards outlined by their retrospective governing body. Low-intensity practitioners should ensure they are aware of relevant codes of conduct and professional practice guidance and that they always act within these. Whilst there are some differences across ethical frameworks and codes of practice, all highlight core values that LI practitioners should abide by. These include: respecting all those that we work with including rights to confidentiality; acting within our boundaries of competence and maintaining proficient practice; avoiding harm and managing risk; and acting within appropriate professional boundaries, with honesty and integrity.

Service Considerations and Early Intervention

Consideration should be given as to where a LI practitioner role (or team) will operate most effectively. How can access to early intervention referrals be facilitated whilst supporting an effective implementation of the role to avoid dilution or its merging or blurring with existing services? It may be appropriate for LI roles to be utilised across a range of settings including education, universal services, community settings, youth venues and appropriate community medical practices; ideally, where low level mental health difficulties are most likely to be first identified and in settings where those with early indications of mental health difficulties may not typically seek or access support within more traditional, clinic-based settings.

The flexibility to implement the LI role according to service need and context is an important aspect of the LI initiative (see Chapter 17) with shared learning and good practice examples between local areas contributing to development. However, it is *critical* for the CYP LI role to maintain the remit of working with referrals at a stage of early intervention. The challenge of achieving and sustaining this is acknowledged; increasing prevalence and demand for support from more complex presentations is well reported (Health Foundation, 2022). However, both the efficacy of the LI role and the feasibility of managing a high caseload rely on working with an appropriate cohort of mild to moderate early intervention referrals.

'A services experience of developing a low-intensity practice provision'

This LI service, based in London, targeted support for early presentations of anxiety, low mood, and behaviour difficulties. Several challenges emerged, particularly in relation to the variation in clinical thresholds across services. A central point of access (CPA) across local mental health (MH) services was set up which facilitated joint working and supported effective triage of referrals and agreements towards which would be the most appropriate pathway. This endeavour resulted in a noticeable increase in appropriate referrals for LI practitioners and increased the speed of delivery of early intervention services. Technology-related challenges remained one of the biggest headaches with services using different IT systems, but the communication between health, social care and the charity sector sitting together to screen referrals was of huge benefit. The LI practitioners supported the CAMHS duty clinicians in gathering information to decide appropriate care pathways and were invaluable in this role, as well as delivering interventions to mild-moderate presentations. A more recent development has been delivering online workshops (e.g., managing child's anxiety/behaviour/sleep) to young people and/or parents/carers who are waiting for other services. The LI practitioners are now an established and valuable part of the MH provision in the area and the setting up of the CPA has really improved access and signposting to appropriate services in a timely manner.

Carolyn Edwards, Supervisor and Service Lead

Summary

Low-intensity practice for CYP and families comprises a set of core principles and characteristics that distinguishes it from other modalities. Building on foundations of evidence-based, collaborative and outcome informed practice, the LI practitioner will typically utilise a range of CBT informed self-help resources and manualised interventions to deliver a course of support of between four and eight sessions. Successful delivery of LI practice is requisite on both practitioner and provider attending to a range of key elements including implementing and maintaining suitable referral criteria, robust and consistent assessment and supervision processes that incorporate the wider family and systemic context, an understanding of ethical and legal considerations and the application of appropriate and supportive liaison, signposting, and case closure processes.

References

Atkinson, M., Wilkin, A., Stott, A., Doherty, P., & Kinder, K. (2002). *Multi-agency Working: A Detailed Study*. National Foundation for Educational Research. www.nfer.ac.uk/publications/CSS02/CSS02.pdf

BABCP. (2021). *Standards of Conduct, Performance and Ethics*. British Association for Behavioural and Cognitive Psychotherapies. https://babcp.com/About/Governance-and-Policy/Policy-and-Documents

Bennett-Levy, J., Richards, D., Farrand, P., Christensen, H., Griffiths, K., Kavanagh, D., Klein, B., Lau, M., Proudfoot, J., Ritterband, L., White, J., & Williams, C. (2010). *Oxford Guide to Low Intensity CBT Interventions*. Oxford University Press.

BPS. (2018). *Code of Ethics and Conduct*. British Psychological Society. www.bps.org.uk/guidelines-and-policies

Bronfenbrenner, U., & Morris, P.A. (2006). The bioecological model of human development. In W. Damon & R.M. Lerner (Eds.)., *Handbook of Child Psychology*, Vol. 1: *Theoretical Models of Human Development*. (6th ed.). (pp. 793–828). John Wiley and Sons.

Clark, D.M. (2018). Realizing the mass public benefit of evidence-based psychological therapies: The IAPT program. *Annual Review of Clinical Psychology*, 14, 159–183. https://dx.doi.org/10.3109%2F09540261.2011.606803

Da Silva, D. (2012). *Helping People Share Decision Making*. The Health Foundation, London. www.health.org.uk/publications/helping-people-share-decision-making

Department of Health. (2014). *Five Years Forward View*. www.england.nhs.uk/wp-content/uploads/2014/10/5yfv-web.pdf

Department of Health. (2015). *Future in Mind: Promoting, Protecting and Improving Our Children and Young People's Mental Health and Wellbeing*. National Health Service England. https://assets.publishing.service.gov.uk/government/uploads/system/ uploads/attachment_data/file/414024/Childrens_Mental_Health.pdf

Farrand, P. (2020). Low-intensity CBT Skills and Interventions. Sage.

Faulconbridge, J., Law, D., & Laffan, A. (2015). *The Child and Family Clinical Psychology Review*, number 3 summer 2015. What good looks like in psychological services for children and young people and their families. Section 4: Types of intervention. *British Psychological Society*. www.researchgate.net/publication/283634680_What_good_looks_like_in_psychological_services_for_children_young_people_and_their_families_special_edition_of_the_child_and_family_clinical_psychology_review

Fonagy, P., Cottrell, D., Phillips, J., Bevington, D., Glaser, D., & Allison, E. (2016). What Works for whom: A critical review of treatments for children and adolescents. Guilford Press.

Fuggle, P., & Hepburn, C. (2019). *Clinical Outcomes for the Wellbeing Practitioner Programme for Children, Young People, and Their Parents/Carers*: Update report December 2019. Anna Freud National Centre for Children and Families. https://manuals.annafreud.org/cwp/#National%20CWP%20Outcomes%20Report%202019

Gondek, D., Edbrooke-Childs, J., Fink, E., Deighton, J., & Wolpert, M. (2016). Feedback from outcome measures and treatment effectiveness, treatment efficiency, and collaborative practice: A systematic review. *Administration and Policy in Mental Health and Mental Health Services Research*, 43(3), 325–343. https://link.springer.com/article/10.1007/s10488-015-0710-

Grist, R., Stallard, P., Croker, A., & Denne, M. (2019). Technology delivered interventions for depression and anxiety in children and adolescents: A systematic review and meta-analysis. *Clinical Child and Family Psychology Review*, 22(2), 147–171. https://doi-org.uoelibrary.idm.oclc.org/10.1007/s10567-018-0271-8

Health and Social Care Alliance Scotland. (2017). *Developing a Culture of Health: The Role of Signposting and Social Prescribing in Improving Health and Wellbeing*. www.alliance-scotland. org.uk/wp-content/uploads/2017/10/ALLIANCE-Developing-a-Culture-of-Health.pdf

Health Foundation. (2022). *Children and Young People's Mental Health*. www.health.org.uk/ news-and-comment/charts-and-infographics/children-and-young-people-s-mental-health

Jacob, J., De Francesco, D., Deighton, J., Law, D., Wolpert, M., & Edbrooke-Childs, J. (2017). Goal formulation and tracking in child mental health settings: When is it more likely and is it associated with satisfaction with care? *European Child Adolescent Psychiatry 26*(7), 759–770. https://doi.org/10.1007/s00787-016-0938-y

James, A.C., Reardon, T., Soler, A., James, G., & Creswell, C. (2020). Cognitive behavioural therapy for anxiety disorders in children and adolescents. *Cochrane Database of Systematic Reviews*. https://doi.org/10.1002/14651858.CD013162.pub2

Kuhn, E.S., & Laird, R.D. (2014). Family support programs and adolescent mental health: Review of evidence. *Adolescent Health Medicine and Therapeutics. 5*, 127–142. https://doi.org/ 10.2147%2FAHMT.S48057

Law, D., Faulconbridge, J., & Laffan, A. (2015). The child and family clinical psychology review, 3. What good looks like in psychological services for children and young people and their families. Section 3: Delivering effective psychological help in different parts of the system. *British Psychological Society*. www.researchgate.net/publication/283634680_What_good_looks_like_in_psychological_services_for_children_young_people_and_their_families_special_edition_of_the_child_and_family_clinical_psychology_review

Law, D., & Wolpert, M. (Eds.). (2014). Guide to Using Outcomes and Feedback Tools with Children, Young People and Families (2nd ed.). CAMHS Press.

Lockhart, G., Jones, C., & Sopp, V. (2021). A pilot practice-based outcomes evaluation of low-intensity cognitive behavioural interventions delivered by postgraduate trainees to children and young people with mild to moderate anxiety or low mood: An efficient way forward in mental health care? *The Cognitive Behaviour Therapist, 14*(E34). doi:10.1017/S1754470X21000301

Muris, P., Meesters, C., & van Melick, M. (2002). Treatment of childhood anxiety disorders: A preliminary comparison between cognitive-behavioural group therapy and a psychological placebo intervention. *Journal of Behaviour Therapy and Experimental Psychiatry, 33*(3–4), 143–158. doi: https://doi.org/10.1016/s0005-7916(02)00025-3

National Involvement Standards. (2015). *4Pi Involvement for Influence*. Department for Health. www.nationalvoices.org.uk/sites/default/files/public/ 4pinationalinvolvementstandardsfull report20152.pdf

NHS England. (2014). CYP-IAPT Principles in child and adolescent mental health services. Values and standards. "Delivering With and Delivering Well". www.england.nhs.uk/wp-content/uploads/2014/12/delvr-with-delvrng-well.pdf

Oud, M., De Winter, L., Vermeulen-Smit, E., Bodden, D., Nauta, M., Stone, L., van den Heuvel, M., Al Taher, R., de Graaf, I., Kendall, T., Engels, R., & Stikkelbroek, Y. (2019). Effectiveness of CBT for children and adolescents with depression: A systematic review and meta-regression analysis. *European Psychiatry, 57*, 33–45. https://doi.org/10. 1016/j.eurpsy.2018.12.008

Rocks, S., Glogowska, M., Stepney, M., Tsiachristas, A., & Fazel, M. (2020). Introducing a single point of access (SPA) to child and adolescent mental health services in England: A mixed-methods observational study. *BMC Health Services Research, 20*, 623 https://doi.org/10.1186/ s12913-020-05463-4

Shafran, R., Myles-Hooton, P., Bennett, S., & Öst, L.G. (2021). The concept and definition of low intensity cognitive behaviour therapy. *Behaviour Research and Therapy, 138*. https://doi. org/10.1016/j.brat.2021.103803

Silverman, W.K., Kurtines, W.M., Ginsburg, G.S., Weems, C.F., White, P., Delight, L., & Carmichael, H. (1999). Treating anxiety disorders in children with group Cognitive-Behavioural Therapy: A randomized clinical trial. *Journal of Consulting and Clinical Psychology*, *67*(6), 995–1003. https://doi.org/10.1037//0022-006x.67.6.995

Weisz, J., Jensen Doss, A., & Hawley, K. (2006). Evidence-based youth psychotherapies versus usual clinical care: A meta-analysis of direct comparisons. *American Psychologist, 61*(7), 671–689. https://doi.org/10.1037/0003-066x.61.7.671

Zolkoski, S.M., & Bullock, L.M. (2012). Resilience in children and youth: A review. *Children and Youth Services Review*, *34*(12), 2295–2303. https://psycnet.apa.org/doi/10.1016/j.childyouth.2012.08.009

Part 2
Low-Intensity CYP Assessment and Key Practice Considerations

3

Assessment in Low-Intensity Practice

Laura Raymen

Introduction

This chapter will outline the structure of a low-intensity (LI) assessment with children/young people and their parents/carers. It will explore how to gather client-centred information in relation to children/young people's presenting mental health difficulties and their impact. The chapter will then explain how to give information about LI cognitive behavioural therapy, create a collaborative problem statement and SMART goals and make shared decisions about LI assessments next steps, treatment planning and endings.

An Overview

The ability to conduct a comprehensive assessment, is a key feature of LI practice and LI Cognitive Behavioural Therapy (LICBT). An assessment is often the first meeting between a practitioner, a Child/Young Person (CYP) and their parents/carers and is an opportunity to gather information about their presenting mental health difficulties and the impact upon their day-to-day life. Assessment sessions allow practitioners to establish if the CYP is suitable for LICBT, or whether they need to be signposted to alternative support. Parents/carers may or may not be present for LICBT assessment sessions, which can take place in person, via video calling platforms, or over the telephone (Baguley et al., 2010). LICBT assessments should be completed within sixty minutes.

Throughout the assessment process, practitioners should aim for CYP to be collaboratively involved in all decisions that affect them (NHS England, 2014). Client-centred interviewing is designed to identify the presenting mental health difficulty, whilst involving clients as active partners in this process (Richards & Whyte, 2011). It is a way of trying to understand the CYP as a unique individual, using their knowledge and experience to guide the assessment. Where appropriate, parents/carers can also offer insight into the impacts of the presenting difficulty, especially when assessing primary school aged children. It can be useful to remember that whilst a practitioner may be the expert in LICBT, only the CYP is the expert in their individual experiences.

ASSESSMENT IN LOW-INTENSITY PRACTICE | 31

It is important to develop a range of 'common' and 'specific' factors skills to help facilitate a client-centred assessment (Richards & Whyte, 2011). Common factors refer to the mix of interpersonal skills that are common across therapeutic modalities such as, offering empathy, reflection, eye contact and a non-judgemental attitude; whilst specific factors refer to the elements of practice that differ across therapy types such as, knowledge of specific LICBT interventions (Richards & Farrand, 2010).

Following a session introduction, the structure of the assessment session (see Figure 3.1) can be split into three key areas:

- Information gathering – Practitioners should aim to gather information around the CYP's presenting mental health difficulty e.g., Autonomic, Behavioural, Cognitive and Emotional (ABCE) symptoms, the impacts and level of risk present.
- Information giving – Practitioners should give information about LICBT, the descriptive formulation cycle, evidence-based LICBT treatment options and/or signpost to more appropriate support.
- Shared decision making – Practitioners and CYP should aim to reach a shared understanding of the main presenting mental health difficulty, set realistic goals and support next steps in terms of treatment planning.

Key Points

- LI assessment involves information gathering, information giving and shared decision making
- LI assessment can be conducted with or without parents/carers, in person, via video calling platforms or over the telephone
- LI assessment uses a client-centred approach
- LI assessment draws on a combination of common and specific factors skills
- LI assessment is up to 60 minutes in duration

Vignettes

The following hypothetical CYP vignettes will be referred to and used as examples throughout this chapter:

1. Elna is an 8-year-old girl, who has started speaking to her Mum about feeling worried. The problem started happening 6 months ago when her Mum had an illness, and even had a short hospital stay at one stage. The illness lasted around two months, following which Mum started to feel better and has now made a full recovery. Elna started to have trouble sleeping when Mum became

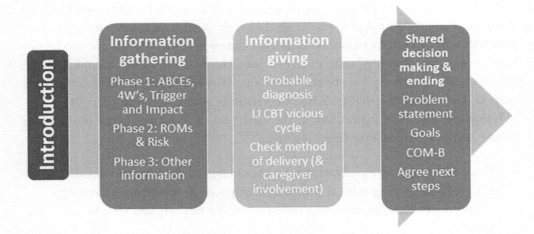

Figure 3.1 Structure of a low-intensity assessment session

ill and will often creep into Mum's bed at night. Over time it has become harder for her to attend school as she worries whether her Mum is okay. School have also found it harder to manage her behaviour when she is in. Due to her worries, she has found it harder to sleep in her own bed lately. She has also started ordering her toys in her room and becomes upset if this is altered in any way. Mum is concerned for the impact on Elna's friendships and education. Elna was born in South Africa and moved to England with Mum when she was two and has no contact with her father.

2. Theo is a boy who has just turned 12, and is reporting feeling low in mood. He is initially unsure of any triggers for his feelings other than a fall out with his best friend. He also started secondary school two months ago. Over time he has stopped several activities, including playing for his local football team, scouts, and swimming. He sees less of his friends in person, though he does spend a lot of time talking to two friends when gaming online, which he spends most of his free time doing. He continues to attend school, but is reluctant to speak to children he knows, as he believes that they are all close to the friend he fell out with. He has also been wary of speaking to other children in his class that did not attend his old school. He states that he has never had many friends and can find it hard to get to know people. He lives at home with Mum and Stepdad, who he gets on well with. They note that his appetite seems to be reduced and is restricted to a more narrow range of foods. He also has an older stepsister who has just turned 17.

3. Chris is 16 years old, and uses they/them pronouns. They live at home with Mum and Dad, and two younger siblings, aged 14 and 10. As exams have

been approaching Chris has been noticing increasing levels of anxiety and low mood. On top of this it has become harder to spend time with friends. In part this is due to the concern that if they were to go out, they would feel anxious and something bad would happen. This has led to less activity, withdrawal, and a lack of enjoyment. Whilst Chris has thought about going out with their closest friend, they report not being able to get away from the idea that it would not go well.

4. Lina is a 14-year-old girl, in year nine of secondary school and is a practising Christian. She lives at home with her Mum, and Gran. Her dad is married to Lina's step-mum Layla and Lina has a younger stepbrother (Sol, who is 8). Dad, Layla and Sol recently moved, so they now live further away, and visiting is more difficult. She has a positive relationship with her older brother who is away at university and her best friend Alec. Lina likes Graphics, Art, and History, she does not like German because she feels the teacher picks on her. Lina started feeling less like doing things she used to enjoy about 6 months ago, at the start of the school year, and it's gradually got worse. She has struggled to keep up with schoolwork and finds it difficult to stay focused and pay attention in lessons. Her grades are slipping, and her teachers have noticed a difference in her work. Lina lacks energy, even when she has slept well. She thinks she's a failure and isn't going to pass her exams or get a decent job. Lina also feels like a bad friend, because she struggles to find the energy or enthusiasm to meet up with friends and thinks she's not any fun to be around. Because she finds it difficult to be cheerful and be 'a good friend' Lina is spending more and more time at home on her own. Lina is not getting as much enjoyment out of activities she used to like (sketching, music, meeting up with her friends), and is getting annoyed at little things that she feels shouldn't bother her. She knows this is not 'normal' and tries to hide her frustration but tends to snap at her mum and grandmother for small things. Because she doesn't want to upset her family Lina spends a lot of time in her bedroom.

Introductions

Introductions should be clear, friendly, and set up the structure and purpose of the LI assessment session. It is best practice that practitioners introduce themselves by name and preferred name, as well as giving some information about their role as a LI practitioner (or trainee if applicable) (Farrand et al., 2010). An explanation of how practitioners work as part of a wider team within their service and the role of their clinical supervisor, can help to provide some useful context.

It is important to confirm the CYP's full and preferred name, as well as the names of any caregivers present, so that everyone has been introduced. To support inclusivity within clinical practice, consider the benefit of confirming the CYP's preferred pronouns where appropriate (Brown et al., 2020). If parents/carers are present, outlining their role within the assessment session can help to manage expectations and remove barriers to treatment participation (Nock & Kazdin, 2001). For example, normalising how most questions will be directed towards the CYP, with the parent/carer there to support when required.

To help set the structure of the assessment, it is useful to introduce a clear session agenda (Richards & Whyte, 2011) and to consider ways to share this visually with the CYP to increase accessibility e.g., on a big piece of paper, a whiteboard, or use of the share screen function (video calling platforms). Session agendas should include all the LICBT assessment items, which are briefly discussed to help set CYP and parent/carers' expectations, for example:

- Introductions
- Confidentiality
- What are you finding difficult?
- Routine Outcome Measure (ROMs)
- Risk assessment
- Problem statement
- SMART goals
- What is LICBT?
- Next steps

To support collaborative practice practitioners are encouraged to check if there is anything else that the CYP, or their parents/carers, would like to add to the assessment agenda. Encouraging CYP to tick off items as they progress through the session can help to promote active participation.

Good time-management skills are essential to covering all the agenda items within the timeframe (Telford & Wilson, 2010). Identifying when you will reach the 60-minute mark and checking this is okay with CYP can help to support this process. Practitioners may also wish to normalise note taking and hence occasional breaks in eye contact, explaining that they will still be actively listening. If practitioners are recording the assessment for supervision or university assignment purposes, it is best practice to confirm the CYP and parents/carers' (if present) verbal consent on the session recording.

Confidentiality and Consent to Share Information

Discussing the role of confidentiality and consent is an essential element of all clinical introductions (BABCP, 2017). Before undertaking an initial assessment, practitioners must ensure that confidentiality and consent have been discussed with the CYP and/or their parents/carers.

Different types of consent should be elicited from CYP and their families as a routine part of initial assessments. This should be revisited if a CYP was assessed elsewhere in the service but is new to working with a LI practitioner: including consent to treat and consent to share information. Consent to treat includes explaining what the session will involve and whether the CYP is happy to proceed. It is particularly important when the CYP may have been referred by an external party rather than self-referral. Under-16s can consent to treatment independently of parents/carers, provided they are deemed to be Gillick competent (readers are signposted to their mandatory service safeguarding training). If the CYP is attending alone without a parent/carer, it is important that practitioners have details of who the CYP would prefer to be contacted if needed (e.g., school, GP, parent/carer). Practitioners should check within their employing organisation for the arrangements in place that clearly outline the processes and principles for information sharing. Practitioners should be aware of how information is shared within an organisation (for example, expectations for note-keeping, information shared within supervision) and the processes for sharing information with others who may be involved in a CYP's life/care.

Regarding confidentiality, it is imperative that CYP understand what practitioners will do with the information they share and the conditions under which their confidentiality is broken. To help keep the assessment process client centred, practitioners are encouraged to check the CYP's understanding of confidentiality before explaining what this means within their sessions. Practitioners should check their services confidentiality policies, but in general all CYP information should remain confidential within the service, unless the following risk is identified:

- Risk to self
- Risk to others
- Risk from others

Practitioners are encouraged to give examples of who they may need to share information with if imminent/significant risk is disclosed e.g., the CYP's caregivers, GP and/or school safeguarding leads. To support transparency, it can be useful to explain that practitioners would seek to inform the CYP if they needed to break confidentiality and involve them in this process where appropriate.

It is recommended that confidentiality should be explained as keeping information 'safe and secure,' avoiding terms such as 'secret' and 'private' which may be misleading. CYP should be made aware that information is routinely shared within the service e.g., during supervision. For an example of how to explain confidentiality please see the box below.

Introducing Confidentiality

'Do you know what the term confidentiality means? What this means for our work together is that everything you talk about today remains safe and secure between us and my service. I will not be sharing this information beyond my team, unless I was worried about your safety. Keeping young people safe is the most important part of my job. There are three conditions when I would need to break confidentiality: If I felt you were a risk to yourself, if someone posed a risk to you, or if you posed a risk to someone else. I would always try to let you know before I shared your information further and I would involve you in that process as much as possible. Do you have any questions?'

Some practitioners may be concerned that giving examples of what would need to be shared, might prevent CYP from disclosing information; however, ensuring CYP have accurate information about what actions would be taken, can in fact increase disclosure through collaborative transparency and shared expectations (Blanchard & Farber, 2020). As McGillivray et al. (2022) reported, one of the biggest reasons for non-disclosure of suicidal ideation in CAMHS clients was fear of hospitalisation; the authors recommend clear discussions with CYP about the rules and limits of confidentiality to help alleviate distorted fears which may increase the likelihood of concealment.

Explaining the Limits of Confidentiality with Examples

'As I mentioned, there are some times when I would have to share information outside of our service. For example, if someone told me that they have thoughts of hurting themselves or that life would be better without them here, I would want to support them with managing those difficult thoughts and to come up with a plan to help, but I would not need to necessarily share that information outside of our team. However, if someone told me they were planning to end their life next Tuesday evening then I would need to communicate that information with others, possibly parents or carers so that there is a plan for keeping that young person safe. This would also apply if someone shared that they, or someone they knew were being hurt by someone. Finally, if someone shared with me that they really wanted to seriously hurt themselves or someone else, even if there was no active plan in place to do so, I might need to share this so we could keep people safe from harm. If I need to share information outside of the team like this, I will let you know first, and we would get your involvement in the process as much as possible. Do you have any questions for me around confidentiality?'

Considerations of when to breach confidentiality can be complex at times and should be taken to supervision. Vallance (2016) outlines four useful CAMHS case scenarios that can be valuably discussed in supervision for practitioners new to this work.

ASSESSMENT IN LOW-INTENSITY PRACTICE 37

Key Points: Introduction

- Introduce self by name and role
- Confirm CYP name and preferred name
- Explain the conditions of confidentiality
- Create a collaborative session agenda
- Set a clear timeframe/normalise note taking
- Confirm verbal consent to record (if relevant)

Interpersonal Skills

The nature of the relationship that practitioners form with a CYP and often their parents/carers, is the foundation on which all assessment, intervention, and outcome is built. Evidence suggests that the therapeutic relationship is as important as specific factors e.g., knowledge of intervention techniques, when it comes to treatment outcomes (Norcross & Lambert, 2019). Traditionally, the therapeutic alliance may be described as dyadic (between two people); However, in LICBT the relationship is triadic, consisting of interactions between the CYP, practitioner and the LICBT intervention materials. Known widely as guided self-help, this structured process allows the CYP, with the support of their practitioner to work towards overcoming their presenting mental health difficulties (Baguley et al., 2010).

Examples:

The following example statements that could develop the therapeutic alliance were all taken from Elna, Theo, Chris, and Lina's assessment sessions:

- 'I think lots of young people can find preparing for exams stressful and hard' – normalising
- 'It sounds like getting to sleep is really tricky for you at the moment Lina' – empathy
- 'So, you have told me you have stopped spending time with your friends, but still speak to a few online, have I understood that right?' – reflection
- 'I can see that you are experiencing some really difficult thoughts at the moment Chris' – empathy
- 'So far Elna, you have told me that you are worrying about your Mum getting ill and this is making it harder to go to school and sleep in your own bed. You have also noticed that your toys need to be in a certain order on your shelf. Is there anything else you would like to share with me?' – summarising
- 'So, you have stopped playing for your local football team because you don't have the motivation to train anymore, have I understood that correctly?' – reflection

LOW-INTENSITY PRACTICE WITH CYP AND FAMILIES

It is the successful application of both verbal and non-verbal competency skills that helps to build and maintain a strong therapeutic alliance. It is important to note that practitioners should aim to creatively engage the CYP at the appropriate developmental level (please see Chapter 6 for more information about creativity and adaptation). Practitioners should also aim to build a working relationship with any involved parents/carers, as their involvement can be important when supporting CYP with tasks outside of sessions. Furthermore, time management can also be considered an interpersonal skill, with the practitioner avoiding keeping the CYP for longer than necessary.

Key Points: Interpersonal Skills

- Verbal common factor skills include empathy, reflection, summarising, and normalising
- Nonverbal common factor skills include appropriate eye contact, facial expressions, and seating arrangements
- Development of the therapeutic alliance can be supported with use of age-appropriate creative techniques
- Time-management skills are also important – completing the assessment within 60 minutes

Information Gathering

One of the main aims of a LI assessment is to gain a disorder-specific understanding of the CYP's mental health difficulties. This helps to assess the CYP's suitability for LICBT support and informs the identification of the most evidence-based treatment intervention.

Each mental health difficulty has a common pattern of Autonomic (A), Behavioural (B), Cognitive (C) and Emotional (E) symptoms. Padesky and Mooney's (1990) *Five-Part* model, or Williams and Garland's (2002), *Five Areas* model, highlight the bidirectional links between ABCE symptoms within an individual's environmental context. See Figure 3.2 below for Theo's example descriptive formulation, linked to getting up on a Saturday morning. This is the type of information practitioners should aim to gather during this section of the assessment.

Funnelling

This information is gathered through a LICBT questioning style known as 'funnelling.' Funnelling involves moving from open to closed questions, as a way of gaining a clear and comprehensive understanding of CYPs presenting mental health difficulties.

ASSESSMENT IN LOW-INTENSITY PRACTICE | 39

Figure 3.2 Theo's presenting Descriptive Formulation

Source: Adapted with permission from Padesky and Mooney (1990) Five-Part Model, copyright Christine A. Padesky.

Practitioners should aim to open and close several situational specific funnels rather than gathering a mix of symptoms, experienced over a range of situations. For example, what are Theo's ABCEs when he is in school, when he speaks to new people and when he wakes up at the weekend? Gathering separate ABCE cycles in this way helps to build up a detailed picture of CYPs presenting mental health difficulties to inform the descriptive formulation, including any comorbidity, such as low mood and anxiety. To maintain a client centred approach, funnelling cannot be fully scripted as you are led by the information each CYP provides based on their individual experiences. Practitioners may also gather useful information from parents/caregivers who may be in attendance; however, it is recommended that any additional information is checked

LOW-INTENSITY PRACTICE WITH CYP AND FAMILIES

with the CYP, to keep your funnelling client centred. Please see the following transcript from Theo's LICBT assessment session for an example of the funnelling technique:

Example:

Practitioner: Could you tell me in your own words what you have been finding difficult recently? – general open question

Theo: I'm just feeling really rubbish all the time.

Practitioner: That sounds tough. Can you tell me more about feeling rubbish? – specific open question

Theo: I just do not have any energy to do anything anymore. Like go to football training or swimming at the weekends.

Practitioner: So you are finding it hard to play football or go swimming, you mentioned thoughts such as 'I do not have any energy', are you having any other thoughts? – specific open question

Theo: Umm, I guess I just do not see the point. Things never go right for me, and I am never going to be selected to play in the first team.

Practitioner: I wonder if you could tell me how often you are having these types of thoughts? – closed question

Theo: Probably most days at the moment. It is worse at night when I cannot sleep, or when my Mum tries to wake me up on a Saturday morning.

Practitioner: It must be difficult having those thoughts most days. How does it make you feel? – closed question

Theo: Frustrated... and sad, I guess. I just cannot seem to shift this feeling that nothing is going to get better for me.

Practitioner: It might not feel like it now, but that is quite a normal feeling for people who are low in mood. Is there anything that makes it worse? – closed question

Theo: Yeah being on my own, not leaving the house all day.

Practitioner: Okay, so sometimes you do not leave the house all day. Is there anything else that you have stopped doing since feeling rubbish? – specific open question

Theo: Seeing my friends, I kept ignoring their text messages and I don't like talking to people in school who didn't go to my old primary school.

Practitioner: Just to make sure I have this right; you have been feeling really rubbish and sad recently. You have been experiencing some negative thoughts such as 'I can't be bothered, and nothing is going right for me.' As a result, you have been struggling to find the energy to play football, going swimming and spend time with your friends. Is there anything else you would like to add? – summary/general open question

The Four W Questions

Alongside exploring the CYP's ABCE symptoms as part of the descriptive formulation, it is useful to gather the Four W Questions. These can be used to help structure questioning funnels:

- What? – identifying the main problem/problems and the symptoms being experienced (here and now).
- When? – Linked to time e.g., a time of the day (morning/evening) when symptoms are experienced to a lesser or worse extent.
- Where? – linked to location e.g., a particular place where symptoms are better or worse.
- With whom? – specific people that may make symptoms better or worse.

The FIDO Questions

To help clinch the finer details, Frequency, Intensity, Duration and Onset (FIDO) questioning can help to assess the severity of symptoms being presented. This can be used on a wider level e.g., how often do you have panic attacks? And on a specific symptom level e.g., how long does your heart race for?

- Frequency – How often does the problem/symptom occur in a day/week/month/year?
- Intensity – How strong/intense is the problem/symptom on a scale of 1–10?
- Duration – How long does the problem/symptom last for?
- Onset – When did this start/what triggers the symptoms on a day-to-day basis?

Triggers and Impact

As part of a comprehensive LICBT assessment, practitioners should also explore what triggers the CYP's symptoms and the impact that this is having on their day-to-day lives. Please note that a day-to-day trigger differs from the initial onset of the CYP's presenting difficulty. Impact should be gathered around the following key life areas:

- Education
- Home life
- Social life
- Hobbies/interests

Where possible try to gather the consequence of the impact, for example, Theo may share that he is falling behind at school, yet, with some further questioning the practitioner may be able to establish the consequence of this is that Theo is worried he will not reach his predicted grades and is having more negative thoughts about his future.

Routine Outcome Measures (ROMs)

In line with the LICBT minimum data set, standardised Routine Outcomes Measures (ROMs) should be completed as part of the initial assessment and at every session to ensure practitioners are working within a stepped care model of mental health service delivery. NHS England (2014) outlines how ROMs should be used to draw on CYP and parent/carer self-report, used to directly inform clinical work and to evaluate the effectiveness of interventions and services. See Table 3.1 for the recommended minimum data set for LICBT assessment sessions. Please note, all these questionnaires can be found on the Child Outcomes Research Consortium (CORC) website.

Table 3.1   Routine Outcome Measures (ROMs): Minimum data set for low-intensity assessment

	Depression and Anxiety	**Parenting/Behavioural Difficulties**
ROM	Revised Children's Anxiety and Depression Scale **RCADS** (Full) Self-reported	Strengths and Difficulties Questionnaire **(SDQ)** Parental/teacher
Age range	8–18	Parent or teacher of a CYP 2–17 years
Type of measure	Likert scale, 47 items	Likert scale, 25 items
Assessing	6 problem specific scales: Separation anxiety, Social Phobia, Generalised Anxiety Disorder, Panic Disorder OCD and Major Depressive Disorder	4 symptom specific scales (conduct, emotional, peer problems, hyperactivity) and one positive scale prosocial
Author	Chorpita et al. (2000)	Goodman (2001)
ROM	Revised Children's Anxiety and Depression Scale **RCADS** (Full) Parent-reported	Strengths and Difficulties Questionnaire **(SDQ)**
Age range	Caregiver of a CYP aged 8–18	11–17
Type of Measure	Likert, 47 items	Likert, 25 items divided between 5 scales
Assessing	6 problem specific scales: Separation anxiety, Social Phobia, Generalised Anxiety Disorder, Panic Disorder, OCD and Major Depressive Disorder	4 symptom specific (conduct, emotional, peer problems, hyperactivity) and 1 positive scale prosocial
Author	Chorpita et al. (2000)	Goodman (2001)
ROM	Young Children's Outcome Rating Scale **(YCORS)** Children's Outcome Rating Scale **(CORS)** Outcome Rating Scale **(ORS)**	Oppositional Defiance Disorder – parent reported **(ODD)**
Age	YCORS – 5 and under CORS – 6-12 ORS 13+	Any, completed by parent/caregiver
Type of Measure	Visual Analogue Scale, 4 items	Likert scale, 8 items
Assesses	General mental health: personal wellbeing, interpersonal relationships, social relations and overall sense of wellbeing	Behavioural difficulties diagnostic criteria taken from the DSM-V
Author	Miller et al. (2003)	Behavioural difficulties diagnostic criteria taken from the DSM-V
ROM	Goal Based Outcomes **(GBO)**	Brief Parental Self-Efficacy Scale **(BP-SES)**
Age	All	All, completed by parent/carers

Table 3.1   (Continued)

	Depression and Anxiety	Parenting/Behavioural Difficulties
Type of Measure Assesses	(0–10) one scale per goal	Likert, 5 items
Assesses	No progress towards goal (0), goal achieved (10)	Parental/caregiver report of parental self-efficacy
Author	Law and Jacob (2015)	Woolgar et al. (unpublished data)
ROM	Child Session Rating Scale **(CSRS)** Session Rating Scale **(SRS)**	Child Session Rating Scale **(CSRS)** Session Rating Scale **(SRS)**
Age	Child Session Rating Scale **(CSRS)**: 6-12 Session Rating Scale **(SRS)**: 13+	Child Session Rating Scale **(CSRS)**: 6-12 Session Rating Scale **(SRS)**: 13+
Type of Measure	Likert, 4 items	Likert, 4 items
Author	Duncan et al. (2003)	Duncan et al. (2003)

Caption: A table which includes all the ROMs used to support work with depression, anxiety, and behavioural difficulties. The age range, type of measure, what it assesses, and author are included as part of the table.

Source: Adapted with permission from Richard & Whyte (2011) IAPT Reach out guide. Reach_Out_3rd_edition.pdf (exeter.ac.uk)

Worthern and Lambert (2007) found ROMs help to improve clinicians' ability to detect the worsening of symptoms and provide them with information that may have otherwise been missed. Non-burdensome and meaningful use of ROMs has also been found to reduce drop out (Miller et al., 2006) and enhance shared decision making (Coulter, 2010). Additionally, standardised ROMs are used to support the continued evaluation of the effectiveness of LICBT interventions and contribute towards whole service evaluations. However, these questionnaire measures should not be used as a stand-alone diagnostic tool and instead considered within the context of the other information gathered during the assessment session (Law & Wolpert, 2014). It is important to collaboratively review the results of the measures with the CYP/parents/carers e.g., checking scores align with their experience and funnelling around any particularly high scoring items. It can be helpful to encourage CYP/parents/carers to complete the ROMs before the session, so practitioners have time to outline the rationale behind their regular completion and review scores together in session. See the box below for a clinical example.

Clinical Example

'Thank you for completing the questionnaires that I sent out Lina, these measures are one tool that helps me to make sure that you receive the most suitable support. If we decide to work together, ROMs allow us to track how things are going each week and comparing scores on a graph can help to measure progress over time. Did you have any questions when completing the questionnaires? ... I can see that for "I feel worthless" you scored "always" could you tell me a bit more about that? ... Overall, this questionnaire suggests that you are experiencing symptoms of something called low mood/depression. Is this something you have heard of before? Does this fit with your experience?'

Key Points: Information gathering

- Funnelling is a LICBT questioning technique which aims to gather client centred information, moving from open to closed questioning
- Low-intensity assessment aims to identify key ABCE disorder specific symptoms to build a collaborative descriptive formulation
- LI assessment explores the 4 W's – What, When, Where, With Whom
- Clinching the finer details FIDO – Frequency, Intensity, Duration, Onset
- Gathering day-to-day triggers and impact – Education, Family Life, Social Life, Hobbies and Interests
- It is important to complete and review ROMs

Risk Assessment

A thorough and comprehensive risk assessment is an essential feature of all assessment and subsequent intervention sessions (Farrand et al., 2010). Assessing CYP safety in terms of risk to self, risk from others and risk to others, both currently and in the past, is the most important part of the LI practitioner role and helps to assess CYP suitability for LICBT support. It is recommended that CYP are given the option for their parent/carer to remain or leave the room for this section, to maximise the opportunity for risk disclosure. Please see Chapter 4 – Risk Assessment and Management, for more detail and information.

Additional Information

Once a clear understanding of the CYP's presenting difficulties is established, practitioners should seek to gather the following additional information to check the CYP's suitability for LICBT support:

- The initial onset of the current episode – when did it start?
- Why is the CYP seeking help now – what is their motivation?
- Have they received/are they receiving any other mental health support – LICBT needs to remain single stranded in approach
- Are they taking any prescribed medication – any queries should be signposted to their General Practitioner (GP)
- Age-appropriate enquiry into use of alcohol and illicit drug use – could be masking symptoms/a risk concern

Information Giving and Shared Decision Making

The Problem Statement

To condense the detailed information gathered during a LI assessment, a summary of the CYP's main presenting difficulties should be developed in the form of a problem statement (Farrand et al., 2010). This summary not only helps the practitioner and CYP to reach a shared understanding of their main presenting mental health difficulty, but also forms a baseline to compare progress against during subsequent intervention sessions (Beckwith & Crichton, 2010). All LI practitioners should seek to treat one mental health presentation at a time, adopting a single stranded approach (Baguley et al., 2010). Therefore, the problem statement should remain the same unless the focus of treatment changes e.g., switching to support low mood rather than anxiety. The problem statement should aim to summarise the following key areas:

- The main presenting difficulty
- Trigger
- Autonomic, Behavioural, Cognitive, Emotional symptoms
- Impact

To support client centred practice the problem statement should be written in the CYP's own words, and the opportunity given for the CYP to complete the sentence starters with the support of the practitioner. Doing so can help the CYP to take increased ownership of their problem statement and support collaborative practice. Practitioners may wish to adapt the terminology of 'problem statement' to make this more CYP friendly, examples include:

- My summary
- Summary statement
- What is going on for me

Please see the box below for Theo's example problem statement. This information should aim to summarise the information gathered earlier when funnelling, rather than providing an opportunity to gather new information.

Theo's Problem Statement

My main problem is feeling low most days since starting secondary school in September. I feel tired and lethargic and have stopped going to football training, scouts, and swimming. I have thoughts such as, 'I can't be bothered' and 'nothing ever goes well for me,' this often leaves me feeling sad and frustrated. The impact of this is I am not making any new friends and spending more time alone in my bedroom which is making me feel isolated.

Once the problem statement has been created, practitioners are encouraged to seek the CYP's view that this is an accurate representation of their experiences and that they are happy for this to form the focus of subsequent intervention sessions. See the box below for a problem statement template, with some suggested sentence starters.

Problem Statement Template

- My main problem is...
- This is triggered by...
- In my body I experience...
- I have thoughts such as...
- I have stopped/started doing...
- Emotionally I feel...
- The impact of this is...

Goal Setting

Setting collaborative treatment goals is a key feature of all Cognitive Behavioural Therapy (Beck et al., 1979). Goal setting has been found to support investment in the therapeutic process and overall treatment outcomes (Michalak & Holtforth, 2006). At the initial assessment, the practitioner should seek to develop three relevant 'SMART' goals that the CYP would like to work towards:

- **S**pecific
- **M**easurable
- **A**chievable
- **R**ealistic
- **T**imely

Use of the SMART framework can help to formulate a 'desire to feel better' into something more specific for which progression towards can be objectively measured. Behavioural based goals e.g., 'to start doing more of something' are easier to fit within the SMART framework, than more abstract goals such as, 'to feel less worried.' Asking questions such as, 'What would you be doing if you felt less worried?' can help to support the development of relevant and meaningful goals for LI support. Once goals are agreed upon, progress towards these should be rated on the Goal Based Outcome (GBO) (Law & Jacob, 2013) and then tracked at each intervention session. An example of SMART goals can be found in the box below:

Theo's SMART Goals

- To go to football training at my local club once a week (Thursday evening), even if I do not feel like going.
- To arrange to meet my friend Charlie at the skate park once a month, rather than just talking when gaming.
- To complete half an hour of homework/revision when I get in from school 16:00–16:30 so I have more time to enjoy myself at the weekends

Probable Diagnosis

As LICBT interventions are disorder specific, accurate problem identification is required to match the CYP's mental health presentation to the most evidence-based treatment option. Within LICBT this is achieved through the giving of a 'probable diagnoses' in line with the ICD-10 (WHO, 1992) diagnostic categories. Phrases such as, 'It appears that you are experiencing symptoms in line with something called social anxiety' may be used. Please note that LI practitioners are not qualified to give formal mental health diagnoses and this distinction should be made clear in the initial assessment.

It is recommended that practitioners check the young person's and if relevant parent/carers', understanding of the mental health presentation identified e.g., 'Have you heard of social anxiety?' Consider offering some psychoeducation around common symptoms and impacts to help normalise their experiences and instil hope for positive change. It is important to note that should a practitioner be unsure of which probable diagnosis to give, or which comorbidity to focus upon, best practice is for practitioners to seek support from their clinical supervisor. CYP do not require a probable diagnosis to access LICBT support, but it can be offered where appropriate and helpful to do so.

Information Giving – Descriptive Formulation

It is important that CYP leave the LI assessment with an awareness of the type of support that is offered. Only when the CYP has a clear understanding of what LICBT is, and what is involved, can they make informed decisions about their care. Time should therefore be allocated to giving information about how LICBT is focused upon the 'here and now' (Richards, 2010) and how it uses a range of evidence-based tools and techniques to help CYP manage their mood and experiences. The aim of LICBT is that CYP will continue to use the techniques they learn once the intervention sessions have been completed. On occasion it may be deemed appropriate to work with the parents/carers to help them to support their CYP for example, via parent-led CBT or parenting interventions.

A section of information giving should be focused upon introducing the descriptive formulation, with age-appropriate information being provided around the maintenance of the relevant mental health presentation. For example, explaining how current avoidance behaviours may be offering short-term relief, but resulting in longer-term maintenance of the CYP's symptoms. Practitioners are encouraged to outline how LICBT aims to break this vicious cycle through changes to either the cognitions, behaviours, or a combination of the two.

Giving practical information about the nature of LICBT support can help a CYP to decide whether this is the most suitable support for them at this point in time, for example:

- How many sessions you can offer (standard is six–eight)
- Where these will take place (school/home/community/online/telephone)
- What will be involved (regular setting of home practice tasks)
- Who will be there (caregivers, same/different practitioner)

Giving such information offers an opportunity to seek the young person's preferences, support shared decision making and increase the accessibility of your LICBT support. For some tips to support information giving please see the box below:

Tips to Support Information Giving

- Consider checking the CYP's/parents/carer's understanding of LICBT before giving information
- Try to make this section as visual and interactive as possible e.g., with use of a descriptive formulation diagram
- To consolidate understanding, encourage the CYP to input their ABCE symptoms into the descriptive formulation diagram
- Consider use of the share screen function if using a video calling platform

---

COM-B Model

The guided self-help format of LICBT requires motivation and commitment from the CYP (and potentially their parents/carers) to instigate behavioural change. At assessment it is important to consider any potential barriers to CYP participation in LICBT support, and this can be achieved through use of the COM-B system, a framework for understanding behaviour change (Michie et al., 2011) see Figure 3.3.

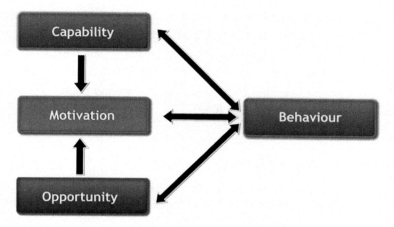

Figure 3.3 The COM-B model of Behaviour

The COM-B system suggests that there are three interacting conditions required to achieve behavioural change (Michie et al., 2011). Capability, the physical and psychological ability to complete a behaviour; Opportunity, external influences on behaviour that are part of the individual's physical and social environment; and Motivation, automatic and reflective processes that drive and direct behaviour. Applying this system to a LI assessment may take the following format:

Example COM-B Assessment Questions:

- Asking Lina if there is anyone at home who could support her with the home practice tasks – Opportunity
- Checking if Theo feels like this is the right time for him to engage in this type of support – Motivation
- Adapting your information giving so the language and resources used are accessible for 6-year-old Elna – Capability
- Asking if Theo can get to your sessions independently – Opportunity
- Checking if Chris is willing to complete tasks outside of sessions – Motivation

---

Practitioners are encouraged to use this model to guide questioning around any potential barriers to accessibility and not to introduce the specific COM-B system to CYP in session.

Next Steps and Ending

The LI assessment should end with the practitioner, CYP and any parents/carers making a shared decision about the next steps. This may involve the practitioner taking

LOW-INTENSITY PRACTICE WITH CYP AND FAMILIES

the information gathered to case management supervision, before meeting with the CYP and parents/carers again to discuss LICBT suitability and the different evidence-based treatment options. Providing a session summary can help to contextualise the session and check if the CYP and their parent/carers have any further questions. A Session Rating Scale (SRS) should be completed to gather useful feedback to support future adaptions (Duncan et al., 2003).

Shared Decision Making and Ending

- Work towards the creation of a collaborative problem statement
- Collaborative development of three SMART goals for treatment
- Information giving around the descriptive formulation diagram
- Giving of practical information – how many sessions, delivery methods, role of home practice tasks
- Shared decision making around the next steps and ending

Summary

This chapter has provided an overview of a LI CYP assessment session. Through the process of information gathering, information giving and shared decision making the practitioner should have a clear understanding of the CYP's presenting mental health difficulties and the impact of these upon their day-to-day life. The importance of client centred, collaborative practice has been highlighted, with an emphasis on the development of both common and specific factor skills to develop a therapeutic alliance with both CYP and any parents/carers. ROMs should be completed to support accurate problem identification and as part of the minimum data set for LICBT. The creation of a problem statement and SMART goals help to form a baseline to measure progress against. LI assessment sessions are the first step towards ensuring CYP have fair access to evidence-based mental health support. Early intervention aims to equip CYP with lifelong practical tools and techniques to reduce the impact of mild to moderate mental health presentations.

For further resources, please visit the CEDAR website at: https://cedar.exeter.ac.uk/resources/cyp/

References

BABCP. (2017). *Standard of Conduct, Performance and Ethics*. Retrieved from: https://babcp.com/Portals/0/Files/About/BABCP-Standards-of-Conduct-Performance-and-Ethics%20Feb%202021.pdf?ver=2021-02-24-142904-080

Baguley, C., Farrand, P., Hope, R., Leibowitz, J., Lovell, K., Lucock, M., O'Neill, C., Paxton, R., Pilling, S., Richards, D., & Turpin, G. (2010). *Good Practice Guidance on the Use of Self-help Materials Within IAPT Services.* NHS.

Beck, A.T., Rush, A.J., Shaw, B.F., & Emery, G. (1979). *Cognitive Therapy of Depression.* Guilford Press.

Beckwith, A., & Crichton, J. (2010). The negotiation of the problem statement in cognitive behavioural therapy. *Communication and Medicine, 7*(1), 23–32.

Blanchard, M., & Farber, B.A. (2020). "It is never okay to talk about suicide": Patients' reasons for concealing suicidal ideation in psychotherapy. *Psychotherapy Research, 30*(1), 124–136.

Brown, C., Frohard-Dourlent, H., Wood, B.A., Saewyc, E., Eisenberg, M.E., & Porta, C.M. (2020). "It makes such a difference": An examination of how LGBTQ youth talk about personal gender pronouns. *Journal of the American Association of Nurse Practitioners, 32*(1), 70–80.

Chorpita, B.F., Yim, L., Moffitt, C., Umemoto, L.A., & Francis, S.E. (2000). Assessment of symptoms of DSM-IV anxiety and depression in children: A revised child anxiety and depression scale. *Behaviour Research and Therapy, 38*(8), 835–855.

Coulter, A. (2010). Do patients want a choice and does it work?. *British Medical Journal, 341.* 10.1136/bmj.c4989

Duncan, B.L., Miller, S.D., Sparks, J.A., Claud, D.A., Reynolds, L.R., Brown, J., & Johnson, L.D. (2003). The session rating scale: Preliminary psychometric properties of a "working" alliance measure. *Journal of Brief Therapy, 3*(1), 3–12.

Farrand, P., Williams, C., Bennett-Levy, J., & Richards, D.A. (2010). Low intensity CBT assessment: In person or by phone. In J. Bennett-Levy, D. Richards, P. Farrand, H. Christensen, K. Griffiths, D. Kavanagh, B. Klein, M. A. Lau, J. Proudfoot, L. Ritterband, J. White & C. Williams (Eds.), *Oxford Guide to Low Intensity CBT Interventions* (pp. 89–96). Oxford University Press.

Goodman, R. (2001). Psychometric properties of the strengths and difficulties questionnaire. *Journal of the American Academy of Child and Adolescent Psychiatry, 40*(11), 1337–1345.

Law, D., & Jacob, J. (2013). *Goals and Goal Based Outcomes (GBOs).* CAMHS Press.

Law, D., & Wolpert, M. (2014). *Guide to Using Outcomes and Feedback Tools.* Retrieved from: https://www.corc.uk.net/media/1950/201404guide_to_using_outcomes_measures_and_feedback_tools-updated.pdf (corc.uk.net)

McGillivray, L., Rheinberger, D., Wang, J., Burnett, A., & Torok, M. (2022). Non-disclosing youth: A cross sectional study to understand why young people do not disclose suicidal thoughts to their mental health professional. *BMC Psychiatry, 22*(1), 1–11.

Michalak, J., & Holtforth, M.G. (2006). Where do we go from here? The goal perspective in psychotherapy. *Clinical Psychology: Science and Practice, 13*(4), 346–365.

Michie, S., Van Stralen, M.M., & West, R. (2011). The behaviour change wheel: A new method for characterising and designing behaviour change interventions. *Implementation Science, 6*(1), 1–12.

Miller, S.D., Duncan, B.L., Brown, J., Sparks, J.A., & Claud, D.A. (2003). The outcome rating scale: A preliminary study of the reliability, validity, and feasibility of a brief visual analog measure. *Journal of Brief Therapy, 2*(2), 91–100.

Miller, S.D., Duncan, B.L., Brown, J., Sorrell, R., & Chalk, M.B. (2006). Using formal client feedback to improve retention and outcome: Making ongoing, real-time assessment feasible. *Journal of Brief Therapy, 5*(1), 5–22.

NHS England (2014). *CYP IAPT Principles in Child and Adolescent Mental Health Services. Values and Standards. "Delivering with and delivering well".* Retrieved from: delvr-with-delvrng-well. pdf (england.nhs.uk)

Nock, M.K., & Kazdin, A.E. (2001). Parent expectancies for child therapy: Assessment and relation to participation in treatment. *Journal of Child and Family Studies, 10*(2), 155–180.

Norcross, J.C., & Lambert, M.J. (Eds.). (2019). *Psychotherapy Relationships That Work:* Volume 1: *Evidence-based Therapist Contributions.* Oxford University Press.

Padesky, C.A., & Mooney, K. (1990). Presenting the cognitive model to clients. *Cognitive Therapy Newsletter International, 6,* 13–14.

Richards, D.A. (2010). Access and organization: Putting low intensity interventions to work in clinical services. In J. Bennett-Levy, D. Richards, P. Farrand, H. Christensen, K. Griffiths, D. Kavanagh, B. Klein, M. A. Lau, J. Proudfoot, L. Ritterband, J. White & Chris Williams (Eds.), *Oxford Guide to Low Intensity CBT Interventions* (pp. 19–34). Oxford University Press.

Richards, D.A., & Farrand, P. (2010). Choosing self-help books wisely: Sorting the wheat from the chaff. In J. Bennett-Levy, D. Richards, P. Farrand, H. Christensen, K. Griffiths, D. Kavanagh, B. Klein, M. A. Lau, J. Proudfoot, L. Ritterband, J. White & Chris Williams (Eds.), *Oxford Guide to Low Intensity CBT Interventions* (pp. 201–207). Oxford University Press.

Richards, D.A., & Whyte, M. (2011). National Programme Student Materials to Support the Delivery of Training for Psychological Wellbeing Practitioners Delivering Low Intensity Interventions. Rethink Mental Illness.

Telford, J., & Wilson, R. (2010). From classroom to 'shop floor': Challenges faced as a low intensity practitioner. In J. Bennett-Levy, D. Richards, P. Farrand, H. Christensen, K. Griffiths, D. Kavanagh, B. Klein, M. A. Lau, J. Proudfoot, L. Ritterband, J. White & Chris Williams (Eds.), *Oxford Guide to Low Intensity CBT Interventions* (pp. 469–474). Oxford University Press.

Vallance, A.K. (2016). 'Shhh! please don't tell…' confidentiality in child and adolescent mental health. *BJPsych Advances, 22*(1), 25–35.

Williams, C., & Garland, A. (2002). A cognitive–behavioural therapy assessment model for use in everyday clinical practice. *Advances in Psychiatric Treatment, 8*(3), 172–179.

Woolgar, M., Humayun, S., Scott, S., & Dadds, M. (unpublished data). *A new brief parenting efficacy scale.* Retrieved from: Brief Parental Self Efficacy Scale (BPSES) (corc.uk.net)

World Health Organization. (1992). The ICD-10 Classification of Mental and Behavioural Disorders: Clinical Descriptions and Diagnostic Guidelines. World Health Organization.

Worthen, V.E., & Lambert, M.J. (2007). Outcome oriented supervision: Advantages of adding systematic client tracking to supportive consultations. *Counselling and Psychotherapy Research, 7*(1), 48–53.

4

Risk Assessment and Management

Hannah Vickery (née Whitney)

Introduction

This chapter will describe the different types of risk and risk factors which require attention within a low-intensity assessment with CYP and their families. It will outline how to structure and undertake a risk assessment appropriate for low-intensity practice and settings and gather risk information in an age-appropriate, culturally competent and client-centred way. Finally, the chapter will explain how to communicate risk assessment information clearly and create risk management plans under supervision.

Overview

Although the ability to assess and appropriately manage risk are considered core competencies for all staff holding a caseload within child and adolescent mental health services (Roth et al., 2011), the practice will vary considerably depending on the service context. For example, specialist assessments of adverse childhood experiences may be completed within Looked After Children teams, and specific structured risk assessments may be undertaken within youth offending settings. As covered in Chapter 3, before undertaking an initial assessment, in which the risk assessment should sit, practitioners must ensure that confidentiality and consent have been discussed with the child, young person and/or family. For the purposes of this text, the focus is on conducting risk assessments and management plans within Low-Intensity Practice with Children and Young People (LI-CYP). In this context, the risk assessment should serve the primary functions detailed below.

Functions of a Low-Intensity Risk Assessment:

- Further engaging the child/adolescent and/or their parent/carer; risk assessments provide opportunities for validation and normalising as well as the implementation of support and protection where necessary
- Gathering information about the child or young person (CYP)'s safety with regards to historic and current risk to self, others and from others

- Creating a clear record of the risk assessment information at the time of assessment within client notes including details of appropriate communication and agreed actions
- Using shared decision making and supervision to establish and employ the most appropriate risk management actions

---

A good risk assessment combines consideration of a range of psychosocial factors as part of a clinical interview to capture the CYP's care needs and assess the following types of risk:

- risk to self (including self-harm, suicidal ideation and behaviour, drug and alcohol use, and self-neglect)
- risk from others (including neglect, abuse, bullying, online grooming, sexual exploitation etc.)
- risk to others (including thoughts of harming others)

This chapter will outline engagement and confidentiality aspects as essential prerequisites to risk assessments before going on to detail the types of risk factors that require appraisal, an outline of the types of risk to assess, example questions and a discussion regarding the importance of cultural humility and sensitivity within the process. It will finish with discussion about risk management and the low-intensity practitioner's role within this. The case study of Lina will be referred to throughout this chapter.

Engagement

Given that one of the main objectives of the initial assessment process, and a significant predictor of positive outcomes, is the engagement of the child, young person or family (Shirk et al., 2011), it is important that low-intensity practitioners consider this priority whilst assessing risk. The interpersonal common factor skills of active listening, the use of reflective summaries, and the maintaining of a warm and non-judgemental position are essential to support CYPs in undertaking these discussions. Where practitioners have anxieties about conducting risk assessments (e.g., a fear of upsetting the client or concerns about forgetting to ask something), asking necessary questions about risk to self is often avoided unless raised by the client (Quinnett, 2019) or alternatively there may be an over-reliance on risk assessment pro-formas. The former is very concerning given the plethora of literature illustrating that individuals will often not disclose risk information unless directly asked (e.g., Lois et al., 2020; McElvaney, 2015; O'Reilly et al., 2016) and the latter scenario can reduce the interpersonal warmth within the interaction thereby reducing the likelihood of transparent client disclosure (McGillivray et al., 2022; Shea, 2012). Practitioners concerned about whether asking about self-harm or suicidal ideation might increase the risk should be reassured by the substantial research illustrating the opposite (Polihronis et al., 2020). The creation of a trusting and validating space will support accurate risk assessment but practitioners should not wait for a 'magic moment' of strong therapeutic alliance before asking risk questions; for some clients, asking the questions is itself experienced as strengthening to the alliance (Lothian & Reed, 2002).

In the UK, a range of risk assessment tools are utilised within mental health services (Graney et al., 2020), with the majority (39 per cent) being locally developed versions of standardised measures. In line with National Institute for Health and Care Excellence (NICE) guidelines, these are only intended to support a client-centred understanding of the risks and what can be done to reduce these risks in the creation of a risk management plan (NICE, 2012). Risk assessment tools should not be used to predict future suicide or self-harm behaviour nor should they be used to determine who should/should not be offered treatment (NICE, 2012); they can however inform which part of the service may be most appropriate to support the young person (e.g., not all practitioners will have training in supporting children and young people who are engaging in self-harm requiring medical attention). Low-intensity practitioners should utilise risk assessment tools as expected within their employing organisations and use these to guide the funnelling (also known as hierarchical) questioning style (Bryan & Rudd, 2006). In instances of significant risk, other aspects of the session (assessment or intervention) will need to be delayed in order for the content to be fully explored and a risk management plan collaboratively developed.

Factors Influencing Risk

There are several considerations which inform a clinical team's understanding of clinical risk; risk factors (those individual, familial, and external aspects of a child or young person's life that are deemed to increase the perceived level of risk) and protective factors (those aspects that are understood to reduce the perceived level of risk). Risk and protective factors can be understood as static or dynamic depending on the changeability of the factor (e.g., IQ level vs. relationship status).

Some factors, known as adverse childhood experiences (ACEs) have been consistently demonstrated to increase all types of risk (to self, to others and from others). ACEs are defined by Young Minds (2018, p.22) as "highly stressful, and potentially traumatic, events or situations that occur during childhood and/or adolescence. They can be a single event, or prolonged threats to, and breaches of, the young person's safety, security, trust or bodily integrity." ACEs are sadly very common with one UK study reporting that 47 per cent of people have experienced at least one (Bellis et al., 2014). It is important to highlight that not everyone who has experienced ACEs will pose such risks, nor need CAMHS support; however, adopting an approach to assessment which recognises these factors and their potential impact on individuals

LOW-INTENSITY PRACTICE WITH CYP AND FAMILIES

is being recognised as increasingly recommended (Palfrey et al., 2019). For a comprehensive and accessible review of ACEs and their impact, please see Young Minds (2018) 'Addressing Adversity' collection. As a takeaway learning point for risk assessments, it is important to ask children, young people and families about not only what has brought them to the service today but briefly to also ask what tough experiences they have had before today that might help us to make sense of the their difficulties.

Example ACEs

Migration, asylum or loss of significant relationships outside of a family's control
Discrimination; racism, disablism, sexism, misgendering
Parental mental health difficulties or substance use
Traumatic loss of a loved one
Surviving an illness or accident
Being a young carer for a parent or sibling
Physical, sexual or emotional abuse or neglect
Witnessing domestic abuse

It is beyond the scope of this chapter to cover all risk factors associated with the various experiences which can present in LI-CYP. However, suicide risk is the aspect most comprehensively covered within LI assessment and intervention sessions (Papworth, 2018), and so specific risk factors for this area will be discussed briefly in more detail. When considering suicide risk, I have suggested elsewhere (Vickery, 2022) that practitioners may find following the acronym IIPAP (said aye-aye pap as a mnemonic for remembering ideation, intent, plans, actions and protectives; see next section) helpful in assessing risk as it facilitates discussion around many central risk factors in risk to self (including intent, plans and actions). These questions can be supplemented with additional enquiry into other risk factors such as worthlessness (Liu et al., 2006), hopelessness (Weinstein et al., 2015), parental psychopathology (Sarker et al., 2010), family history of suicide (Hua et al., 2019) and aggressive behaviour (Whalen et al., 2015) if these aspects are not raised elsewhere in the assessment. Given that many suicide attempts by young people are a result of impulse rather than planning (Beckman et al., 2019), it is also important that questions designed to assess impulsivity are included such as 'How often do you lose control? Have there been times when you have done things in the spur of the moment which you later regret?'

As with many risk factors, personal (e.g., child neurodiversity) and environmental (e.g., family conflict) interact with one another (Ridge-Anderson et al., 2016). It may be that difficult family relationships create children and young people with more suicidal ideation, or it may be that other factors contributing to a young person's suicidality (e.g., all or nothing thinking/irritability) lead to difficulties within the family system.

Core Components of a Risk Assessment

Whilst we may not have answers regarding causality, developing an understanding of the various risk factors at play, can support practitioners, along with consideration of protective factors (e.g., social supports, help-seeking behaviour) to make sense of the risks posed and the best means of supporting the CYP to be safe.

Core Components of a Risk Assessment

Whilst low-intensity practitioners would not be expected to assess or complete intervention work with CYP presenting with significant risk (e.g., active suicidal ideation with intent and recent attempt on life, self-harm behaviour which requires medical attention, domestic violence in the home, CYP carrying a weapon into school), these aspects of client presentations will feature within assessment sessions, particularly if the service supports self-referral. It is also important to remember that client presentations change over time; someone who initially presents with no reported risk to self, to others or from others, may share different experiences at subsequent sessions. Therefore, in all low-intensity work, risk should be reviewed in brief at all sessions (see box below) by presenting a summary of the previous risk information and asking if anything has changed. If the client reports any change, each of the areas should again be covered in full.

Reviewing Risk in Intervention Sessions

'Last time we met Lina, you shared that you have had no thoughts of self-harm and I really appreciated your honesty in sharing with me that you have had some fleeting thoughts of not wanting to be here. You told me you have not considered any plans or actions towards ending your life and you remind yourself of the Bible reference that states "Why should you die before your time?" which you shared helps you when you have these thoughts. Have there been any changes in this? You also shared that you felt safe from others and that whilst you understandably sometimes have thoughts of bad things happening to the bullies at school, you shared you have never taken any action to harm others. Can I check, is that information still correct?'

At the initial assessment, where risk or safety (developmental level dependent) is explicitly detailed as an agenda item, it is important that clients have a degree of predictability of what the process will involve. Brent et al. (2011) suggest starting with highlighting the importance of the topic and asking for permission to continue with the questioning (e.g., 'often young people we see here have some really tough stuff going on that affects how safe they feel. To help keep people safe, we need to cover some questions about times you might have been at risk of harm from yourself, from other people or maybe to other people. Would it be ok if we go on now to talk through some of these questions?'). Giving CYP autonomy and space to voice any concerns they might have about risk assessment questions can support them in turn to be more open about the content (Pettit et al., 2018).

Experienced practitioners recognise the importance of asking the necessary questions whilst remaining client-centred with O'Reilly and colleagues (2016) suggesting that clinicians can either ask questions about risk flexibily when relevant emotional content is raised by the client (introducing the risk assessment questions in an incremental way) or, in the absence of such opportunities, staff should introduce the subject in a graded, relaxed, clear and confident manner; both of these approaches can facilitate effective risk assessments and both adopt a funnelling questioning style building from open questions about client experiences of distress through to closed

Table 4.1 Areas and example questions covered in risk assessments (adapted from Vickery, 2022)

Area	Elements to cover and example questions
Suicidality – Ideation, Intent, Plans, Actions, Protectives (IIPAP); PAP questions should be asked if ideation or intent are present for the young person	Ideation: You mentioned earlier about feeling overwhelmed and beyond sad sometimes. At those times, what thoughts do you have about the future? I know some young people who feel overwhelmed have had thoughts of ending their life. Is this something you have experienced? When was the last time you had them? What thoughts do you have about ending your life, can you give me an example? Intent: How likely do you think it is that you will act on these thoughts of ending your life? If you were to rate this from 0 (I would never ever try and end my life) vs. 10 (I will definitely end my own life at some point). Plans: Have you made any plans, recently or in the past, about how you would do this? What other ways have you thought about ending your life? Any other ways? Actions: What actions have you taken, recently or in the past, towards this? Have you visited the train station/stockpiled medication/looked for places you would hang yourself? Protectives: What things have helped keep you here; what things have stopped you acting on these thoughts?
Self-harm – IIPAP (as above) – PAP indicated if any ideation or intent	Some young people I work with, tell me that when they are feeling frustrated, they hurt themselves as a way of trying to cope; this includes a range of things including hair-pulling, punching walls in frustration or cutting. Is harming yourself something you have ever done? When was the last time you hurt yourself like that? Are there other ways you hurt yourself?
Self-neglect – Eating, sleeping, self-care	How well have you been able to look after yourself whilst you have been feeling this way? Have you noticed changes in your personal hygiene, eating, getting the sleep you need?
Drug and alcohol use –	Do you ever drink alcohol or take drugs? When was the last time?
Risk from others – Emotional, physical, sexual, social media safeness, neglect	Has anyone ever hurt you? Are there times when you feel unsafe? Have there been times when you have felt uncomfortable or scared of someone online? Do you have everything you need at home? What happens at home if you get in trouble?
Risk to others – IIPAP (as above) – PAP indicated if any ideation or intent	It sounds like you have had an incredibly tough time with bullies at school, I can hear how much they have hurt you emotionally and also physically. Sometimes young people who have been hurt by others go on to have thoughts of hurting other people back. I'm wondering if you've ever had thoughts of hurting anyone? Have you ever been in trouble with school or the police for fighting?

specific questions regarding risk and safety. See below for examples of these methods and notice within them the efforts made by the practitioner to make the risk assessment process as collaborative as possible; for practitioners wanting more information on how to broach these conversations, interested readers are signposted to Kiyimba et al.'s (2021) chapter and also to supervision where roleplay rehearsal can really help increase practitioner confidence.

Introducing Risk Assessment Questions

Incremental approach – suggested for when practitioners have indications that risk is present (e.g., previous suicidal ideation, self-harm behaviour, bullying or evidence of bruising) and/or when the client shares their experiences of intense distress. Involves starting with the emotional content and building on these to ask about ideation, intent, plans, actions and protective factors.

Practitioner: It sounds really hard Lina in those moments when you feel really flat and frustrated. With all that going on for you, how do you show your frustration?

Lina: I don't know really. Sometimes I scream into a pillow or throw things about in my room.

Practitioner: Ok so you scream and throw things about. Sometimes people who feel the way you describe, might have thoughts of lashing out at objects or at people. Has that happened at all for you?

Lina: Definitely not people! I've made some dents in the door of my bedroom cupboard where I've hit it a few times yea but never a person or anything.

Practitioner: Ok thanks for sharing that Lina. How was your hand after hitting the cupboard door?

Lina: It hurt a bit but that felt quite good, it felt like I had achieved something. I don't... I don't want to hurt anyone else, I just want to get some of the anger out and it was just a bit of a bonus that it also kind of helped. Sometimes I don't do it and can just do the screaming thing the school nurse mentioned or call Alec or something.

Practitioner: Ok, I can really hear you Lina, you definitely don't want to hurt anyone else and the main reason you have hit things has been to release some of the anger you've been feeling. I want us to get a bit more of an understanding of the hitting, like how often it happens and what has led up to those times, and then we can chat a bit more about the pain feeling 'quite good' and see if there are other ways you have hurt yourself. How does that sound?

Lina: Uh... yea ok.

Practitioner: Let's start with the hitting, when was the last time you hit the cupboard and can you remember what had led up to that moment?" Externalising approach – suggested in situations where discussions about risk do not readily present within the session, still utilising a gradual introduction.

> Practitioner: Ok so next on our agenda we have the item of safety. In this section we have a few questions that as a service, we ask everybody we work with so we can make sure that the young people we work with are safe. Some of the questions might not feel like they fit for you; this is ok, you can just let me know if that's the case, and sometimes we might need to repeat some questions just so I can check I have understood you correctly. The areas we need to cover are known as 'to self', 'to others' and 'from others'. Where would you like us to start?"

As the practitioner elicits more information about suicidality, self-harm, or thoughts of harming others for example, they can check the comprehensive understanding of the risk information using the FINDIE acronym detailed below.

Depending on the scope of the risk assessment and the work that the practitioner might be completing in their context, discussions about the potential functions of self-harm behaviour can be explored within a low-intensity framework. See Table 4.3 for an example of the use of an ABC chart with Lina to make sense of the aggressive behaviour towards objects. The detail in brackets was discussed in supervision rather than shared with Lina but as an exercise it would help to inform the planned alternative behaviours in her safety plan (need to meet the same function where possible to be most effective for the CYP).

If a parent/carer accompanies a CYP to their LI assessment, practitioners will need to decide on whether to ask the risk assessment questions with them present or not depending on the age and presenting difficulty of the young person. Barrio (2007) discusses the importance of considering family involvement in risk assessment highlighting that they can be an important source of information and can reduce the burdensomeness of a lengthy assessment interview. However, having parents/carers present can hinder the CYP's information sharing. One option is to outline to the CYP that 'The next section of questions is about risk and safety and so we usually

Table 4.2 Clinical example of FINDIE areas and answers

Area	Clinical example
Frequency (how often?)	Thoughts about hurting self approximately once a fortnight. Usually after double German on Thursdays or after a fight with Mum.
Intensity (how strong?)	2/10 most of the time, sometimes 6/10 if things are really tough.
Number (how many?)	5–6 scratches, approximately 4–5cm in length on my right arm using my left fingernails.
Duration (how long?)	Thoughts last for anywhere from 10 mins–1.5 hours; scratching itself lasts less than 1 minute.
Impact (how hard?)	Feels better in the short term as I have a sense of achievement. Long-term impact = upsets Mum if she finds out, can't wear short sleeves for the following few days and feel guilty.
Exceptions (when not?)	Most of the time. When I speak to Alec, when I'm doing art stuff (when I can be bothered), when I'm mind-numbing myself watching old episodes of Friends or Glee.

RISK ASSESSMENT AND MANAGEMENT

Table 4.3 Clinical example of an ABC chart to explore the function of Lina's self-harm punching objects behaviour

Antecedent	Behaviour	Consequence
Mum nagging at me about the state of my room	Punching pillows and cupboard door	Reduction in anger (negative reinforcement) Mum 'hears and sees me' – she gets all concerned and caring if/when she sees my hand or the cupboard (positive reinforcement)

suggest that we do this bit without Mum/Mummy 2/Dad/Nana unless you want them to stay'; this allows the CYP the choice and also gives the parent/carer an impression about what is going to be discussed. In some referrals, for example for child anxiety or behavioural difficulties, the LI practitioner may predominantly work with the parent/carer and may in some exceptional cases rely entirely on their report of CYP risk experiences rather than CYP self-report; in these instances, this would need to be clearly documented in the notes and raised in supervision. It may also warrant liaison with school/college/other agencies, so the practitioner has additional viewpoints informing the risk assessment.

When asking questions about risk from others, practitioners should first be aware of indicators of abuse covered in mandatory/statutory training but also concisely summarised in the Department for Education (2015) guidelines. Considering that adult survivors of childhood abuse often cite never having been asked as one of the primary reasons they never told anyone of the abuse (Lothian & Read, 2002), it is crucially important that practitioners do not avoid these questions and are prepared with how to respond in the instance of disclosure. Ensure you are familiar with your safeguarding lead contacts as well as the expectations of your job role within service in communicating and managing abuse disclosures.

Responding to Disclosures

- Listen carefully without expressing your own views or feelings. If you appear shocked or angry it may prevent them from continuing or they may rescind what they have said.
- Clearly reassure them that they have done the right thing by telling you and that it is not their fault – it is important that these messages are communicated clearly to the CYP.
- Let them know you take them seriously and that you'll do all you can to keep them safe.
- Explain what you will do next; for younger children explain that you need to speak with some colleagues to help and for adolescents explain that you will need to report the abuse.
- In accordance with local safeguarding policies, report and record what you have been told as soon as possible; making notes as soon after speaking to the child as possible to ensure that the content is as accurate as possible.

Risk Management

The communication of risk assessment information is fundamental to the successful management of risk. Low-intensity practitioners should record all risk assessment information in full on their electronic health record system; this should include details of negative responses (e.g., Lina reported no experiences of neglect to self or from others) as well as those answers indicating the presence of risk. In accordance with local employing organisation policies and procedures, cases presenting with risk should be reported accordingly and for low-intensity practitioners the expectation is that all cases will be discussed weekly in caseload management supervision, prioritising new assessments and those presenting with any change in risk. Similarly, practitioners should closely adhere to local safeguarding processes should any information indicate that a CYP, or another child, young person or vulnerable adult, has been or is being abused, or is at imminent risk of serious harm. On rare occasions, this may involve keeping the young person with you (if the appointment is in person) whilst you inform the safeguarding lead and discuss next steps if it is deemed that the young person is not safe to leave.

In the presence of identified risk to self, and in some services, this is completed with all clients; the development of a safety plan is an important part of risk management. A safety plan is a document designed in collaboration between client and practitioner to identify potential triggers to escalating risk, outline existing coping strategies and sources of support and to provide details of where the client can access out-of-hours support if needed. Safety plans have been evidenced as more effective than treatment as usual and no-harm contracts in which the client is asked to contract to keep themselves safe (Stanley et al., 2018). Who completes the safety plan with the client will depend on the service model and also on the nature and level of risk. For example, in the case of Lina, it may be appropriate for the low-intensity practitioner to develop the safety plan (depending on service protocols), whereas in instances of self-harm requiring medical attention and a disclosure regarding online grooming, this would be more appropriately actioned by a senior member of the team. As part of risk management plans, in the presence of self-harm or suicidal ideation, involvement of parents/carers in reducing access to means is encouraged within NICE guidelines where parental involvement has been agreed as appropriate (NICE, 2012).

Possible Content for Inclusion in a Safety Plan (Use Service Templates Collaboratively with the Client Where These Exist)

- A list of potential triggers and early warning signs (things the CYP or family report as precursor symptoms to the onset of suicidal ideation or self-harm behaviour)
- Details and tangible reminders of protective factors

- Plans for safe environment (e.g., removing/reducing access to means)
- Details of what has worked well in the past to reduce suicidal thoughts and/or the likelihood of self-harm behaviour – this part should be developed in conjunction with the CYP based on what works for them rather than a generic list of distraction techniques
- Contact details of sources of support including:
  (a) Social/personal supports (friends and family members)
  (b) Service/professional support (with contact details)
  (c) Emergency contacts (e.g., out-of-hours services)
  (d) Helplines (with details provided)

Summary

This chapter has outlined the core aspects of risk assessment that should be covered within low-intensity assessments and regularly reviewed for change throughout intervention work. The primary objective of this type of risk assessment is to identify and understand the various factors which influence their risk of harm, to self, from others and to others.

Adverse childhood experiences (ACEs) are common and understanding CYPs' experiences of these and how they can shape vulnerability to harm from others, suicidal ideation and self-harm behaviour is an important part of any CYP risk assessment.

Acronyms such as IIPAP (ideation, intent, plans, actions, and protectives) and FINDIE can be helpful for practitioners to ensure that relevant content is elicited and should be used within a funnelling questioning format (moving from emotion-based questions through to those asking more specifically about detail).

Finally, risk management is a process shared within a team and whilst low-intensity practitioners will have fundamental skills in the creation of risk management plans, they will not have advanced or specialist skills in this area and so these plans should be closely supervised through weekly case management.

For further resources, please visit the CEDAR website at: https://cedar.exeter.ac.uk/resources/cyp/

References

Barrio, C.A. (2007). Assessing suicide risk in children: Guidelines for developmentally appropriate interviewing. *Journal of Mental Health Counselling, 29*(1), 50–66.

Beckman, K., Lindh, A.U., Waern, M., Stromsten, L., Renberg, E.S., Runeson, B., & Dahlin, M. (2019). Impulsive suicide attempts among young people – A prospective multicentre cohort study in Sweden. *Journal of Affective Disorders, 243*, 421–426.

Brent, D.A., Poling, K.D., & Goldstein, T.R. (2011). Treating depressed and suicidal adolescents: A clinician's guide. Guilford Press.

Bryan, C.J., & Rudd, M.D. (2006). Advances in the assessment of suicide risk. *Journal of Clinical Psychology, 62*(2), 185–200.

Department for Education. (2015). *What to do if you're worried if a child is being abused; advice for practitioners*. Available at www.gov.uk/government/publications/what-to-do-if-youre-worried-a-child-is-being-abused–2

Graney, J., Hunt, I.M., Quinlivan, L., Rodway, C., Turnbull, P., Gianatsi, M., Appleby, L., Hua, P., Bugeja, L., & Maple, M. (2019). A systematic review on the relationship between childhood exposure to external cause parental death, including suicide, on subsequent suicidal behaviour. *Journal of Affective Disorders, 257*, 723–734.

Kapur, N. (2020). Suicide risk assessment in UK mental health services: A national mixed-methods study. *The Lancet Psychiatry, 7*(12), 1046–1053.

Kiyimba, N., Karim, K., & O'Reilly, M. (2021). 'Just ask': How to talk to children and young people about self-harm and suicide risk. In *Improving Communication in Mental Health Settings* (pp. 88–105). Routledge.

Liu, X., Gentzler, A.L., Tepper, P., Kiss, E., Kothencné, V.O., Tamás, Z., & Kovacs, M. (2006). Clinical features of depressed children and adolescents with various forms of suicidality. *The Journal of Clinical Psychiatry, 67*(9), 1442–1450.

Lois, B., Urban, T., Wong, C., Collins, E., Brodzinsky, L., Harris, M.A., Adkisson, H., Armstrong, M., Pontieri, J., Delgado, D., Levine, J., & Liaw, K.R. (2020). Integrating suicide risk screening into paediatric ambulatory subspecialty care. *Paediatric Quality and Safety, 5*(3), 1–8.

Lothian, J., & Read, J. (2002). Asking about abuse during mental health assessments: Clients' views and experiences. *New Zealand Journal of Psychology, 31*(2), 98–104.

McElvaney, R. (2015). Disclosure of child sexual abuse: Delays, non-disclosure and partial disclosure. What the research tells us and implications for practice. *Child Abuse Review, 24*(3), 159–169.

McGillivray, L., Rheinberger, D., Wang, J., Burnett, A., & Torok, M. (2022). Non-disclosing youth: A cross sectional study to understand why young people do not disclose suicidal thoughts to their mental health professional. *BMC Psychiatry, 22*(1), 1–11.

National Institute for Health and Care Excellence. (2012). *Self-harm in over 8s: Long-term management. Clinical guideline 133*. Available at www.nice.org.uk/guidance/cg133.

O'Reilly, M., Kiyimba, N., & Karim, K. (2016). 'This is a question we have to ask everyone': Asking young people about self-harm and suicide. *Journal of Psychiatric and Mental Health Nursing, 23*(8), 479–488.

Palfrey, N., Reay, R.E., Aplin, V., Cubis, J.C., McAndrew, V., Riordan, D.M., & Raphael, B. (2019). Achieving service change through the implementation of a trauma-informed care training program within a mental health service. *Community Mental Health Journal, 55*(3), 467–475.

Papworth, M. (2018). Assessment and management of risk. In M. Papworth & T. Marinnan (Eds.), *Low-Intensity Cognitive Behaviour Therapy: A practitioner's guide*. SAGE Publishing.

Pettit, J.W., Buitron, V., & Green, K.L. (2018). Assessment and management of suicide risk in children and adolescents. *Cognitive and Behavioural Practice 25*(4), 460–472.

Polihronis, C., Cloutier, P., Kaur, J., Skinner, R., & Cappelli, M. (2020). What's the harm in asking? A systematic review and meta-analysis on the risks of asking about suicide-related behaviors and self-harm with quality appraisal. *Archives of Suicide Research, 26*(2), 325–347.

Ridge-Anderson, A., Keyes, G.M., & Jobes, D.A. (2016). Understanding and treating suicidal risk in young children. *Practice Innovations, 1*(1), 3–19.

Roth, A., Calder, F., & Pilling, S. (2011). NHS education for Scotland competence framework for workers in CAMHS settings. Available at www.ucl.ac.uk/clinical-psychology/competency-maps/camhs-map.html (Accessed: 12 February 2022).

Shea, S.C. (2012). The interpersonal art of suicide assessment: Interviewing techniques for uncovering suicidal intent, ideation and actions. In R.I. Simon & R.E. Hales (Eds.), *Textbook of Suicide Assessment and Management*. American Psychiatric Publishing.

Shirk, S.R., Karver, M.S., & Brown, R. (2011). The alliance in child and adolescent psychotherapy. *Psychotherapy*, *48*(1), 17–24.

Stanley, B., Brown, G.K., Brenner, L.A., Galfalvy, H.C., Currier, G.W., Knox, K.L., Chaudhury, S.R., Bush, A.L., & Green, K.L. (2018). Comparison of the safety planning intervention with follow-up vs usual care of suicidal patients treated in the emergency department. *JAMA Psychiatry*, *75*(9), 894–900.

Quinnett, P. (2019). The role of clinician fear in interviewing suicidal patients. *Crisis*, *40*(5), 355–359.

Vallance, A.K. (2016). 'Shhh! Please don't tell'. Confidentiality in child and adolescent mental health. *BJPsych Advances*, *22*(1), 25–35.

Vickery, H. (2022). Low-Intensity Assessment. In S.D. Bennett, P. Myles-Hooton, J.L. Schleider, & R. Shafran (Eds.), *Brief and Low-Intensity Interventions for Children and Young People*. Oxford University Press.

Weinstein, S.M., Van Meter, A., Katz, A.C., Peters, A.T., & West, A.E. (2015). Cognitive and family correlates of current suicidal ideation in children with bipolar disorder. *Journal of Affective Disorders*, *173*, 15–21.

Whalen, D.J., Dixon-Gordon, K., Belden, A.C., Barch, D., & Luby, J.L. (2015). Correlates and consequences of suicidal cognitions and behaviors in children ages 3 to 7 years. *Journal of the American Academy of Child and Adolescent Psychiatry*, *54*(11), 926–937.

5

Overview of Low-Intensity Interventions, the Evidence Base and Treatment Planning

Markku Wood and Mike Turnbull

Introduction

This chapter will provide an overview of the overarching evidence base for low-intensity (LI) interventions with Children and Young People (CYP) and their families. Based on the emerging evidence base and the national curriculum, an intervention mapping tool will be presented, along with an overview of the LI interventions available to the LI-CYP practitioner, for the common mental health difficulties they are trained to work with. Building on Chapters 3 and 4, the chapter then provides an overview of the process of shared decision making in relation to treatment planning. An example is then presented of how to operationalise the intervention map and to collaboratively select an appropriate intervention, using the information gathered in assessment, the evidence base and the preferences of the CYP and their family.

Overview of LI Evidence Base

With the LI practitioner role still in its early years of development and expansion it stands to reason that the evidence base too, for LI in CYP, is also in its infancy (Fuggle & Hepburn, 2019). As such, many of the evidence-based interventions described have been extrapolated and carefully adapted, based on adult LI research (Firth et al., 2015; James et al., 2015; Oud et al., 2019; Papworth & Marrinan, 2019; Van Straten et al., 2015) for use with CYP. For example, though there is a sound and rapidly expanding evidence base for the clinical and cost-effectiveness of internet-delivered interventions for depression and anxiety disorders within adult populations (Griffith et al., 2010; Newby et al., 2016) much less exists for children and young people.

That said, a number of national and local evaluations have found promising outcomes in terms of clinically reliable and significant change across services, conditions and treatments (Fuggle & Hepburn, 2019; Turnbull et al., 2023; Gay et al., 2022).

Moreover, 'pockets' of robust evidence exist for particular conditions and approaches. For example, considering Behavioural Activation for depression, on top of a raft of robust evidence from the adult literature (Richards et al., 2016), specific evidence is emerging for CYP (Martin & Oliver, 2019; Pass et al., 2018; Oud et al., 2019; Tindall et al., 2017). Similarly, in respect of the treatment of childhood anxiety disorders, evidence exists for the use of CBT (James et al., 2020) and Parent-Led Cognitive Behavioural Therapy (PL-CBT) (Thirlwall et al., 2013; Thirlwall et al., 2017). More recently research is looking at adaptations of PL-CBT used online, with preliminary work in this area already published (Hill et al., 2022).

In comparison to the adult domain, evidence around computerised CBT (CCBT) is also sparse but emerging. However, some promising evidence does exist for the effectiveness of CCBT across mood and anxiety disorders (Attwood et al., 2012; Wright et al., 2020). This book focuses specifically on Pesky-Gnats as an established and well researched example of practitioner assisted CCBT for young people (Chapman et al., 2016; McCashin et al., 2020; 2021), whilst other online mental health packages have been developed to provide a range of useful internet-based resources e.g., Living Life to the Full for Young People. With the ongoing expansion of LI approaches aimed at CYP and families, other new digital CBT applications, including Lumi Nova: Tales of Courage, Think Ninja, Online Social Anxiety Cognitive therapy for Adolescents (OSCA), Online Support and Intervention for Child Anxiety (OSI) and SilverCloud, have received conditional recommendation from NICE for use in the NHS to help children and young people with symptoms of mild to moderate anxiety (NICE, 2022).

In a recent systematic review and meta-analysis Bennett et al. (2019) looked at both unguided and guided self-help interventions for CYP. Efficacy was investigated across 50 studies (n = 3396) which showed medium to large positive effects on CYP levels of depression, anxiety and disruptive behaviour. Bennett et al. identified several key findings that are encouraging and advocate for the continued investment in these valuable new LI practitioner roles. These include the suggestion that; LI self-help interventions have the potential to begin to help to manage the (growing national) unmet need in CYP mental health services (CYP-MHS), can be efficacious in the treatment of common CYP mental health difficulties, within this, that guided self-help is more likely to be efficacious than self-guided self-help, but that self-help is potentially less helpful than higher intensity treatments.

Given the emerging evidence base, it seems reasonable, and in fact a priority, to expand this workforce and continue this valuable research area to review and demonstrate the effectiveness of LI interventions. More in-depth coverage of the evidence base for the specific low-intensity interventions will be presented in the individual intervention chapters that follow in Part 3.

Intervention Map

Children's Wellbeing Practitioners (CWPs) and Education Mental Health Practitioners (EMHPs) are trained to a national curriculum which was developed taking into account trends of the most common mental health difficulties that CYP are facing nationally. This, coupled with the interventions which have an evidence base and those developed specifically for (or adapted to) early intervention and low-intensity in CYP-MH. LI practitioners are therefore skilled at working with multiple presentations of mental health difficulties and use specific (often manualised) evidence-based interventions to work with a defined group of mild to moderate conditions (i.e., anxiety, depression and behavioural difficulties). Following an assessment (see Chapter 3) the LI practitioner follows a process to collaboratively select the most appropriate intervention to support the CYP and/or their family. Figure 5.1 below provides an overview of the interventions that are available to LI practitioners broken down by condition.

The intervention map illustrates that the LI practitioners are trained to treat CYP with difficulties relating to low mood and a variety of anxiety disorders including panic, GAD, social anxiety, specific phobias, separation anxiety. They are also trained to work with behavioural difficulties and general interventions to improve quality of life. Each of these conditions have associated interventions that are most likely to be effective, based on evidence and shared decision making. The intervention map therefore guides the LI practitioner to the interventions that are likely to be most effective in managing the difficulties the CYP is presenting with. Take, for instance, depression. You will see that the treatment branch offers suggested treatments of behavioural activation, cognitive restructuring, and behavioural experiments.

Overview of Interventions

The following section builds on the values and principles outlined in Chapter 2 and highlights some of the key/common interventions that are used for particular presentations and how the LI practitioner will select the appropriate intervention. Each of the interventions discussed below is focussed on a specific presentation or presentations and has its own emerging evidence base, however each also has common threads of theory and practice principles. LI interventions use a combination of unguided and guided self-help resources and worksheets and/or follow a clear protocol or manualised intervention pathway. They predominantly draw on cognitive behavioural theory and approaches, adapted to LI and early intervention for

OVERVIEW OF LOW-INTENSITY INTERVENTIONS | 69

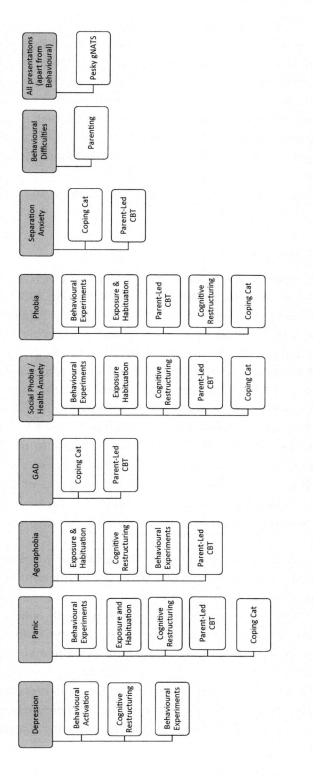

Figure 5.1 Low-intensity intervention map

CYP. Delivery methods can include group, face to face, telephone and video sessions and can draw upon computerised materials and platforms, and other self-help materials. By the nature of the mild to moderate severity of the presentation and the evidence base, the interventions often follow a brief course of between four to eight sessions which are shorter in duration than HI therapies, with sessions normally lasting between 30 to 45 minutes, depending upon the protocol. That said, in some instances clinical decisions might be made, with the support of supervision, to extend interventions beyond the eight-session mark. Self-help is used throughout the interventions detailed below (delivered via workbooks, worksheets, CCBT, mobile apps etc.) and where applicable, these are signposted throughout the chapters and can be found at: http://cedar.exeter.ac.uk/resources/cyp/.

Selecting a Depression Intervention

With key symptoms of depression impacting individuals' functioning, activity levels and motivation, an intervention like Brief Behavioural Activation (Brief BA) (Pass & Reynolds, 2020) for Adolescent Depression can be selected in collaboration with the CYP to help them make changes by expanding and diversifying stable sources of positive reinforcement (see Chapter 8). Whilst based on the seminal work of Jacobson et al. (1996), Brief BA for Adolescents draws on more recent values-based approaches (Lejuez et al., 2011). This eight-session protocol simplifies the more complex behavioural model of depression into a three-part child friendly maintenance cycle. Initial sessions are focussed on socialisation to the BA model and identifying positively reinforcing valued activities that are likely to be anti-depressant. Later sessions are focussed on trying out and increasing contact with a diverse range of valued activities that tap into the concepts of achievement, closeness to others and enjoyment, which lead to positive reinforcement and are in turn anti-depressant. The protocol also incorporates parental support, problem solving and relapse prevention.

In later chapters further options are presented for the LI practitioner when working with low mood, for instance if negative thoughts/cognitions are presenting the LI practitioner might choose to look at an intervention such as cognitive restructuring. Cognitive restructuring for the low-intensity practitioner is primarily concerned with the processing and challenging of unhelpful surface level Negative Automatic Thoughts (NATs). To this end CWPs and EMHPs predominantly find themselves primarily working with thinking styles and challenging NATs using adapted versions of the thought record. Other change methodologies such as positive data logs and/or pros and cons exercises can also be considered under supervision. If there are behavioural barriers, CWPs and EMHPs may also choose to integrate behavioural experiments (see below and Chapter 11).

Selecting an Anxiety Intervention

When considering interventions for anxiety, there are multiple options for the LI practitioner to consider. Each of these interventions are presented in detail in later chapters, however a summary is provided for reference below. The idiosyncratic nature of the anxiety presentation along with the evidence base, collaboration and supervision will guide the LI practitioner to the choice of anxiety interventions for each CYP.

Behavioural Experiments

Behavioural Experiments (BEs) are probably the most versatile and powerful change technique available to the low-intensity practitioner as they are based on a cognitive behavioural learning paradigm meaning that cognitive and behavioural factors are targeted simultaneously (Bennett-Levy et al., 2004; Salkovskis et al., 1999). BEs are one of the change techniques employed by the low-intensity practitioner across the treatment of anxiety disorders including panic disorder, social phobia, and separation anxiety disorder. BEs involve setting up (based on the descriptive formulation) opportunities to test and challenge unhelpful behaviours and thoughts. Experiments are set up in a careful, collaborative and stepped way, so that the YP does not become overwhelmed, but equally is not under stimulated, thus not making meaningful change (Donoghue et al., 2011).

Graded Exposure and Habituation

Anxiety is, by nature, extraordinarily difficult to tolerate and manage, especially when the anxiety impacts functioning and quality of life. Therefore, understandably, CYP and their families spend great efforts avoiding and escaping triggers that can cause perceived distress. Sadly, this can lead to an increase in anxiety in the longer term, with the CYP unable to realise that their worry is likely a perceived and not an actual threat. Exposure (in this context) then, is a carefully planned and collaborative process of exposing the individual to the feared stimulus in a graded fashion, often using analogies such as a fear ladder or fear steps. This process then allows the individual to gradually increase their tolerance of and thus reduce their fear of that stimulus. This process is called habituation (Maples-Keller & Rauch, 2020). Exposure and Habituation can be very useful in managing multiple feared situations, objects, internal and external feared triggers, and are often used in in the treatment of specific phobia.

Parent-Led CBT

Alongside group and individual interventions aimed at the children and young themselves, interventions such as Parent Led CBT (PL-CBT) aim to support parents and carers become experts in helping their children (Creswell et al., 2019). PL-CBT is aimed at supporting the parents of children and young people between the ages of 6 and 12 years experiencing specific phobia, panic, generalised anxiety disorder, social anxiety disorder and separation anxiety disorder. The programme can be delivered individually or in groups and is accompanied by an individual treatment manual (Halldorsson et al., 2019) and a group treatment manual (ibid.) alongside an excellent self-help guide for parents that can be used as a stand-alone resource (Creswell & Willetts, 2019). More recently online delivery methods for PL-CBT are being developed in the form of the 'Online Support and Intervention for Anxiety: OSI' package that is currently under evaluation through the Child Anxiety Treatment in the context of COVID-19 (Co-CAT) randomised control trial (Hill et al., 2022). Given that PL-CBT is based on the concept of upskilling parents, the programme has often been introduced as a first line treatment for anxiety disorders in many LI services across the country. More recently, work has begun on adapting these approaches to help CYP with OCD and ASD.

Selecting an Intervention for Supporting Behavioural Difficulties

Behavioural difficulties can present in multiple ways and have just as many causes. They can have wide ranging impacts on the CYP and the family and can have a marked impact on quality of life, restricting access to education, healthcare and lifestyle outcomes (Felce et al., 2011). However, these are often the manifestation and expressions of distress, from anxiety and low mood to difficulties in communication (potentially related to neurodiversity), to complexities in parenting, boundaries and family distress.

LI behavioural interventions often have theoretical origins in social learning theory, behaviourism and cognitive behavioural theory/practice. The interventions focus on psychoeducation and support for parents predominantly, increasing their understanding of the origins of the behaviour and how to manage these. LI practitioners can offer advice around different approaches for parents to take, based on the assessment information gathered. These approaches can also be beneficial in supporting education.

Other Low-Intensity Interventions:

Computerised/Online/Digital CBT/CCBT

Within the adult world of LI practice, computerised or online CBT (CCBT) has been a core part of the adult Psychological Wellbeing Practitioner role since the introduction of the adult Improving Access to Psychological Therapies (IAPT) project (Papworth

& Marrinan, 2019). Similarly, NICE (2023) in their Early Value Assessment (EVA) of Guided self-help digital cognitive behavioural therapy for children and young people with mild to moderate symptoms of anxiety or low mood concluded that four digital CBT techologies can be used while further evdience is being generated. Unfortunately, the options for children and young people are far more limited and given the need for more developed cognitive skills and independent working computerised CBT is perhaps more applicable to older children and adolescents. That said, since the onset of COVID-19 interest in remotely accessed therapies for children and young people has risen with greater expansion facilitated by the CWP and EMHP workforce. Generally, CCBT can be delivered in three different ways:

1. Pure self-help mode: The user is just given logins and expected to work through on an independent basis.
2. Guided self-help or support mode: The user is supported by and has regular support sessions with the supporter.
3. Supported in session delivery: The user will have regular sessions with support to work through materials.

To consider any computerised/online intervention, the LI practitioner must first assure themselves of the young person's capacity to work independently even if they are being supported as is normally the case. The most common packages used include Pesky gNATs (https://peskygnats.com), Living Life to the Full for Young People (LLTF-YP) (https://www.llttfyp.com) and more recently SilverCloud's (https://silvercloud.com) CYP-specific modules. Pesky gNATs (see Chapter 13) is aimed at children and young people between the ages of 9–17 and takes the form of a computer game where the young person works their way through a variety of CBT informed content which is presented in a child friendly format. LLTF-YP, which is part of a suite of online content, can be used in pure self-help, in clinician supported mode or run as a group intervention. SilverCloud offers a variety of online programmes for anxiety, low mood, stress and body image, and comes with an extensive suite of additional modules and resources. SilverCloud can run in all three modes and incorporates routine outcome measures (ROMs) and risk checking protocols. Whilst there is robust evidence for adult modules of SilverCloud, research is currently underway to establish the effectiveness of the recently developed child and adolescent modules.

Lifestyle Management

Lifestyle management interventions can be utilised across MH conditions and are often delivered alongside other interventions. These interventions focus on improving (more holistically) basic but important areas of our life such as sleep, exercise or diet.

74 | LOW-INTENSITY PRACTICE WITH CYP AND FAMILIES

Interventions can take the form of psychoeducation of support with signposting to other services that might be able to help such as school nurses, the GP or sleep clinics. The principle behind these approaches is to improve overall wellbeing and potentially remove obstacles that can hinder engagement with other psychological interventions. Consider if Theo would like to return to football and is doing well in developing his meaningful activities, however, if his sleep is compromised then he may feel more irritable, less able to concentrate and more fatigued.

Developing Intervention Plan and Shared Decision-making Process

It is essential that interventions are selected collaboratively using shared decision making. After the initial assessment the LI practitioner should take all the information gathered, including the routine outcome measures and problem statement, to case management supervision to aid decision making and develop an evidence-based treatment plan. Liaison with other services and agencies, e.g., schools, may also be necessary to gain a full picture of the difficulties and their impact on the CYP and family.

Revisiting the Problem Statement, Descriptive Formulation, and Goals

As noted in Chapter 3, to enable shared decision making, by the end of the initial assessment, the LI practitioner should have:

- Developed a collaborative problem statement.
- Developed up to three SMART goals for treatment.
- Offered initial information giving around the ABCE cycle / descriptive formulation.
- Offered practical information on LI interventions – e.g., how many sessions, delivery methods and the role of home practice tasks etc.
- Begun discussion around the possible next steps for progressing with the intervention.

In order to select the most appropriate intervention, the LI practitioner will follow a clear procedure in collaboration with the CYP, their family, and other important stakeholders (e.g., education teams). The assessment process will have provided the LI practitioner with a better understanding of what difficulties the CYP and family are presenting with and support the development of the problem statement and the generation of goals. The problem statement will then guide the LI practitioner to the sorts of follow up questions they should be asking and subsequently direct them to an appropriate intervention. For example, in the case of Theo (presented in Chapter 3 and expanded below), the vignette description suggests difficulties surrounding low mood and disengaging in some of the activities he used to enjoy, such as face to face contact with his friends. Reconnecting with friends could form one of his goals and part of the intervention. The information gathered in assessment will therefore guide the LI practitioner to a working hypothesis and the building of a descriptive formulation. The process of sharing the ABCE cycle and development of the descriptive formulation with input of the CYP/family and support in supervision will further guide the LI practitioner to select the most appropriate intervention.

Revisiting the Routine Outcome Measures

In selecting the most appropriate intervention the LI practitioner is acting as a 'scientist practitioner'. As such the practitioner will be data driven in their decision making. ROMs will therefore form an integral part of the intervention planning process, helping guide the practitioner and the CYP to descriptions and greater understanding of the difficulties and their impact. If we take Theo as an example, we might expect the Revised Children's Anxiety and Depression Scale (RCADS) to be indicating levels of low mood above the clinical cut-off with elevated scores around social anxiety also (see Figure 5.2).

Using ROMS with Theo, such as in this case the RCADS, will support the practitioner's decision-making process and allow them to focus their efforts on a more specific intervention pathway. In Theo's case with the dominant difficulties being around low mood and associated inactivity, the practitioner could choose to focus on the depression pathway on the map. ROMS will help the practitioner to broaden their understanding of the specific components of the low mood, how they impact Theo, and can allow further discussion, reaching greater depth of shared understanding

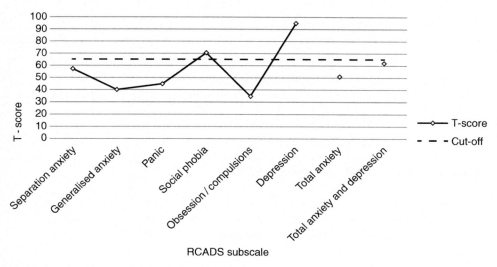

Figure 5.2 Summary of Theo's RCADS scores

LOW-INTENSITY PRACTICE WITH CYP AND FAMILIES

with Theo. ROMS can also help the practitioner to ask important questions they might not have got around to asking had they not utilised the ROMS.

Revisiting the COM-B Model

To support treatment planning, the practitioner should also utilise the Capability Opportunity and Motivation - Behaviour Change (COM-B) model/process (Michie et al., 2011) to guide questioning around any potential barriers to accessibility. In the case of Theo, example COM-B questions/considerations might be:

- Can Theo engage with the 'therapeutic/CBT' language and understand the rationale for changing behaviour – Capability
- Practitioner: 'Are you still a member of the football club, can you return whenever you like?' – Opportunity
- Practitioner: 'Does this feel like this is the right time for him to make the changes we have discussed?' – Motivation

The outcomes of the COM-B question will guide the practitioner to look at possible treatment options. In this case the model gives three options: behavioural activation, cognitive restructuring, and behavioural experiments.

Final Steps of Intervention Planning

Practitioners need to consider what interventions are available and how they map onto the evidence base for the problem highlighted as the primary treatment target. A subsequent meeting should then be held with the CYP to discuss LI suitability and the different evidence-based treatment options. Before the practitioner decides which intervention to choose, they should summarise and present the information they have gathered to the CYP to reach a shared decision. As discussed, shared decision making is essential to engagement and motivation, and will likely improve outcomes. An example of how the practitioner might include Theo in the decision-making process is presented below:

Shared Decision Making – Including ROMS

Practitioner: Thanks Theo for completing all those questions with me, I'd like to discuss some of the things the questions have suggested about the experiences you have. Is that okay?

Theo: Okay.

Practitioner:	It looks like you have scored more highly here on areas related to your mood. Does that fit with you?
Theo:	Yes, I often feel low and can't be bothered to do anything.
Practitioner:	Do you think feeling low has anything to do with you not wanting to do anything?
Theo:	Maybe.
Practitioner:	I think maybe you are right... when we feel low it is difficult to motivate ourselves to do anything, and we often stop doing things we previously enjoyed. Are there things you have stopped doing?
Theo:	Play football with my mates.
Practitioner:	You would like to play football again?
Theo:	Yeah.
Practitioner:	Do you think playing a game of football and being around your team-mates might make you feel happier?
Theo:	Yeah, maybe.
Practitioner:	Great, the evidence we have from research conducted with other young people that feel low, is that doing things that they value can make them feel happier. We call this intervention Behavioural Activation. Can we look at this possibility together?
Theo:	Okay, Yeah, I'd love to play football again, but not sure how I'll go back.

The LI practitioner will go on to discuss next steps for engaging in Behavioural Activation (BA) and make sure that Theo understands what is involved and how the intervention process will progress. The ROMS, COM-B and relationship developed with Theo in the initial session/sessions will be instrumental in having shared purpose and motivation to change.

Summary

This chapter has outlined the process by which the LI practitioner can move from their assessment to choosing an evidence-based intervention in a shared/collaborative way. Understanding the evidence base can help both the practitioner and the family to find shared purpose and rationale. Similarly, a good overall knowledge of the interventions available will help the LI practitioner to select the support package that has the best chance of helping the CYP and their family. Finally, practising the skills of shared decision making so that this is interpersonally an empowering experience for all can create the space for better outcomes and improved interpersonal success.

For further resources, please visit the CEDAR website at: https://cedar.exeter.ac.uk/resources/cyp/

References

Bennett, S.D., Cuijpers, P., Ebert, D.D., McKenzie Smith, M., Coughtrey, A.E., Heyman, I., Manzotti, G., & Shafran, R. (2019). Practitioner review: Unguided and guided self-help interventions for common mental health disorders in children and adolescents: A systematic review and meta-analysis. *Journal of Child Psychology and Psychiatry*, *60*(8), 828–847. doi: 10.1111/jcpp.13010. Epub 2019 Feb 18. PMID: 30775782

Bennett-Levy, J., Westbrook, D., Fennell, M., Cooper, M., Rouf, K., & Hackmann, A. (2004). Behavioural experiments: Historical and conceptual underpinnings. In J. Bennett-Levy, G. Butler, M. Fennell, A. Hackman, M. Mueller, & D. Westbrook (Eds.), *Oxford Guide to Behavioural Experiments in Cognitive Therapy* (pp. 1–20). Oxford University Press. https://doi.org/10.1093/med:psych/9780198529163.003.0001

Chapman, R., Loades, M., O'Reilly, G., Coyle, D., Patterson, M., & Salkovskis, P. (2016). 'Pesky gNATs': Investigating the feasibility of a novel computerised CBTintervention for adolescents with anxiety and/or depression in a Tier 3 CAMHSsetting. *The Cognitive Behaviour Therapist*, *9*(35). http://doi.org/10.1017/S1754470X16000222

Creswell, C., Parkinson, M., Thirlwall, K., & Willetts, L. (2019). *Parent-led CBT for Child Anxiety: Helping Parents Help their Kids.* Guilford Press.

Creswell, C., & Willetts, L. (2019). Helping Your Child with Fears and Worries: A Self-help Guide for Parents. Robinson.

Donoghue, K., Stallard, P., & Kucia, J. (2011). The clinical practice of cognitive behavioural therapy for children and young people with a diagnosis of Asperger's Syndrome. *Clinical Child Psychology and Psychiatry*, *16*(1), 89–102.

Felce, D., Perry, J., Lowe, P., & Jones, E. (2011). The impact of autism or severe challenging behaviour on lifestyle outcome in community housing. *Journal of Applied Research in Intellectual Disabilities 24*(2), 95–104.

Firth, N., Barkham, M., Kellett, S., & Saxon, D. (2015). Therapist effects and moderators of effectiveness and efficiency in psychological wellbeing practitioners: A multilevel modelling analysis. *Behaviour Research and Therapy*, *69*, 54–62. https://doi.org/10.1016/j.brat.2015.04.001

Fuggle, P., & Hepburn, C. (2019). *National CWP Outcomes Report 2019.* Anna Freud National Centre for Children and Families. https://manuals.annafreud.org/cwp/index.html#National%20CWP%20Outcomes%2eport%202019:%5B%5BNational%20CWP%20Outcomes%20Report%202019%5D%5D%20Home

Gay, H., Janbakhsh, M., Smith, N., & Turnbull, B. (2022). *CWP Regional Report 2020 2021.* CEDAR Create. https://swcypiapt.com/resources/publications/

Griffith, K.M., Farrer, L., & Christensen, H. (2010). The efficacy of internet interventions for depression and anxiety: A review of randomised controlled trials. *Medical Journal of Australia*, *192*(S11), S4–S11. https://doi.org/10.5694/j.1326-5377.2010.tb03685.x

Halldorsson, B., Elliott, L., Chessell, C., Willetts, L., & Creswell, C. (2019). Helping your Child with Fears and Worries: A Self-help Guide for Parents, Treatment Manual for Therapists, Version 1.0. https://centaur.reading.ac.uk/87041/

Hill, C., Chessell, C., Percy, R., & Creswell, C. (2022). Online support and intervention (OSI) for child anxiety: A case series within routine clinical practice. *Behavioural and Cognitive Psychotherapy*, *50*(4), 429–445. https://doi.org/10.1017/S1352465822000157

Jacobson, N.S., Dobson, K.S., Truax, P.A., Addis, M.E., Koerner, K., Gollan, J.K., Gortner, E., & Prince, S.E. (1996). A component analysis of cognitive-behavioral treatment for depression. *Journal of Consulting and Clinical Psychology*, *64*(2), 295–304. https://doi.org/10.1037//0022-006x.64.2.295

James, A.C., James, G., Cowdrey, F.A., Soler, A., & Choke, A. (2015). Cognitive behavioural therapy for anxiety disorders in children and adolescents. *The Cochrane database of systematic reviews* (6), CD004690. https://doi.org/10.1002/14651858.CD004690.pub3

James, A.C., Reardon, T., Soler, A., James, G., & Creswell, C. (2020). Cognitive behavioural therapy for anxiety disorders in children and adolescents. *Cochrane Database of Systematic Reviews*, *11*, CD013162. https://pubmed.ncbi.nlm.nih.gov/33196111/

Lejuez, C.W., Hopko, D.R., Acierno, R., Daughters, S.B., & Pagoto, S.L. (2011). Ten year revision of the brief behavioral activation treatment for depression: Revised treatment manual. *Behavior Modification*, *35*(2), 111–161. https://doi.org/10.1177/0145445510390929

Martin, F., & Oliver, T. (2019). Behavioral activation for children and adolescents: A systematic review of progress and promise. *European Child and Adolescent Psychiatry*, *28*(4), 427–441. https://doi.org/10.1007/s00787-018-1126-z

Maples-Keller, J.L., & Rauch, S.A.M. (2020). Habituation. In J.S. Abramowitz & S.M. Blakey (Eds.), *Clinical Handbook of Fear and Anxiety: Maintenance Processes and Treatment Mechanisms* (pp. 249–263). American Psychological Association. http://doi.org/10.1037/0000150-014

McCashin, D., Coyle, D., & O'Reilly, G. (2020). A qualitative evaluation of Pesky gNATs in primary care: The experiences of assistant psychologists providing computer-assisted CBT to children experiencing low mood and anxiety. *Internet Interventions*, *22*(Dec), 100348. https://doi.org/10.1016/j.invent.2020.100348

McCashin, D., Coyle, D., & O'Reilly, G. (2021). *Pesky gNATs* for children experiencing low mood and anxiety: A pragmatic randomised controlled trial of technology-assisted CBT in primary care. *Internet Interventions*, *27*(March), 100489. https://doi.org/10.1016/j.invent.2021.100489

Michie, S., Van Stralen, M.M., & West, R. (2011). The behaviour change wheel: A new method for characterising and designing behaviour change interventions. *Implementation Science*, *6*(1), 1–12. https://doi.org/10.1186/1748-5908-6-42

Newby, J.M., Twomey, C., Yuan Li, S.S., & Andrews, G. (2016). Transdiagnostic computerised cognitive behavioural therapy for depression and anxiety: A systematic review and meta-analysis. *Journal of Affective Disorders*, *199*, 30–41. https://doi.org/10.1016/j.jad.2016.03.018

NICE. (2022, November 4). NICE conditionally recommends digital cognitive behaviour therapies for use in the NHS to help children and young people with symptoms of mild to moderate anxiety. https://www.nice.org.uk/news/early-value-assessment-digital-cbt-children-young-people-with-anxiety-and-low-mood

National Institute for Health and Care Excellence (2023). Guided self-help digital cognitive behavioural therapy for children and young people with mild to moderate symptoms of anxiety or low mood: early value assessment: Health technology evaluation (HTE3). https://www.nice.org.uk/guidance/hte3

Oud, M., de Winter, L., Vermeulen-Smit, E., Boddend, D., Nautae, M., Stone, L., van den Heuvel, M., Al Taher, R., de Graaf, I., Kendall, T., Engels, R., & Stikkelbroek, Y. (2019). Effectiveness of CBT for children and adolescents with depression: A systematic review and meta-regression analysis. *European Psychiatry: The Journal of the Association of European Psychiatrists*, *57*, 33–45. https://doi.org/10.1016/j.eurpsy.2018.12.008

Papworth, M., & Marrinan, T. (2019). Low-Intensity Cognitive Behaviour Therapy: A Practitioner's Guide. (2nd ed.). Sage.

Pass, L., Lejuez, C.W., & Reynolds, S. (2018). Brief behavioural activation (Brief BA) for adolescent depression: A pilot study. *Behavioural and Cognitive Psychotherapy*, *46*(2), 182–194. https://doi.org/10.1017/S1352465817000443

Pass, L., & Reynolds, S. (2020). Brief Behavioural Activation for Adolescent Depression: A Clinician's Manual and Session-by-Session Guide. Jessica Kingsley Publishers.

Richards, D.A., Ekers, D., McMillan, D., Taylor, R.S., Byford, S., Warren, F.C., Barrett, B., Farrand, P.A., Gilbody, S., Kuyken, W., O'Mahen, H., Watkins, E.R., Wright, K.A., Hollon, S.D., Reed, N., Rhodes, S., Fletcher, E., & Finning, K. (2016). Cost and outcome of behavioural activation versus cognitive behavioural therapy for depression (COBRA): A randomised, controlled, non-inferiority trial. *Lancet, 388*(10047), 871–880. https://doi.org/10.1016/S0140-6736(16)31140-0

Salkovskis, P.M., Clark, D.M., Hackmann, A., Wells, A., & Gelder, M.G. (1999). An experimental investigation of the role of safety-seeking behaviours in the maintenance of panic disorder with agoraphobia. *Behaviour Research and Therapy, 37*(6), 559–574. https://doi.org/10.1016/s0005-7967(98)00153-3

Thirlwall, K., Cooper, P.J., Karalus, J., Voysey, M., Willetts, L., & Creswell, C. (2013). Treatment of child anxiety disorders via guided parent-delivered cognitive-behavioural therapy: Randomised controlled trial. *The British Journal of Psychiatry, 203*(6), 436–444. https://doi.org/10.1192/bjp.bp.113.126698

Thirlwall, K., Cooper, P., & Creswell, C. (2017). Guided parent-delivered cognitive behavioural therapy for childhood anxiety: Predictors of treatment response. *Journal of Anxiety Disorders, 45*, 43–48. https://doi.org/10.1016/j.janxdis.2016.11.003

Tindall, L., Mikocka-Walus, A., McMillan, D., Wright, B., Hewitt, C., & Gascoyne, S. (2017). Is behavioural activation effective in the treatment of depression in young people? A systematic review and meta-analysis. *Psychology and Psychotherapy: Theory, Research and Practice, 90*(4), 770–796. https://doi.org/10.1111/papt.12121

Turnbull, M., Kirk, H., Lincoln, M., Peacock, S., & Howey, L. (2023). A pilot evaluation of the role of a children's wellbeing practitioner (CWP) in a child and adolescent mental health service (CAMHS). *Clinical Child Psychology and Psychiatry, 28*(3).

Van Straten, A., Hill, J., Richards, D.A., & Cuijpers, P. (2015). Stepped care treatment delivery for depression: A systematic review and meta-analysis. *Psychological Medicine, 45*(2), 231–246. https://doi.org/10.1017/S0033291714000701

Wright, B., Tindall, L., Hargate, R., Allgar, V., Trépel, D., & Ali, S. (2020). Computerised cognitive-behavioural therapy for depression in adolescents: 12-month outcomes of a UK randomised controlled trial pilot study. *BJPsych open, 6*(1), e5. https://doi.org/10.1192/bjo.2019.91

6

Creativity and Adaptation within CYP Low-Intensity Practice

Alex Boyd

Introduction

Chapter 3 describes the content of the low-intensity assessment and the necessary skills needed to ensure an effective collaborative assessment is completed. However, how can Low-Intensity (LI) practitioners do this in a creative way? What should they do when they find themselves with a child who won't talk? What if the young person is avoidant and the practitioner feels they are struggling to develop a good therapeutic alliance, gather the information needed or engage in an effective way?

This chapter will consider how we can adapt low-intensity practice in creative and child focused ways, not only to conduct an effective assessment, but use creativity to increase the benefits of LI interventions. There is plentiful literature on the use of creative approaches to cognitive behvioural therapy (CBT) and there is not scope to consider all possibilities within this chapter. The chapter will address how we can use some creative approaches to engage young people and make cognitive behavioural concepts accessible and meaningful.

Individual LI practitioners will benefit most from considering these adaptations alongside the individual interests of the young person they are working with and utilising supervision to support meaningful change.

Children and young people (CYP) may find it hard to express their feelings and concerns in verbal language, they may not know why they feel certain ways or how to communicate their difficulties. Using the information available both within the session and from those people involved in supporting the young person is essential to ensure adaptations are effective, helpful and meaningful. Furthermore, developmental consideration of the age and stage of the CYP as well as any possible communication and/or neurodevelopmental difficulties is needed. Culture and diversity should be key to any adaptations as meaning and understanding can differ, an awareness of not making any assumptions should be held in mind, being led by the family and their understanding is key (Naeem et al., 2019).

Approaches are outlined below under headings for ease of description, however, overlap exists between them all.

Engagement

It is important to remember that while a young person may be accessing LI support and experiencing low mood or anxiety, it doesn't mean the work can't be fun. If the approach is too clinical or uses concepts that are beyond the CYP's understanding, the practitioner may struggle to engage them and create meaningful change. Chapter 3, Assessment in Low-Intensity Practice details the non-verbal and verbal common factor skills that help to build a strong therapeutic alliance and create a safe therapeutic space. The following ideas can help establish engagement, build upon the common factors, and facilitate collaboration.

Drawing: using pen and paper is a good way to start to communicate in a simple collaborative way. For example, the task of drawing each other's worlds.

- How: both the practitioner and the child take a piece of paper and draw their worlds, there are no rules, they can look however they want them to, they can be round like the world, or take up the whole page. It is a simple exercise to engage and get to know the young person and the young person to get to know the practitioner. Taking time to draw each other's world and compare notes, can help to establish rapport and start to understand what interests the young person. For example, if their world contains video games, how can these be built upon throughout the work to engage and support information gathering and later interventions? This can be adapted for online work by using the white board function and taking it in turns.

Ice breakers: using a variety of ice breaker questions can take the pressure off the first meeting:

- How: getting to know them by asking general questions such as, what is your favourite TV show; do you have any pets? what is your favourite part of school? Do you have any hidden talents? What is your favourite sport? How would you spend a rainy day? If you could be invisible for a day, what would you do? This can be extended into games where you can add ice breakers into play. For example, snakes and ladders when you go up a ladder or down a snake you take a question from a bag/list. Alternatively, practitioners can create a simple numbered board and you roll the dice and move to the square. The square then corresponds to a question. Ice breakers can then be taken further in starting to understand a young person's feelings such as the example in the box below. By allocating specific questions to feelings, the LI practitioner can start to assess a young person's understanding of feelings and when they might be present for them.

CREATIVITY AND ADAPTATION | 83

Conversation cards: simple cards with information on to start a conversation can offer focus and depth to engagement.

- How: Cards with questions on can support the start of a conversation such as what do you hope for? What is the most important thing to you right now? How would you know if meeting me today had been good/helpful/a success? These can be drawn from a bag or place them all face down on a table and turn them over.

Game: Starting to Understand Feelings

- Aim: to explore feelings and if certain feelings are present for the young person
- How: roll the dice and ask the corresponding question. Can be done via video call or in person
- Materials needed: numbered dice & a crib sheet

Example Crib Sheet (can be expanded with two or more dice)

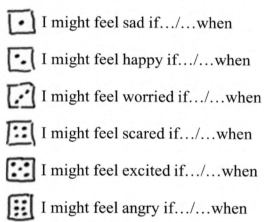

Figure 6.0 Example Crib Sheet

Gathering Information

Building on the information above, information can be gathered to understand the *five areas descriptive formulation (the hot cross bun)* (Padesky & Mooney, 1990). A more creative way to do this can be by using of large pieces of paper or areas of a tabletop or four different areas on the floor and taking each section in turn. The practitioner can connect the areas using string and getting the young person to move between the four areas demonstrating the links.

Emotional Symptoms/Feelings

The following examples provide some creative ways to gather and understand feelings (for gathering **emotional symptoms**) and establish the level of emotional expression the young person has. If the practitioner or young person are unsure about accessing and understanding their feelings, the following ideas can also give a vehicle for exploring emotional literacy.

- Emoji faces – use a list of emojis to identify which ones the young person feels they experience
- Masks with feelings faces – use masks to draw out the feelings and link them to situations
- Drawing feelings on faces – use blank face outlines as a way to help if the young person is reluctant to draw anything on their own
- Using puppets or figures as a way of externally describing feelings, e.g., use the figure or puppet to ask how the puppet might be feeling if they were in the same situation as the young person
- Feeling cards, wheels or a feeling clock can be used to show young people the feeling and associated facial expression. It can give options where young people feel unsure, for example, selecting cards with facial expressions and definitions on or moving the hands of the clock to the feeling they are experiencing.
- Use of stories, films and video resources – for example the Disney film Inside Out provides accessible format in snippets for feeling exploration. There are plenty of other supportive materials available on the internet.

Autonomic Symptoms/Bodily Sensations

Creative ways to gather (for gathering **autonomic** bodily sensations) and what might be happening in the body can be done by expanding on the ideas above, e.g., where might the puppet/figure feel that feeling in their body? Body maps can also help establish where in the body the young person is experiencing symptoms, the practitioner can draw an outline of a body, draw around the young person's body on large paper and then note the areas the young person experiences symptoms. An example of this can be seen in Figure 6.1. Stories can be a helpful way to understand what might be happening in a young person's body and their use is further detailed below.

The figure of the body map illustrates the outline of person with their hands held out.

Figure 6.1   An example of a body map

Cognitive Symptoms/Understanding Thoughts

In understanding the young person's thoughts, gathering the **cognitive** component of the young person's difficulties, practitioners can build on the examples used above to gather feelings and bodily sensations. For example, asking the young person what would the puppet/figure think? If the puppet was feeling that way, what thoughts might be going through its mind? If you were experiencing that feeling, what might you be thinking?

Kendall and Hedtke's (2006) Coping Cat manual provides an excellent illustration of how you can use cartoons to illicit understanding of thoughts. Stallard's (2002) think good feel good also uses cartoons and figures to support young people in becoming aware of and the role of their thoughts. Young people may not be sure of what is meant by thoughts, as a result the LI practitioner may need to educate them (see using stories below) or they may find it hard to distinguish between thoughts and feelings. For example, young people might respond to the question of what were they thinking with "I was sad". Adding thought bubbles to simple pictures can help to expand the information and support the idea that we have thoughts, not just feelings. Figure 6.2 is a simple illustration of this.

Figure 6.2 shows a boy with thought bubbles coming from their head. It shows an arrow pointing towards a picture of a school accompanied by the caption 'what might Mo be thinking?'

In order to access thoughts effectively, the LI practitioner needs to ensure the young person can identify a specific situation, ensure they are objectively defined and ensure thoughts are not confused with feelings. Generally, thoughts should be open to questioning, they are often evaluations, judgements and interpretations and offer an opportunity to consider them differently (Friedberg et al., 2009).

Using role play and their own examples, the LI practitioner can help to educate young people about thoughts. E.g., *I was running late for our session today and I thought*

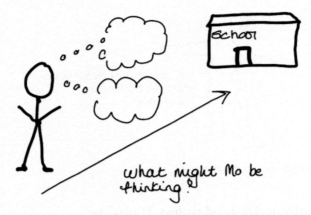

Figure 6.2 Using thought bubbles and simple drawings can help elicit thoughts

you might be annoyed? This made me feel a little anxious. Imagery can be used to elicit thoughts. For example, if you close your eyes and pretend you are in that situation, what is running through your mind? This can be taken further with the use of *in vivo* techniques to access them in situ.

Behaviours

In gathering information about a young persons behaviours is unable to say what happens or happened, the practitioner can help them to identify the behaviours creatively, again by building on the above (e.g., what did the puppet then do?) or asking the young person to describe what happens as if it were a TV programme, movie or drawing out a cartoon or comic strip. Using role play or acting can also support the the young person to describe or externalise the behaviour. Working with parents/carers can also support this, whereby the parent/carer maybe able to add the behaviour to the end of the story or use the puppet to act it out. Making paraells with stories (see below) or TV programmes or films to descibe their behaviour can be another vehicle for understanding. They can also add humour e.g., sitcoms such as *The Big Bang Theory*.

Using Creativity and Adaptations to Expand LI Approaches

Young people may find it hard to express in verbal language how they think, feel or understand their difficulties; they might not know why they do things. This is where the power of stories, analogies and metaphors can further help bring concepts to life, make parallels to their experiences, and help them to work towards utilising tools to overcome their difficulties.

Using Stories and Characters

Stories are familiar ways of understanding information for CYP and can easily be integrated into therapeutic work. They are the foundation of their early learning and often spark their play and imagination. They allow the translation of complex concepts and support learning. As Friedberg (1994) notes, stories help to provide a safe vehicle to communicate and potentially express prohibited thoughts and feelings. A good story can enhance the power of interventions and in order to do this it needs to be relevant, concrete and aesthetically pleasing (Blenkiron, 2005).

Stories can be used to:

Educate and draw similarities in meaning as part of the young person's experience and psychoeducation. The idea of a cave man in describing the self-protective mechanisms underpinning the fight, flight, freeze response is regularly used in anxiety education.

Gather information. Reading and creating stories together which tell the young person's story can help them to narrate, externalise and tell other people how they are feeling. The box below demonstrates this approach with Elena.

Develop courage and build a narrative to the young person's own treatment. For example, in the Disney Story of Moana, when blight strikes Moana's island, and she sets out to find a way to bring a mystical relic back to her island to save the people, she is confronted with many challenges she needs to overcome in order to successfully complete her journey. Moana provides an abstract example whereby the young person can identify with her courage in order to find their own. Another abstract example is the story of Marvel's Hulk. When an experiment goes wrong and Bruce Banner finds himself with the ability to transform into the Hulk, rather than being scared he uses the Hulk's strength for good and to support people.

A story about a child overcoming their fears about going to school and how they did this would provide a more concrete example for a child who is struggling with school related anxiety. A child who is finding it hard to open up and talk may benefit from stories which illustrate this (e.g., *Ruby's Worry* by Tom Percival or *The Huge Bag of Worries* by Virginia Ironside). When reading stories about another character's experience, the practitioner should ensure they ask curious questions, such as 'how do you think the character was feeling when…?' 'What do you think was going through their mind?' This helps to build a bridge between the story and the young person's own experiences.

Stories can be taken further to build a treatment plan; they can help reinforce and increase understanding of the treatment when young people are finding it hard to implement strategies. The story can act as a vehicle to coach young people through repetition. This can be done in conjunction with figures or puppets as used above and can support generalisation. For example, the author has used

LOW-INTENSITY PRACTICE WITH CYP AND FAMILIES

the story of the Hulk to help a young person know that being overwhelmed with big feelings can be managed and strategies put in place; 'what would the Hulk do?' was used as a reminder and shortcut for the employment of intervention tools to manage the anxiety. An example of how stories were used to engage Elna can be seen in the box below:

Example of How Stories Were Used to Engage Elna

The following script demonstrates the use of stories to support engagement, information gathering, working towards a treatment plan. The story of Jilly was one where Jilly was anxious about making mistakes and as a result was avoiding things for fear of getting things wrong or feeling anxious.

Practitioner: Hi Elna, I wondered if we might read a story in today's session. Do you like stories?
Elna: Yes, we visit the library to look at new books.
How do you think Jilly was feeling?
Practitioner: I have a story here all about a girl called Jilly.
(They start to read the story together)
Elna: She is sad and worried about making a mistake in her homework?
Practitioner: Have you any idea or can you guess what Jilly might be thinking in this picture as she sits down to do her homework?
Elna: She looks sad and worried, a little like she might cry.
Practitioner: Do you ever feel the same way as Jilly?
Elna: Yes.
Practitioner: What goes through your mind when you feel like that?
Following the use of the story, the practitioner uses this as a foundation to build a narrative about Elna's own anxiety.
Practitioner: If we were to write another story about Jilly, where Jilly had some worries like you, what do you think it would be about?
Elna: She might be worried about going to bed?
Practitioner: Okay, are there any other parts we can add to the story?

This was then built upon with the following questions:

- How would you describe it for Jilly? What would the worries look like?
- Shall we think about what was happening when Jilly's worries started?
- Are there times Jilly's worry is worse?
- Is there anything which helps the worries?
- How would Jilly know if the worries had got smaller?

Together the practitioner can expand the story using some of the 4W questions and FIDO to gather information. Once the problem information can be gathered, the story can be expanded to add support for the intervention.
Practitioner: Now we have another story of why Jilly is worried, shall we think about how to end the story with how she stopped being so worried?

CREATIVITY AND ADAPTATION | 89

Stories don't always need to be in written form, young people who don't like use of written material may benefit from stories which are acted out. How would the story look if it was a TV show or play? Or was broken down into bite size parts like those used on social media? Using video recording equipment as the reinforcer when more traditional approaches to stories aren't helpful or engaging for the young person can be fun and act as reminders.

Metaphors and Analogies

A metaphor is defined as a figure of speech in which one thing is said to express meaning in another. We use metaphor in many aspects of our daily lives. For example; *'he is a night owl'*, to indicate that someone regularly stays up late at night. They are a way of interpreting and understanding our lives by attaching meaning to our experiences, they are often abstract but support our learning and ability to generalise therapeutic work. From an early age children can and do equate meaning to something else. For example, picking up a toy and pretending it is a telephone. Metaphors can help a young person to conceptualise and remember important information relevant to their treatment (Blenkiron, 2005).

A young person's ability to understand and make use of metaphor will increase with age, the metaphors which may be helpful to teenagers may not be fully understood by a 7-year-old. Metaphors work best when they are grounded in the young person's interests and are culturally relevant. They should be concrete and collaborative (Friedberg & Wilt, 2010). For example, the metaphor of thoughts being like text messages or emails as seen in the example below with Chris may be relevant to an older child who uses email and text messaging but less so to a younger child.

They hold most power when the young person is able to make the connection as to what the metaphor represents and can be used to support learning and gain insights. For example, the metaphor of being half way up a ladder when the rungs break can be expanded to understand how someone might be feeling when their usual behaviour has become unhelpful or unsafe. Using good Socratic questioning can help to explore the content and meaning to help amplify the emotion and make links to their own lives.

A further illustration of a young person-led metaphor is the case of Lina who used the metaphor of 'it is like someone has pushed my buttons, like the television is on mute'. This gave the practitioner the opportunity to explore what this meant to Lina. Asking questions about what the TV represented, what the lack of sound meant, what kept the TV on? What did 'mute' really mean to her? She was able to use this as a vehicle to describe that she was finding it hard to engage with school as she was feeling low in mood and lacking in motivation; she described this as quiet (muted) and just watching everything happening. Using the metaphor, they were able to use behavioural activation to manage her mood and expand on the metaphor looking at what could increase the sound on the TV (linking this to activity), change the channel and use different programmes as analogies for change. Other examples include the use of dark glasses as a metaphor for low mood and removing them as a way of demonstrating challenging negative cognitions. The use of a Chinese finger trap can be a good metaphor for being stuck in a cycle of anxiety or low mood and the development and use of alternative thinking; you need to look differently and push the finger trap in to release the fingers. Use of a flat battery or heavy heart, being lost in a maze, a deflated balloon or black hole can offer short cuts to understanding the range of symptoms associated with low mood. Blenkiron (2005) compares depression to being like a bad hair day, and in doing so highlights that hair can change and so can mood. Other examples might include a water butt or bucket overflowing indicating stress levels. Colours can be used to illustrate mood, example, what colour would the anxiety be? Symptoms on the body – colours can be added to body maps. Use of the weather can offer a range of examples used to express emotions (e.g., sunshine for happiness, rain for sadness, wind for anxiety and a storm for all emotions) and the use of weather predictions or reports can be a helpful way to gather information about feelings. Interventions can represent being prepared for the weather (such as an umbrella or coat). Stallard (as cited in Killick et al., 2016) highlights the usefulness of the traffic light as a metaphor. Red is stop and can denote catching unhelpful thoughts, green is go and the alternative coping thoughts. It can be used to build alternatives and extended further with problem solving; red being stop and identify the problem; amber being used to explore the problem and look for solutions; and green being the stage of implementing the solution or undertaking a behavioural experiment. A thermometer can be used in the same way considering temperature to indicate the level of feeling or the ability to implement intervention techniques.

Alongside metaphor, similes and analogies can become a helpful adjunct to LI interventions when interwoven in the use of language and again can be extremely useful in supporting the translation of complex information for young people. An analogy is a comparison where one thing is compared to another to build learning. For example, using the analogy of learning to ride a bike can draw parallels with therapy in that you need to learn a new skill, keep trying and persevere to ride without stabilisers. Therapeutic work can be seen as the stabilisers used to support the development of skills before riding alone. For further reading and understanding of the power of metaphor and its use in cognitive behavioural interventions please see Friedberg and Wilt (2010), Blenkiron (2005) and Killick et al. (2016).

Example of a Script Used with Chris and the Use of Metaphor

Chris: I just feel as though I have all these thoughts in my head, it's like I am on overload, I can't think properly, it's like I'm glitching?

Practitioner: So, your brain is like a computer or tablet which is glitching?

Chris: Yes, exactly that, it's like some apps are frozen and I have too many open windows, it isn't working well.

Practitioner: Which apps or windows are struggling most?

Chris: The school ones, it's the exam pressure, the friends one, it's like it's all slowed down, a bit like my life. I am doing so much less than I used to, this creates another window which makes me feel bad about not being like I used to be. It's like the loading wheel you get on the screen is just stuck going round and round.

Practitioner: So, everything feels stuck? Are there any emails or messages which keep coming in over and over again?

Chris: The emails or messages... hmmm... it's like there are lots all at once as well as the open screens.

Practitioner: So, if we view the messages as your thoughts, are there ones which come in over and over and slow the computer down most?

Chris: Worry ones I guess, I can't get away from this feeling that something will go wrong if I meet up with friends, something bad would happen.

Practitioner: How many of these messages do you think are coming into the computer?

Chris: I don't know, a lot... maybe 200?

Practitioner: Do you think there are any other messages coming in?

Chris: Maybe, I think I only see the bad ones.

Practitioner: What do you mean by bad ones? Can you explain a bit more?

Chris: I guess you would describe them as worried or anxiety type ones.

Practitioner: So, the computer is going slow, there are lots of messages, but you are mainly reading the ones about something bad will happen? Ones which make you worried and anxious?

Chris: Yes.

Practitioner: How about we work out how to close some of those apps and filter some of those messages; do you think any of those 200 messages say something else? What would a different, less anxious message say? What would a message say that was helping take you towards your goals?

Summary

This chapter briefly outlines some ideas about adapting your LI approaches to make your work with them meaningful, engaging and fun. By creatively approaching engagement and information gathering using tools such as drawing and play as well as stories and metaphor for creative interventions LI practitioners can expand their reach and support better outcomes for CYP. Further consideration and adaptations will be needed depending on the method of engagement (e.g., online via video methods, by telephone or in person), which will likely differ. For further resources, please visit the CEDAR website at: https://cedar.exeter.ac.uk/resources/cyp/

References

Blenkiron, P. (2005). Stories and analogies in cognitive behaviour therapy: A clinical review. *Behavioural and Cognitive Psychotherapy, 33*(1), 45–59.

Friedberg, R.D. (1994). Storytelling and cognitive therapy with children. *Journal of Cognitive Therapy, 8*, 209–217.

Friedberg, R.D., McClure, J.M., & Garcia, J.H. (2009). *Cognitive Therapy Techniques for Children and Adolescents: Tools for Enhancing Practice.* Guilford Press.

Friedberg, R.D., & Wilt, L.H. (2010). Metaphors and stories in Cognitive Behavioural Therapy with children. *Journal of Rational Emotive and Cognitive Behavioural Therapy, 38*, 100–113.

Kendall, P.C., & Hedtke, K.A. (2006). *The Coping Cat Workbook* (2nd ed.). Workbook Publishing.

Killick, S., Curry, V., & Miles, P. (2016). The mighty metaphor: A collection of therapists' favourite metaphors and analogies. *The Cognitive Behaviour Therapist, 9*, 1–13.

Naeem, F., Phiri, P., Rathod, S., & Ayub, M. (2019). Cultural adaptation of cognitive behavioural therapy. *British Journal of Psychiatry Advances, 25*, 387–395.

Padesky, C.A., & Mooney, K. (1990). Presenting the cognitive model to clients. *Cognitive Therapy Newsletter International, 6*, 13–14.

Stallard, P. (2002). *Think Good, Feel Good: A Cognitive Behaviour Workbook for Children and Young People.* Wiley.

7

Key Tips and Working with Common Difficulties

Kirsty Roberts and Annette MacKinley

Introduction

This chapter will look at some of the key skills needed for low intensity practice and the common difficulties that can arise during the low-intensity assessment and intervention process with children and young people (LI-CYP). The first part of this chapter will discuss key tips and interpersonal skills which are important for building a therapeutic alliance and conducting an effective assessment, such as gaining consent and sharing information about confidentiality, developing common factor skills, and encouraging collaboration with the young person and their parents or carers. The second part of this chapter will look at some of the possible solutions to the challenges that can arise during information gathering and information giving, as well as shared decision-making within a session.

Key Tips for Developing the Therapeutic Alliance and Conducting an Effective Low-Intensity Assessment

Consent

When a young person attends an appointment for the first time, they are likely to be processing thoughts about the session and may be a little anxious about what they will be asked. It is helpful to spend a little time chatting so that the young person can have a little time to adjust to their surroundings. At the beginning of the assessment, it is important to receive consent from the young person and the important adult in their life for accessing and storing their personal information, for providing them with the support and the intervention, and for any sessions being recorded. This will include discussing how their information will be stored and used, and who will be viewing recordings, the purpose of this, and how this will be stored including the length of time before the recording is deleted.

These can be difficult concepts to explain, however from an early age young children can begin to understand what it feels like to share something about themselves and how upsetting it can be when this is shared. We share information and stories with those people we trust and who we believe will respect the information we have given them. Therefore, taking time to discuss consent in language that the young person understands is one of the ways we can begin to build up the trust needed for a strong and supportive therapeutic alliance. For example, for vignette one, language would be adapted for Elna to gain her consent, alongside her mother being present and giving consent for an assessment and intervention. Due to her age, time may also be spent before the session and during the session to engage Elna with games and tasks to get to know her more and help her to feel more relaxed, mum may be involved in these too if she is to stay.

Confidentiality

Having a respect for what is being said is vital, and the practitioner does well to discuss this early when meeting the young person and the important adults in their life. When explaining confidentiality to a young person, it may be wise not to confuse it with keeping secrets. Confidentiality can imply that the listener will not share what they have been told which is not possible if there are risk factors present. However, it is essential that the young person understands that what they say is important to help build an understanding of the difficulty they are experiencing, and that by being able to say anything they need to, the practitioner will be able to give them the help they need. By expressing how their words are respected and valued, the foundations of a trusting alliance can be developed. This is more appropriate than suggesting they can say anything because it will be kept secret.

A further reason to avoid confusing confidentiality with secrecy is when asking about whether the young person feels as though they are at risk of harm from other people. If this is a concern, it is possible that their silence has been achieved through a coercive use of the need for secrecy, and therefore secrecy can have traumatising implications.

Common Factor and Non-verbal Skills

Being present with the young person as they are expressing how their difficulties are making them feel and the impact they are having on their life, is naturally very important. Eye contact helps the flow of communication and shows the young person that they are being listened to. Taking notes can interrupt this flow and should therefore be kept to a minimum.

When a practitioner is in training or is a novice there is a temptation to take down everything that the young person says. As the practitioner becomes more experienced, they understand that not only is their notetaking interfering with the interpersonal aspects of the relationship, but that if there are too many notes then they cease to be helpful and may not be referred to again.

By actively listening, a picture of the young person's life can begin to develop and an understanding of how their difficulty features in their everyday life emerges through gaining this insight and understanding. Other than noting demographic details, age of onset, and the risk assessment responses, most of the details are less important than maintaining eye contact in these early sessions (Symons, 2020). When the details which will inform the problem statement are being gathered, these can be written on the descriptive formulation model in front of the young person so that they are able to see how these aspects interact.

Paraphrasing, reflecting, and summarising the young person's words can show how they are being heard and understood. This can be conveyed more effectively if done so through a genuine and authentic understanding rather than merely repeating notes.

Demonstrating empathy can also be challenged if the focus is on taking down everything that is being said. Empathy does not have to be verbal; sitting with silence, being still, nodding, and mirroring the young person's body language and posture can be powerful indicators of being present and having empathy for what the young person is saying. Normalising the experience can be helpful, but it can also be invalidating and can be taken to be suggesting that the difficulty is not worthy of help. Unless the practitioner is focused primarily on the young person's body language and the nuances of this while telling their experiences, the cues can be missed, and the therapeutic alliance impacted.

Collaboration

When the young person first comes to meet their practitioner, they are unlikely to know what to expect. Most adults that a young person meets outside of their family will be either a teacher, a carer, a social worker, a sports coach, a group leader, or church or community elders. There is no reason to assume that they will see their practitioner in a way other than as someone with more power than themselves.

While the role should be explained in the first session, the young person will only understand the collaborative nature of the therapeutic alliance through the modelling of this by the practitioner over time.

One way of achieving this is through the use of team-related language, for example, *we, us,* and *our.* Giving the young person choices within the session can help too, such as reading out the problem statement and goals, setting and ordering the agenda items, or managing the time. The young person may feel nervous about doing these until they are sure what is expected, but with gentle encouragement they may become more confident. The practitioner needs to resist the temptation to rescue the young person by making all the decisions themselves.

The use of session rating scales and feedback forms can be a little challenging for anyone to fill in with the person they are evaluating in front of them. Having a discussion based on observations to support this can be helpful, for example 'I noticed you were a little distracted during the task today. What do you think we could have talked about or done to help you more today?'

Role of Parent/Guardian/Professional (i.e., Teacher)

A low-intensity assessment may include any important adults in the young person's life. This may be the parents or carers only, but it may include professionals too. Encouraging a shared understanding can be key to the young person receiving the support they need (Symons, 2020).

Some adults have an accurate understanding of the young person's difficulties. Perhaps, they have a relationship which encourages open dialogue and where the young person's experiences are validated. It is possible that a parent had similar experiences as a child and can empathise with what they are going through. Ideally, the parent would be able to distinguish any differences between their own experiences and those of the young person, but the practitioner will need to be mindful of this not being the case. If the young person has difficulty expressing themselves, having the adult in the assessment session too can be helpful because they can provide valuable prompts to encourage the young person to share important details.

Having the adults in the room does not come without challenges, however. Behaviour is communication (Hollo et al., 2014), and it can be the behaviour that first alerted the adults to there being a problem. In some circumstances it can be the behaviour that the adult is wanting to be addressed. For the young person they may be only too aware of the impact their behaviour is having on those around them, and they may want the consequences of this impact to stop. It is possible that the thoughts and feelings at the core of the difficulty are not being considered. For the practitioner, all of this is important information, but their skills at funnelling for the detail will also be essential.

None of the information being shared by the young person and the adults is irrelevant and understanding this will help the practitioner to balance the needs of the adults to share their knowledge, experiences, and hypotheses, without undervaluing what the young person is saying. The adults will have experience of assessments from their interactions with professionals in many settings, and they may have thought about what they wish to say. The young person may have no experience of this and have no idea of what is expected of them. It is worth noting that a potential disadvantage of the adults being able to express themselves first is that the young person may then understand that the adult's perspective is the only one, and they may believe their perspective must be wrong.

Having an open and honest conversation with the young person and the adults could mitigate the likelihood of this happening, especially if it is stressed that all information is important for building an accurate representation of what is happening for the young person and how best to move forward.

Common Challenges in Low-Intensity Assessment and Possible Solutions

Information Gathering

Funnelling

Funnelling within Low-Intensity Cognitive Behavioural Therapy (LICBT) can be a main area that raises difficulties which can then have an impact on the treatment chosen, therapeutic relationship, engagement, and outcomes. Funnelling is first used during the assessment session and a key skill for LI practitioners to be proficient in. Practitioners should understand why they are asking certain questions and the patterns of which questions are being asked to what effect (such as open or closed questions). The question type used can impact the type of response the CYP gives, such as whether you are hoping that they will elaborate and open up more or whether you are hoping for a specific response to a closed question, such as risk. This answer of the CYP to a closed question is usually then re-opened with a specific open question to find out more about that response.

Effective funnelling is imperative and practitioners can nurture this skill through the use of the Declarative-Procedural-Reflective (DPR) model (Bennett-Levy, 2006). This helps the practitioner to consider whether a funnelling issue comes from a skills deficit with a gap in either their knowledge (in which case research could be done to enhance their knowledge), procedural skills development (with role plays, for example), or an area that requires deeper individual reflection. Clinical skills supervision is a useful space to explore funnelling skills (see Chapter 18 – Supervision, for more information), alongside the decisions made within case management supervision directly affected by the quality of the funnelling. Self-practice, self-reflection (SP-SR) could also be used in the roleplays to see how it feels to be on the receiving end of funnelling from peers (Bennett-Levy et al., 2014).

The information gathered and probable diagnosis, goals, and problem statement will all be guided by the practitioner ensuring all the information is in line with the main focus, to guide the intervention chosen. If the CYP has more than one presenting difficulty (such as low mood and anxiety), then multiple funnels should be pursued to ensure all of the information has been gathered succinctly. A funnel relating to one area, such as low mood, should be gathered in its entirety before being summarised and a separate funnel opened. This should then be discussed with the CYP when all funnels have been completed and their choice for focus of treatment discussed, to aid the problem statement and goals. The evidence-based interventions can then be discussed within the latter half of the assessment. For example, for vignette 3 (Chris), there is an experience of both anxiety and depression, so funnelling would be key to ensuring the practitioner is clear on Chris's experiences of both, with a clear collaborative decision on which one is most pertinent for Chris to work on. This would then be a good opportunity to discuss how it would be helpful to remain on the chosen intervention, despite a temptation to switch and try and alleviate the other presenting difficulty not focused upon and why low intensity working has this rationale.

Funnelling can however help to explore any changes during the intervention sessions. If any changes occur then the baseline problem statement and goals should not be changed, as these are the baseline for the assessment session (Farrand, 2020). If the CYP wants to change the focus for treatment (such as focusing on their low mood rather than anxiety), then this would be discussed with the Supervisor in the first instance before agreeing to this. Changing the focus and therefore the recommended intervention would normally be avoided within LICBT due to the limited sessions, highlighting why, for effective funnelling at assessment to ascertain the treatment focus and goals with a discussion happening at the shared decision making stage of the assessment, it is beneficial to see through the intervention chosen rather than switching. For example, you may explain that as their low mood improves with the correct intervention, they may then wish to focus on their anxiety, which may feel more prevalent as the low mood is improving. Normalising this at assessment can be positive and manage expectations. It may be that the CYP then seeks further treatment for the other presenting difficulty (if there is more than one) after a consolidation period in the future, depending on service protocols.

ROMs

The Routine Outcome Measures (ROMs), also covered in Chapter 3, are taken at every session, with a target of over 90 per cent of data collection in line with the minimum data set for working with CYP at low intensity (Woodford, 2017). Practitioners should always use the measures alongside their clinical judgement (Law and Wolpert, 2014), being careful about the interpretation of the results (Spiegelhalter, 2005). The RCAD measures need to be adjusted to account for the YP's age and gender, as the raw scores will be adjusted to be correctly interpreted for the normalised data based on those variables. The RCADS can feel quite lengthy for a YP, as a 47-question survey in full at assessment, and Law and Wolpert (2014) suggest using curiosity with the ROMs, discussing the appropriate measures to use with parents and ensuring meaning is given to the ROMs for YP in your introduction of them.

There are lots of benefits to using ROMs in the session, which can be shared with the YP, such as allowing for changes to be made promptly Bower and Gilbody (2005). The parent can sometimes feel that they are being tested or judged when the ROMs are introduced and given, so extra sensitivity will need to be used in advising what they are measuring and why. There can sometimes be discrepancies between the YP's scores and the parent's scores, in which case the YP's scores would take priority with the parent's scores being used to add more information to these. How the measures will be stored and interpreted on the clinical database should be explained in a brief, developmentally appropriate manner, with the results brought in a graph form or discussed on a shared screen if working remotely.

Extra care should be taken to use neutral language when discussing scores, as over-use of praise when scores improve may have negative consequences on engagement if scores were to worsen in the future, or the YP may complete these to please the practitioner if the power dynamics leant towards a teacher/student scenario. These dynamics can be more easily slipped into with some clinical presentations, such as Social Anxiety Disorder, where the YP may actively try and seek practitioner approval and score 'well'. As previously mentioned earlier within the chapter, the SRS given at the end of a session will need to be thought about in its administration to support honest feedback. Collaborative conversations can be helpful around the benefits of the YP letting the practitioner know if things need adjusting, to try and discourage the YP from completing them as they think the practitioner would like them to be (positively skewed). Preparation, as always, is key with low-intensity working, so if working face to face, having these pre-printed for ease with high volume working in packs is always helpful. If working remotely, practitioners may be creative with the completion of these securely, either by the YP giving the verbal responses with a shared screen or giving access for online completion.

Risk

Risk assessments must be comprehensively and collaboratively carried out at all assessment and subsequent intervention sessions (see Chapter 4, Risk Assessment and Management, for more detail and information). Risk areas include risk to self, risk from others and risk to others, both in the past and present. For example, for vignette 2 (Theo), there would be additional factors to consider, such as ensuring Theo is not at risk during his online gaming, alongside his food intake reduction. The CYP may find the bridging statement into the risk assessment to be more empathic and sensitive with some normalising information around risk. This helps the CYP to understand that you will be non-judgemental about the information shared and that other CYP may experience something similar. This also leaves the door open in case the CYP wishes to disclose risk at future sessions, or if there is a change. As with the ROMs, neutral language may be helpful throughout, as it is tempting to respond with praise or 'good' when the CYP says they are not experiencing any risk, which may again change the power dynamics or mean the CYP is less likely to want to disclose in the future if they feel you would not approve, for example. Thanking the CYP and their parent(s) if present after the risk assessment is usually well received and praises the CYP in a neutral way for their participation, not attached to the answers they gave.

Information Giving and Shared Decision Making

Problem Statement, Goals and Probable Diagnosis

As discussed previously and within Chapter 3, these two important areas are set at assessment and would not normally be changed within intervention sessions (unless the treatment focus changes, which should be avoided where possible via effective funnelling and collaborative decision making in the event of comorbidities). Setting the problem statement is a fine line between giving enough guidance and summarising information already gathered. Some practitioners may have the sentences pre-written with spaces to make this area clearer and help the CYP to understand the structure, whilst others may prefer to allow the CYP to set the statement whilst giving guidance. Summarising these into a problem statement as a focus of treatment can give a moment of clarity and reflection for the CYP, so empathy and sensitivity should be fostered. It is common to see the practitioner pleased at the progress of the problem statement and giving praise, without reflecting on how it might feel for the CYP to hear it presented in this way.

Common difficulties usually occurring with goal setting are that they are not SMART, in-line with the problem statement set or the intervention. Clinical skills supervision is an appropriate and useful space to continue to develop this skill. The more experienced a practitioner becomes, the more the skills of aligning all the elements of an assessment will develop, but as above this requires practice and an awareness of intervention-relevant factors. All of these elements when focused towards a main funnel and focus (such as low mood) bridge the conversation in a more digestible way for the CYP to begin to discuss what the main presenting difficulty might be, using developmentally appropriate language.

Some practitioners or services do not use the term "problem statement" and adapt this to statements such as 'my statement' to remove the word 'problem', which may worry some CYP. Some practitioners effectively use storytelling and creativity (see

Chapter 6) to help the CYP to understand that it is not them that is the 'problem', but it is the difficulties they are experiencing which is what you will focus on together, to help create some separation and reassurance around the use of this word.

The probable diagnosis section can create some difficulties with the CYP and/or parent confusing the boundaries of the role, such as believing this to be a medical or official diagnosis. The practitioner should be sensitive to this and explain the purpose of summarising what it sounds like the main difficulty might be, based on the information discussed and the experiences of the CYP and their parent. Normalisation would be helpful at this point with some statistics which are developmentally appropriate, such as how many people in the CYP's class might be feeling the same way.

The Capability, Opportunity, Motivation and Behaviour Model

The Capability, opportunity, Motivation and Behaviour model (COM-B model) is a really useful behaviour change model to utilise within the LICBT framework (Papworth & Marrinan, 2019). Exploring the different components with the CYP and parent (capability, opportunity, and motivation) can help with foresight at the assessment stage into any difficulties which may occur with treatment. For example, the COM-B model would be a really useful tool to consider particularly what motivations Elena might have to engage in the intervention. If the behaviours she is engaging in are bringing her a short-term relief from the anxiety, it is important to ensure she is on board and understands the intervention so it is a collaborative effort.

It is useful to use the COM-B model at the end of every treatment session to problem solve for the next session. Potential difficulties related to finding solutions to the issues can arise, such as the logistics of attending a session or access to technology. Accessing the CYP's motivation levels can also require some creativity, with adaptation to language on what motivation means, such as 'Is this something you would like to try? How much out of 10 do you feel like you would like to meet next week?'. This can help gauge how ready the CYP is and whether they have understood the session and the tasks. The identification of low motivation can open the conversation with the CYP further about any worries they may have about working with the practitioner, or something that has come up in the session which may be making them feel like they don't want to continue (if it was particularly upsetting, for example). Roleplaying can be utilised to aid practitioner proficiency in the model and to use it well, whilst keeping the CYP and parent engaged.

Summary

This chapter has overviewed key tips and interpersonal skills which are important for building a therapeutic alliance and conducting an effective low-intensity assessment, alongside some of the possible solutions to the challenges that can arise during the information gathering, information giving and shared decision-making stages of the assessment. These key tips and ideas should help to further practitioners' awareness of common issues, with suggestions to develop their clinical practice further. For further resources, please visit the CEDAR website at: https://cedar.exeter.ac.uk/resources/cyp/

References

Bennett-Levy, J. (2006). Therapist skills: A cognitive model of their acquisition and refinement. *Behavioural and Cognitive Psychotherapy*, *34*(1), 57–78.

Bennett-Levy, J., Thwaites, R., Haarhoff, B. & Perry, H. (2014). *Experiencing CBT from the Inside Out: A Self-Practice/Self-Reflection Workbook for Therapists*. Guilford Publications.

Bower, P., & Gilbody, S. (2005). Stepped care in psychological therapies: Access, effectiveness, and efficiency: Narrative literature review. *The British Journal of Psychiatry*, *186*(1), 11–17. https://doi.org/10.1192/bjp.186.1.11

Farrand, P. (2020). *Low-Intensity CBT Skills and Interventions: A Practitioner's Manual*. Sage.

Hollo, A., Wehby, J.H., & Oliver, R.M. (2014). Unidentified language deficits in children with emotional and behavioral disorders: A meta-analysis. *Exceptional Children*, *80*(2), 169–186. http://dx.doi.org/10.1177/001440291408000203

Law, D., & Wolpert, D. (2014). *Guide to Using Outcomes and Feedback Tools with Children, Young People and Families*. CAMHS Press.

Papworth, M., Marrinan, T., & Papworth, M. (2019). *Low-Intensity Cognitive Behaviour Therapy: A Practitioner's Guide*. Sage.

Spiegelhalter, D.J. (2005). Funnel plots for comparing institutional performance. *Statistics in Medicine*, *24*(8), 1185–1202.

Symons, Z. (2020). Common and specific factors: The importance of what you do and how you do it. In P. Farrand (Ed.), *Low-Intensity CBT Skills and Interventions: A Practitioner's Manual* (pp. 79–92). Sage.

Woodford, J. (2017). *Wellbeing Practitioner–Children and Young People (WP-CYP) Data Handbook*. South West CYP-IAPT Collaborative. swcypiapt.com/wpcontent/uploads/2017/08/WP-CYP-Data-Handbook-v3.pdf

Part 3
Low-Intensity CYP Interventions

8

Brief Behavioural Activation (Brief BA)

Laura Pass and Shirley Reynolds

Introduction

This chapter will give an overview of Brief Behavioural Activation (Brief BA). The behavioural theory of depression, learning theory and the principle of reinforcement will be outlined, followed by the evidence base behind BA. The Brief BA model and approach will then be explored with the key stages of BA treatment, including monitoring activity, identifying values, and planning/actioning valued activities being outlined. Finally, the chapter will consider how to individualise treatment for each young person and troubleshooting for common difficulties and barriers that may be experienced.

The Theory Behind the Disorder

Learning Theory

Brief BA for depression in young people is based on *Learning Theory*, or *Behavioural Theory* (Olson, 2013). BA is based on a type of learning called '*operant conditioning*' (ibid.) which is learning through reinforcement and punishment. '*Reinforcement*' increases the likelihood that a behaviour will be repeated. There are two types of reinforcement: positive reinforcement and negative reinforcement. Parents and teachers often use positive reinforcement or 'rewards' to encourage children to behave in certain ways. Star charts, praise, and attention are used as positive reinforcement. Positive reinforcement is associated with emotions like joy, contentment, and pride. Negative reinforcement also makes it more likely that a behaviour will be repeated but is more subtle. Negative reinforcement refers to the removal of a situation or experience that is aversive or unwanted, for example, a child avoids walking down a specific street so that they avoid a bully, or a teenager studies really hard for their exams. Because walking home a different way means they don't meet the bully the child feels less frightened. Similarly, when the young person studies hard they feel less anxious about failing and this makes it more likely they will study hard again.

Their behaviour has been *negatively reinforced*. Negative reinforcement is associated with relief, something bad, e.g., fear, has gone away.

How Does Learning Theory Explain Why Depression Keeps Going?

We can use the two concepts of positive and negative reinforcement to understand why depression does not go away. For example, Lina has gradually become less involved in different activities, and her activities have become less enjoyable. This means that the positive reinforcements (rewards) she used to get are now missing. Lina has less positive reinforcement and less reward, as a result she experiences fewer positive emotions.

Lina's mum is worried about how Lina is behaving especially when she looks sad and withdraws from the family, so has started to pay her a bit more attention. She checks in with Lina, texts her from work, and brings her little treats. Although Lina finds this a bit annoying, she also enjoys Mum's attention. Lina is receiving positive reinforcement from her mum when she behaves in a 'depressed' way. This makes it more likely that she will repeat these behaviours (even though neither of them intends for this to happen).

Lina is also getting *negative reinforcement*. Because she feels she is not good company, is a failure, is irritable and grumpy, and isn't 'a good friend' she spends a lot of time alone. This means she doesn't have to worry about snapping at her friends or her family – and feels relief – this is 'negative reinforcement'. Negative reinforcement means that Lina is more likely to spend time alone again.

This pattern of low reward and negative reinforcement is very common in young people who are depressed. As Figure 8.1 below shows it also creates a vicious cycle.

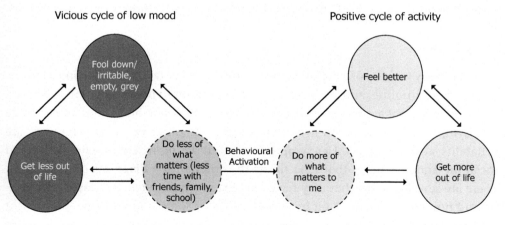

Figure 8.1 The Brief BA cycle (Pass & Reynolds, 2020)

Sourec: © Pass and Reynolds (2020)

How Does Brief Behavioural Activation Use Learning Theory to Overcome Depression?

In Brief BA we work alongside a young person to help them receive more rewards and reinforcement. We use positive reinforcement, to help engage young people in treatment and then to help them 'do more of what matters'. By 'doing more that matters' young people experience more rewards, and this increases their 'positive affect' or mood. We aim to replace activities that do not 'matter' to the young person with activities that do matter, and that are rewarding. By increasing positive reinforcement, we reduce opportunities for negative reinforcement. Throughout this chapter, we will describe the key stages of Brief BA and show how learning theory is used throughout the treatment.

The Evidence Base Behind BA

Behavioural activation is a well-established and effective treatment for adults with depression (e.g., Uphoff et al., 2020). There is much less evidence that relates to depression in adolescents. In the USA, McCauley et al. (2016) found that BA was as effective as other evidence-based treatments assessed. Similarly, Chu and colleagues (2016) evaluated group BA for adolescents with anxiety and depression. At the end of BA treatment young people reported significant reductions in depression and anxiety, and symptoms were significantly lower in the BA group compared to the waiting list control group. In the UK, Kitchen et al. (2021) found that BA was acceptable to young people recruited from the NHS and Pass et al. (2018) reported that Brief BA was acceptable and effective in an outpatient NHS clinic when delivered by mainly low-intensity clinicians. Therefore, whilst there is a need for larger randomised studies in the UK, the evidence suggests that Brief BA is likely to be a useful low-intensity treatment for young people.

Case Study

Lina has many features of a major depressive disorder. Being irritable, feeling a failure, trouble concentrating, and low energy are all symptoms of depression. Lina also isn't enjoying her usual activities – this is known as 'anhedonia' and is one of the three core symptoms of depression in young people. The other two core symptoms are irritability and low mood. Her symptoms are interfering in Lina's schoolwork and social life and it is likely that Lina meets the criteria for a diagnosis of depression. There are several factors that may have led Lina to begin to feel depressed. Her family and home life are changing in important ways. Some important people are not around as much. She has been missing social events and school and is worried about her schoolwork. But can we understand why Lina stays depressed to overcome her difficulties and start enjoying life again?

In low intensity treatment it is helpful to consider what behaviours are keeping Lina depressed. If we can help Lina to change those, we can probably help her overcome her symptoms and start enjoying life again.

The Assessment Process

Lina met Alex (an Education Mental Health Practitioner; EMHP) for an assessment at school after the Mental Health Support Team (MHST) received a referral from Lina's tutor. Lina had completed the Revised Child Anxiety and Depression (RCADS; Chorpita et al., 2000) self-report version and her mum the parent version ahead of the assessment. These showed that Lina was scoring in the 'elevated' range for depression symptoms. Some individual items were particularly noticeable; Lina scored herself a '3' (always) for 'Nothing is much fun anymore', 'I cannot think clearly' and 'I have no energy for things'. Lina scored herself a 2 (most of the time) for 'I feel worthless', Lina's mum scored this item 0. When asked about this difference, Lina explained that she kept those thoughts to herself as she didn't want to burden mum.

Both Lina's and her mum's RCADS also indicated elevated anxiety scores. They both rated Lina a 2 for 'I worry I will do badly at schoolwork' and 'I have trouble going to school'. However, when asked about these, Lina described a realistic concern over dropping grades and attendance which both her mum and school had raised over the last few months.

To help identify Lina's main difficulties, Alex created a Problem Statement with Lina (see Box 8.1) including a recent situation where Lina felt 'grey' (last weekend when Lina's friends had invited her to meet up, but she couldn't get the energy or enthusiasm to go, so told them she had an asthma attack). They also considered what goals Lina wanted from Brief BA, trying to make them as SMART as possible.

Lina's Problem statement:

- *My main problem is* feeling grey, irritable and empty most of the time.
- *Physically* I feel unmotivated and tired.
- *Emotionally* I feel grey and empty.
- *I think* 'I can't be bothered', 'I'm a bad friend', 'I'm letting everyone down'
- *As a result,* I am isolating myself. This is impacting on my life in that I am not spending time with friends or family and not going to all my lessons.

Brief BA Treatment Goals:

1. To meet up with friends outside of school once a week
2. To get to all my lessons
3. To have dinner with family downstairs twice a week

Lina described struggling to concentrate on schoolwork, conversations with friends, and even TV shows. Lina had received a diagnosis of dyslexia earlier in secondary school, but her usual strategies were not working. Lina reported no physical health issues except asthma. Alex completed a risk assessment and Lina reported no self-harm or suicidal thoughts, actions or plans, no risk to others, and no risk from others. Lina reported that she wasn't making much effort on self-care (showering less often, spending less time and effort on her hair and clothes), which her mum also noted.

The Process of Delivering BA: A Step by Step Guide

Lina and Alex (EMHP) met for six Brief BA sessions at school with a review session a month later. Sessions were twice a week at the beginning, then weekly with a break at half-term.

Stage 1: Getting to Know You and What Matters to You (Sessions 1–3)

Symptoms of depression make it challenging for young people to get involved in treatment. Any psychological treatment is hard work and requires lots of motivation, planning, commitment, and hope – all of these qualities are low in young people who are depressed. However, if a young person does not attend sessions, they can't benefit from them. Therefore, a priority in early sessions of Brief BA is to overcome these barriers and 'engage' young people in treatment.

When we start Brief BA, we do two important things. First, we look out for different ways to give the young person lots of positive reinforcement. We use praise, attention, and interest in them, validate their experiences and demonstrate empathy. We reinforce any non-depressed behaviour and any efforts to engage in Brief BA. Second, we explain why they feel as they do in a very simple way (the vicious cycle of depression) and how we can change this by working together. We show them the vicious cycle and draw it again, with their specific words and experiences included.

It's hard to look after yourself, spend time with friends and family, take part in hobbies, study and learn, or enjoy normal everyday activities when you feel bad. In the vicious cycle, we can see that a young person who has started to withdraw from their usual activities stops 'doing things that matter', gets less out of life, and that this feeds in to negative emotions. Young people with depression use different words to describe how they feel – in Figure 8.1 we see 'irritable, empty, grey'. Other common words that young people use are 'sad', 'lonely', 'flat'.

These different negative emotions then get in the way of doing things that matter. So young people do less and less of the things that matter to them. As a result, they get less out of life, and this makes them feel even worse. The young person is in a depression 'trap'. Their behaviour makes sense – but it is making them feel worse and worse. By the time a young person is identified as needing help they might have been stuck in this trap for months or even years.

Importantly, we can also use the cycle to find a way to escape the depression trap. We explain that we are going to work with them, as a team, to help them do 'more that matters'; that this will help them get more out of life, and that slowly this will help them to feel better. Explaining the 'depression trap' and discussing how it fits their experience helps young people (and their parents) see that there is a very good reason for how they are feeling and that their feelings are understandable. Where possible we use parents to support the young person doing Brief BA, so it is very helpful to have them on board. We also encourage parents to provide positive reinforcement for non-depressed behaviour. We explain to the young person and their parent (if present) that depression is very hard, that they are trapped in a vicious cycle (in the left in the diagram above) and that if it was easy for them to change they would already have done so.

In session 1, Alex explained to Lina and her mum the rationale behind Brief BA, showed how it applied to Lina's difficulties (see transcript), and drew out the Brief BA cycle using Lina's own examples.

Transcript: Explaining the Brief BA Rationale

Alex: Brief BA is about doing more of what matters to *you*. So we'll first spend some time together looking at what matters to you. We sometimes call this your 'values'. Values are what you believe are important, and shape the kind of person you want to be... There is no right or wrong, and everyone's values are a little different as they are personal to you. The key for us is to find out what is important to you. How does that sound?

Lina: Umm... I'm not sure I even know what's important to me.

Alex: That's completely fine and very common, as it's not something we talk much about every day. We have some tools to help us discover this together. Once we have some idea of what's important to you, we can use this to help prioritise valued activities, to do more of what matters to you every day.

To 'get to know' the young person we pay close attention to everything they tell us about their life and circumstances. Between sessions we ask them to monitor and record their activities and their moods. They can do this in lots of different ways, the important thing is to help us get to know them better. Alex introduced the idea of activity monitoring to Lina and her mum, explaining it was a 'getting to know you' tool, to help find out how Lina was spending her time and to get to know more about

LOW-INTENSITY PRACTICE WITH CYP AND FAMILIES

her. Alex explained that this would help show what matters to Lina (and what does not), as well as providing a useful baseline to work from. Alex explained the idea that activities can be rewarding in different ways (see ACE-I box for more details).

Alex explained that most things may not feel very rewarding (high on any of the ACE ratings) currently, because depression symptoms get in the way. However, reviewing the log together would show what activities helped Lina feel *'a bit less grey'*, and what was *'even a tiny bit rewarding, better than a zero'*. Alex also used this time alone with Lina to check in on risk by reviewing the answers Lina had given to these questions in the assessment, and they continued to check in on risk at every session.

What Are ACE-I Ratings?

- **A**chievement (a sense of success or accomplishment, including ticking something off your 'to-do list', or the relief from getting something hard or unpleasant done)
- **C**loseness (a sense of connection with others, including humans, animals/nature, spiritual connection; closeness might be felt while in the presence of others, or when alone
- **E**njoyment (a sense of pleasure, fun, and/or relaxation)
- **I**mportance (a sense of this specific activity mattering to you, does it fit with how you want to be living your life/the kind of person you want to be?)
  - Sometimes activities can be Important even if they don't score highly on Achievement, Closeness or Enjoyment (e.g., because they fit with a broader value or longer-term goal)

At the end of their first session Alex asked Lina to complete an activity log for the days up until their next session. In the second session, Lina and Alex reviewed Lina's activity log (which Lina had made on her phone so Alex made a copy).

Transcript: Reviewing Activity Log

Alex: How did you find recording your activities?

Lina: It was ok... to see the link between what I did and how I felt. Seeing it gave me a bit of perspective. I feel like I'm not doing much that's important to me, but I don't know how to change that.

Alex: Ok, we can work on that together. Was there anything else you noticed?

Lina: Scrolling on my phone made me feel bad when I did it for a long time. It's just a habit I don't even realise I'm doing sometimes.

Alex: That's interesting. Has that made you think about what you might want to do differently?

Lina: Yeah, I want to *connect* more with people rather than just scroll. I tried sending a few messages to friends when I caught myself scrolling, to stop digging myself into that hole, which helped.

Alex: Wow, an excellent example of Brief BA in action! It's brilliant that you're already taking important steps towards doing more of what matters to you. This is something we can build on by looking together at what is important to you. It sounds like connecting with friends might be one of them?

Lina: Yeah, it's... connecting with friends that matters, not putting up appearances or just going through the motions to fit in.

Making Brief BA individual for every young person

- Get ahead: Consider aspects of diversity from assessment/referral, plan for adaptations that might be useful (e.g., interpreter, accessibility)
- Keep them in mind: How can Brief BA be as easy as possible for *this* young person?
- Use data: Review activity logs to understand the unique circumstances of the young person, and reflect on how to incorporate these into Brief BA
- Follow their lead: Be led by the young person's values, and ideas for valued activities: These can be surprisingly diverse and creative
- Be flexible: Brief BA can be delivered in different ways, with different materials: Don't be afraid to adapt; by supporting a young person to understand and do more of what matters to them
- Use supervision: Practitioners should reflect on their own background, values, and characteristics and how these might draw them to endorse certain values/valued activities more than others
- Don't assume: Every young person is different (e.g., chronological age/ school year tells little about developmental stage and level of autonomy allowed at home)
- Be curious! Young people are usually the experts in how practitioners can meet their needs

Identifying Values

In Brief BA we use a structured way to help young people identify 'what matters to them' (the Values sheet). We also listen out for clues about activities that are linked to their values. Alex and Lina used the Values handout to explore Lina's values, first with Lina writing a few things down and then reviewing and looking at her activity logs for more ideas. They then discussed how Lina's values could be turned into small and achievable concrete activities, that did not need much time, money or effort. Alex highlighted Lina texting her friends as a great example of a valued activity (linked to Lina's value of 'connecting with friends').

Alex asked Lina if there were any small activities she wanted to try before their next session, and Lina said she wanted to text a friend at least once a day. Alex suggested that Lina try an 'in-session' valued activity before the session ended. Lina decided to reply to a text from her friend Ashley. Lina reported being pleased that she had done this, and that she felt that she was being a better friend by replying. Alex took this opportunity to positively reinforce Lina's behaviour. This helped Lina see how small, achievable activities that link with her values could make small but important positive changes in mood.

Stage 2: Doing More of What Matters (Session 4+)

In Brief BA, the aim is not to do 'more' but to do *'more that matters'*. Sometimes this might mean doing less of the things that don't matter, to make room for activities that are more important to the young person.

Why do 'more that matters' to the young person? There are many reasons, including:

1. It is more specific and personal to the young person and an excellent way to get to know them better.
2. Finding out 'what matters' to the young person keeps the session focused on them, is likely to improve the relationship between the Brief BA clinician and the young person, and keep them coming back to sessions.
3. What matters to the young person will be more intrinsically reinforcing for them and have a greater effect on their mood.
4. Young people are often already 'doing things' but these are not things that matter to them – and are therefore not giving them positive reinforcement.
5. What matters to the young person is likely to be more motivating to them.
6. Working out what matters to you is an important 'task' of adolescence when we develop our identity; thus, this is developmentally important and is important beyond the end of treatment.

The key to change in Brief BA is to support and scaffold the young person to start to make small but important changes in their behaviours. When we know what matters to the young person, we can work with them to identify 'valued activities'. These are small, manageable behaviours that they can plan to do which are in line with their values ('what matters to them'). Valued activities are positively reinforcing, and therefore likely to be repeated.

Depression takes away or reduces energy, motivation, and hope. For young people with depression to be able to 'do more that matters' we need to provide a lot of help and support. Practitioners and the young person should try to identify a small, valued activity that they can complete, during the session (as Alex did with Lina). Doing a valued activity in the session means that the clinician can support the young person and adapt the activity if necessary. This makes it more likely that the young person will attempt the valued activity, provides an opportunity to reinforce the young person and their effort, and gives the young person an immediate experience of success (and reward). By doing the valued activity together, the clinician and young person share an important experience, and this builds the therapeutic relationship and helps them identify other valued activities that the young person can do between sessions.

Trouble Shooting Barriers to Doing Things Differently

While Lina reported understanding the 'idea' of Brief BA, she struggled to implement the valued activities they had identified. In session 4, Alex explored this further.

Stage 3: Review and Repeat, Troubleshooting, Planning for Ending (Sessions 6–8, Review)

Much of the 'work' of Brief BA is a continuation of identifying values (new discoveries about these might come up in any session, as the young person tries out doing things differently), planning and doing valued activities. This 'review and repeat' cycle includes troubleshooting difficulties that arise and if needed, trying new approaches to problem-solve around barriers. Contracts and Problem-Solving are both tools that can be used in the face of barriers to a young person engaging in valued activities.

Remember that the pace of progress will vary depending on a young person's depression symptoms, support network and individual circumstances; some will make rapid progress while others may only feel able to make small steps towards doing more of what matters to them. Practitioners should not expect too much too soon, and make sure they praise and encourage every effort a young person makes towards doing more of what matters to them.

Involving Others

After Lina had experienced the 'feel good' benefits of Brief BA by doing valued activities within a session, she started to do more of these outside of sessions. At Lina's request, Alex emailed Lina's mum copies of the handouts and some of the valued activities Lina planned to try out. Lina's mum was happy to help, and they got into a habit of checking in about this every day.

When Lina was at her dad's she found it harder to do as many valued activities, partly because she didn't always have everything to hand at the other house. She also found it difficult to ask her dad to help as she worried it would be asking too much. Alex had been sending the Brief BA worksheets to dad but Lina wasn't sure he always read them as it depended what shifts he was working that week. Lina suggested her step-mum Layla might be someone who could help, and Alex and Lina used a contract to consider ways in which she could do this.

LOW-INTENSITY PRACTICE WITH CYP AND FAMILIES

Alex and Lina talked about how to check Layla was happy to help in these ways, and actioned the following:

- Lina took a photo on her phone of the contract and sent it to Layla
- Alex emailed a copy of the contract and all session handouts to Layla
- Alex arranged a brief video call with Layla to talk this through

Making the Most of the Environment

Alex asked Lina for ideas about who else could help support her and they came up with some specific ideas. These included asking her form tutor Mr Mangera about the study skills group, speaking to the school librarian about audio versions of English books, and asking her head of year about the buddy scheme for new Year 7s that Lina wanted to help with. Alex and Lina also brainstormed ways Lina could use the school environment to support valued activities through the day (e.g., researching her science project on the school computers, using a music room to help a friend practise, buying a healthy snack from the canteen). Lina found using her school planner particularly helpful for this as she looked at it throughout the day.

As Brief BA sessions progressed, Lina made good progress on valued activities but found activities where she needed help from others to arrange more difficult. Alex suggested they use Problem-Solving to work through this.

Making Routine Outcome Measures (ROMs) Meaningful

Alex explained why we use routine outcome measures at the start of Brief BA. Alex and Lina completed the RCADS depression subscale and the Outcome Rating Scale at the start of each session, and a brief therapeutic alliance measure (Session Rating Scale) at the end of every session. Alex always asked for feedback from Lina about what she liked about the session, and what could be improved.

In session 5, Alex noticed that Lina's depression symptoms seemed worse and asked Lina what she thought was going on. Lina said she had not been able to visit her dad at the weekend because of train disruptions. As her weekend plans changed at the last minute, she had not organised anything with her friends. Lina explained that she didn't get in touch with friends to see if they were free as she didn't want 'to seem desperate'. Instead, she ended up scrolling social media, checking what her friends were up to, and thinking about what she was missing. Lina said she had felt 'really deflated, and I just gave up bothering to think what else I could do, it felt too hard'.

Alex and Lina spent the rest of the session reviewing valued activities Lina could do if plans changed last minute. Lina came up with some new ideas for 'quality family time' if a visit to dad's wasn't possible (video call her dad or older brother at university, watch Gran's favourite TV show with her, help mum cook dinner), as well as 'connecting with friends'.

Ending Brief BA

Planning for the end of Brief BA is very important, as it's likely the clinician has provided a lot of positive reinforcement that will end when sessions finish. Alex explained the number of Brief BA sessions from the beginning, and noted with Lina at the start of every session how many they had left (e.g., 'So today is session 3 of the 6 we have together, so we're half-way through'). Alex regularly asked '*What could help you keep doing X after our sessions have finished?*', and encouraged Lina's parents, step-mum and teachers to understand and act on the Brief BA principles for ongoing support after the sessions ended. Lina and Alex discussed how Lina might continue to monitor her mood and behaviours. Lina made an action plan of things she would do if she noticed the depression trap beginning again.

At the review one month after the final session (with Lina and her mum, plus an email update from Lina's dad and step-mum), Lina's and her mum's RCADS scores reported scores on the depression and anxiety scales that were below the clinical level. Lina reported '*feeling less grey and empty. I look forward to doing things more now. It can still feel an effort but I'm starting to enjoy some things again, especially when I know it's something that matters to me.*' Lina's mum described '*feeling more confident in knowing how to support Lina going forwards, and keep going with the positive changes*'. Lina's dad and step-mum were also involved in supporting Lina and were looking at how to make it easier for Lina to visit. Alex discharged Lina, and sent a Brief BA treatment summary to Lina, her parents and step-mum, and her form tutor/deputy head of year.

Like many other young people Lina will continue to face difficulties and challenges. As well as helping young people to overcome the depression trap, Brief BA can help them to develop new skills and understanding to protect themselves. As with all early help, identifying depression quickly and offering Brief BA before problems become entrenched and young people lose significant years of development is an important aim of education and CYP mental health services.

Brief BA Key Take Home Points

- Set the bar as low as possible: Depression is hard work and gets in the way of treatment, so make it as easy as possible for the young person to take part
- Get to know the young person: Be curious
- Make it work for who is in the room
- The Brief BA clinician is a key source of positive reinforcement: Encourage and praise at every opportunity
- Do more of what matters, especially in session
- Enlist and engage supporters
- Expect risk and keep it on the table
- Review regularly through feedback, ROMs and supervision
- Remember, it's simple but it's not easy!

Summary

In this chapter, we have outlined the behavioural theory of depression and the principles of reinforcement that underpin the Brief BA approach. Through Lina's case example, we have worked through the key stages of Brief BA step by step and shown how learning theory is used throughout the treatment. Brief BA provides a structure and techniques to guide a low-intensity clinician to build a positive therapeutic relationship with a young person, alongside using the principle of positive reinforcement. Brief BA is a straightforward but powerful treatment to help a young person break their depression cycle, do more of what matters to them, and get more out of life.

For further resources, please visit the CEDAR website at: https://cedar.exeter.ac.uk/resources/cyp/

References

Chorpita, B.F., Yim, L., Moffitt, C., Umemoto, L.A., & Francis, S.E. (2000). Assessment of symptoms of DSM-IV anxiety and depression in children: A revised child anxiety and depression scale. *Behaviour Research and Therapy*, *38*(8), 835–855. https://doi.org/10.1016/S0005-7967(99)00130-8

Chu, B.C., Crocco, S.T., Esseling, P., Areizaga, M.J., Lindner, A.M., & Skriner, L.C. (2016). Transdiagnostic group behavioral activation and exposure therapy for youth anxiety and depression: Initial randomized controlled trial. *Behaviour Research and Therapy*, *76*, 65–75. https://doi.org/10.1016/j.brat.2015.11.005

Kitchen, C.E., Tiffin, P.A., Lewis, S., Gega, L., & Ekers, D. (2021). Innovations in practice: A randomised controlled feasibility trial of behavioural activation as a treatment for young people with depression. *Child and Adolescent Mental Health*, *26*(3), 290–295. https://doi.org/10.1111/camh.12415

McCauley, E., Gudmundsen, G., Schloredt, K., Martell, C., Rhew, I., Hubley, S., & Dimidjian, S. (2016). The adolescent behavioural activation program: Adapting behavioral activation as a treatment for depression in adolescence. *Journal of Clinical Child and Adolescent Psychology*, *45*(3), 291–304. https://doi.org/10.1080/15374416.2014.979933

Olson, M.H. (2013). *Introduction to Theories of Learning* (9th ed.). Routledge. https://doi.org/10.4324/9781315664965

Pass, L., Lejuez, C.W., & Reynolds, S. (2018). Brief behavioural activation (Brief BA) for adolescent depression: A pilot study. *Behavioural and Cognitive Psychotherapy*, *46*(2), 182–194. doi:10.1017/S1352465817000443

Pass, L., & Reynolds, S. (2020). *Brief Behavioural Activation for Adolescent Depression: A Clinician's Manual and Session-by-Session Guide*. Jessica Kingsley Publishers.

Uphoff, E., Ekers, D., Robertson, L., Dawson, S., Sanger, E., South, E., Samaan, Z., Richards, D., Meader, N., & Churchill, R. (2020). Behavioural activation therapy for depression in adults. *The Cochrane Database of Systematic Reviews*, *7*(7). https://doi.org/10.1002/14651858.CD013305.pub2

9

Exposure and Habituation

Sarah Holland

Introduction

This chapter will focus on the use of Exposure and Habituation (EH) with children and young people (CYP) at Low-Intensity. The steps to completing EH with CYP will be identified and demonstrated. This will be applied to the case of Elna, introduced earlier within the assessment chapter of this book. Theory supporting the use of EH and the current state of evidence for its use will also be considered. Example worksheets will be included to support the practitioner in developing delivery of the intervention.

Overview

'Anxiety' refers to an individual's physiological and behavioural response to an actual or potential threat (Barlow, 2002; Steimer, 2002). Although this response can be useful in motivating an individual to avoid danger, it can also be triggered unnecessarily by a variety of non-threatening or low-risk stimuli (Bouchard et al., 2004). Individuals with anxiety disorders may experience persistent and excessive fear in relation to a perceived threat, which leads to repeated avoidance (American Psychiatric Association, 2013). The more an individual avoids a feared situation or stimulus to reduce anxiety, the more reliant they become on this as a coping strategy, and the avoidance behaviour is therefore negatively reinforced (Barlow, 2002).

Exposure and Habituation (EH) is a low-intensity, single strand intervention to treat mild to moderate anxiety disorders. It involves the repeated and prolonged confrontation with a situation or stimulus that provokes fear or anxiety, even though the perceived threat is objectively safe and poses low risk (Maples-Keller & Rauch, 2020). The feared stimuli could be a living person or animal (e.g., clowns, dogs), an inanimate object (e.g., furniture, vehicles), physiological (e.g., breathlessness, palpitations) or situational (e.g., social situations, crowds, separating from caregiver) (Abramowitz, 2013). At low-intensity, EH can occur in different formats depending on the nature and specific presentations of anxiety, including *in vivo* exposure, which involves facing feared stimuli in real life situations; and imaginal exposure, which involves facing mental stimuli and imagined situations (e.g., unwanted thoughts, images) (Papworth, 2020). After repeated exposure, an individual's anxiety reduces naturally, which is a process known as habituation (Maples-Keller & Rauch, 2020). Although the particular stimuli and situations used in exposure tasks will vary across different presentations, the method of implementing exposure is similar. Someone with social worries may talk to a peer, whilst a child with separation anxiety may attend school. A person with a dog phobia may walk in a park where dogs are, or a CYP with panic with agoraphobia may attend a shopping centre. The task is always related to the specific difficulty.

Empirical Evidence

Exposure and Habituation (EH) has a strong evidence base for the effective treatment of anxiety disorders, where behavioural avoidance is a crucial maintaining factor (Kaczkurkin & Foa, 2015). The largest body of research evaluating the effectiveness of exposure therapy has been conducted with adult participants, where research has demonstrated positive outcomes for a range of anxiety disorders, such as social anxiety (Mayo-Wilson et al., 2014), specific phobia (Wolitzky-Taylor et al., 2008), panic disorder (Pompoli et al., 2016), agoraphobia (Breuninger et al., 2019) and health anxiety (Weck et al., 2015).

EH is frequently given in combination with other approaches under a wider category of Cognitive Behavioural Therapy (CBT). As a result, much of the evidence supporting the use of EH originates from studies of CBT more generally. A meta-analysis by Wang et al. (2017) evaluated the effectiveness of CBT for childhood anxiety disorders for 7,719 participants from 115 studies, where CBT was found to be significantly more effective than a control group. Moreover, a further meta-analysis of 111 treatment outcome studies concluded that exposure-based therapy is a well-established and highly efficient treatment for child and adolescent anxiety (Higa-McMillan et al., 2016).

Despite the combination of techniques used in CBT, exposure has been considered key to the effective treatment of anxiety disorders in CYP (Kendal et al., 2005; Whiteside, Ollendick et al., 2020). Whiteside, Sim, et al. (2020) examined 75 studies that included CYP with an anxiety disorder treated with CBT or a comparison condition. The authors concluded that 'a greater amount of in-session exposure was related to significantly larger effect sizes between CBT and waitlist control across reporters and from pre- to post-treatment for child report' (Whiteside, Sim et al., 2020, p. 2).

Early data collected by the University of Exeter (unpublished) has examined the use of EH at low intensity by CYP Wellbeing Practitioners measured using the Revised Children's Anxiety and Depression Rating Scale (RCADS) (Chorpita et al., 2000). The data indicated RCADS scores were significantly lower post-therapy compared to pre-therapy for CYP presenting with separation anxiety (n= 31), panic disorder (n=35), and social anxiety (n=26). This initial data suggests that EH is an effective LICBT intervention for CYP; however, due to the small sample size, covariates such as the number of sessions attended were unable to be controlled. A larger sample is required to explore the difference in pre-post therapy scores, whilst controlling for potentially confounding variables. This will allow greater certainty that changes in subscale scores post-therapy are due to EH, rather than other factors such as the number of sessions attended. Evidence would therefore seem supportive of the use of EH, with significant promise in working at low-intensity with CYP.

Intervention Process

Focus will now be placed upon the step-by-step process of completing an EH intervention with the case of Elna identified within the assessment chapter. From assessment the following problem statement and goals were identified:

Problem statement:

My main problem is that I hate being away from mum. This is triggered when I need to go anywhere on my own, like going to school. I experience physical symptoms such as feeling sick. Sometimes I don't go to school or I get picked up early, and I have to sleep in mum's bed at night. I have thoughts that something terrible will happen to my mum when I'm not with her. I feel worried and sad. This means that I can't always do the things I want to, like going to parties and sleepovers with my friends.

Treatment goals:

1. To sleep in my own bed all night at least three times a week (within one month).
2. To go to school for four full days a week, by the end of our work together (6–8 weeks)
3. To go to my friend Lucy's house for her birthday sleepover (in 1 month).

Step 1: Psychoeducation and Treatment Rationale

Once EH has been discussed and agreed in collaboration with the CYP (and parent/caregiver if appropriate), the next step will be to provide a clear treatment rationale for EH, and a clear expectation of the homework they will be asked to complete between sessions. The practitioner should provide psychoeducation of how the CYP's anxiety can be maintained, by examining how their thoughts (cognitions), emotions, physiological symptoms, and behaviours are interconnected (known as the vicious cycle of anxiety). Figure 9.1 illustrates Elna's descriptive formulation diagram of anxiety around 'going to school' used to support these links. In this example, Elna's physiological and cognitive responses motivate her to avoid going to school (*feared situation*); however, this avoidance strategy prevents her from recognising that the feared consequence that her mum would be poorly might not happen. Template worksheets are provided on the accompanying website resources and can be found on https://cedar.exeter.ac.uk/resources/cyp/ (Appendix A). These can be adapted according to the CYP's developmental and cognitive level.

Key Tips:

- Provide a clear treatment rationale
- Explore the role of thoughts, feelings, behaviour and physical sensations
- Identify the key role of avoidance and exposure
- Consider adaptations needed to meet the CYP needs

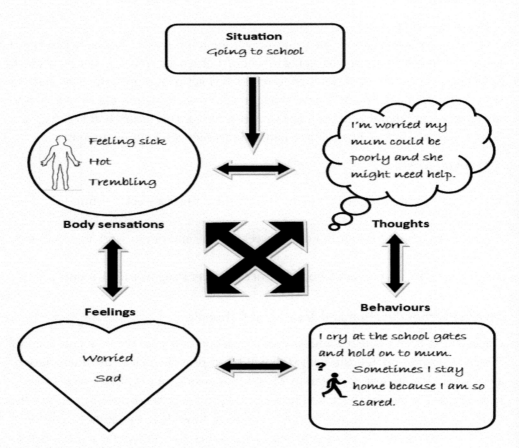

Figure 9.1 Descriptive formulation diagram of Elna's anxiety

Step 2: Exposure Hierarchy

EH involves creating a list of feared situations and organising these into a fear hierarchy, where the CYP rates their perceived level of anxiety for each task. Tasks should be relevant to the CYP's treatment goals (Papworth, 2020) in that they are steps towards a clear goal. Exposure often begins with confronting moderately distressing stimuli or situations on the hierarchy and gradually working up to more difficult situations. Figure 9.2 illustrates a hypothetical exposure hierarchy for Elna, which she called her 'fear ladder'. Hierarchy worksheets are provided on the accompanying website (Appendix B) and can be adapted according to the young person's cognitive and developmental level and interests.

Step 3: Setting up Exposure Conditions

An important element in developing exposure within the intervention is to consider some key rules for implementation. Exposure activities should meet the following conditions: graded, prolonged, repeated, and without distraction (Richards & Whyte, 2011).

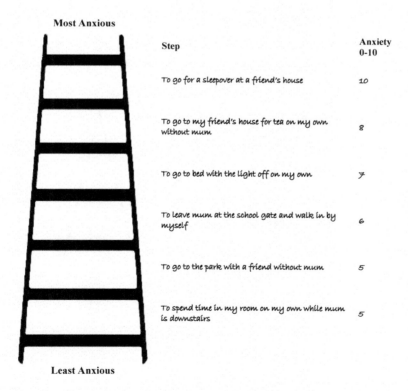

Figure 9.2 Elna's exposure hierarchy, known as her 'fear ladder'

Graded

The feared situations on the hierarchy should be graded, where the tasks that the CYP finds the most fearful or anxiety provoking should be placed at the top of the hierarchy, followed by activities that are of medium difficulty and then the easiest at the bottom of the hierarchy. For example, a CYP with social anxiety can begin by speaking to a peer in the classroom for a prolonged period of time, before working towards delivering a presentation in front of the entire class. Once a CYP has created their hierarchy, the practitioner and CYP then agree on a plan for conducting and repeating the exposure within the hierarchy, before moving up to the next step. For something to be a useful exposure exercise, it should give the CYP enough symptoms of anxiety to enable habituation to take place. This should not be too overwhelming such that exposure is prevented and should not lead to an absence of anxious arousal.

Prolonged

It is important that the CYP remains in the feared situation for long enough until anxiety naturally reduces through the process of habituation. When an individual is confronted with a feared situation, it can be difficult to stay in the situation for a prolonged length of time, however if they leave before beginning to feel a reduction in anxiety, it is likely that they will continue to avoid the situation in the future (with leaving a situation being negatively reinforced through the reduction in anxiety). Figure 9.3 illustrates how anxiety reduces after leaving a situation immediately

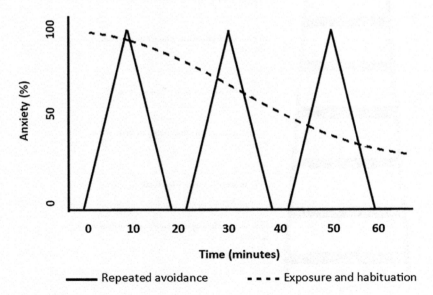

Figure 9.3 An illustration of a CYP's anxiety levels associated with repeated avoidance and a prolonged exposure task

over three time periods ('Repeated avoidance'), which prevents the CYP from learning that the feared consequence is unlikely to happen. This means that anxiety is equally high with each subsequent exposure. When a CYP stays in the situation for a prolonged period (as a rule of thumb until the anxiety has at least halved), their anxiety will eventually reduce through the process of habituation ('Exposure and habituation').

Repeated

For habituation to take place, the CYP will need to repeatedly expose themselves to the feared stimuli or situation between sessions. The CYP should continue to complete the same step of their hierarchy until their anxiety score at the start of the exercise reduces to a sufficiently manageable level before they consider moving on to the next step of their hierarchy. Figure 9.4 illustrates how levels of anxiety can reduce following repeated exposures to a feared stimulus or situation. This is different from the experience of repeated high levels of anxiety in a given situation perpetuated by escape and avoidance of a situation.

It is important for the CYP to try to repeat the exercise at each step as many times as possible to get the full benefit. If the exercise is no longer causing the CYP more than 40 per cent anxiety at the start of the exercise, then it may be time to move to the next step on their hierarchy. Establishing what constitutes an acceptable and manageable level of anxiety will be important to establish with the CYP.

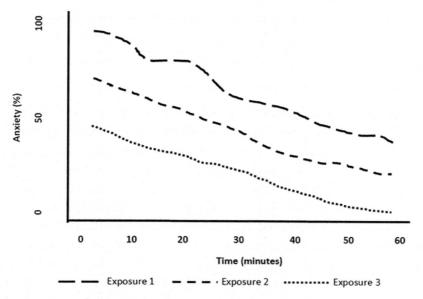

Figure 9.4 Habituation of anxiety over time during three repeated exposure exercises

Without Distraction

When someone feels anxious it is understandable for them to try to do things to make them feel better. This could be using distraction techniques or engaging in safety behaviours, which can reduce anxiety in the short term. For example, one may use distraction techniques such as reliance on using a mobile phone, wearing headphones, or seeking reassurance from others. In the long term, however, this is not helpful for the CYP, as they are unable to fully experience their symptoms of anxiety, which prevents habituation from taking place (Maples-Keller & Rauch, 2020).

For EH to work successfully, it is important that the exercise is planned to ensure the CYP is not distracted in any way. It can be difficult to drop these safety behaviours straight away, so it may be beneficial to gradually reduce them as the young person moves up each step of their hierarchy, working towards removing the safety behaviour altogether. This has been considered as an 'approach' safety behaviour, as opposed to an 'avoidant' safety behaviour and it increases the proximity of exposure to a feared event (Rachman et al., 2008). For example, if a CYP cannot walk to school without their parent with them, then they may have this as an easier activity as long as it still gives them enough anxiety for them to habituate. Some steps further up their hierarchy could then be walking to school on their own (if appropriate).

Key Tips:

- Create a hierarchy of steps towards a clear goal
- CYP is the expert in grading task
- Exposure should be graded, repeated, prolonged and without distraction
- It may be necessary to consider approach safety behaviours to start

---

Step 4: Plan Exposures

Once a step on the hierarchy has been identified, the CYP will be supported to create an exposure plan, recording the specific activity they will complete to face their fears. Once the CYP has planned when they will complete the exercise, they can fill in the date and time on their worksheet (see accompanying website Appendix C).

It is important for the CYP to record their rating of anxiety before the exercise, just as they start the exercise, and once they have completed the exercise. The CYP should stay in the feared situation for as long as it takes for their anxiety to reduce. Typically, their second anxiety rating should reduce by 50 per cent before stopping the exercise (Richards & Whyte, 2011), though this may take repeated exposure to achieve. Anxiety scales can be adapted according to the young person's age and cognitive development. For younger children, a score from 0–10 may be more suitable than a percentage. Figure 9.5 illustrates an example of an exposure plan for Elna.

Date & Time	Duration	Exercise	Level of Anxiety			Comments
			Before Exercise	Start of Exercise	End of Exercise	
Saturday 10:30am	90 minutes	Watch a film in my room on my own	6	5	4	I wish mum was with me, but I enjoyed watching the film

Figure 9.5 Elna's exposure exercise. Anxiety level is recorded at three time periods on a scale of 0–10.

Step 5: Review Progress, Reward Effort and Move Up Hierarchy

After the CYP has effectively habituated to each exposure task, their effort should be rewarded before moving to the next step of their hierarchy. Rewarding is an important part of the EH process as it increases a CYP's motivation and engagement and allows them to gain a sense of achievement from their success (Kendall et al., 2005). Success can be defined as any step towards facing anxiety, including removing or reducing a safety behaviour, any effort to face a situation that was previously difficult, or tolerating anxiety in a situation instead of escaping. The CYP's developmental level will determine what types of rewards could increase motivation. For example, younger CYP may like to receive special stickers as a reward, whereas older CYP may prefer extra screen time (e.g., television or games). In the case of Elna, a suitable reward could be to earn stickers on a sticker chart or to go to a special place (e.g., going to a park after school, or going to a café to have a hot chocolate).

Key Tips:

- Use an exposure plan to support tasks
- Use anxiety ratings to judge exposure completion
- Reward efforts to engage with exposure

Troubleshooting

Developmental and Cognitive Level of CYP

It is important that the CYP understands the rationale of the intervention (Kendall et al., 2005). Practitioners should therefore be flexible in adapting their language and use of resources to ensure the intervention remains child centred and culturally appropriate. When communicating with CYP and their parents or caregivers, it is important to consider their level of cognitive and emotional development, including any learning disabilities, neurodevelopmental conditions, sight or hearing problems and delays in language development (National Institute for Health and Care

Excellence [NICE], 2013). Adaptations for cultural diversity should also be considered when completing any intervention. Practitioners should be aware that some children may struggle to identify their emotions and therefore could have difficulties rating the intensity of their anxiety for the exposure tasks. It is therefore important that practitioners adapt their approach according to the CYP's level of understanding. This could include adapting anxiety scales, such as the use of feelings thermometers (see accompanying website Appendix D).

Involvement of Parents/Caregivers

Research has shown that CBT with active parental involvement is associated with long-term maintenance of positive treatment outcomes (Manassis et al., 2014). The involvement of parents and caregivers is especially helpful when working with younger children, as they will be able to support the CYP to facilitate their activities on their exposure hierarchy (Rudy et al., 2017), particularly as many of the exposure tasks will occur outside of sessions (e.g., at home).

It is important that practitioners discuss boundaries and expectations with parents and caregivers regarding their role in the intervention (Gola et al., 2016). Research suggests that parents and caregivers can play a role in the development and maintenance of anxiety in CYP (Ginsburg & Schlossberg, 2002), such as through modelling anxious behaviours themselves (Fisak & Grills-Taquechel, 2007). It is therefore important that parents receive some psychoeducation around the potential behaviours that may be inadvertently reinforcing anxiety. When working with Elna, the practitioner could provide psychoeducation to her mother regarding how anxiety can be maintained (such as providing reassurance and/or allowing Elna to avoid situations she finds difficult). Elna's mother could be encouraged to use other strategies, such as praising Elna for her achievements with her homework, using rewards to increase motivation. Working closely with family can further support opportunities for the practitioner to learn cultural norms and expectations within the family to support practitioner understanding and development.

Ethical Considerations

Practitioners should be aware of the confidentiality of the CYP if conducting exposure tasks outside of the session, as there is a risk that others may identify the CYP as undergoing therapy, without the consent of the CYP. Practitioners should therefore pre-warn the CYP and decide how they will respond if they see someone they know during an exposure exercise (Gola et al., 2016; Thomassin et al., 2017). Exposure exercises should not be harmful or deemed to be unsafe in any way (Gola et al., 2016). For example, it could be unsafe for a child with a specific phobia of dogs to stroke a large unknown dog, as the animal could potentially be aggressive.

Child and young person engagement

Even with a clear understanding of the rationale for treatment, some CYP can be uncertain or reluctant to participate in exposure tasks and may struggle to complete home practice tasks between sessions. In this instance, it can be helpful to consider the application of the COM-B model (Michie et al., 2011; Michie et al., 2014) to recognise any difficulties with capability, opportunity and motivation that might impact on their behaviour and engagement in the intervention. The COM-B model indicates that for a behaviour to occur, a person must have the capability to participate (e.g., knowledge and skills), the opportunity (e.g., in their environment), and motivation. It is beneficial for practitioners to review the COM-B model for each homework task that is set in sessions (Papworth, 2020). The use of encouragement and rewards is usually an effective motivator for CYP's to engage in the exposure tasks (Bouchard et al., 2004). See accompanying website resource 'COM-B for Elna' for further detail.

Practitioners should ensure that the CYP does not start with an exposure exercise which is too challenging early in treatment. If the CYP engages in an exercise which elicits too much anxiety, it is more likely that they will avoid the exposure or engage in distraction techniques or safety behaviours. There is a chance that the attempted exposure task may elicit more distress than they anticipated (Canella et al., 2020), which could also result in them withdrawing from the situation before habituation occurs. In these instances, the practitioner can explore modifying the task or breaking it down into smaller steps so it feels more manageable (Papworth, 2020). The steps involved in the hierarchy can be moved and re-ordered according to new ratings from the experience of exposure as needed.

Summary

This chapter has illustrated the use of Exposure and Habituation (EH) with Children and Young People (CYP), using a clinical case example to demonstrate its application at low intensity. EH has strong empirical support as an effective treatment for a range of anxiety disorders in adults, children, and adolescents. In order for habituation to occur successfully, it is important that exposure exercises are graded, prolonged, repeated, and without distractions. Troubleshooting potential challenges to applying EH has been outlined, such as consideration of the CYP's cognitive development, parent and caregiver involvement, ethical considerations, and CYP engagement. For a copy of handouts and accompanying materials for the chapter please go to https://cedar.exeter.ac.uk/resources/cyp/

For further resources, please visit the CEDAR website at: https://cedar.exeter.ac.uk/resources/cyp/

References

Abramowitz, J.S. (2013). The practice of exposure therapy: Relevance of cognitive-behavioral theory and extinction theory. *Behavior Therapy, 44*(4), 548–558. https://doi.org/10.1016/j.beth.2013.03.003

American Psychiatric Association, DSM-5 Task Force. (2013). *Diagnostic and Statistical Manual of Mental Disorders: DSM-5™* (5th ed.). American Psychiatric Publishing, Inc. https://doi.org/10.1176/appi.books.9780890425596

Barlow, D.H. (2002). *Anxiety and Its Disorders: The Nature and Treatment of Anxiety and Panic* (2nd ed.). Guilford Press.

Bouchard, S., Mendlowitz, S.L., Coles, M.E., & Franklin, M. (2004). Considerations in the use of exposure with children. *Cognitive and Behavioral Practice, 11*(1), 56–65. https://doi.org/10.1016/S1077-7229(04)80007-5

Breuninger, C., Tuschen-Caffier, B., & Svaldi, J. (2019). Dysfunctional cognition and self-efficacy as mediators of symptom change in exposure therapy for agoraphobia – Systematic review and meta-analysis. *Behaviour Research and Therapy, 120*, 103443. https://doi.org/10.1016/j.brat.2019.103443

Canella, R., Essoe, J.K., Grados, M., & McGuire J.F. (2020). Overcoming challenging in exposure therapy. In T.S. Peris, E.A. Storch & J.F. McGuire (Eds.), *Exposure Therapy for Children with Anxiety and OCD* (pp. 383–404). Academic Press.

Chorpita, B.F., Yim, L.M., Moffitt, C.E., Umemoto, L.A., & Francis, S.E. (2000). Assessment of symptoms of DSM-IV anxiety and depression in children: A Revised Child Anxiety and Depression Scale. *Behaviour Research and Therapy, 38*(8), 835–855. https://doi.org/10.1016/s0005-7967(99)00130-8

Fisak, B., & Grills-Taquechel, A.E. (2007). Parental modelling, reinforcement, and information transfer: Risk factors in the development of child anxiety? *Clinical Child and Family Psychology Review, 10*(3), 213–231. https://doi.org/10.1007/s10567-007-0020-x

Ginsburg, G.S., & Schlossberg, M.C. (2002). Family-based treatment of childhood anxiety disorders. *International Review of Psychiatry, 14*(2), 143–154. https://doi.org/10.1080/09540260220132662

Gola, J.A., Beidas, R.S., Antinoro-Burke, D., Kratz, H.E., & Fingerhut, R. (2016). Ethical considerations in exposure therapy with children. *Cognitive and Behavioral Practice, 23*(2), 184–193. https://doi.org/10.1016/j.cbpra.2015.04.003

Higa-McMillan, C.K., Francis, S.E., Rith-Najarian, L., & Chorpita, B.F. (2016). Evidence base update: 50 years of research on treatment for child and adolescent anxiety. *Journal of Clinical Child and Adolescent Psychology, 45*(2), 91–113. https://doi.org/10.1080/15374416.2015.1046177

Kaczkurkin, A.N., & Foa, E.B. (2015). Cognitive-behavioral therapy for anxiety disorders: An update on the empirical evidence. *Dialogues in Clinical Neuroscience, 17*(3), 337–346. https://doi.org/10.31887/DCNS.2015.17.3/akaczkurkin

Kendall, P.C., Robin, J.A., Hedtke, K.A., Suveg, C., Flannery-Schroeder, E., & Gosch, E. (2005). Considering CBT with anxious youth? Think exposures. *Cognitive and Behavioral Practice, 12*(1), 136–148. https://doi.org/10.1016/S1077-7229(05)80048-3

Manassis, K., Changgun Lee, T., Bennett, K., Zhao, X.Y., Mendlowitz, S., Duda, S., Saini, M., Wilansky, P., Baer, S., Barrett, P., Bodden, D., Cobham, V.E., Dadds, M.R., Flannery-Schroeder, E., Ginsburg, G., Heyne, D., Hudson, J.L., Kendall, P.C., Liber, J., & Wood, J.J. (2014). Types of parental involvement in CBT with anxious youth: A preliminary meta-analysis. *Journal of Consulting and Clinical Psychology, 82*(6), 1163–1172. https://doi.org/10.1037/a0036969

Maples-Keller, J.L., & Rauch, S.A.M. (2020). Habituation. In J.S. Abramowitz & S.M. Blakey (Eds.), *Clinical Handbook of Fear and Anxiety: Maintenance Processes and Treatment*

Mechanisms (pp. 249–263). American Psychological Association. https://doi.org/10.1037/0000150-014

Mayo-Wilson, E., Dias, S., Mavranezouli, I., Kew, K., Clark, D.M., Ades, A.E., & Pilling, S. (2014). Psychological and pharmacological interventions for social anxiety disorder in adults: A systematic review and network meta-analysis. *The Lancet Psychiatry, 1*(5), 368–376. https://doi.org/10.1016/S2215-0366(14)70329-3

Michie, S., Atkins, L., & West, R. (2014). *The Behaviour Change Wheel: A Guide to Designing Interventions.* Silverback Publishing.

Michie, S., van Stralen, M.M., & West, R. (2011). The behaviour change wheel: A new method for characterising and designing behaviour change interventions. *Implementation Science, 6*(42). https://doi.org/10.1186/1748-5908-6-42

National Institute for Health and Care Excellence. (2013). *Social Anxiety Disorder: Recognition, Assessment and Treatment* (NICE Guideline CG159). www.nice.org.uk/guidance/CG159

Papworth, M.A. (2020). Graded exposure therapy. In P.A. Farrand (Ed.), *Low-Intensity CBT Skills and Interventions: A Practitioner's Manual* (pp. 207–222). SAGE.

Pompoli, A., Furukawa, T.A., Imai, H., Tajika, A., Efthimiou, O., & Salanti, G. (2016). Psychological therapies for panic disorder with or without agoraphobia in adults: A network meta-analysis. *Cochrane Database of Systematic Reviews, 4*(4), CD011004. https://doi.org/10.1002/14651858.CD011004.pub2

Rachman, S., Radomsky, A.S., & Shafran, R. (2008). Safety behaviour: A reconsideration. *Behaviour Research and Therapy, 46*(2), 163–173. https://doi.org/10.1016/j.brat.2007.11.008

Richards, D., & Whyte, M. (2011). Reach out. National Programme Student Materials to Support the Delivery of Training for Psychological Wellbeing Practitioners Delivering Low Intensity Interventions (3rd ed.). Rethink Mental Illness. https://cedar.exeter.ac.uk/media/universityofexeter/schoolofpsychology/cedar/documents/Reach_Out_3rd_edition.pdf

Rudy, B.M., Zavrou, S., Johnco, C., Storch, E.A., & Lewin, A.B. (2017). Parent-led exposure therapy: A pilot study of a brief behavioral treatment for anxiety in young children. *Journal of Child and Family Studies, 26*, 2475–2484. https://doi.org/10.1007/s10826-017-0772-y

Steimer, T. (2002). The biology of fear- and anxiety-related behaviors. *Dialogues in Clinical Neuroscience, 4*(3), 231–249. https://doi.org/10.31887/DCNS.2002.4.3/tsteimer

Thomassin, K., Jones, A., & Suveg, C. (2017). 'You want me to do what?!' Ethical considerations when conducting exposure tasks with youth with anxiety. *Evidence-based Practice in Child and Adolescent Mental Health, 2*(1), 30–42. https://doi.org/10.1080/23794925.2016.1250015

Wang, Z., Whiteside, S.P.H., Sim, L., Farah, W., Morrow, A.S., Alsawas, M., Barrionuevo, P., Tello, M., Asi, N., Beuschel, B., Daraz, L., Almasri, J., Zaiem, F., Larrea-Mantilla, L., Ponce, O. J., LeBlanc, A., Prokop, L.J., & Murad, M.H. (2017). Comparative effectiveness and safety of cognitive behavioral therapy and pharmacotherapy for childhood anxiety disorders: A systematic review and meta-analysis. *JAMA Pediatrics, 171*(11), 1049–1056. https://doi.org/10.1001/jamapediatrics.2017.3036

Weck, F., Neng, J.M.B., Richtberg, S., Jakob, M., & Stangier, U. (2015). Cognitive therapy versus exposure therapy for hypochondriasis (health anxiety): A randomized controlled trial. *Journal of Consulting and Clinical Psychology, 83*(4), 665–676. https://doi.org/10.1037/ccp0000013

Whiteside, S.P.H., Ollendick, T.H., & Biggs, B.K. (2020). *Exposure Therapy for Child and Adolescent Anxiety and OCD.* Oxford University Press.

Whiteside, S.P.H., Sim, L.A., Morrow, A.S., Wigdan, H.F., Hilliker, D.R., Murad, M.H., & Wang, Z. (2020). A meta-analysis to guide the enhancement of CBT for childhood anxiety: exposure over anxiety management. *Clinical Child and Family Psychology Review, 23*(1), 102–121. https://doi.org/10.1007/s10567-019-00303-2

Wolitzky-Taylor, K.B., Horowitz, J.D., Powers, M.B., & Telch, M.J. (2008). Psychological approaches in the treatment of specific phobias: A meta-analysis. *Clinical Psychology Review, 28*, 1021–1037. https://doi.org/10.1016/j.cpr.2008.02.007

10

Cognitive Restructuring

Chelsie Smith and Rosie Jones

Introduction

This chapter will discuss the intervention Cognitive Restructuring (CR), the therapeutic process of recognising and challenging unhelpful or negative thoughts. Thoughts play a critical role in influencing how individuals feel and act. The experience of anxiety or low mood has been seen to be directly related to the presence of negative or unhelpful cognitions (Chahar Mahali et al., 2020). The intensity of these thoughts can be distressing, impacting on how an individual acts and feels, which in turn maintains or reinforces their vicious cycle of low mood or anxiety (Beck et al., 1979). CR can help to reduce the strength of belief in unhelpful thoughts, as well as the emotional impact of them. This chapter will focus upon supporting delivery of the CR intervention. Consideration will be given to theory and the existing evidence base. Application of the intervention will be illustrated in considering the cases of Theo and Chris who were introduced within the assessment chapter.

Working with Thoughts

A common question for practitioners seeking to work with children, is to consider at what age children are likely to benefit from working cognitively (i.e., with thoughts). To be able to benefit from CBT, some key cognitive skills have been proposed as necessary (e.g., Stallard, 2009). Typically, these include:

1. The ability to distinguish between thoughts, feelings, and behaviours
2. Awareness of one's thoughts and the ability to spot these
3. Understanding of the bidirectional relationship between thoughts, emotions, and behaviour

This has led to suggestions that children under age seven (or even older) may lack the cognitive maturity to benefit from CBT (Choo, 2014; Halder & Mahato, 2019). This view seems to stem from developmental psychological theory, such as the work of Piaget (1952). Here, cognitive development is conceptualised as occurring in stages, which are broadly linked to age. More complex thinking skills are seen as present within the 'formal operational thought' stage, which suggests children from age twelve and up may benefit from the use of CBT. Later theorists suggest an ability to benefit from a younger age. For example, Vygotsky's (1978) 'zone of proximal development' and Donaldson's (1978) use of the social context would suggest that younger children may also be able to benefit.

Age alone, however, may not be the best guide to address this question. Neurodiversity, and the varying pace of cognitive development would support a more individualised approach. This would necessitate a reframing of the question to ask, 'What scaffolding or support can I offer this child to support their access?' The cognitive tasks required for effective CBT may be present in young children with the right support structure in place. Wellman et al. (1996) identify that young children aged three are able to identify thought bubbles as showing a person's thinking and can distinguish these from actions or behaviour. Furthermore, they can understand that people may think differently about the same event, and that thoughts can be accurate or untrue. Flavell et al. (2001) report that five-year-old children have developed the ability to identify and express their thoughts. This inner dialogue is seen as supportive of 'self-talk', a common feature of CBT literature (Stallard, 2013).

The accessibility of LI CBT for children, and the ability to work through cognitive change, is likely to be directly linked to the adaptations or 'scaffolding' offered. The use of cartoons and thought bubbles can support children's understanding and engagement (Scheeringa et al., 2001). Other approaches to scaffolding, such as the use of stories and play have also been noted (Hirschfeld-Becker et al., 2010). Friedberg and McClure (2015) used sentence starters to prompt the identification of thoughts to good effect. The same authors also identify that it may be helpful to simplify the steps involved in cognitive work, considering a 'catch it, check it, change it' approach. This further supports low-intensity intervention, which seeks to break down cognitive work into clear and structured steps.

CBT, including the use of cognitive methods, has established clinical effectiveness in younger children for a number of diagnostic presentations. This includes obsessive compulsive disorder in children aged five to eight (Freeman et al., 2008) and three- to seven-year-old children with anxiety disorders (Hirschfeld-Becker et al., 2010; Minde et al., 2010). Positive outcomes have also been found in children with more complex presentations (Cohen & Mannarino, 1996; Deblinger et al., 2001; Scheeringa, 2011). Research supports the use of CR as an effective intervention within a practitioner's toolbox (Ougrin, 2011) with positive effects for CYP (Herring et al., 2022; Peris et al., 2015; Simon et al., 2020). NICE guidelines for mild and moderate depression in children (NICE, 2019) and social anxiety (NICE, 2013) support the use of CBT as a key treatment.

This literature supports the application of cognitive methods across the age range, and highlights how scaffolding can support accessibility and engagement for young people. It would therefore seem that more important than the criterion of age, is the openness of the practitioner to scaffold, adapt and support the young person's engagement creatively in working through the intervention steps.

The Assessment Process

A CR intervention can be used across a range of anxiety presentations and depression. This is due to the key role that thoughts play in maintaining difficulties. Whilst the techniques remain the same, the specific thoughts to be targeted with the intervention approach will vary. CYP who experience anxiety may interpret situations as threatening or dangerous and may have beliefs around being unable to cope (Stallard, 2021), an example might be *'I cannot deal with this, I am going to have a panic attack'*. CYP who experience low mood may judge themselves negatively, overlook positives, and attribute failures to personal internal causes whilst attributing positive events to external causes (Stallard, 2021). Emotional experiences can therefore act as a beacon for the exploration of the presence of key thoughts.

The Process of Conducting the Intervention

The LI approach to CR can be identified as having four key stages as outlined below. In this collaborative approach, CYP are taught the skills in each stage to recognise and challenge their unhelpful thoughts (Clark, 2013).

Step 1: Psychoeducation

The first step in CR is psychoeducation: a method to facilitate understanding and sharing a rationale for the approach. This process may include discussing the CYP's challenges or sharing key facts regarding cognitions (see Fuggle et al., 2013). Before moving on to challenging thoughts, it is imperative that the practitioner and CYP have a shared understanding of the rationale behind CR.

One method for supporting psychoeducation completed within session is to ask the CYP to complete a descriptive formulation diagram. This could be explored during a time they notice they are feeling low or anxious. This will help to highlight the role that thoughts play in maintaining difficulties, and the need to challenge these. Completing this for exceptions (times when mood may be better, or the problem lessened) can also illustrate the value of thoughts in protecting mood and maintaining positive experiences. A key step in psychoeducation therefore is to establish the role that thoughts play and the need to step back and challenge them. This can be exemplified by looking at Theo's descriptive formulation diagram, which was used to support information giving about how CBT may help him to meet his goals, including the identification of his automatic thoughts and how they impact upon the other domains (see Figure 10.1).

COGNITIVE RESTRUCTURING

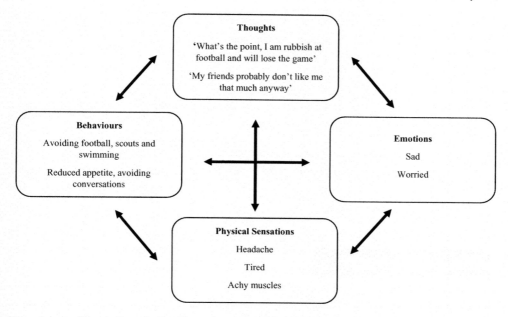

Figure 10.1 Theo's Descriptive Formulation Diagram

Source: Unhelpful Thoughts: Challenging and testing them out, Paul Farrand, Joanne Woodford and Katie Jackson https://cedar.exeter.ac.uk/media/universityofexeter/schoolofpsychology/cedar/documents/liiapt/2018CLES041_CEDAR_Unhelpful_Thoughts_BW.pdf

Theo's practitioner can consider with him how CR can help to break this cycle by looking closely at his negative thoughts, exploring the evidence around them, and considering how to rebalance these and alleviate difficulties.

Practitioner: We have spoken a little bit about how these thoughts, for example 'My friends probably don't like me that much anyway', can keep some of these problems going. They can really change your feelings and behaviours in ways that don't fit with your goals. So, the main aim of CR and the work we are going to be learning together is how to help break this cycle by looking at these thoughts really closely. To work out if they are telling you the truth. How does that sound?

Theo: Okay I guess. How do we look at my thoughts closely?

Practitioner: Good question! We still start by learning about thoughts and then you will begin to catch some of these and write them down so you can learn a little bit more about what types of thoughts you experience. After this, you will become a detective and look for evidence for and against your thoughts to see if they are actually true or not.

A common human experience is to have habits or patterns in our thinking. To a large extent this makes sense, as it reduces the demands on our busy brains. However, when our mood is low, these patterns tend to be part of the vicious cycles we have identified. These can be called 'unhelpful thinking styles or thinking traps' and noting these is another important part of the psychoeducation stage. Within the CBT literature there are a number of examples of lists of common thinking traps. A template for a list of 'thinking traps' to share with a CYP is on the accompanying website for the chapter (https://cedar.exeter.ac.uk/resources/cyp/). These could be supported or amended with images relating to the CYP's interests, or images to be used developed together in session. Scaffolding could be used in the form of stories or cartoons with speech bubbles to support this step.

Key Points in Step 1:

- Seek a shared understanding of CR with the CYP
- Explore together the key role of thoughts
- Link the use of CR to goals and how this may help
- Apply this to a recent lived experience of the CYP
- Normalise difficulties with intrusive thoughts
- Start to explore thinking traps

Step 2: Thought Recording

This second stage involves supporting the CYP to observe, identify and record their negative cognitions. It is important for a CYP to be able to recognise their thoughts as and when they occur, as the method of thought challenging is underpinned by becoming consciously aware of one's cognitions (Fuggle et al., 2013).

Thought recording can be a challenging skill to learn and it is not unusual for individuals to find this difficult. Some CYP may report they are not aware of their cognitions, or they may mislabel feelings to be thoughts (Westbrook et al., 2011). It is helpful therefore to practise thought recording in session to ensure the CYP fully understands this. This could be modelled through spotting thoughts in conversations, thoughts within stories presented, and using thought bubbles linked to images to explore possible thoughts (Kendall et al., 2013).

The overall purpose of thought recording is more than the process of collecting and writing down examples, but is described by Westbrook et al. (2011) as a 'training exercise'. With practice, individuals are able to note their thoughts, allow distance away from them and challenge them almost automatically.

Practitioner:	The next stage Chris is for us to get a better understanding of what is happening for you when you experience the difficult feelings we explored. To help you do this, we use a technique called thought recording. Have you ever heard of this before?	
Chris:	Is it just writing down your thoughts?	
Practitioner:	Yes, it is about writing down your thoughts. Thought diaries can be a helpful way to keep track of what is going through your mind and how you felt in different situations. Doing this can help you know which types of thoughts keep coming up and which are the most difficult, so we can work to challenge these later on. How does that sound?	
Chris:	Yeah, that sounds ok I guess. I will give it a try. Do I have to write every thought down?	
Practitioner:	It's great to hear that you can give this a try. You should try to record your thoughts when you notice that you start to feel particularly sad or worried. Let's have a look at one type of thought diary together and see what you think.	

Examples of thought diaries are provided on the webpages accompanying this chapter at: https://cedar.exeter.ac.uk/resources/cyp/ (appendix A and B). One approach to developing this step is to start with a three-part thought record (see Figure 10.2). It can be helpful to start with the emotions as this is the sign to the CYP that this is a good moment to catch a thought. Identifying what was happening at the time can support taking a step back to consider the situation. Thinking what the situation was can help to identify the thoughts that a person is experiencing. Once the emotion has provided a cue to start, the CYP can be supported to catch the thought. This can be rehearsed in session by thinking of a recent difficult time. The practitioner can also model the use of this form by thinking of a recent event that caused them some mild difficulty. This can further normalise this experience and support the breaking down of power discrepancies to illustrate this as a common difficulty.

Emotion: How were you feeling? Can you rate this out of 10 where 10 is strongest?	Situation: What was happening at the time that you started to notice your emotions change?	Thoughts: What were you thinking at the time? What is so bad about this?

Figure 10.2 Three-part thought record

Source: © Smith (2023)

Whilst tracking thoughts, CYP should record the intensity of the emotions and rate the belief in the thought. This is helpful to support evaluating the impact of challenging thoughts later on (Leahy & Rego, 2012).

Top Tip!

When supporting CYP to complete thought recording, use emotions as a start point. Asking someone what difficult thoughts they have had this week may be less helpful than asking someone to recall a time when they were feeling low or worried. This situation can then be explored for cognitions.

Figure 10.3 shows an example of a three-part thought record completed by Chris. It can also be helpful to look at the thoughts across different situations to help consider with Chris whether there were any common thinking traps. This could support Chris in spotting any particular trap by asking questions about this, e.g., 'Am I overgeneralising again?' If helpful for the young person, an additional column to the record can be added where the CYP can name any thinking traps spotted.

Chris has completed their thought diary by identifying different situations and the emotions they felt. However, you may have noticed that Chris has included the belief: '*I am so useless*'. It can be helpful to target more situation specific thoughts rather than more broad thoughts. Therefore, if a CYP elicits broad beliefs applying

Emotion	Situation	Thought
How were you feeling? Can you rate this out of 10 where 10 is strongest?	What was happening at the time that you started to notice your emotions change?	What were you thinking at the time? What is so bad about this?
Anxious (6)	*Friday At school*	*I cannot do this exam, my teachers all think I'm rubbish too (65%)*
Worried (7)	*Saturday Friends asked me to go out and hang out with them*	*There's no point going out with my friends because it will go wrong. I will say something embarrassing and panic (85%)*
Sad (8%)	*Monday at School*	*I am so useless (70%)*

Figure 10.3 Chris's completed three-part thought record

Source: © Smith (2023)

COGNITIVE RESTRUCTURING | 137

across a number of situations, a helpful technique is to focus back on the specific situation to gather further information. A clinical example transcript (clinical example 1) is provided on the accompanying chapter resources website address at the end of this chapter to illustrate this further.

Thoughts can be recorded in a variety of ways, and it is important to find a way that works best for CYP. Some young people prefer to make notes on a mobile telephone or to record voice notes. Routine Outcome Measures (ROMs) can also be a helpful tool to help gather CYP's thoughts, as can discussing interests and hobbies. Presenting information visually with less reliance upon language can make it easier for CYP who may have limited cognitive abilities or learning disabilities to engage in CR. Some further guidance is provided on the accompanying website sheet 'adaptations for eliciting and recording thoughts'.

Key Tip:

Seek to provide practice opportunities for recording thoughts. This can start in session and could then be rehearsed further between sessions. It may be helpful to record thoughts as and when they occur, particularly if the CYP finds it hard to identify these after the event. Using notes on a mobile phone can be one way to support this.

Whichever way CYP choose to record their thoughts, it is important to spend time recognising the emotional impact of the cognitions. To ensure the CYP feels understood, the practitioner should validate the difficulty of experiences. Moving away from these thoughts too quickly or beginning the thought challenging step without acknowledging the emotional impact of them, could appear dismissive or critical to a CYP. Time in sessions should always be provided to discuss the CYP's thoughts in the context of their individual experiences.

Key Points in Step 2:

- It may be necessary to offer scaffolding to support the CYP in the skill of recording thoughts
- Modelling thought recording, the use of stories, pictures and thought bubbles can all help
- Use emotions as a cue to search for thoughts
- Thought records offer a structure to support this skill
- Continue to offer empathy and validation for difficulties experienced

Step 3: Evidence For and Against

Step three involves generating evidence for and against the thought. This begins the 'challenging' part of the intervention. As Leahy and Rego (2012) state, cognitive restructuring intends to achieve realistic rather than positive thinking. For example, Theo is experiencing the thought '*my friends don't really like me anyway*' and could be asked to identify all the evidence why his friends do not like him, and then alternatively, all the reasons why this might not be true. In support of the thought, Theo might explain how his friends did not respond to his text, but the reasons against this thought might highlight the times where they did respond or when they met up previously. The overall goal is not to change the belief to become unrealistic or overly positive, but to investigate the reality of the negative assumptions. In this sense any thought must pass 'the test of daily living' in being able to account for lived experience.

To begin this process, the practitioner collaboratively reviews the CYP's thought record completed for home practice. If the CYP has been unable to catch a thought, this becomes a shared task for the session. Drawing support from parents or carers for younger children may be useful. The thought identified should be a thought with sufficient emotion attached to it. The CYP's ratings of emotion can support this process and help to establish and value their expertise as vital to the work.

Key Tip:

When demonstrating step three, it may be helpful to explore a thought that has been scored in mid-range intensity. This may help to avoid triggering too much emotional experience that may prevent learning on how the step works. Once the step has been learnt and rehearsed it may be more likely to be deployed when more intense thoughts are considered.

Once you have identified a thought to explore, the next stage is to encourage CYP to consider evidence in support of that thought. This can be a helpful place to start, as it can support CYP to feel validated that their thought is being taken seriously, rather than just dismissed. It is useful to encourage the CYP to write down all evidence gathered; example worksheets can be seen in website Appendix C and D.

In exploring evidence for a thought, explore with the CYP how they know the thought to be true. It is important to establish that seeking evidence is looking for factual support. This will often be seeking evidence that can be observed by others as clearly demonstrating the thought as true. For example, the thought 'Jem doesn't like me and doesn't want to know me' is not evidenced by Jem not immediately texting back or leaving a message unread. However, Jem messaging back, 'I don't want

COGNITIVE RESTRUCTURING | 139

to meet up with you ever, please don't message me' would be considered evidence. A key tip is to look out for further automatic thoughts disguising themselves as evidence. An example of this could be 'Jem didn't immediately read and respond to my message because they want to avoid me', which is an example of a further thought without evidence.

Once the CYP has recorded the evidence **for** the thought, it is time to move on to seeking the evidence **against** the thought. This follows the same procedure as above, but this time asking; why might this thought not be true? What is the evidence against it? 'Clinical example 3' on the website offers further illustration. This stage can be more challenging as individuals may find it hard to identify any evidence against a thought that they believe strongly. A helpful technique in this case is to focus on decentering, to support CYP to develop a wider perspective (Leahy & Rego, 2012). This means supporting someone to take a different perspective on their thoughts away from one where they are stuck with this problem in this moment. It can mean asking about how others may look at this, or what they may say to another in the same position. See website Appendix E for a helpful worksheet.

Key Tip:

When looking at evidence for and against a thought, it is important to avoid using the language 'positive' and 'negative'. This is because the aim is not to achieve positive thinking, but a more balanced way of thinking that is more in line with lived experiences and the experience of daily life.

Figure 10.4 shows a completed example where Chris has begun to examine and record evidence for and against the thought. However, using this specific worksheet may not work for all clients. Some alternative techniques include making this step more playful by 'playing detective' in collecting evidence and 'putting the thought on trial in court' to make a judgment on it. Such terminology can support a stepping back from thoughts to support a reduction in negative emotional experience.

Key Points in Step 3:

- Explore thoughts linked directly to emotional experience
- Seek 'facts' when exploring evidence for or against a thought
- Further thoughts or emotions are not 'facts' and should be explored as whether they provide factual evidence if presented
- Decentering techniques can support the review of evidence

LOW-INTENSITY PRACTICE WITH CYP AND FAMILIES

Emotion	Situation	Thought	Evidence for	Evidence against
How were you feeling? Can you rate this out of 10 where 10 is strongest?	What was happening at the time that you started to notice your emotions change?	What were you thinking at the time? What is so bad about this? (rate belief 1–10)	What facts are there to show that this thought is right? Beware of thoughts pretending to be facts!	What facts are there to show this thought is not right?
Anxious (6)	Friday At school my English teacher was talking about preparing for exams	I cannot do this exam, I will fail (6)	I failed my last English practice exam I got bad marks in my homework last week	I failed my last practice exam, but I have passed all the exams before that. My teacher said that he sometimes shouts because he thinks if I work hard I can get a good mark. I got good marks for my work for most of the year

Figure 10.4 Example of thought challenging using the five-part thought record with Chris

Source: © Smith (2023)

Step 4: A Balanced Alternative

Now that evidence for and against the thought has been identified, the final step is to review the evidence to find a realistic balanced alternative. Here, the practitioner works with the CYP to review all the evidence collated, and to explore the meaning that can be drawn from this. It is important that the learning is asked Socratically, so that the CYP can draw the conclusion themselves. For example, this may take the form: 'When you look at the evidence for and against this thought what do you notice? What do you make of the weight of evidence? What does this say about your original thought? What do you think about how well this thought sums up the evidence? Can you think of an alternative thought that may sum this up better? Which of these thoughts fits best for your goal' (see 'clinical example 2' on website to illustrate this further).

This identified more balanced alternative is added to the thought record as a final six-part version (see website 'clinical example 4' illustrating this with Chris). See website Appendix F, with a further version in Appendix G.

During this stage, the CYP may not have complete belief in their new balanced thought and may still report a high level of emotion linked to their belief. This is normal and to be expected, as it is likely that many CYP would have been experiencing such thoughts for a long time and will need to continue to practise the four stages of cognitive restructuring. Repeating this will enable the CYP to become more skilled at recognising when they are using unhelpful thinking styles, as well as practising finding evidence for and against these thoughts. Practitioners should encourage and support the CYP to continue practising all stages after the work together has finished, so that eventually these stages will become a helpful habit. A further tip that may help to support change can be adding a further column to the thought record. This can be titled 'feelings and actions now'. This can be used to re-rate emotions after challenging to see the difference and positive impact of the CR step. Actions now may relate to planning ways forward with this new thought and what may now seem more possible (e.g., 'I can take this exam').

This process completes all four stages of CR; psychoeducation, thought recording, finding evidence for and against, and creating a balanced alternative. These steps may be initially challenging for the CYP, but with practice, they can become second nature and adapted to manage a range of situations and emotions. Scaffolding needed is a key focus to support access with some CYP.

Key Points in Step 4:

- Seek a 'balanced' alternative thought that can account for evidence identified and survive daily experience
- Use Socratic exploration to help the CYP to identify the alternative thought for themselves
- Be prepared to repeat use of the steps a number of times to support establishing use of this as a new pattern of response
- Alternative thoughts generated can be judged by the CYP as to whether they support their set goals (particularly when compared to the original thought)

Summary

CR is a valuable intervention option for the LI CBT practitioner. It can apply across a range of presentations, and with appropriate scaffolding, across a range of ages and diverse presentations. CR provides CYP with the tools to identify and challenge thoughts linked to difficult emotions, in order to develop balanced thoughts and work towards their goals. With a four-step approach to the intervention, CR provides an accessible, repeatable approach. By practising steps in session and then setting this for practice between sessions, steps can be consolidated, with any difficulties in use reviewed at the following session. The practitioner can model steps for the CYP in session, rehearse them, and socratically help the CYP to draw learning from reviewing evidence for and against their challenging thoughts. With time and practice, the CYP will learn to identify and challenge thoughts more easily, thus reducing the impact of the vicious cycle, and supporting more balanced thoughts that can stand the test of daily life and support progression to the goals set. For a copy

References

Beck, A.T., Rush, A.J., Shaw, B.F., & Emery, G. (1979). *Cognitive Therapy of Depression*. Guilford Publications.

Chahar Mahali, S., Beshai, S., Feeney, J.R., & Mishra, S. (2020). Associations of negative cognitions, emotional regulation, and depression symptoms across four continents: International support for the cognitive model of depression. *BMC Psychiatry 20*(18). https://doi.org/10.1186/s12888-019-2423-x

Choo, C. (2014). Adapting cognitive behavioral therapy for children and adolescents with complex symptoms of neurodevelopmental disorders and conduct disorders. *Journal of Psychological Abnormalities in Children, 3*, 124. doi:10.4172/2329-9525.1000124

Clark, D.A. (2013). Cognitive restructuring. In S. G. Hoffman (Ed.), *The Wiley Handbook of Cognitive Behavioral Therapy* (pp. 23–44). Wiley-Blackwell.

Cohen J.A., & Mannarino, A.P. (1996). A treatment outcome study for sexually abused preschool children: Initial findings. *Journal of the American Academy of Child and Adolescent Psychiatry, 35*(1), 42–50.

Deblinger, E., Stauffer, L.B., & Steer, R.A. (2001). Comparative efficacies of supportive and cognitive behavioral group therapies for young children who have been sexually abused and their nonoffending mothers. *Child Maltreatment, 6*(4), 332–343.

Donaldson, M. (1978). *Children's Minds*. Fontana.

Flavell, J.H., Flavell, E.R., & Green, F.L. (2001). Development of children's understanding of connections between thinking and feeling. *Psychological Science, 12*(5), 430–432.

Freeman, J.B., Garcia, A.M., Coyne, L., Ale, C., Przeworski, A., Himle, M., Compton, S., & Leonard, H.L. (2008). Early childhood OCD: Preliminary findings from a family-based cognitive-behavioral approach. *Journal of the American Academy of Child and Adolescent Psychiatry, 47*(5), 593–602.

Friedberg, R.D., & McClure, J.M. (2015). *Clinical Practice of Cognitive Therapy with Children and Adolescents: The Nuts and Bolts* (2nd ed.). Guilford Press.

Fuggle, P., Dunsmuir, S., & Curry, V. (2013). *CBT with Children, Young People and Families*. Sage.

Halder, S., & Mahato A.K. (2019). Cognitive behavior therapy for children and adolescents: Challenges and gaps in practice. *Indian Journal of Psychological Medicine, 41*(3), 279–283.

Herring, G.T., Loades, M.E., Higson-Sweeney, N., Hards, E., Reynolds, S., & Midgley, N. (2022). The experience of cognitive behavioural therapy in depressed adolescents who are fatigued. *Psychology and Psychotherapy: Theory, Research and Practice, 95*(1), 234–255.

Hirschfeld-Becker, D.R., Masek, B., Henin, A., Blakely, L.R., Pollock-Wurman, R.A., McQuade, J., DePetrillo, L., Briesch, J., Ollendick, T.H., Rosenbaum, J.F., & Biederman, J. (2010). Cognitive behavioral therapy for 4- to 7-year-old children with anxiety disorders: A randomized clinical trial. *Journal of Consulting and Clinical Psychology, 78*(4), 498–510.

Kendall, P.C., Crawley, S.A., Benjamin, C.L., & Mauro, C.F. (2013). *Brief Coping Cat: Therapist Manual for the 8-session Workbook*. Workbook Publishing.

Leahy, L.R., & Rego, A.S. (2012). Cognitive Restructuring. In T.W. O'Donohue & E. J. Fisher (Eds.), *Cognitive Behaviour Therapy. Core Principles for Practice* (pp. 133–158). John Wiley & Sons.

Minde, K., Roy, J., Bezonsky, R., & Hashemi, A. (2010). The effectiveness of CBT in 3- 7-year-old anxious children: Preliminary data. *Journal of the Canadian Academy of Child and Adolescent Psychiatry, 19*(2), 109–115.

National Institute for Health and Care Excellence (NICE). (2013). *Social Anxiety Disorder: Recognition, Assessment and Treatment* [Clinical guideline CG159]. www.nice.org.uk/guidance/cg159/chapter/Recommendations#identification-and-assessment-of-children-and-young-people

National Institute for Health and Care Excellence (NICE). (2019). *Depression in Children and Young People: Identification and Management* [Clinical guideline NG134]. www.nice.org.uk/guidance/ng134/chapter/Recommendations#step-3-managing-mild-depression

Ougrin, D. (2011). Efficacy of exposure versus cognitive therapy in anxiety disorders: Systematic review and meta-analysis. *BMC Psychiatry, 11*(1), 1–13.

Peris, T.S., Compton, S.N., Kendall, P.C., Birmaher, B., Sherrill, J., March, J., Gosch, E., Ginsburg, G., Rynn, M., McCracken, J.T., Keeton, C.P., Sakolsky, D., Suveg, C., Aschenbrand, S., Almirall, D., Iyengar, S., Walkup, J.T., Albano, A.M., & Piacentini, J. (2015). Trajectories of change in youth anxiety during cognitive-behavior therapy. *Journal of Consulting and Clinical Psychology, 83*(2), 239–252.

Piaget, J. (1952). *The Origins of Intelligence in Children*. W.W. Norton & Co.

Scheeringa, M., Weems, C., Cohen, J., Amaya-Jackson, L., & Guthrie, D. (2011). Trauma-focused cognitive-behavioral therapy for posttraumatic stress disorder in three- through six-year-old children: A randomized clinical trial. *Journal of Child Psychology and Psychiatry, 52*(8), 853–860.

Simon, E., Driessen, S., Lambert, A., & Muris, P. (2020). Challenging anxious cognitions or accepting them? Exploring the efficacy of the cognitive elements of cognitive behaviour therapy and acceptance and commitment therapy in the reduction of children's fear of the dark. *International Journal of Psychology, 55*(1), 90–97.

Stallard, P. (2009). *Anxiety: Cognitive Behaviour Therapy with Children and Young People*. Routledge.

Stallard, P. (2013). Adapting cognitive behavior therapy for children and adolescents. In P. Graham & S. Reynolds (Eds.), *Cognitive Behaviour Therapy for Children and Families* (3rd ed.) (pp. 22–33). Cambridge University Press.

Stallard, P. (2021). *A Clinician's Guide to CBT for Children to Young Adults. A Companion to Think Good, Feel Good and Thinking Good, Feeling Better*. John Wiley & Sons Ltd.

Vygotsky, L.S. (1978). *Mind in Society: The Development of Higher Psychological Processes*. Harvard University Press.

Wellman, H.M., Hollander, M., & Schult, C.A. (1996). Young children's understanding of thought bubbles and of thoughts. *Child Development, 67*(3), 768–788.

Westbrook, D., Kennerley, H., & Kirk, J. (2011). *An Introduction to Cognitive Behaviour Therapy*. Sage.

11

Behavioural Experiments

Rob Kidney

Introduction

This chapter will focus upon the use of Behavioural Experiments (BEs) with children and young people (CYP) at low intensity. Within this chapter the steps to complete a low-intensity BE with a young person will be identified and demonstrated. This will be applied to the case of Chris, introduced within the assessment chapter. Theory underpinning the use of BEs and the current state of evidence for their use will be considered. Example worksheets will be highlighted to support delivery with demonstration of the use of a BE workbook designed for use when working with young people. A link to access the booklet for free and a link to a free app version of the booklet is provided at the end of the chapter.

What Are Behavioural Experiments?

A behavioural experiment is a set of steps to help identify or test the **thoughts** or **predictions** that a child or young person (CYP) may have in a given situation. BEs help to understand the impact of **behaviour** based on these thoughts or predictions in order to test their accuracy. For example, a CYP may have a fear of losing control of their bladder. This is an example of a **thought**. They may fear that if they go out with friends, they will become anxious and wet themselves. This is an example of a **prediction** in a given situation. This prediction may lead them to avoid social situations or going out. This is an example of **behaviour**. A BE can provide a direct test of this prediction through purposeful behaviour. This may mean going out and being with friends without seeking toilets. Through this experiment of **behaviour**, the CYP can learn about the validity of their prediction. In this instance, perhaps that they do not lose control, or that no-one notices if this happens. Through BEs we can support CYP to understand how their behaviour can impact upon predictions. This enables them to find out about the accuracy of predictions and possible alternative understandings that can support change.

The author would like to thank artist Isobel Woolley for the artwork in this chapter.

Within low-intensity (LI) practice, BEs are focused upon the identification and testing of specific thoughts or worries that a CYP has. Once a thought has been identified, it is explored in terms of the predictions that it makes. For example, for a CYP feeling anxious, they may predict that something bad or feared will happen. If a CYP is feeling low in mood, they may predict that nothing will be any fun, or that it won't be worthwhile in any way. The LI focus is to teach the use of skills in testing these predictions by experimenting with behaviour. This is a direct test of what the prediction (the problem) says will happen. In this way the validity of the prediction can be tested, and alternative explanations can be explored. This often means changing and challenging behaviours that provide short-term emotional relief through avoidance and negative reinforcement. Completion of experiments may therefore be experienced as challenging, and it is essential that the CYP has a shared understanding of the rationale for any experiment. Several experiments may need to be conducted over time, as the CYP works through a series of behavioural experiments graded from mild to more moderate challenges. Whilst a LI focus may not necessarily complete all steps in a hierarchy, it should equip the CYP with the self-help skills to continue this work and may consider ways to continue to draw support from the network around them. This could include parents/carers, family members, school staff or even trusted peers. At LI, it may be helpful to think of BEs as following seven steps that need to be completed.

The Seven Steps of a Behavioural Experiment:

1. Identify the thought (prediction) and when it happens
2. Plan how to test the prediction (experiment)
3. Identify what will happen if the prediction is true
4. Identify what will happen if the prediction is not true
5. Carry out the experiment
6. Review the outcome – what happened?
7   Which prediction did the outcome fit with and what can you learn from this?

These steps will be explored with the case of Chris, exploring a workbook where steps have been simplified further to support accessibility of BE to support CYP.

The Benefits of Using BEs with Children and Young People

BEs offer several possible benefits to young people, which may make them an appropriate intervention to consider using when discussing intervention choices with CYP. Some of the main benefits offered with the use of BEs are:

- *Identifying thoughts when this is difficult.* Sometimes avoidance may be a well-established strategy. Its use offers short-term benefits (often a reduction in anxiety), and therefore is likely to be repeated. Long-term avoidance may make it hard to identify exactly what the thought is that goes with a feeling. However, when approaching a feared situation through experimentation, access to cognitions can be more prominent and accessible.
- *Establishing that a feared catastrophe/depressive thought is unlikely to happen/does not come true.* Long standing avoidance may also lead to an inability to learn that feared outcomes do not take place. It may be that it is not until an experiment to directly test fears has taken place, that predictions of feared events can begin to be weakened.
- *Discovering the importance of maintaining factors.* Behavioural experiments help to understand the need to enable both cognitive and behavioural change in supporting CYP to meet their goals. A social encounter that does not update feared predictions is less likely to be helpful (e.g., being in a social situation but staying well clear of others). Challenging thoughts but maintaining safety behaviours or avoidance may also be less likely to bring meaningful change (e.g., challenging thoughts based on past history but maintaining avoidance of contacting others).
- *Finding out whether an alternative way of doing things works better.* Cognitive challenges alone may lead to a 'head-heart split', where although cognitive challenge can lead to someone knowing in their head that something may not be true (rationally), they do not feel it in their heart (or fully believe it) until they have lived experience of testing this understanding (Bennett-Levy, 2003; Rachman & Hodgson, 1974). Similarly, changing behaviour may allow exposure to feared events, but may not integrate back into cognitive understanding unless directly targeted at this (MacMillan & Lee, 2010; Padesky, 1994).
- *Generating evidence for an alternative explanation – constructing new beliefs.* This is facilitated though the review of behavioural experiences as a direct test of predictions.
- *Developing resilience and further experimentation.* Repeated experimentation and working through a hierarchy of experiments offers the opportunity for repetition to strengthen resilience.

Evidence – What Evidence Is There for BEs?

Most literature offering support for BEs has focussed upon adult populations and is often explored within a range of high-intensity work. This has led Bennett-Levy et al. (2004) amongst others to consider BEs as one of the most powerful treatment tools in Cognitive Behavioural Therapy (CBT). Evidence-based HI CBT treatment models holding behavioural experiments as a central element of treatment include panic disorder, social phobia (Clark, 1997), obsessive-compulsive disorder (Salkovskis et al., 1999b), and post-traumatic stress disorder (Ehlers & Clark, 2000). Evidence in support of the effectiveness of BEs therefore sits within a wider CBT treatment package. This means that whilst BE may form part of an evidence-based effective treatment protocol, the question remains whether BEs alone are an active ingredient for change, and if so, how active are they in relation to other components of therapy? However, the inclusion of behavioural experiments across a wide range of evidence-based protocols for a range of presenting issues suggests a potential broader treatment value.

LI use of BEs may also offer the opportunity for a more parsimonious approach to the use of the active ingredients of treatment to support the mental wellbeing of CYP. In seeking to enhance clinical effectiveness, Kuyken et al. (2009) provide a critical analysis of the assumed value of high-intensity formulation driven approaches. Within this analysis a study by Schulte et al. (1992) is identified, which provides an interesting perspective. The study compared three different options for the treatment of phobia. In one option a bespoke personalised formulation (functional analysis) driven treatment was offered, in a second option a standardised *in vivo* exposure protocol (without formulation) was offered, and in a third option, a bespoke treatment based on the formulation of another (different) trial participant was given. The most effective treatment from the study was the second, which focussed upon standardised treatment strategies only. This is an option much more aligned to LI CBT guided self-help treatments with an emphasis on use of key intervention components. LI CBT guided treatment based upon active treatment ingredients (in this case behavioural experiments) may therefore have the potential to support defined, parsimonious, and highly effective treatment options.

Several authors have considered evidence for the effectiveness of behavioural interventions as a treatment strategy with CYP (British Psychological Society, 2002; Stallard, 2005). Studies exploring the effectiveness of behavioural or cognitive only strategies, suggest that there is potential for greater effectiveness when combining both these strategies in the form of behavioural experiments. MacMillian and Lee (2010) reviewed 14 studies and considered that evidence suggested behavioural experiments to be more effective than behavioural methods alone across a number of different diagnostic presentations. Whilst more research to consider the value of different components of CBT will support understanding of this further, research above points to the potential value of behavioural experiments in the intervention toolkit of a LI CBT practitioner supporting CYP.

The most promising data to support the use of BEs at LI CBT with children, comes from that collected through practice. Early data collected from the use of BEs by

Evaluations of Children's Wellbeing Practitioners at the University of Exeter (CEDAR, 2022), has suggested the effectiveness of BE as a LI CBT intervention. Data, which will be published in detail at a later date, examined 141 young people undertaking a LI BE intervention for mental health needs as measured by the Revised Children's Anxiety and Depression Rating Scale (RCADS, Chorpita et al., 2000). Following the use of a BE intervention across presentations, a pre-post mean decrease of over 15 points on the RCADS whole scale score was noted. Breakdown by specific diagnosis as measured by the RCADS showed a reliable improvement in 58 per cent of depression cases, 58 per cent of Social Anxiety disorder, 63 percent of panic disorder, 57 per cent of obsessive-compulsive disorder, 65 per cent of generalised anxiety disorder and 56 per cent of Separation Anxiety Disorder cases. This initial data suggests a wide range of applicability and effectiveness for the use of BEs in LI CBT to support the mental health and wellbeing of children and young people. Over time, further data collection may add the opportunity to explore variations according to age, length of treatment, co-morbidity, and severity.

Adaptation of BEs When Working with CYP

There is much literature considering the need to adapt CBT, some of which is referred to below. It is important to note, as highlighted by Friedberg et al. (2000), that without adaptation many CYPs' ability to access materials may be reduced. Verbal and written materials alone may be less appealing or provide a barrier to understanding intervention (Reinecke et al., 2003). The need for young people to have the ability to identify and work with thoughts has been considered to potentially restrict the use of CBT to older and more cognitively skilled CYP, unless the work is adapted to support access (Choo, 2014).

Specific adaptations proposed by Choo (2014) include: modified use of language to more accessible terms (see also Freeman et al., 2008), minimising steps involved in interventions to reduce complexity, visual presentation of material, and prompts to support use. Scheeringa et al. (2011) highlight increased understanding for young children when images are used to support explanations. Freeman et al. (2008) illustrate the value of using puppets and characters to demonstrate and develop coping skills. Use of comic strips and social stories have been highlighted by Gray (1998) to support understanding, particularly in more neurodiverse children, and have been seen as useful strategies to support creativity in CBT (Donoghue et al., 2011).

In developing the BE workbook, adaptations to support engagement and accessibility have been considered, and crucially feedback sought from young people throughout development. This provided guidance on the style and nature of images, use of language and the balance between the use of text and images.

Figure 11.1 Characters Zee and Tao, who illustrate the stages of Behavioural Experiments

Adaptations within the booklet include:

- The use of characters to provide a social story and context (see Figure 11.1)
- Characters provide a rationale for the use of BEs to discuss with CYP
- Images to support engagement (commissioned artist) and visual presentation
- Adapted language and simplification of concepts to key messages
- Externalisation of 'the problem' as the difficulty (and not the CYP)
- Characters normalise the presence of difficulties
- Characters demonstrate each intervention step and model solving difficulties with these
- Chunking of information to support learning and recall
- An invitation to join the characters in exploration through experiments
- Parsimonious development of intervention steps reduced from 7 to 5 (see Table 11.1)

Clinical Use of BEs

BEs have the potential to work with any of the example cases provided in the assessment chapter, where thoughts and predictions are maintaining the difficulty. However, in this chapter the case of Chris will be used to illustrate the use of intervention steps alongside the use of characters within the BE booklet. Some key information

Table 11.1 The steps to complete a behavioural experiment

Seven steps to a Behavioural Experiment	Adapted Booklet steps
1. Identify the thought (prediction) and when it happens	1. What thoughts when?
2. Plan how to test the prediction (experiment)	2. Design the experiment
3. Identify what will happen if the prediction is true	3. Make predictions (Steps 3 and 4 simplified)
4. Identify what will happen if the prediction is not true	
5. Carry out the experiment	4. Run the experiment
6. Review the outcome – what happened	5. What did I learn? (Steps 6 and 7 simplified)
7. Which prediction did this fit with and what can you learn from this?	

known at referral is that Chris is 16 years old and uses they/them pronouns. They live at home with Mum and Dad, and two younger siblings, aged 14 and 10. As exams have been approaching, Chris has noticed increasing levels of anxiety and low mood. On top of this, it has become harder for Chris to spend time with friends. In part this is due to the concern that if they were to go out, they would get anxious and something bad would happen. This has led to less activity, withdrawal, and a lack of enjoyment. Whilst Chris has thought about going out with their closest friend, they report not being able to get away from the idea that it would not go well.

Through shared discussion, Chris expressed a main goal of wanting to increase social activity with friends. They felt that feeling more socially connected would support their ability to manage exams when stress levels were higher. Assessment highlighted the prediction that if Chris were to go out with friends, then this would lead to being verbally attacked by others, with social rejection from all future events. In this sense, the social concerns were seen as primary and leading to reduced contact with others and a consequential drop in mood. In discussing treatment options, Chris felt that BEs could be helpful and was willing to explore this option. Therefore, in this instance, the dual role of thoughts and behaviour in social avoidance, the identified key goal for treatment, Chris's access to thoughts and predictions, and preference in treatment choice made by Chris, all highlighted the suitability of the use of BEs.

Orientation to BEs

Orienting CYP to the use of BEs to support wellbeing can be approached in several ways. This could include a discussion of the intervention and how it may help, or with the use of stories and metaphor to explore use (Blenkiron, 2005; Stott et al., 2010). Within the booklet a social story around the characters is used at the start of the booklet. Here, a simple diagram is used to show the model and is illustrated by the characters Zee and Tao (see Figure 11.2).

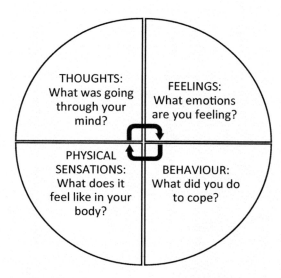

Figure 11.2 Diagram to show the therapeutic model

This can be used to illustrate how to break down difficulties and to orient the YP to the approach. Once the examples of characters have been discussed (see Figures 11.3 and 11.4), the practitioner can then support the CYP to consider how this may apply to their own concerns.

The characters then explore the idea that thoughts may not always be true. This is developed though externalisation, by considering the idea that 'the thought may be the problem, and may be lying to us'. This sets the context of needing to test thoughts to find out about them and guides the work to the first step of intervention.

Step 1: Catch What the Thoughts Are and When They Happen (What Thoughts When)

The focus here is to consider with the CYP what their thoughts are and what predictions these thoughts make. Thoughts and predictions may be linked to specific goals or things that the CYP wants to achieve (e.g., to go to a social event with a friend). Equally, predictions may be identified through the things that young people are avoiding. For a CYP avoiding certain foods this could be, for example, a thought of choking and a prediction that they will not be able to swallow certain foods.

Prompts to support this step can be helpful, and within the booklet Zee and Tao are asked questions to support their response. This supports them (and CYP) to develop a sense of when the thoughts come in, what they say, and what predictions are made based upon these. This is an important step to facilitate the planning of subsequent experiments. The characters illustrate their experience of identifying their thoughts and the predictions that these thoughts make (Figure 11.5).

Zee's story

One day I had an argument with my friend. Later, she said some mean things on social media. What made it worse was that some other people liked what she wrote.

I started to think that this meant that everyone thought badly of me, and that no one would want to be with me or talk to me.

Then I just didn't feel like I could be near anyone. I stopped talking to friends, and eventually they stopped talking to me. This just seemed to tell me I was right all along.

It looked like this:

Figure 11.3 Zee's concerns

Each step of the intervention is linked to the BE worksheet. This worksheet is intended to become the prompt that the CYP can use to support all BE steps once the workbook has been completed. This can be given as a hard copy, electronically, and as an alternative that may be more appealing to young people, it can also be on a mobile phone via an app. This is available free on the Android play store and Apple store under the title 'CBT behavioural experiments'. The app contains the

BEHAVIOURAL EXPERIMENTS | 153

Tao's story

For me it was a bit different.
I just had this feeling that there was something wrong with me. That if I went out the house I would panic and maybe even go mad or lose control of my bladder.

I just kept getting all these images of me looking crazy or wetting myself. It really upset me. I felt so anxious I stopped going out in case it happened. Slowly it just got harder and harder. Then I always stayed in.

It looked like this:

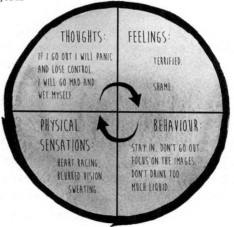

Figure 11.4 Tao's concerns

same images and guidance as the booklet and enables CYP to keep a library of their experiments. Links are provided at: http://cedar.exeter.ac.uk/resources/cyp/

The characters and CYP are then prompted to put their 'what thoughts when' into part 1 of the form. Each part of the booklet is introduced one chunk at a time with the matching intervention step. The characters identify their responses and space is left for the CYP to add their own 'what thoughts when' (see Table 11.2).

Table 11.2 Worksheet part 1 applied to Zee

What thoughts when?
Part 1
Whenever I think about talking to or messaging a friend, I think that they just won't want to talk to me.

Figure 11.5 Tao and Zee considering their step 1 thoughts

For Tao, his 'what thoughts when' identify, 'When I want to go to the shops, I think I'll panic, lose control and wet myself'. In working with Chris, their presentation shows similarity to Zee's. This helps to normalise Chris's difficulties further and supports ideas for completing each step. Exploring their thoughts and predictions was helped by using the frame of 'If (I do a specific activity) then (this terrible thing will happen)'. In this sense the prediction is conditional (if X then Y), but is applied to a specific event, rather than as a general rule. This specificity is important in setting up subsequent tests of predictions. Chris identified that unlike Zee, they didn't feel that their friends would immediately reject the idea of meeting, but that once they started meeting with friends, it would become so anxiety provoking that Chris would become overwhelmed. Chris predicted that they would show such an unusual display of anxiety, that friends would think badly of Chris, and mock and reject them (Table 11.3).

Table 11.3 Worksheet part 1 applied to Chris

What thoughts when?
Part 1
When I think about meeting with friends, I think I will get so anxious and act so strange that they will mock me and reject me.

Key Tips:

- Try to ensure that the thought identified is a clearly defined thought rather than a general thought
- Using an 'If __ then __' format can help
- Try to make the 'then' part clearly observable (and ideally a behaviour)

BEHAVIOURAL EXPERIMENTS | 155

Step 2: Design It

The next step in working through BEs is to design the experiment to test the thought or prediction. This means considering how you can tell if the thought is telling you the truth. Note that the choice of language here is designed to externalise the thought further. This can create some emotional distance to see the thought as outside of the person and as something that can be looked at and examined, or indeed experimented upon.

This first experiment may well need to be a graded one. Experimenting upon the most feared version of the thought or prediction may be too big a first step. The intention is to teach the CYP the skills of the self-help practice. Therefore, seeking a manageable but still challenging first experiment will support the opportunity for engagement with the intervention and learning of the key steps. This dilemma is identified by Zee, who expresses finding it hard to think of a first step as it all felt frightening to her. This can help to normalise this experience for CYP. In the booklet Zee discussed how she looks for a smaller first step and identifies sending a message to someone she used to talk to as a possibility. In this way Zee models a manageable first experiment, which is still going to test her prediction (see Table 11.4). This modelling and problem solving can be discussed with the CYP to help with progressing through this step (part two).

This is explored with Chris, and an experiment discussed and planned, as illustrated in table 11.5.

Table 11.4 Worksheet part 2 applied to Zee

What thoughts when? Part 1	Experiment plan (design it) Part 2
Whenever I think about talking to or messaging a friend, I think that they just won't want to talk to me.	Send a message to Nia tonight saying 'Hey, how's things?'

Table 11.5 Worksheet part 2 applied to Chris

What thoughts when? Part 1	Experiment plan (Design it) Part 2
When I think about meeting with friends, I think I will get so anxious and act so strange that they will mock me and reject me.	Meet one trusted friend (Sam) at home.

Key Tips:

- Experiments may need to be graded to support engagement
- Ensure any experiments will be able to clearly test the thought or prediction
- Consider whether carer support will be needed, and if so, discuss this with the CYP

Step 3: Make Predictions

A key element of completing behavioural experiments is to ensure that **before** the experiment takes place, that there is a shared understanding of:

- How the CYP will know if the thoughts and predictions are true, and
- How the CYP will know if the thoughts and predictions are not true.

Setting the basis for evaluation of the experiment before it has been completed helps to ensure that findings are less likely to be discounted or ignored. This understanding also supports later evaluation of the meaning of the outcome of the experiment. In seeking to determine ways to judge the meaning of experiments in advance, seek to identify observable facts (this is often behaviour). The meaning drawn from experiments may be impacted upon by bias in observation. For example, if an experiment was designed to test predictions of feared social rejection, the evidence to show that it may be true should be based on clear observable behaviour. An example of clear observable behaviour may be someone saying, 'I'm sorry but I don't want to be your friend'. A more neutral behaviour that may be affected by cognitive bias may be the expectation 'they will give me a funny look'. Here, a glance away may be misinterpreted or seen differently by others observing this. Here, the behaviour is subject to an individual's interpretation of an ambiguous event, and so should be avoided as the basis for judging a planned experiment.

The booklet's characters model this process in identifying clear descriptions of what will happen in relation to their predictions (see Figure 11.6). These can be used in discussion with CYP to support development of their own clear predictions.

Zee and Tao explore how they know if their predictions are true or not. Tao addresses the reality that completing experiments may be likely to raise anxiety, but that this experience of anxiety does not automatically mean that the prediction is true. The booklet prompts the CYP to add their description of how they will know if their thought or prediction is right into part 3 of the worksheet. Characters then explore how they know if their thoughts or predictions are not right. This is added to part 4 of the worksheet (Table 11.6 for Zee).

The completion of this step with Chris could lead to the following example of the worksheet being developed.

In Chris's example, clear observable actions can be identified in advance of meeting their friends.

Key Tips:

- Establish what proves and disproves a prediction before doing the experiment
- Stick to observable facts to judge outcomes, rather than any unclear outcomes that may be affected by further unhelpful thoughts or worries

---

BEHAVIOURAL EXPERIMENTS | 157

Figure 11.6 Zee and Tao identify their step 3 predictions

Table 11.6 Illustration of Zee's step 3 predictions completed on the worksheet

What thoughts when? Part 1	Experiment plan (Design it) Part 2	If the thoughts are right, then... Part 3	If the thoughts are not right, then... Part 4
Whenever I think about talking to or messaging a friend, I think that they just won't want to talk to me.	Send a message to Nia tonight saying 'Hey, how's things?'	She will send a message back, telling me not to message her again.	She messages me back in a nice way, or even ends up sending a few messages.

LOW-INTENSITY PRACTICE WITH CYP AND FAMILIES

Table 11.7 Illustration of Chris's step 3 predictions completed on the worksheet

What thoughts when? Part 1	Experiment plan (Design it) Part 2	If the thoughts are right, then... Part 3	If the thoughts are not right, then... Part 4
When I think about meeting with friends, I think I will get so anxious and act so strange that they will mock me and reject me.	Meet one trusted friend (Sam) at home.	Spending time with friends will lead to their saying I am strange and that they do not ever want to meet up again, and soon leave.	Spending time with friends will be okay, they will talk to me, not leave, and would agree to meet up again.

Step 4: Run the Experiment

This step requires the CYP to complete their planned experiment. The experiment could be completed within the session timeframe to support completion. For experiments completed outside of the session, it is helpful to consider the planning of this in detail. This can include shared consideration of:

- When the experiment will be completed (day, time)
- How the CYP will remember to complete the task and any prompts needed
- Whether any support from parents/caregiver/friends is needed (are there any costs or resources needed?)
- What may get in the way of completing the experiment
- Problem solving potential barriers
- When the outcome will be completed on the worksheet
- Why it may be helpful to complete the experiment and what learning could come from this
- How completing the task fits with the CYP's goal for treatment

Step 5: What Did I Learn?

Within this step the outcome of the experiment is compared to the prediction and ideas for evaluating this, as developed in step 3. As these have been set prior to the experiment, this should be more accessible to the CYP in reviewing what happened. This step is modelled by the characters in the booklet and includes managing initial difficultlies. In Zee's case, her friend did not initially respond to her. She notices that she started to feel low, but that she stuck with the experiment and her friend responded later. In clinical practice, this may mean contacting different friends to give additional opportunities to explore the prediction and noticing that familiar old predictions can soon be jumped to. Tao noticed that his experiment was hardest before he started, but that once he got going things began to feel easier. This can also help to normalise any anticipatory anxiety that a CYP may experience.

The CYP and their practitioner then work together to consider the meaning of the outcome of the experiment and how this fits with their initial prediction. Knowing

BEHAVIOURAL EXPERIMENTS | 159

in advance how to judge whether predictions are correct or not helps with this step. This is reviewed by the booklet characters, who draw out their learning to model this step to support discussion with the practitioner.

Zee is able to review the outcome of her experiment to draw the conclusion: 'My prediction did not come true. It made me think that maybe I could start to contact other people or meet up sometimes. I'm not saying it's all easy now, but I do think I can do more experiments like this to find out. I don't need to just believe the upsetting thoughts I have.' This reflects both the learning and her experience of this being challenging, whilst opening up more possibilities. Similarly, Tao reflected upon the experiment to note: 'My prediction did not come true. I did feel anxious because I was doing something scary. Even though it was hard, I found that I could do it. I now think I can manage this walk without my worries coming true. I am going to try some more experiments to do some longer walks with more people about. This seems more possible for me now.'

Here the characters demonstrate relating their experiment back to their feared predictions. (What does this mean about your prediction?) They also seek to support the final step of the intervention where the lens is turned towards the future. What does this mean for you now? What does this mean you could do next? (see table 11.8). These considerations should be aligned to the CYP's goals for treatment and their future. This discussion is used to complete the final element of the experiment log worksheet.

In enquiring about Chris's learning, the practitioner considers with them what the outcome of the experiment was (what happened). They can then consider together whether this outcome fitted with part 3 (if the thoughts are right then...) or part 4 (if the thoughts are not right then...). Looking forwards it can be helpful to explore what this means about their predictions, and what might be possible now. This may well mean continuing to explore further behavioural experiments in line with their goal. For Chris, this exploration is explored in table 11.9.

Table 11.8 Illustration of Zee's step 5 learning completed on the worksheet

What thoughts when? Part 1	Experiment plan (Design it) Part 2	If the thoughts are right, then... Part 3	If the thoughts are not right, then... Part 4	What did I learn? (Part 5)
Whenever I think about talking to or messaging a friend, I think that they just won't want to talk to me.	Send a message to Nia tonight saying 'Hey, how's things?'	She will send a message back, telling me not to message her again.	She messages me back in a nice way, or even ends up sending a few messages.	After an hour she messaged me back. It was a nice message. My thoughts were not right. We have messaged since and are going to meet up. I don't need to just believe the upsetting thoughts I have; I can test them.

Table 11.9 Illustration of Chris's step 5 learning completed on the worksheet

What thoughts when? Part 1	Experiment plan (Design it) Part 2	If the thoughts are right then... Part 3	If the thoughts are not right then... Part 4	What did I learn? Part 5
When I think about meeting with friends, I think I will get so anxious and act so strange that they will mock me and reject me.	Meet one trusted friend (Sam) at home.	Spending time with friends will lead to their saying I am strange and that they do not ever want to meet up again, and soon leave.	Spending time with friends will be okay, they will talk to me, not leave, and would agree to meet up again.	The prediction was not true. I worried at first but, this passed in time. Sam was friendly and didn't say anything about my behaviour. We chatted for a couple of hours. We are meeting up at Sam's house next week.

Through the steps of completing a BE, Chris may be helped to develop other predictions in line with their goals and next steps. This could even be helped by developing a competing new adaptive prediction (based upon the outcome of experiments) of what could happen and testing this. Rating the strength of belief in each prediction (original and new prediction) could provide a further measure of progress.

Key Tips:

- Ensure the CYP considers the meaning of the experiment, and what this may mean moving forwards in seeking to generalise learning to other situations or experiments
- Experiments may need to be repeated to develop confidence in alternative predictions
- Consider how learning can be consolidated with further experiments
- Focus upon the CYP learning the steps of completing BEs, rather than rushing through as many experiments as possible

Summary

This chapter has identified what a BE is, when it may be used, and the evidence base underpinning the use. The steps involved in completing a BE with a CYP at LI have been detailed. Adaptations and supporting materials have been described with each step. This has been applied to a case identified in the assessment chapter, with further examples provided from the workbook designed to support the intervention. This workbook is available for free with an app version also available for free at the Android play store and the Apple app store, see http://cedar.exeter.ac.uk/resources/cyp/

References

Bennett-Levy, J. (2003). Mechanisms of change in cognitive therapy: The case of automatic thought records and behavioural experiments. *Behavioural and Cognitive Psychotherapy, 31*, 261–277.

Bennett-Levy, J., Butler, G., Fennell, M., Hackman, A., Mueller, M., & Westbrook, D. (2004). *Oxford guide to behavioural experiments in cognitive therapy*. Oxford University Press.

Blenkiron, P. (2005). Stories and analogies in cognitive behaviour therapy: A clinical review. *Behavioural and Cognitive Psychotherapy*, *33*, 45–59.

British Psychological Society. (2002). *Drawing on the evidence*.

Choo, C. (2014). Adapting cognitive behavioural therapy for children and adolescents with complex symptoms of neurodevelopmental disorders and conduct disorders. *Journal of Psychological Abnormalities in Children*, *3*, 124. https://doi.org/10.4172/2329-9525.1000124

Chorpita, B. F., Yim, L. M., Moffitt, C., Umemoto, L. A., & Francis, S. E. (2000). Assessment of symptoms of DSM-IV anxiety and depression in children: A revised child anxiety and depression scale. *Behaviour Research and Therapy*, *38*, 835–855.

CEDAR. (2022). CWP regional report 2020–2021. https://swcypiapt.com/resources/publications/

Clark, D. M. (1997). Panic disorder and social phobia. In D. M. Clark & C. G. Fairburn (Eds.), *The science and practice of cognitive behaviour therapy* (pp. 121–153). Oxford University Press.

Donoghue, K., Stallard, P., & Kucia, J. (2011). The clinical practice of cognitive behavioural therapy for children and young people with a diagnosis of Asperger's syndrome. *Clinical Child Psychology and Psychiatry*, *16*(1), 89–102.

Ehlers, A., & Clark, D. M. (2000). A cognitive model of post-traumatic stress disorder. *Behaviour Research and Therapy*, *38*, 319–345.

Freeman, J. B., Garcia, A. M., Coyne, L., Ale, C., Przeworski, A., Himle, M., Compton, S., & Leonard, H. L. (2008). Early childhood OCD: Preliminary findings from a family-based cognitive-behavioral approach. *Journal of the American Academy of Child and Adolescent Psychiatry*, *47*(5), 593–602.

Friedberg, R. D., Crosby, L. E., Friedberg, B. A., Rutter, J. G., & Knight, K. R. (1999). Making cognitive behavioral therapy user-friendly to children. *Cognitive and Behavioral Practice*, *6*(3), 189–200.

Gray, C. (1998). Social stories and comic strip conversations with students with Asperger syndrome and high-functioning autism. In E. Schopler, G. B. Mesibov, & L. J. Kunce (Eds.), *Asperger syndrome or high-functioning autism?* (pp. 167–198). Plenum Press.

Kuyken, W., Padesky, C. A., & Dudley, R. (2009). *Collaborative case conceptualisation: Working effectively with clients in cognitive behavioural therapy*. Guilford Press.

Padesky, C.A. (1994). Schema change processes in cognitive therapy. *Clinical Psychology and Psychotherapy*, *1*, 267–278.

McMillan, D., & Lee, R. (2010). A systematic review of behavioural experiments versus exposure alone in the treatment of anxiety disorders: A case of exposure while wearing the emperor's new clothes? *Clinical Psychology Review*, *30*(5), 467–478.

Rachman, S. J., & Hodgson, R. (1974). Synchrony and desynchrony in fear and avoidance. *Behaviour Research and Therapy*, *12*, 311–318.

Reinecke, M. A., Dattilio, F. M., & Freeman, A. (Eds.). (2003). *Cognitive therapy with children and adolescents: A casebook for clinical practice* (2nd ed.). The Guilford Press.

Salkovskis, P. M. (1999). Understanding and treating obsessive-compulsive disorder. *Behaviour Research and Therapy*, *37*, S29–S52.

Scheeringa, M., Weems, C., Cohen, J., Amaya-Jackson, L., & Guthrie, D. (2011). Trauma-focused cognitive-behavioral therapy for posttraumatic stress disorder in three-through six year-old children: A randomized clinical trial. *Journal of Child Psychology and Psychiatry*, *52*(8), 853–860

Schulte, D., Kunzel, R., Pepping, G., & Schulte-Bahrenberg, T. (1992). Tailor-made versus standardized therapy of phobic patients. *Advances in Behaviour Research and Therapy*, *14*(2), 67–92.

Stallard, P. (2005). *A clinician's guide to think good-feel good: Using CBT with children and young people*. John Wiley & Sons.

Stott, R., Mansell, W., Salkovskis, P., Lavender, A., & Cartwright-Hatton, S. (2010). *Oxford guide to metaphors in CBT building cognitive bridges*. Oxford University Press.

12

Brief Coping Cat

Kate Phillips and Philip C. Kendall

Introduction

This chapter focuses on the use of Brief Coping Cat (BCC) with children and young people (CYP). Within this chapter we identify and demonstrate the steps needed to complete a low-intensity BCC intervention. This will be supported with use of the case of Elna, who was first introduced in the assessment chapter. Both the theory underpinning the use of BCC and the current evidence for use of the intervention will be considered. Example worksheets are on the accompanying website https://cedar.exeter.ac.uk/resources/cyp/ to support delivery.

Client Scenario: Reprise

Elna is an 8-year-old girl, who has started speaking to her Mum about feeling worried. The problem started approximately six months ago when her Mum was ill and had a short hospital stay. The illness lasted about two months, following which Mum started to feel better and has now made a full recovery. Elna started to have trouble sleeping when Mum first became ill. She would often wake and, with some worries, creep into Mum's bed. Recently it has become harder for Elna to attend school – she worries whether her Mum is okay. School staff have found it hard to manage Elna's behaviour when she is at school. Elna has found it harder to sleep in her own bed, and Mum has become concerned for the impact of Elna's behaviour on her friendships and education. Upon further assessment, Elna worries that if she is not with her mother, she may become suddenly ill or even die. Elna stays as close to her mother as possible, sleeping in her bed most nights and becoming upset if her mother moves from her eyeline within the home. In addition, morning drop-off at school has become very difficult. Elna will express resistance to school as soon as she wakes. She is slow to get ready and frequently becomes tearful on the way to school. At drop-off, Elna clings to her mother and resists separation. Throughout the day Elna seeks frequent reassurance about her mother's health and is visibly anxious. These persistent concerns distract Elna from her schoolwork, and she expresses concern with making mistakes. If she thinks she did something incorrect she will erase excessively or even tear up her paper. When her teacher prompts her to move along in her work, she becomes upset and distressed at times.

Theory Behind the Disorder

Fear and anxiety are present in normative child development. As children develop, the content of their anxieties and fears tends to reflect changes in their perceptions of what is going on around them (Campbell, 1986) starting out more global, imaginary, uncontrollable, and powerful, and over time becomes more specific, differentiated, and realistic (Bauer, 1976). Although anxiety is an expected part of typical development, it becomes a disorder when the experience is exaggerated beyond that which would be expected for the given situation and/or interferes with the CYP's functioning. Further, anxiety disorders are characterized by worries and fears that are not commensurate with the facts of the situation and/or interfere with activities of daily living. These fears manifest in cognitive (e.g., excessive worries, rumination) and/ or physical (e.g., muscle tension, difficulties sleeping, shakiness) symptoms. Worries cover a broad range of domains including, school, social evaluation, perfectionism, and separation from caregivers.

The most common anxiety disorders in CYP are generalized anxiety disorder (GAD: characterized by excessive worries about everyday life matters), social anxiety disorder (SAD: characterized by fears of negative evaluation and judgment by peers) and separation anxiety disorder (SEP: characterized by fear of separation from a parent or caregiver; American Psychiatric Association, 2013; Kendall, Compton, et al., 2010). In CYP, GAD presents as pervasive, uncontrollable worries that can occur in an array of domains, including concern about performance, family or social relations, physical health, or ruminations about future or past behaviour. CYP with GAD find the worry hard to control. SEP presents as extreme anxiety in anticipation of or upon separation from an attachment figure. Often CYP who experience separation anxiety disorder fear that danger or harm will come to themselves or a loved one, which would prevent the CYP from seeing the loved one again, specifically in the context of separation. Such fear may lead to refusal to be away from the caregiver for developmentally appropriate periods of time. In SAD, the source of anxiety/fear is social evaluation that may include a fear of embarrassing or humiliating oneself in front of others.

Anxiety disorders in CYP are characterized by cognitive distortions and avoidant behaviours. Cognitive distortions include thinking that is dysfunctional or biased. These distortions must first be identified, recognized as problematic, and subsequently corrected. Anxious CYP focus their attention on threatening or fearful stimuli in their environments (Ehrenreich & Gross, 2002) with hypervigilance to environmental cues that signal some sort of threat. It is this maladaptive thinking that leads to interference and avoidance, and thus must be a treatment target. Research

LOW-INTENSITY PRACTICE WITH CYP AND FAMILIES

has indicated that anxious CYP experience their emotions more intensely and perceive themselves as less able to manage situations than non-anxious CYP (Suveg & Zeman, 2004). Anxious CYP exhibit more dysregulated management and less adaptive coping across anger, sadness and worry situations than CYP without an anxiety disorder. It follows that anxious CYP benefit from interventions that improve their knowledge of and ability to regulate their emotions.

Brief Coping Cat

This 8-session program treats anxiety in CYP. The approach is cognitive-behavioural; an integration of behavioural approach (e.g., exposure tasks, relaxation training, homework, role play activities, practice and reward) and amending the cognitive processing factors associated with anxiety (anxious self-talk, emotional distress, anticipatory dread). The goal is to teach CYP to recognize signs of anxious arousal and use these signs as cues to use anxiety management strategies.

BCC is derived from the 16-session *Coping Cat*, a cognitive-behavioural therapy (CBT) program for youth anxiety (Kendall & Hedtke, 2006; for additional details see Podell et al., 2010). The *Coping Cat* has been evaluated in several RCTs (e.g., Kendall, Hudson, et al., 2008; Walkup et al., 2008; Kendall et al., 2013; for additional details see Beidas, et al., 2013). BCC retains the central structure, course and theory behind *Coping Cat*, reducing treatment length from 16 to 8 sessions, showing favorable outcomes, acceptability and feasibility (Crawley et al., 2013). This has additional relevance for the low-intensity CBT practitioner, as the length of intervention, applicability to mild to moderate presentations, and strong evidence base make this a highly suitable approach.

Key Point: Components of BCC

- Affective education
- Awareness of anxious bodily sensations
- Identification and modification of anxious self-talk
- Problem solving
- Practice of newly acquired skills in increasingly anxiety-provoking situation (i.e., homework role-plays; exposure tasks/behavioural experiments)
- A working relationship.

Theory Behind the Intervention

The goal of BCC is to teach CYP to manage anxiety. Treatment is not intended to eliminate anxiety, but to teach how to identify signs of anxiety (e.g., somatic sensations, cognitive distortions, avoidance) and to implement strategies to decrease interference. BCC first focuses on affective education. CYP learn about emotions, with a focus on anxiety and its functions and features. This learning provides an opportunity for practitioners to normalize anxiety and model effective coping, with research supporting the inclusion of psychoeducation in anxiety interventions (Dannon et al., 2002). Skills training focuses on (a) awareness of bodily reactions to feelings and physical symptoms of anxiety; (b) recognition and evaluation of 'self-talk,' or what CYP think and say to themselves when anxious; (c) problem-solving skills, including modifying anxious self-talk and developing plans for coping; (d) and self-evaluation and reward for effort.

Skills are introduced and implemented using the FEAR Plan with each letter representing a step in the intervention (see accompanying website information sheet 1 'fear plan steps' for more information). The **F-Step** (i.e., Feeling frightened?) distinguishes anxious feelings and body 'clues' that indicate rising anxiety. This step helps CYP identify anxiety within themselves and use these clues to engage in coping. CYP identify anxious self-talk using the **E-Step** (i.e., Expecting bad things to happen). Strategies consist of teaching CYP to 'test out' negative self-talk and challenge unrealistic or dysfunctional negative self-statements. The E-step helps CYP to both identify anxious thoughts that exacerbate anxiety and reduce distress by changing self-talk to coping self-talk. Support for this is provided though research identifying an association between changes in self-talk and a decrease in anxiety symptoms (Kendall et al., 2016; Kendall & Treadwell, 2007; Peris et al., 2015; Ruocco et al., 2018).

Once able to identify somatic cues and self-talk associated with anxiety, the **A-step** (i.e., Attitudes and Actions that can help) aids CYP in generating alternatives for managing or reducing anxiety. This step introduces problem-solving, which prompts CYP to ask themselves questions: (1) What is the problem? (2) What are all the things I could do about it? (3) What will probably happen if I do these things? (4) Which solution do I think will work best? and (5) After I have tried it, how did it go? Problem-solving has been shown to be an efficacious intervention (Hogendoorn et al., 2014; Provencher et al., 2004) and is associated with maintenance of post-treatment improvement (Kleiner et al., 1987). The **R-step** (i.e., Results and Rewards) presents CYP with reinforcement for effort (not solely for performance). Approach, not avoidance, is encouraged through appropriate rewards. CYP are guided to rethink their experience in anxiety-inducing situations, focusing on effort and growth rather than perfection.

The FEAR plan is applied in exposure tasks. Planned exposures are individualized to each CYP, allowing them to use their new coping skills in 'real life' anxiety-provoking situations. Exposure tasks are related to favorable clinical outcomes in anxious CYP (Peris et al., 2017; Whiteside et al., 2020) and are the most common feature of effective intervention for CYP anxiety (Chorpita & Daleiden, 2009). During planned exposure,

CYP are encouraged to identify and report on their own anxious experience (F-Step and E-Step), problem solve to plan for approach rather than avoidance (A-Step) and approach the feared stimuli or situation. Following approach, CYP are rewarded for brave behaviour and encouraged to compare their expectations to their lived experience during the planned exposures (R-Step). Assigned homework ('show-that-I-can' tasks) related to topics from session and planned exposures solidify learning across skill building (1–3) and exposure (4–8) sessions. Parent/guardian involvement supports learning about anxiety and intervention, with increased reward for brave behaviours, homework completion, and the facilitation of planned exposures at home.

> ### Key Point: Strategies of BCC
>
> - Graduated sequence of training tasks and assignments
> - Contingent rewards
> - Homework assignments ('Show-That-I-Can' – STIC tasks)
> - Coping modeling

The Process

To model the implementation of BCC, we use the previously described case of Elna.

Session 1: Orient to Program and Normalize Anxiety

During this session the practitioner oriented Elna and her Mum to BCC. The practitioner's main goal was to ensure the child wants to return for the following session. The practitioner first engaged Elna in a 'get-to-know-you' game, intentionally not addressing her fear or worry. Elna was oriented to the various toys and games available and allowed to pick a game, which they reserved for the last five minutes of session. The practitioner oriented Elna to the program and reviewed each step of the FEAR plan. Anxiety was defined and the goal of the program was described.

> Practitioner: Elna, now that we have a sense of what anxiety is, how many people in the world do you think experience anxiety?
>
> Elna: I don't know, maybe a few?
>
> Practitioner: Actually, almost **everyone** experiences anxiety, at least a little anxiety. In fact, if we did not have some anxiety, we might do things that are dangerous, like drive too fast or not look both ways before crossing the street. The trouble with anxiety is that sometimes, when the anxiety volume gets turned up too loud,

BRIEF COPING CAT | 167

	it starts getting in the way of us doing things we want to do. It's like anxiety gives us a false alarm. Know what I mean? Elna, has the fire alarm ever gone off in your home or school… when something happened like burnt toast?
Elna:	Yes, or even sometimes when my Mum gets the potatoes extra crispy.
Practitioner:	Exactly! And even though there isn't a real fire, the alarm sounds. Our anxiety is like a fire alarm, it keeps us safe when things are dangerous, like if there was a real fire. However, we don't want our alarm to go off when there is **no danger;** a false alarm, like with the burnt toast. One goal for us may be to have fewer false alarms. We can work together and learn to know when you are anxious and what to do about it. Can you think of anything that makes you anxious?
Elna:	I am worried about being away from my Mum. When at school my head gets full of thoughts that she might get sick… and not pick me up… or even that she might die.

Elna was encouraged to describe how these worries get in the way or 'mess up' things that she wants to be doing. The practitioner and Elna worked together to make a fear hierarchy (things that cause anxiety) and collaboratively rated the feared situations (Table 12.1). Finally, the practitioner and Elna agreed to a "Show-That-I-Can" (STIC) practice assignment – Elna was to describe one situation during the week when she was feeling anxious. They concluded with the game of Elna's choosing.

The practitioner met with Elna's Mum and oriented her to the steps and goals of the program. Though not required, it is helpful for parents to be kept abreast of the program features, and to have reasonable expectations. We provide parents with

Table 12.1 Illustration of an initial hierarchy with Elna

Initial FEAR Hierarchy

Situation	Fear Rating (0–10)
Stay in office while Mum steps out for 1 minute	2
Stay in living room while Mum is in her bedroom for 1 minute	3
Stay in office while Mum leaves waiting room for 3 minutes	3
Stay in office while Mum steps out for 5 minutes	5
Stay in living room while Mum is in her bedroom for 5 minutes	6
Stay in the office while Mum leaves the building for 5 minutes	7
Stay in the flat while Mum walks to the mailbox and back	8
Stay in the office while Mum leaves for the shops for 20 minutes	9
Stay in office while Mum goes to run errands (not sure when will come back)	10

printed information. Two options include Kendall, Podell et al., 2010 and Khanna & Kendall, 2021.

When asked, Elna's Mum expressed concern over Elna's refusal to separate, stating it is making things difficult in the morning and at night. The practitioner explained how Elna's Mum could help Elna with this through her weekly STIC tasks and help Elna to face her fears.

Session 2: Introduce F and E-Steps

After reviewing the previous week's STIC task, the practitioner moved to chat with Elna about how she experiences anxiety (see Worksheets 12.1 and 12.2 on website), providing examples as needed. The practitioner serves as a coping model, illustrating the use of this skill to support the CYP to do the same.

> Practitioner: These feelings people get in their body, like shaky hands or butterflies in their stomach can actually be clues that we are feeling anxious. When we can notice we are becoming anxious then we have cues that signal us to use coping skills – skills we all can learn. This is the F-Step, answering the question are you Feeling frightened?

The practitioner then described the F-Step (see Worksheet 12.3 on website) and guided Elna through noticing what her body feels like when she is anxious. The practitioner introduced the concept of 'self-talk,' including anxious self-talk and coping self-talk. The practitioner asked Elna to think about someone famous and the thoughts that person might have that would make an experience more distressing (i.e., anxious self-talk) and to also think of thoughts that would help the person reduce anxiety (i.e., coping self-talk). This could, for example, be a footballer about to take an important penalty, or a singer about to go on stage. The practitioner continued with this idea, highlighting how coping thoughts can change behaviour and eventually applied the same process to Elna's anxiety (see website Worksheets 12.4 and 12.5 for resources).

> Practitioner: Often when we are worried it is because we are thinking thoughts that scare us or make us expect the worst. These thoughts may be possible, but they are not likely. Coping thoughts can help us feel less worried, and they are often more likely. Some examples of coping thoughts that can help when we are anxious are 'This will be hard, but I can get through it,' 'I have done something like this before and can probably do it again,' and 'It's probably not as bad as the worst.'

Note: It is important that the client finds coping thoughts are believable for them.

The practitioner then explained the E-Step (see Worksheet 12.6) and guided Elna to notice her anxious self-talk when she is worried. They agree that Elna will do a STIC task to practice the F- and E-Steps (see Worksheet 12.7).

Session 3: Introduce A and R-Steps

After reviewing the previous week's STIC task (this is important, to always follow-up), the practitioner and Elna discussed the A-Step (see Worksheets 12.8 and 12.9). They consider how once someone has recognized anxious feelings and self-talk, it can be helpful to change the situation by thinking differently and problem solving. When reviewing problem solving, the practitioner and Elna reflected on solutions that encourage her to approach (and not avoid) difficulties. Some suggestions included changing anxious self-talk to coping self-talk, taking deep breaths to encourage approach, and trying things out rather than avoiding them. They practiced problem solving around Elna becoming worried about her mother during the school day.

The practitioner then introduced the R-Step (Worksheet 12.10), discussing how rewards are something you are given when you're pleased with what you've done. The practitioner presented the idea of Elna rewarding herself for efforts to cope despite feeling afraid. The practitioner emphasized effort over perfection. In other words, the most important thing is having a go, rather than getting things 'right.' They worked together to make a reward menu of things Elna would like to earn, including smaller and larger items (Worksheet 12.11). Items can include social rewards (e.g., play time with a parent), privileges (e.g., extra minutes of screen time) and material rewards (e.g., an ice cream treat). Rewards need not be costly – they should be contingent on effort and non-avoidance.

The practitioner assigned Elna the STIC task of using the FEAR plan (Worksheet 12.12) and reviewing rewards (Worksheet 12.13).

Session 4: Finalize Fear Hierarchy and Begin Exposure Tasks

The practitioner and Elna reviewed the previous session's STIC task and 'tweaked' her fear hierarchy. In previous sessions Elna frequently asked if her Mum was outside and was allowed to check the waiting room once each session. The first exposure they identified to complete together was Elna's Mum leaving the waiting room and staying out of sight for some time. Elna rated this as a 3/10 in terms of intensity. This exposure task was conducted after thinking through the FEAR-Plan. Note that the practitioner supports as many exposures as fit in a session; which may be repeating one exposure, completing multiple exposures, or intensifying the original exposure task. Intensifying refers to ways the practitioner can change the exposure task to increase the difficulty, or statements from the practitioner that are likely to elicit fear.

170 LOW-INTENSITY PRACTICE WITH CYP AND FAMILIES

Intensifying ensures that CYP are sufficiently able to practice employing approach strategies and coping behaviour while experiencing fear.

Practitioner:	Alright, let's watch your Mum leave the waiting room. She has agreed to stay outside the door and come back in several minutes. She will walk out of the waiting room, check her watch, and then come back. Are we good to go?
Elna:	Alright.
Practitioner:	Okay, cool. You can stay in the therapy room and then get to pick a small prize from the prize shelf. And, as we agreed, if you ask where your Mum is, I will only be able to answer you one time.
F:	Feeling Frightened: The practitioner asked Elna how she was feeling in her body and prompted her to rate her anxiety on a scale of 0–10.
Practitioner:	Elna, how is your body feeling? How would you rate your anxiety right now on a scale of 0–10?
E:	Expecting Bad Things to Happen: Practitioner asked Elna what her anxiety was telling her.
Practitioner:	Elna, what is your anxiety saying to you right now?
A:	Attitudes and Actions That Help: The practitioner asked Elna if she would like to try something to calm her body down (she may choose to take three deep breaths, count to ten, etc....). This should only happen before the exposure starts if needed to encourage approach. The practitioner asked Elna to brainstorm some things to say back to her anxiety, and they collaborated to develop a list of ideas.
Practitioner:	Elna, what can you do to calm your body down before we start? Do you want to take three deep breaths with me?
Elna:	Okay.
Practitioner:	Elna, what is your anxiety telling you might happen if your Mum leaves the waiting room?
Elna:	I'm scared something might happen and she will never come back.
Practitioner:	Okay, thanks for sharing, I understand that that thought may be hard. What are some things you can say back to your anxiety to make it less? Can you tell yourself something that is truer from what has happened before or that helps you be brave?

BRIEF COPING CAT | 171

Responses might be 'she always comes back', 'I am safe in this office', or 'I can handle being away from my Mum for a few minutes'.

During the Exposure: The practitioner provided enthusiasm, confidence, encouragement, and coping modeling of brave behaviour going into the exposure task. Once it began, the practitioner encouraged Elna to focus on her mother leaving. Additionally, as agreed, she only answered one question about Elna's Mum's whereabouts, redirecting the questions back to Elna thereafter. The practitioner asked Elna for fear ratings.

R: Results and Rewards: After the exposure task was completed the practitioner rewarded Elna for her efforts, and asked Elna how she thought she did. This was followed by lots of positive comments and specific praise. Without judgment, the practitioner then asked Elna to compare how it was versus how she expected it to be.

Practitioner: Elna, that was so awesome! How do you think it went?

Elna: I was scared about Mum, it felt like a really long time.

Practitioner: I'm not surprised that it felt to you like a long time, and you were being very brave. You have done so well for wanting to work on this even though it is scary. So how did you think this would go when we started?

Elna: I thought something terrible might happen.

Practitioner: Okay, so was the experience like you thought it would be?

Elna: Not totally. She came back, and she was okay. Also, I thought I would cry but I didn't.

Note: In future exposure tasks practitioner might say: Is it getting easier or harder the more you practice?

Sessions 5–7

The STIC task was reviewed and Elna engaged in the next exposure on her fear hierarchy. The practitioner and Elna then agreed on the next STIC task and described to Elna's mother the new exposure STIC tasks to practice during the week.

Session 8

The previous STIC task was reviewed, and the practitioner completed a final exposure with Elna. The practitioner then recapped the program, highlighting Elna's successes. Elna was encouraged to complete a final project (e.g., a video commercial, a poster, a collage) where she communicated her understanding of the FEAR-Plan and how it worked for her. The practitioner met with Elna's Mum to review progress and plan for relapse prevention. At the end, Elna earned a certificate for her completion of the program and hard work.

Trouble Shooting

Realistic Fears

Some of Elna's fears revolve around her mother's health stemming from her previous illness. It is important to validate Elna's realistic fear. The practitioner helped Elna to distinguish between realistic fears/concerns and fears that result from misinterpretation or over generalization. Coping can be used to reduce unrealistic fears and help Elna tolerate realistic fears without interruption to her daily life.

Multiple Targets

Elna initially presented with a number of anxious symptoms including distress around separation, fears about her mother's health, and perfectionism. BCC includes strategies and principles that can be applied across multiple anxieties and fears. When CYP learn these strategies and principles (e.g., coping thoughts, problem solving, and facing fears) they can generalize their learning to worries not specifically addressed in session. Furthermore, practitioners can work with caregivers to design opportunities for bravery (exposure tasks) around additional fears that caregivers can continue to implement at home.

School Refusal

Elna had difficulty with separating from her mother to attend school. It is important for the practitioner to work with the school to support Elna in applying her new skills to that setting. One example would be the practitioner working with Elna to define and role play 'brave morning behaviour' and Elna receiving positive support from her teacher for each day she has a 'brave morning.' Additionally, the practitioner might consult with the teacher to aid her in addressing Elna's reassurance seeking by prompting Elna to use coping skills.

Summary

Whilst fear and anxiety are a normal experience for all CYP (and adults), problems can occur when the fear interferes with the individual's functioning, as illustrated by Elna's difficulties. This is characterized by cognitive distortions and avoidant behaviours that maintain her concerns. BCC offers use of the FEAR plan for CYP to provide affective education to normalize the experience of anxiety and spot clues in the body to use as a cue to apply coping skills. The program offers an evidence-based approach to identify anxious self-talk, challenge negative statements and generate thoughts and actions that can help. Approaching worrying situations, problem solving and rewarding efforts undertaken can help the low-intensity practitioner to support CYP (and those supporting them) to develop the skills to overcome real life anxiety provoking situations to alleviate fear and meet their goals.

For resources, please visit the CEDAR website at: https://cedar.exeter.ac.uk/resources/cyp/

References

American Psychiatric Association. (2013). *Diagnostic and Statistical Manual of Mental Disorders* (5th ed.). https://doi.org/10.1176/appi.books.9780890425596

Bauer, D.H. (1976). An exploratory study of developmental changes in children's fears. *Journal of Child Psychology and Psychiatry, 17*(1), 69–74.

Beidas, R.S., Mychailyszyn, M.P., Podell, J.L., & Kendall, P.C. (2013). Brief cognitive-behavioral therapy for anxious CYP: The inner workings. *Cognitive and Behavioral Practice, 20*(2), 134–146.

Campbell, S.B. (1986). Developmental issues in childhood anxiety. In R. Gittelman (Ed.), *Anxiety Disorders of Childhood* (pp. 24–57). Guilford Press.

Chorpita, B.F., & Daleiden, E.L. (2009). Mapping evidence-based treatments for children and adolescents: Application of the distillation and matching model to 615 treatments from 322 randomized trials. *Journal of Consulting and Clinical Psychology, 77*(3), 566–579.

Crawley, S.A., Kendall, P.C., Benjamin, C.L., Brodman, D.M., Wei, C., Beidas, R.S., Podell, J.L., & Mauro, C. (2013). Brief cognitive-behavioral therapy for anxious youth: Feasibility and initial outcomes. *Cognitive and Behavioral Practice, 20*(2), 123–133.

Dannon, P.N., Iancu, I., & Grunhaus, L. (2002). Psychoeducation in panic disorder patients: Effect of a self-information booklet in a randomized, masked-rater study. *Depression and Anxiety, 16*(2), 71–76.

Ehrenreich, J.T., & Gross, A.M. (2002). Biased attentional behavior in childhood anxiety: A review of theory and current empirical investigation. *Clinical Psychology Review, 22*(7), 991–1008.

Hogendoorn, S.M., Prins, P.J., Boer, F., Vervoort, L., Wolters, L.H., Moorlag, H., Nauta, M.A., Garst, H., Hartman, C.A., & de Haan, E. (2014). Mediators of cognitive behavioral therapy for anxiety-disordered children and adolescents: Cognition, perceived control, and coping. *Journal of Clinical Child and Adolescent Psychology, 43*(3), 486–500.

Kendall, P.C., & Hedtke, K.A. (2006). *Cognitive-behavioral therapy for anxious children:* Therapist manual. Workbook Publishing.

Kendall, P.C., & Treadwell, K. (2007). The role of self-statements as a mediator in treatment for anxiety-disordered CYP. *Journal of Consulting and Clinical Psychology, 75*, 380–389.

Kendall, P.C., Hudson, J.L., Gosch, E., Flannery-Schroeder, E., & Suveg, C. (2008). Cognitive-behavioral therapy for anxiety disordered CYP: A randomized clinical trial evaluating child and family modalities. *Journal of Consulting and Clinical Psychology, 76*(2), 282.

Kendall, P.C., Compton, S.N., Walkup, J.T., Birmaher, B., Albano, A.M., Sherrill, J., Ginsburg, G., Rynn, M., McCracken, J., Gosch, E., Keeton, C., Bergman, L., Sakolsky, D., Suveg, C.,

Iyengar, S., March, J., & Piacentini, J. (2010). Clinical characteristics of anxiety disordered youth. *Journal of Anxiety Disorders, 24*(3), 360–365.

Kendall, P.C., Podell, J., & Gosch, E. (2010). *The Coping Cat: Parent Companion*. Workbook Publishing.

Kendall, P.C., Crawley, S., Benjamin, C., & Mauro, C. (2013). *Brief Coping Cat: The 8-session Therapist Manual*. Workbook Publishing.

Kendall, P.C., Cummings, C., Villabo, M., Narayanan, M., Treadwell, K., Birmaher, B., Compton, S., Piacentini, J., Sherrill, J., Walkup, J., Gosch, E., Keeton, C., Ginsburg, G., Suveg, C., & Albano, A.M. (2016). Mediators of change in the child/adolescent anxiety multimodal treatment study. *Journal of Consulting and Clinical Psychology, 84*, 1–14.

Khanna, M., & Kendall, P.C. (2021). *The Resilience Recipe: A Parent's Guide to Raising Fearless Kids in the Age of Anxiety*. New Harbinger Publications.

Kleiner, L., Marshall, W.L., & Spevack, M. (1987). Training in problem-solving and exposure treatment for agoraphobics with panic attacks. *Journal of Anxiety Disorders, 1*(3), 219–238.

Peris, T.S., Compton, S.N., Kendall, P.C., Birmaher, B., Sherrill, J., March, J., Gosch E., Ginsburg, G., Rynn, M., McCracken, J.T., Keeton, C.P., Sakolsky, D., Suveg, C., Aschenbrand, D., Iyengar, S., Walkup, J.T., Albano, A.M., & Piacentini, J. (2015). Trajectories of change in CYP anxiety during cognitive-behavior therapy. *Journal of Consulting and Clinical Psychology, 83*(2), 239.

Peris, T.S., Caporino, N.E., O'Rourke, S., Kendall, P.C., Walkup, J.T., Albano, A.M., Bergman, R.L., McCracken, J.T., Birmaher, B., Ginsburg, G.S., Sakolsky, D., Piacentini, J., & Compton, S.N. (2017). Therapist-reported features of exposure tasks that predict differential treatment outcomes for CYP with anxiety. *Journal of the American Academy of Child and Adolescent Psychiatry, 56*(12), 1043–1052.

Podell, J.L., Mychailyszyn, M., Edmunds, J., Puleo, C.M., & Kendall, P.C. (2010). The coping cat program for anxious CYP: The FEAR plan comes to life. *Cognitive and Behavioral Practice, 17*(2), 132–141.

Provencher, M.D., Dugas, M.J., & Ladouceur, R. (2004). Efficacy of problem-solving training and cognitive exposure in the treatment of generalized anxiety disorder: A case replication series. *Cognitive and Behavioral Practice, 11*(4), 404–414.

Ruocco, S., Freeman, N.C., & McLean, L.A. (2018). Learning to cope: A CBT evaluation exploring self-reported changes in coping with anxiety among school children aged 5–7 years. *The Educational and Developmental Psychologist, 35*(2), 67–87.

Suveg, C., & Zeman, J. (2004). Emotion regulation in children with anxiety disorders. *Journal of Clinical Child and Adolescent Psychology, 33*(4), 750–759.

Walkup, J.T., Albano, A.M., Piacentini, J., Birmaher, B., Compton, S.N., Sherrill, J.T., Ginsburg, G.S., Rynn, M.A., McCracken, J., Waslick, B., Iyengar, S., March, J.S., & Kendall, P.C. (2008). Cognitive behavioral therapy, sertraline, or a combination in childhood anxiety. *New England Journal of Medicine, 359*(26), 2753–2766.

Whiteside, S.P., Sim, L.A., Morrow, A.S., Farah, W.H., Hilliker, D.R., Murad, M.H., & Wang, Z. (2020). A meta-analysis to guide the enhancement of CBT for childhood anxiety: Exposure over anxiety management. *Clinical Child and Family Psychology Review, 23*(1), 102–121.

13

Pesky gNATs: A CBT Computer Game for Young People

Gary O'Reilly

Introduction

This chapter will focus upon Pesky gNATs, which is a computer game designed to support practitioners delivering Cognitive Behaviour Therapy (CBT) to children and young people (CYP) aged 7–12 years of age experiencing Anxiety or Low Mood (O'Reilly & Coyle, 2015a). This chapter describes how it could be used to help two young people introduced within the assessment chapter. It will focus upon helping Elna to manage her anxiety and Theo with his low mood when working with a low-intensity (LI) presentation. It begins with a description of the theory and structure of Pesky gNATs before describing Elna and Theo's journey through the game.

Theory

Pesky gNATs is designed to take Beck's general CBT model (Beck et al., 1979) originally developed for psychological interventions with adults, and offer it in a format suited to children aged 7 to 12 years (Beck, 2011; Beck & Haigh, 2014). To do this Pesky gNATs filters Beck's CBT model through ideas from Developmental Psychology and Social Learning Theory. Specifically, it adapts CBT for children with reference to Piaget's staged model of children's cognitive development, Vygotsky's concept of a Zone of Proximal Development, Donaldson's and Dunn's contributions to understanding cognition from the supportive context of a child's social world, and Bandura's Social Learning Theory (Bandura, 1971; 1977; Daniels, 2017; Donaldson, 1978; Dunn, 1988; Flavell, 1963; Piaget, 1970; Piaget & Inhelder, 1969; Vygotsky, 1978). In tandem with delivering Beck's model, Pesky gNATs provides young people with an opportunity to learn relaxation, behavioural activation and mindfulness skills chosen with their practitioner to best suit their needs, as they engage with the programme. Readers who would like further detail on this can download this information from an Open Access book chapter (O'Reilly, 2018).

Research into the effectiveness of the Pesky gNATs program was undertaken through a pilot study by Ryan et al. (2013). Outcomes measures compared 16 children (age 9–17) treated with Pesky gNATs with 13 children allocated to treatment as usual. Evaluation used parental reports of their child's internalising scores as rated by the Child Behaviour Checklist (CBCL; Achenbach & Rescorla, 2001). Scores for the Pesky gNATs group reduced overall, moving from the clinical range to the normal/borderline range. Scores within the treatment as usual group reduced overall but remained within the clinical range. Levels of complexity in both groups as measured by the parent rated CBCL were comparable. Young person rated scales of internalising overall moved from the clinical to non-clinical (normal) range in both groups, further supporting the efficacy of Pesky gNATs in line with existing treatments. Ratings of scores on a working alliance inventory highlighted clinician's rating of alliance when using Pesky gNATs to be equal to or better than treatment as usual.

Broader accessibility of Pesky gNATs has been considered by Cooney at al. (2017) who conducted an RCT using an adapted version of Pesky gNATs for adults with intellectual disability. The results of this study identified medium-sized effects on anxiety post-intervention, with large-sized effects at 3-month follow-up. At a later follow-up 40 per cent of the Pesky gNATs sample continued to show clinically meaningful change, supporting a maintenance of progress. McCashin et al. (2021) conducted a naturalistic study of Pesky gNATs within a service context. This study recruited 122 children aged 8 to 12, who were randomised to intervention or waitlist control. Children in the Pesky gNATs condition played the game with an Assistant Psychologist. Within this study both groups experienced statistically significant reductions in internalising problems over time. Whilst there was a statistically significant result demonstrating that more participants from the intervention group moved from clinical to non-clinical levels of internalising difficulties at Time 2, this effect was not maintained at follow-up. However, results support the potential for positive change and high levels of acceptability of the intervention, with further study warranted.

Game World

Computer games provide a wonderful opportunity to engage a child's imagination as they are introduced to the ideas of CBT. Pesky gNATs takes its name from a play on the idea of NATs (Negative Automatic Thoughts) from CBT. In Pesky gNATs Elna and Theo visit a remote tropical island (*gNATs Island*) in a 3-D game world. Here they meet *David gNATenborough*, a world-famous explorer and wild-life film maker. He introduces Elna and Theo to little bugs (gNATs) who affect our thinking, feeling and behaviour in ways we usually do not notice. David invites them to work with him and his team of researchers in the world's first gNAT lab. A metaphor now unfolds over the course of the game to support their understanding and application of CBT. With help from David and the other game characters, Elna and Theo learn how to trap gNATs (Cognitive Monitoring), how to swat gNATs (Cognitive Restructuring), how to hunt gNATs back to their Hive (identify Core Beliefs) and how to splat a Hive (Restructure Core Beliefs).

Game Structure

Pesky gNATs is designed to be played by Elna and Theo in session with their practitioner. This ensures they receive their LI CBT intervention with all the supportive benefits of a therapeutic relationship and the crucial guidance of a practitioner in applying the ideas of CBT to their current difficulties. There are seven levels to the game. Each level takes about 45–50 minutes to play. This places an intervention within the six to eight session framework of LI, and may be completed within 45 minutes for a mild to moderate presentation. As illustrated in Figure 13.1 each level has the same structure to support the collection of outcome measures, the CBT concept for that session, modelling of this concept, application of the concept to the CYPs context, learning skills and developing practice with assistance from a free Pesky gNATs *App* or hardcopy workbook (O'Reilly & Coyle, 2015b).

A summary of the CBT content of each game level (summary sheet 1) and the relaxation, mindfulness and behavioural activation skills available in every level (summary sheet 2) are available on the accompanying website https://cedar.exeter.ac.uk/resources/cyp/ to support an overview.

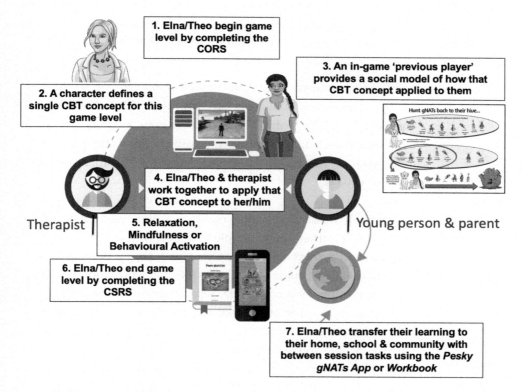

Figure 13.1 Level structure

Source: © Handaxe Community Interest Company (2015).

Level One: Baseline Measures of Anxiety and Mood and the Relationship between Thinking, Feeling and Behaviour

Elna and Theo both begin the game with an invitation to take a 'quiz' about how they are feeling. Their practitioner might ask if they have ever wondered if they are more worried or more sad than other young people their age? Most young people have not usually considered this question before. However, it can be a helpful way to orient them to think about the difficulties they are currently experiencing as, while always important, either common or uncommon compared to others their age. Thinking in this way may normalise some of their experiences and help focus on areas that might benefit from intervention. The 'quiz' in question displayed on-screen within Pesky gNATs is the Revised Children's Anxiety and Depression Scale (RCADS; Chorpita et al., 2000). On completion the game presents their results on screen by RCADS subscale visually represented in three rows labelled 'unlikely,' 'possibly,' or 'probably' respectively equating to the RCADS 'normal,' 'borderline' or 'clinical' ranges based on the scale's normative data. That is, it's unlikely, possibly, or probably the case you are more worried or sad in each area compared to other young people your age.

As illustrated in Figure 13.2 Elna had elevated scores on the 'Separation' subscale and a mild increase on the 'OCD (obsessive compulsive disorder)' scale. In contrast, Theo had an elevation score on the 'Depression subscale. Their practitioner can talk through this with each child, using this information to plan their intervention goals. For Elna the practitioner might say:

> Practitioner: Well done on answering all those questions. Do you see how your answers fall into areas on this chart called 'unlikely,' 'possibly' and 'probably'? That means your answers tell us whether in each area it's unlikely, possibly, or probably the case that you are more worried or sad compared to other young people your age.
>
> Elna: Ok
>
> Practitioner: So in most areas it looks like you are not more worried or sad compared to other young people your age. In those areas your worries and sadness are the same as other young people. In this area here called 'Separation' it looks like you worry more about this than other people your age. Separation worries are worries we have about being away from the people we are the closest to, or worries that something bad will happen to them. Who are the people you feel closest to?
>
> Elna: My mum, I worry she will get sick. She was in hospital.
>
> Practitioner: Ahh I see. That makes sense. When did you last worry about her?
>
> Elna: I don't like it.

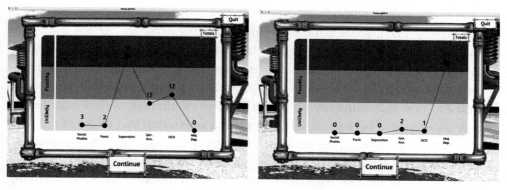

Figure 13.2 Elna (left) and Theo (right) in game completion of the revised children's anxiety and depression scale game level one

Source: © Handaxe Community Interest Company (2015).

Practitioner: Yes when something is scary we sometimes don't like to think about it, or talk about it. Sometimes, if someone we are close to is sick and they get better like your mum has, we worry they will get sick again. To feel safe we might stay close to them, and not want them to be out of our sight. Do you feel like staying close to your mum?

Elna: [shrugs] *A little bit.*

Practitioner: I think it makes sense you feel that way a little bit. Your mum was sick and that was a scary thing to happen. You care very much about her and want her to be ok. So you stay close to her to feel safe and to look after her. Lots of young people feel like you do if one of their parents is sick.

Elna: [nods]

Practitioner: Now that your mum is well again it might be time for you to turn down your worry for her. It may be you don't need to keep so close an eye on her anymore. We can play this game so you can find out. From playing the game you might decide to keep things just as they are now. Or you might decide that your mum is ok even though she was sick and it's ok for you to worry about her a little less. You will always decide for yourself, but the game will help you. Will we play this game to understand your worries about your mum? Does that sound ok?

Elna: ok

In this way the practitioner has used the RCADS embedded in the game to gain a baseline measure that offers some clarity about the nature and extent of Elna's difficulties, to remind her that she has many areas without difficulty, to begin to explore her values (her love for her mum) and validate her fears (that something might happen to her mum), without judging them or insisting they must change, and so avoids making playing the game something that threatens her current strategy to stay safe. Instead, the practitioner invites Elna to use the game to understand herself and what is happening in her life as a potential bridge to change that she can choose to cross if she wishes. A similar conversation with Theo might explore his feelings of sadness and how they influence his life on a daily basis that might similarly open up for him awareness of his current functioning and a consideration of change.

The relationship between our thoughts, feelings and behaviours is the central CBT idea explored with Elna and Theo in level one. This concept is introduced by a game character who explains that most of the time we do not notice what we are thinking, but if we pause for a moment, we can begin to notice our thoughts and how they link to our feelings and behaviour. This is then illustrated on screen by a game character who provides a personal example of a positive thought, feeling, behaviour, and a negative thought, feeling, behaviour relationship from her everyday life. Elna and Theo are then invited to consider this example and use it to guide them in the generation of the relationship between their thoughts, feelings and behaviours with help from their practitioner. Elna and Theo start by describing a positive situation from the last 24 hours and with help from their practitioner identify their thoughts, feelings, and behaviours in that situation. They then do the same for a negative situation from the last 24 hours. Usually this works best if the child can recall a recent experience of a time when they felt anxious or low in mood. Most children, and indeed many adults, confuse thoughts and feelings, so this introduction to thoughts, feelings and behaviours provides children with an opportunity to learn or consolidate their knowledge of the difference. Judith Beck (2011) in her CBT manual for working with adults suggests we ensure clarity on what a thought is and how it differs from a feeling by first inviting our clients to name their thoughts. If they offer a feeling in response, she suggests we invite the client to tell us what the thought is, and then reinvite naming their thoughts. Failing that we invite them to imagine the situation and name the thoughts. If this remains a challenge for the client, the practitioner names what the thoughts may have been with an invitation for the client to correct us if we are wrong. The practitioner then deliberately offers what they guess is the opposite thought of the client, thus eliciting the correction of a more likely thought. This allows its identification and a discussion to clarify what a thought is. In level one Theo struggled to express what his thoughts were and distinguish them from his feelings. His practitioner helped him work through this as follows.

Practitioner: [Repeats the question asked by the game character]. Can you think of a positive situation from the last 24 hours, something you did or that happened that you enjoyed?

Theo: I don't know.

Practitioner: What did you do yesterday?

Theo: I went to school.

Practitioner:	What type of day did you have in school?
Theo:	A boring one – I hate school.
Practitioner:	What did you do after school?
Theo:	I played football. I scored a goal in my match.
Practitioner:	Oh, did you like that?
Theo:	Yes.
Practitioner:	Maybe we could use that for our positive situation? What do you think?
Theo:	Ok. [Theo types playing football and scoring a goal on the computer game screen. The game character asks Theo '*What thoughts did you have at the time?*' Theo types '*happy*'].
Practitioner:	Happy, I think happy is a feeling, and that is going to be the next question, so let's remember your answer. Do you know what a thought is and how it's different from a feeling?
Theo:	Feelings are like happy or sad or angry.
Practitioner:	That's right … and thoughts?
Theo:	… not sure…
Practitioner:	Thoughts are the ideas that go through your mind from moment to moment – like right now I'm thinking 'what's the best way to describe a thought?' What ideas went through your mind when you scored your goal last night?
Theo:	I don't know.
Practitioner:	Let's see if we can work it out. Can you picture what happened? Can you imagine getting the ball and approaching the goal and did you take a shot? [Theo nods]. Can you picture the ball going in?
Theo:	Yeah.
Practitioner:	What ideas went through your mind at that moment?
Theo:	I don't know…
Practitioner:	I could make a guess at what your thoughts might be but only agree with me if it's right. Were you thinking 'This is terrible, I hate scoring goals'?
Theo:	[laughs slightly] No … I was thinking this is good.
Practitioner:	Brilliant – that sounds like your thought. Well done – would you like to put that down? [Theo types this in – and proceeds to the next question 'How did you feel?' he types 'Happy'].
Practitioner:	Well done. Do you see the difference between the idea in your mind when you scored and the feeling that came after it? Lots of people mix those up all the time.
Theo:	Yeah [Proceeds to next question asked by the game character '*What did you do?*']

| Practitioner: | What did you do after you scored your goal, thought 'this is good' and felt happy? |
| Theo: | I jumped about and celebrated with my teammates [both smile and Theo adds this to the screen]. |

Theo and his practitioner then go on to follow a similar process regarding a recent negative situation. In this way Theo has learnt the difference between a thought and a feeling, and how to observe and describe the relationship between his thoughts, feelings, and behaviours. His next task set by a game character is before his next session to record one positive thought, feeling, behaviour relationship and one negative one. The modesty of this task – simply noticing one example of each, increases the likelihood that Theo will be able to complete it. This process of self-observation is the foundation upon which Theo's CBT intervention will be built.

Before level one of the game is completed Theo meets another game character who teaches Relaxation, Mindfulness or Behavioural Activation Skills. As Theo is struggling with low mood his practitioner suggests they try the Behaviour Activation Skills. In contrast, Elna, who is anxious, after recording her positive and negative thought, feeling, behaviour relationships, is guided by her practitioner to choose a relaxation skill and they begin by learning a simple breathing technique. Both children have a hard copy of a workbook (called *The Explorer's Journal*) that reminds them of the content of the session and provides a place to record their positive and negative thought, feeling, behaviour relationship observations. Alternatively, the game has a companion Smartphone App *(The Pesky gNATs App)* available for free on iTunes and Google Play where they can record all their between-session tasks, practice their relaxation, mindfulness or behavioural activation skills and be rewarded for between-session task completion by fun games within the app that unlock as Elna and Theo make progress.

Key Points: Level One

- Measures are embedded within the game to support understanding of the young person's current situation
- The relationship between thoughts, feelings and behaviour is introduced
- A game character illustrates a positive and negative thought-feeling-behaviour cycle to support understanding
- Each level ends with a choice of relaxation, mindfulness or behavioural activation skills

Levels Two and Three: Trapping gNATs: Common types of Negative Automatic Thoughts

Levels two and three of Pesky gNATs build upon the observation of the relationship between thoughts, feelings and behaviours to introduce the idea that some of our

PESKY GNATS

thoughts can make us feel worried or sad in a way that is unhelpful. In the CBT model these are Negative Automatic Thoughts (NATs), and clients engage in thought monitoring to try to observe and consider them. In Pesky gNATs the CYP learns that some of the thoughts they observe can be unhelpful and in the game are described as like being stung by a fly or insect that we did not notice at the time (a gNAT). However, just as we might later spot a bump or a bite from them, we might similarly be able to look back and notice the effect of an unhelpful thought. In the game we call these thoughts 'Pesky gNATs' and in levels two and three Elna and Theo visit the *'gNAT Gallery.'* Here, over the course of two game levels they are introduced to 11 cartoon videos of common types of Negative Thinking presented as different species of gNATs. Each species is introduced with a definition of this type of unhelpful thinking and then illustrated with an example of how they affected a young person after they stung them, illustrated in a cartoon. On the conclusion of each gNAT gallery presentation the young person is asked if they have ever been stung by that type of gNAT (see Figure 13.3).

They also learn how to use their observations of the relationship between their thoughts, feelings and behaviours to set a gNAT trap. An example of a gNAT trap completed by Elna with help from her practitioner is presented in Figure 13.4. Elna has captured some *Predicting the Future gNATs* and an *Everything or Nothing gNAT,* while Theo spotted some *Seeing All the Bad Bits gNATs.* Elna also leaned Progressive Muscular Relaxation and a Body Scan skill at the end of sessions two and three respectively, while Theo continued with his Behavioural Activation.

Figure 13.3 Example from gNAT gallery

Source: © Handaxe Community Interest Company (2015).

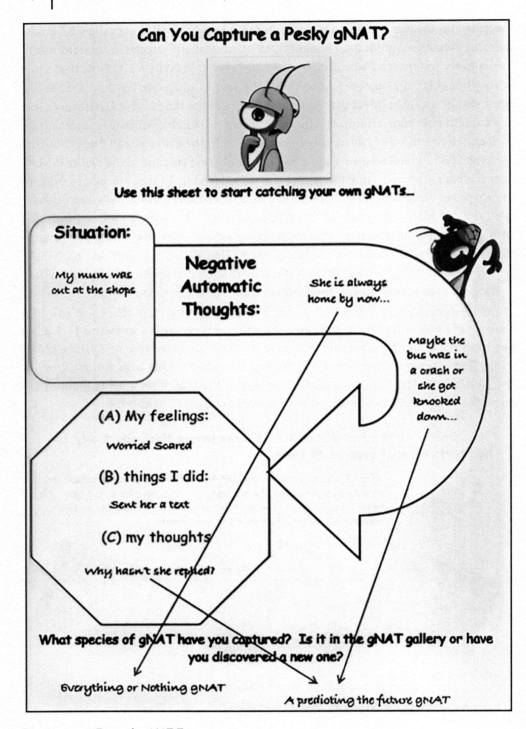

Figure 13.4 Example gNAT Trap

Source: © Handaxe Community Interest Company (2015).

Key Points: Levels Two and Three

- Levels 2 and 3 establish the link between thoughts and emotional experience
- The metaphor of gNATs is used to explore unhelpful thinking patterns
- 'gNAT traps' are used to stop and explore links between thoughts, feelings and behaviour (negative thoughts and their impact)

Level Four: Swatting gNATs: Cognitive Restructuring

Progressing to level (session) four, Elna and Theo have become used to noticing their thinking and how it relates to their anxiety or low mood. Hopefully they are now bringing to their own awareness a growing number of examples of how they are experiencing and interpreting their world. Their practitioner and the game support this development while helping them to regulate their emotions by turning them down through breathing and relaxation with Elna, or turning them up (enjoyment and achievement) for Theo through Behavioural Activation.

In level four Elna and Theo meet Shona, who uses one of her gNAT traps to demonstrate how to consider the usefulness and validity of their thinking in an open-minded balanced way. She does this by rating how much she believes the gNAT she trapped at the time it stung her on a scale of 0–100 per cent, and then asking four gNAT Swatting Questions: (1) What is the evidence for and against this thought? (Always beginning with a full exploration of the evidence for and then progressing to a consideration of the evidence against). (2) Can I look at this situation another way? (3) If I were in a situation like this again what are all the things I could do? And (4) Can I pick a plan that is new? Shona provides her answers to the four gNAT swatting questions in the game. Finally, she revisits her rating of how much she believes her gNATs now she has asked herself the four gNAT Swatting Questions (see Figure 13.5). Elna and Theo use Shona's example to guide them as they work in session with their practitioner to pick a gNAT from their existing traps to mirror the steps of rating, applying the four questions, and re-rating. Both children end the session with an exercise called 'looking at things another way.' This presents them with a visual illusion where different images can be seen in the picture presented. The idea here is to illustrate that without assuming someone is right or wrong, what we see sometimes depends on how we look at something, even when we look at the same thing. Similarly, we might think differently about the same situation depending on how we look at it.

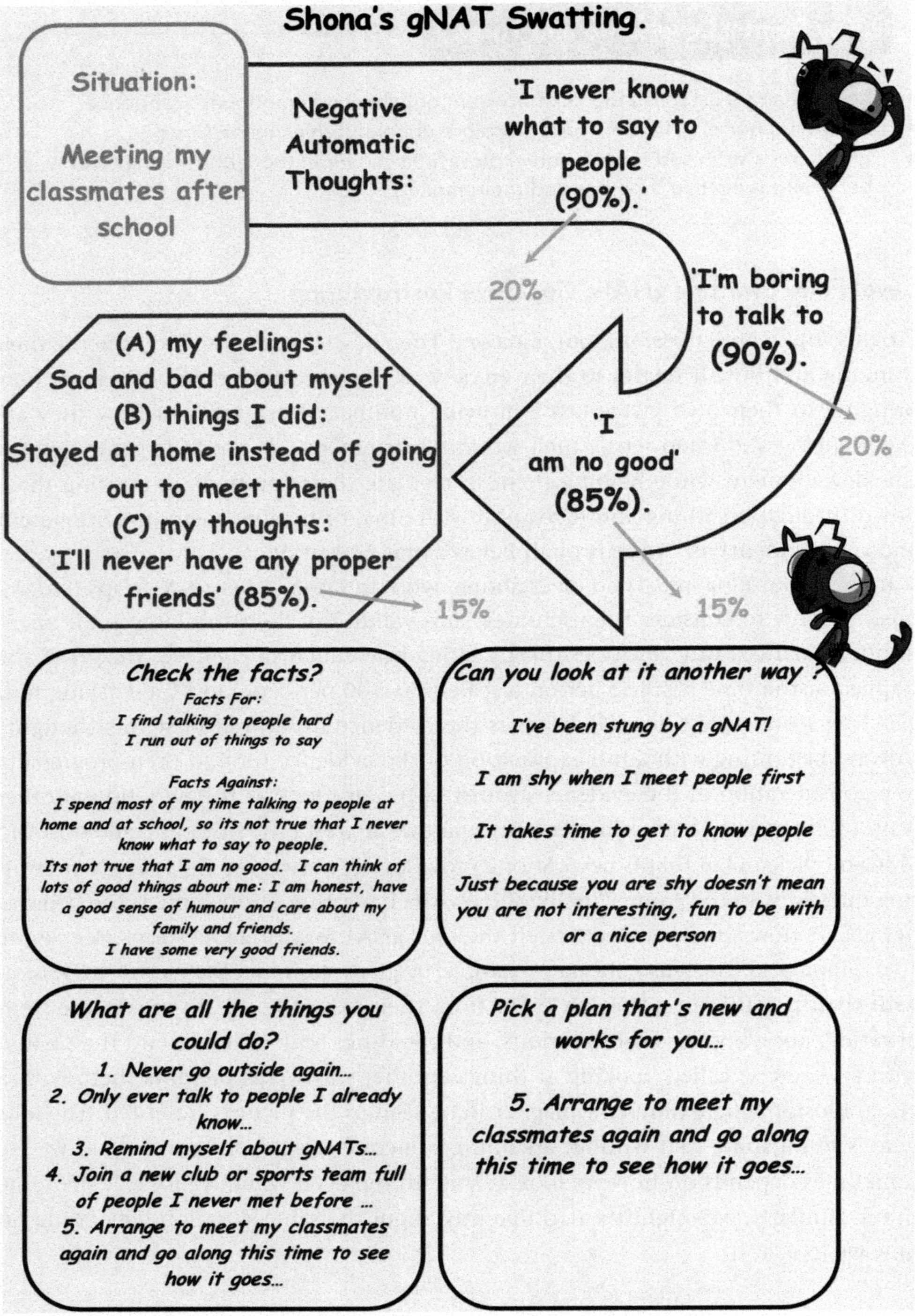

LOW-INTENSITY PRACTICE WITH CYP AND FAMILIES

Shona's gNAT Swatting.

Situation:

Meeting my classmates after school

Negative Automatic Thoughts:

'I never know what to say to people (90%).'

20%

'I'm boring to talk to (90%).

'I am no good' (85%).

20%

(A) my feelings:
Sad and bad about myself
(B) things I did:
Stayed at home instead of going out to meet them
(C) my thoughts:
'I'll never have any proper friends' (85%).

15%

15%

Check the facts?

Facts For:
I find talking to people hard
I run out of things to say

Facts Against:
I spend most of my time talking to people at home and at school, so its not true that I never know what to say to people.
Its not true that I am no good. I can think of lots of good things about me: I am honest, have a good sense of humour and care about my family and friends.
I have some very good friends.

Can you look at it another way ?

I've been stung by a gNAT!

I am shy when I meet people first

It takes time to get to know people

Just because you are shy doesn't mean you are not interesting, fun to be with or a nice person

What are all the things you could do?

1. Never go outside again...
2. Only ever talk to people I already know...
3. Remind myself about gNATs...
4. Join a new club or sports team full of people I never met before ...
5. Arrange to meet my classmates again and go along this time to see how it goes...

Pick a plan that's new and works for you...

5. Arrange to meet my classmates again and go along this time to see how it goes...

Figure 13.5 gNAT Swatting example

Source: © Handaxe Community Interest Company (2015).

PESKY GNATS   187

Key Points: Level Four

- 'gNAT swatting' supports the young person through the steps of cognitive restructuring
- Game characters continue to model and illustrate key skills
- Flexibility in perspective taking is supported throughout

Level Five: Hunting gNATs Back to their Hive: Identifying Core Beliefs

In level five of the game Elna and Theo continue to develop their skills by considering whether any Core Beliefs (Hive beliefs) can be discerned from the gNATs they have trapped and/or swatted to date. In Pesky gNATs this is called *'Hunting gNATs back To Their Hive.'* A game character (Kirsten Katcher) explains that her job on gNATs Island is to discover where gNATs come from. She explains she discovered that all gNATs come from Hives, and although they might look like different species, if they come from the same hive they will try to tell the person they sting a similar message. She then illustrates this by introducing some common Hive Beliefs (e.g., 'I can't cope,' or 'I'm a bad person'). See website 'summary sheet three.' Kirsten gathers together all the gNATs Shona described through the various levels of the game. Kirsten demonstrates how Shona grouped together the ones that sounded similar and traced them back to a single 'I am no good Hive.' In this way Shona came to realise many of her gNATs were giving her this same message (see website sheet 'Shona's hive belief'). With help from their practitioner, they look back over all the gNATs they trapped or swatted so far in the game and group together the ones that sound similar. They then view the array of common Unhelpful Hives before choosing which they think their gNATs come from. For Elna in reviewing her gNATs she sees a common theme of something bad happening to her mum, with the underlying idea of not being able to cope with that. Theo in contrast sees how many of his gNATs were about him not being good enough.

This task ends with a historical story about when people held a belief that the Earth was flat. This is introduced to offer the idea that we are not foolish for having beliefs, they can seem like they are true, but if we look closely we might discover they are not true, are unhelpful or hold us back. The story ends with the positive open-minded idea that Elna and Theo might discover in the next game level their gNATs have suggested a Belief that has held them back. In considering its usefulness and validity, they may discover a whole new world opening up to them just like this happened for people who challenged the idea that the Earth is flat.

Key Points: Level Five

- A new character supports spotting common higher-level beliefs
- Making connections and spotting patterns in thinking is developed further
- The practitioner supports developing cognitive skills through discussion of the game level
- This level normalises the discovery that commonly held beliefs may not be true

Level Six: Splatting Hives and Challenging Core Beliefs.

In level six Elna and Theo explore whether their Unhelpful Hive Belief identified in level five is supported or not by evidence. Game character Kirsten re-introduces the idea that Unhelpful Hive Beliefs are ideas that may seem like they are true until we look more closely at them. We do this in a manner similar to the one we learnt for gNAT swatting, by exploring the evidence for and against our belief. Elna and Theo see the game character Shona work through her consideration of evidence for and against the Belief she identified 'I am no good' (see website 'Shona's hive belief evidence'). Shona first considers all the evidence she can think of that *supports* the idea that she is no good in a structured way, considering evidence from school, friends, family and personally. Elna and Theo, supported by their practitioner, then complete their version of this. Next Shona considers the evidence *against* her identified Belief, reflecting from the same sources of information (school, friends, family and personally). Elna and Theo then follow the same process to explore the evidence *against* their identified Belief. Once completed, Elna and Theo are invited to consider the evidence for and against the belief gathered by Shona and decide what she should do choosing from three options: (1) Splat it because it is an Unhelpful Hive Belief; (2) Gather more evidence; or (3) She should still believe it. Once they assist Shona with this decision, they then complete the same choice regarding their own identified Unhelpful Hive Belief based on the evidence for and against it they have generated in this level of the game.

Key Points: Level Six

- Previously developed skills are applied to higher level beliefs
- Characters model and support practitioner discussion of this step
- Young people are supported in making choices in how to respond to beliefs identified

Level Seven: Healthy Life Plan

The final level of Pesky gNATs reviews some of the key ideas learnt so far, before concluding with development of *'A Healthy Life Plan.'* This is in essence a relapse prevention session with a focus on underlining skills learnt and developing a clear map for psychological health and well-being now and in the future. The *Healthy Life Plan* has six parts: (1) Fun; (2) Personal Goals; (3) Making a Difference; (4) Emotional and Physical Health; (5) Being Me; and (6) Having People in My Life.

This is then modelled by Shona (see website 'Shona's healthy life plan') before CYP complete their own *Healthy Life Plan* in-session with help from their practitioner. The plan could be shared with parents or carers and can continue to be added to. At the conclusion level Elna and Theo are invited to re-take the RCADS, CORS and SRS and compare their pre- and post-intervention responses.

Key Points: Level Seven

- Key learning from the game is reviewed
- Relapse prevention is supported through the 'healthy life plan'
- Plans can be supported by being shared with parents or carers
- Outcome measures are repeated to review change

Summary

The aim of Pesky gNATs is to use combine technology with evidence-based mental health interventions for the good of the community on a sustainable not-for-profit basis. This chapter has highlighted how the use of a computer game world can support CYP (as illustrated by Elna and Theo) through an unfolding metaphor to use LI CBT. Exploring the relationship between thoughts, feelings and behaviour, spotting and challenging common patterns of negative thinking, and challenging themes in belief are supported with relapse prevention and planning for the future. Pesky gNATs and seven hours of related video training on using the programme is available to mental health professionals from www.PeskyGnats.com Other resources are available from that website including a free CBT workbook. Another website, www.MindfulGnats. com contains free access to breathing, relaxation and Mindfulness practice videos from Pesky gNATs which are also available for free from the Apple and Google Play stores in a standalone App called '*Mindful Gnats.*' Our hope is that as many people as possible can access our resources to the benefit of young people like Elna and Theo.

The accompanying website for resources is https://cedar.exeter.ac.uk/resources/cyp/

References

Achenbach, T.M., & Rescorla, L.A. (2001). *Manual for the ASEBA school-age forms and profiles: An integrated system of multi-informant assessment.* University of Vermont, Research Center for Children, Youth & Families.

Bandura, A. (1971). *Social learning theory*. General Learning Press.

Bandura, A. (1977). *Social learning theory*. Prentice-Hall.

Beck, A.T., Rush, A., Shaw, B., & Emery, G. (1979). *Cognitive therapy of depression*. Guilford Press.

Beck, A.T., & Haigh, E.A. (2014). Advances in cognitive theory and therapy: The generic cognitive model. *Annual Review of Clinical Psychology, 10,* 1–24.

Beck, J. (2011). *Cognitive therapy: Basics and beyond* (2nd ed.). Guilford Press.

Chorpita, B.F., Yim L., Moffitt, C., Umemoto, L.A., & Francis, S.E. (2000). Assessment of symptoms of DSM-IV anxiety and depression in children: A revised child anxiety and depression scale. *Behaviour Research and Therapy 38,* 835–855.

Cooney, P., Jackman, C., Coyle, D., & O'Reilly, G. (2017). Computerised cognitive–behavioural therapy for adults with intellectual disability: Randomised controlled trial. *British Journal of Psychiatry, 211*(2), 95–102.

Daniels, H. (2017). Introduction to the third edition. In H. Daniels (Ed.), *Introduction to Vygotsky* (3rd ed.). Routledge.

Donaldson, M. (1978). *Children's minds*. Fontana/Croom Helm.

Dunn, J. (1988). *The beginnings of social understanding*. Harvard University Press.

Flavell, J.H. (1963). The developmental psychology of Jean Piaget. Van Nostrand.

McCashin, D., Coyle, D., & O'Reilly, G. (2021). Pesky gNATs for children experiencing low mood and anxiety: A pragmatic randomised controlled trial of technology-assisted CBT in primary care. *Internet Interventions, Dec 27.* doi: 10.1016/j.invent.2021.100489.

O'Reilly G. (2018). Pesky gnats! Using computer games and smartphone apps to teach complex cognitive behavioural therapy and mindfulness concepts to children with mental health difficulties. In R.J. Harnish, K.R. Bridges, D.N. Sattler, M.L. Signorella, & M. Munson (Eds.), *The use of technology in teaching and learning*. Retrieved from the Society for the Teaching of Psychology website: http://teachpsych.org/ebooks/useoftech

O'Reilly G., & Coyle, D. (2015a). Pesky gNATs: A cognitive behaviour therapy computer game for young people with anxiety or low mood. Handaxe CIC.

O'Reilly G., & Coyle, D., (2015b). The pesky gNATs app: A smartphone app to aid young people with anxiety or low mood in the completion of between session CBT tasks. Handaxe CIC.

Piaget, J. (1970). *Science of education and the psychology of the child*. Orion Press.

Piaget, J., & Inhelder, B. (1969). *The psychology of the child*. Basic Books.

Ryan, A., O'Reilly, G., Coyle, D., & Delahunty, A. (2013). *A pilot-study of a computer-assisted CBT game in a child and adolescent mental health setting*. School of Psychology; University College Dublin.

Vygotsky, L.S. (1978). *Mind in society: The development of higher psychological processes*. Edited and Translated by M. Cole, V. John-Steiner, S. Scribner & E. Souberman. Harvard University Press.

14

Lifestyle Management Intervention

Julia Butler

Introduction

This chapter will focus upon how to assess, provide information and give support to children and young people (CYP) for lifestyle-related issues within the context of low-intensity cognitive behaviour therapy (LICBT). The stages involved in completing a lifestyle management intervention with CYP will be explored in relation to the case studies introduced within the assessment chapter. The evidence base for lifestyle management interventions for CYP will be examined to help inform when this type of intervention may be suitable and relevant. Examples of handouts and links to resources are identified and some materials are provided on the website accompanying the book at: https://cedar.exeter.ac.uk/resources/cyp/

An Overview

Information about lifestyle areas such as sleep, diet, and exercise, is gathered during the assessment stage, and can help to build a more holistic picture of how these factors may impact on a young person's mental health and wellbeing. Lifestyle management (LM) may be supported through psychoeducation to facilitate change as part of an intervention, or it may be the specific focus of treatment if it meets low-intensity criteria and it is the area that the CYP wishes to work on specifically. CYP can also be signposted to relevant resources and more specialist support for a particular area of difficulty that may be outside the remit of low-intensity working, such as sleep clinics.

LM as an intervention may not be disorder specific and will focus on behavioural change with the aim to improve mental health and wellbeing. There may be a comorbid presentation of symptoms, yet the young person may feel they would like to focus on improving sleep, exercise, or eating habits to improve their mood and general wellbeing. This may even be a way for the young person to 'test out' what it is like to work with a practitioner.

Conversations around lifestyle management can be a sensitive topic, so it is important that this is handled carefully and that the focus of treatment remains person-centred and tailored to the individual's needs. As with all low-intensity cognitive behaviour therapy (LICBT), adaptations to resources for age, developmental stage, and individual differences must be considered. Sleep, diet, exercise patterns, and routines will vary considerably from person to person, within families, diverse cultures, and communities and across different times of the year, for example during times of celebration, religious festivals, or holiday times.

Ensuring that any intervention work is done at a time when the young person can engage for the duration of the 6–8 weeks, and that they will have the time, necessary support, and access to the opportunity they need to succeed in managing change is crucial to achieving positive outcomes. This may involve parents/carers, or support for CYP from other individuals, such as school staff, so that they may participate in relevant activities and maintain change.

Providing support to make a change in lifestyle habits may be considered within specific interventions where this is the goal for the young person, such as scheduling physical activity as part of the Behavioural Activation (BA) intervention for low mood and depression. For younger children, it may be a goal for treatment within an intervention such as Parent-Led CBT, for example a goal of the CYP staying in their own bed all night to promote sleep.

The relationship between physical and mental health – what does the evidence say?

It is widely recognised that good quality sleep, a balanced diet and regular exercise are an important part of maintaining good physical and mental health for everyone. Evidence suggests there is a bidirectional relationship between physical and mental health, with 30 per cent of people experiencing problems with their physical health also experiencing common mental health problems such as depression and anxiety (Barnett et al., 2012; Naylor et al., 2012). Raising awareness and supporting healthy habits and lifestyle choices in children and young people can help improve physical and mental health and wellbeing long-term (O'Neill et al., 2014).

Physical Activity

Studies show that physical activity has a positive impact on young people's mental health and wellbeing and that some sedentary behaviours, such as screen-based activities, can impact negatively (Rodriguez et al., 2019). Research also suggests an association between physical activity and improved cognitive functioning in adolescents, which is important for attention, memory, and regulatory behaviours (Biddle et al., 2019). Increasing physical activity may have beneficial effects for lower levels of depression in young people (Biddle et al., 2019). Evidence suggests a longer-term benefit from lifestyle management, as attitudes to physical exercise established in childhood are predictive of the amount of physical exercise undertaken within adulthood (Pretty et al., 2009). Encouraging regular physical activity each week can therefore help establish patterns that will be embedded long-term, support positive mood, and improve cognitive function.

Guidelines (Department of Health and Social Care, 2019) suggest that CYP aged 5–18 should engage in at least 60 minutes of moderate physical activity a week comprised of aerobic and muscle strengthening exercises (see webpage – Handout 1: Physical Activity Guidelines). A link to guidelines for CYP with disabilities can be found in further resources at the end of this chapter. Reducing time spent in sedentary activities like sitting or lying down for long periods is recommended to support regular movement and healthy development of bones and muscles.

The location of activity may bring further additional benefits, where spending time outdoors in natural spaces has been noted to provide positive benefits on both physical and mental health (Bird, 2007; Moss, 2012). Access to green spaces can support positive mental health and wellbeing for CYP, with benefits including improved cognitive abilities such as memory and attention restoration, and behaviour regulation (McCormick, 2017).

Sleep

Sleep hygiene is a lifestyle management approach commonly used in LICBT to support good sleep habits and improve both the quantity and quality of sleep. CYP often present with sleep issues, and it can be difficult to gauge an accurate assessment on the amount and quality of sleep. Guidance suggests that children between 6–12 years of age need between 9–12 hours' sleep and those aged between 13–18 need 8–10 hours' sleep (Great Ormond Street Hospital for Children, 2020). Many young people sleep less than the recommended number of hours, and this has been seen to impact upon their mood and ability to regulate emotions effectively (Baum et al., 2014).

Sleep is vital for good physical and mental health and particularly important during stages of brain development and maturation, such as childhood and adolescence (Dahl & Lewin, 2002). A range of biological, social, and psychological factors affecting young people during adolescence increases their vulnerability to sleep issues (Crowley et al., 2018). Sleep deficit is not therefore uncommon in adolescents, who may not be able get to sleep until late due to changes in their circadian rhythms and are then required to get up early for school (Orchard et al., 2020). Other factors such as caffeine, irregular routines, and use of electronic devices before bedtime can impact on sleep. This may be particularly important to consider within certain demographic groups. Higher incidence of sleep difficulties and difference in sleep patterns in CYP with neurodevelopmental differences has been noted (Gregory & Sadeh, 2016). CYP diagnosed with autism and ADHD often experience greater difficulties with falling asleep, maintaining regular sleep patterns and sleep disorders (Cortese et al., 2013; Elrod & Hood, 2015). These are important areas of consideration within the assessment process.

Difficulties with sleep are correlated with depression and anxiety across the lifespan and the relationship between sleep disturbance and emotional regulation is considered bidirectional (Cousins et al., 2011). Sleep problems are a common symptom of depression in adolescence and can impact on emotional, cognitive, and behavioural function (Gregory & Sadeh, 2016). Orchard et al. (2020) note sleep problems to be a significant predictor of future depression and anxiety symptoms and the subsequent receipt of mental health diagnoses; but that targeted interventions for sleep in young people may have positive outcomes for long-term mental health and wellbeing. It is, therefore, important to consider early interventions to address sleep issues in young people experiencing anxiety and depression to help prevent more serious lifelong difficulties (Forbes et al., 2008).

Diet

Eating a balanced and nutritious diet is important to maintain good health and wellbeing. The impact of diet during childhood and adolescent development is particularly significant. Healthy diets have been seen to be linked to better mental health in children and adolescents (Khalid et al., 2016; O'Neil et al., 2014), whereas unhealthy eating habits, such as high consumption of 'junk food' and irregular eating patterns, are associated with poorer mental health in young people (Zahra et al., 2014). Psychoeducation and signposting to relevant resources to help support healthy eating habits and routines can be helpful in providing CYP and their parents/carers with information to help them make informed decisions about diet choices (see webpage – Handout 2: The Eatwell guide). A healthy, balanced diet helps younger children and teenagers through their growing and developing stages. Further information can be found on the NHS live well, eat well pages (see further resources at the end of this chapter).

LM can now be considered in relation to the presentations of Elna and Theo who we met in the assessment chapter. They have both completed assessments and made choices to begin interventions for different lifestyle related areas. Illustrations will work through the different steps for each case study and include handouts relevant to the lifestyle area of focus.

Elna

Elna is finding that things have improved for her at school recently, but she is still having problems getting to sleep and staying in her own bed, even though she is not worrying as much about mum anymore. She describes that she frequently feels tired and noted that this is impacting on her concentration at school, causing her to feel irritable and upset. Following an assessment, Elna's mum also feels that working on supporting a better sleep routine is something that will help Elna to feel more focussed in school. Elna has recently been invited to a sleepover with a friend but is worried about not being able to sleep without mum there. Mum would like to support Elna to sleep in her own bed so that her own sleep is not disrupted. Elna has identified two goals for treatment:

Goal 1: Sleep the whole night in her own bed at home.
Goal 2: Sleepover at a friend's house without mum there.

During the assessment, the practitioner supports the CYP to complete their own descriptive formulation diagram (Padesky & Mooney, 1990), called a 'hot cross bun' within treatment when adapting language for Elna. This helps to explain the vicious cycle of sleep problems (Figure 14.1). The practitioner can also invite the CYP's parent/caregiver to complete their own diagram to identify thoughts and behaviours in relation to their CYP's sleep disruption (Figure 14.2). In Elna's case, the separation

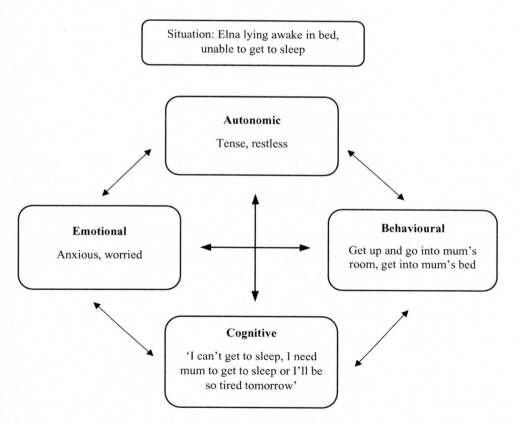

Figure 14.1 Elna's descriptive formulation diagram

Adapted with permission of the copyright holder. Copyright 1986 Christine A. Padesky, www.MindOverMood.com

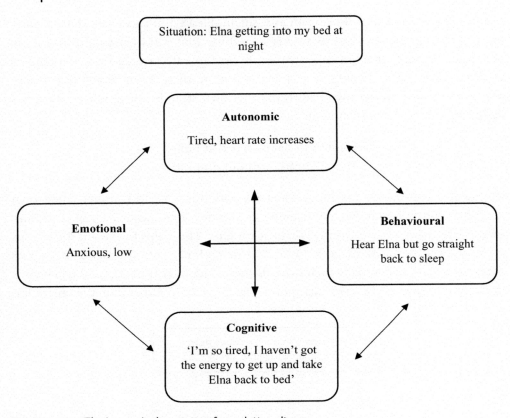

Figure 14.2 Elna's mum's descriptive formulation diagram

Adapted with permission of the copyright holder. Copyright 1986 Christine A. Padesky, www.MindOverMood.com

anxiety Revised Children's Anxiety and Depression Scale (RCADS) subscale was chosen as this was clinically significant when looking at data collected from the full RCADS scores obtained at assessment. This was seen to link to Elna's anxiety about being away from mum.

A circular diagram with four boxes entitled: autonomic, behavioural, emotional and cognitive, which are linked with bi-directional arrows. There is a situation box at the top – Elna getting into my bed at night.

Clinical Practice: Example

Step 1: Psychoeducation

Psychoeducation materials are shared with the CYP/parent/caregiver in the first session to help understand the different stages of sleep we need and some of our body rhythms that help maintain a healthy balance. Handouts 3 and 4 (Sleep part 1, Sleep part 2) can be shared to help the CYP/parent/caregiver understand the mechanisms of sleep and our circadian sleep-wake cycle (see website).

In Elna's case, the practitioner works collaboratively with Elna and her mum to review the descriptive cycle (Figure 14.1) completed in the assessment to help understand what behaviours are maintaining Elna's poor sleep patterns. The significant role of positive praise from a parent/caregiver to encourage effort and independence during the intervention is discussed along with the need for patience – it can take time to make changes and breaking the behaviour change down into small steps can help goals feel more achievable. The role of rewards for achieving steps in the plan can be talked through with the parent/caregiver, with some simple rewards agreed if appropriate to help celebrate steps.

Step 2: Starting a Sleep Diary

The sleep diary is introduced by the practitioner who works through this collaboratively with the CYP/parent/caregiver in the session to gather information about the CYP's sleep from the night before (see website Handout 5: Sleep part 3). Elna has identified that she finds it difficult to stay in her own bed because it has become a habit when she wakes up in the night to go into mum's bed. Elna finds she feels safer and knows everything is okay when she is with her. Mum says she sometimes realises that Elna has crept into her bed but often she is so tired she does not wake up or falls back to sleep immediately. Elna's home activity is to design her sleep diary using Handout 5 as a template and to record her sleep patterns for a week. This will be collaboratively reviewed at the next session.

Step 3: Identify Specific Area of Focus for Changing Behaviour

The sleep diary is reviewed collaboratively in the next session and the practitioner helps the CYP/parent/caregiver to identify the behaviour change they would like to achieve (see Figure 14.3).

The practitioner discusses how to put this change into action and break it down into small achievable steps. Elna and mum continue to keep a record of how things are going over the week to review at the next session. This forms the objective of steps 4–6 of trying out change, recording sleep, and reviewing the identified behaviour change to support better sleep habits and routine.

Step 4: Carry Out Activity to Practice Behaviour Change

In Elna's case, the behaviour change links to her goal of staying in her own bed if she wakes up in the night. This is broken down into the following steps:

1 – Follow agreed bedtime routine and choose a favourite toy for bed.

2 – Say goodnight after a bedtime story, turn off the light and leave the room. If Elna finds it difficult to settle to sleep on her own, a gradual approach to achieving this can be supported by the parent/caregiver as outlined in Step 4 (GOSH, 2020).

LOW-INTENSITY PRACTICE WITH CYP AND FAMILIES

Start date: Day of the week:	Day 1	Day 2	Day 3	Day 4	Day 5	Day 6	Day 7
What time did you go to bed?	8pm	8.30pm	8pm	9pm			
What time did you go to sleep?	9pm	10pm	9.30pm	10pm			
What time did you wake up this morning?	7am	8am	8am	7.30am			
How many times did you wake up in the night?	2	1	2	2			
For how long did you stay awake?	20 mins 15 mins	20 mins	30 mins 15 mins	1 hour			
Did anything wake you up?	Can't remember	Heard mum going to bed	Heard mum going to bed	The wind outside my window			
How good was your sleep? Scale of 0–10*	4	5	4	3			
How did you feel when you woke up? ☺ ⟷ ☹	 😐	 😐	 🙁	 🙁			
Anything else to add?				Terrible night for mum too			

*0 = the worst night's sleep; 10= the best night's sleep

Figure 14.3   Elna's sleep diary extract week 1

Handout: Sleep 3 – Sleep diary extract week 1 (Elna)

Adapted from The Sleep Foundation Sleep Diary https://www.sleepfoundation.org/wp-content/uploads/2020/12/SleepFoundation_SleepDiary.pdf

3 – If Elna wakes up, she has written some self-talk reminders on post-it notes by her bed to help her stay in bed and to remember her goals. She has also pinned the sleepover invitation next to her bed and made a list of what she plans to take.

4 – If Elna gets up and goes into mum's room, mum will get up and quickly settle Elna back into her own bed. She will say goodnight and go back to her own room. She will repeat this if Elna gets up again until Elna stays in her own bed (see repeated return; GOSH, 2020).

5 – Elna has identified a reward for staying in her own bed as a 20-minute play-time in the park after school with her friends on Friday.

Repeated Return Steps

1. When a child wakes and leaves their bed, quickly and quietly return them, tuck them in, say goodnight and leave the room
2. Only speak to say goodnight, remain calm, and repeat as needed until they remain in bed
3. This may be repetitive and tiring but will help the child settle over time. Seek support and take shifts with a partner or family member where needed

Step 5: Record How It Went

Elna records outcomes in the sleep diary in the mornings (Handout 5: Sleep part 3).

Step 6: Review Outcomes and Track Goal Progress – Troubleshooting

The practitioner reviews the diary collaboratively with the CYP each session to track progress and troubleshoot any issues that may have arisen. Routine Outcome Measures (ROMs) are also reviewed collaboratively each week and goal progress tracked on the Goal Based Outcome (GBO) form (Law & Jacob, 2015). Problem-solving techniques can help Elna and her mum to manage difficulties together (see webpage – Handout 6: Sleep part 4). Celebrating success can a help the CYP/parent/caregiver to see what they have managed to achieve.

Step 7: Ending and Relapse Prevention

Elna achieves her first goal of staying in her own bed for a whole week and having a sleepover at a friend's house by the end of six sessions. The practitioner talks through how to maintain the new sleep habits and revisits the descriptive formulation diagrams to see how the vicious cycle of unhelpful behaviours and thoughts have been impacting on sleep. The practitioner looks at identifying triggers and patterns of previous behaviours that may result in relapse into old habits. As part of relapse prevention and moving forward, the CYP/parent/caregiver can make some new goals for the future.

Key Points: Sleep

- Goals are used to support collaboration and focus the work
- Psychoeducation materials provide a rationale for the intervention
- Sleep diaries provide a helpful baseline
- Make a changing behaviour plan for all
- Repeated return helps to set a new pattern over time
- Track progress and provide agreed rewards

Theo

Following an assessment with Theo and Mum, it was agreed to start a Lifestyle Management intervention looking at physical exercise and healthy eating habits. Theo and his mum both felt that Theo's withdrawal and low mood had started with the change to secondary school and Theo giving up some of the sports he used to enjoy. In the assessment, Theo described missing sport and how he was worried about putting on weight now he was doing less exercise, so he was trying not to eat as much. Theo felt that getting fit again would help to lift his mood and he would not spend as much time gaming. Theo's preference was to focus on physical activity as an intervention. He felt this focus would help him get back into doing sport and help get to know people at his new school. He misses his old football team and would like to play again. Theo makes three SMART goals for treatment during the assessment:

Goal 1: Go swimming with his family
Goal 2: Cycle to school
Goal 3: Start training again with his old football team

Theo completes a descriptive formulation diagram in the assessment and uses some graphics from his favourite gaming program to design his own, using an avatar of his choice as the young person representing him. Adapting resources creatively helps support engagement and increases participation, which are key CYP mental health principles underpinning LICBT. For Theo, using an avatar helps him express his descriptive cycle and externalise his feelings through the character he has created (see Figure 14.4). The low mood RCADS subscale was chosen as the outcome measure as this was clinically significant and fitted best with Theo's main presenting difficulty.

A circular diagram with four boxes entitled: autonomic, behavioural, emotional and cognitive, which are linked with bi-directional arrows. There is a situation box at the top – Theo starting secondary school.

Clinical Practice: Working with Activity

Step 1: Psychoeducation

Psychoeducation materials are shared with Theo in the first session to provide some information around how symptoms such as reduced physical activity, loss of energy, motivation and changes in appetite are commonly related to low mood (see webpage – Handout 7: Being active part 1). The practitioner signposts Theo and his parents to guidelines for physical activity (Handout 1), healthy eating guides and further information to support this area for young people and their families (Handout 2). The practitioner may also suggest seeking support from the school nurse or GP if there are any further concerns around a young person's eating.

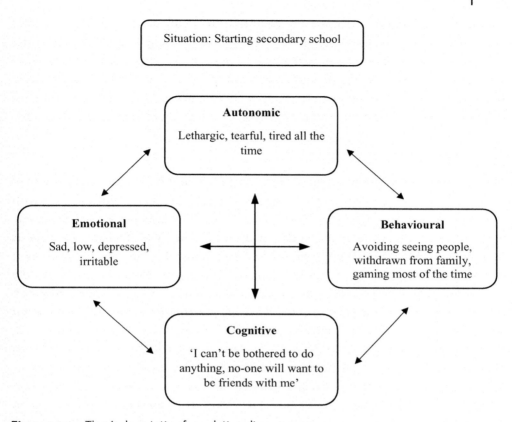

Figure 14.4 Theo's descriptive formulation diagram

Adapted with permission of the copyright holder. Copyright 1986 Christine A. Padesky, www.MindOverMood.com

The practitioner works collaboratively with the young person to consider the descriptive diagram (Figure 14.4) first completed in the assessment. This supports a collaborative review of which behaviours are maintaining inactivity and impacting on the presenting symptoms (low mood). Any unhelpful thoughts linked to these behaviours can be noted. The practitioner talks through how breaking down behaviour change into small steps can help goals to feel more achievable. Discussion is focussed upon modifying behaviours to help make a change. Shared exploration with Theo identifies the possibility of being more physically active to seek to help improve his mood.

Step 2: Writing Down Activities – Steps to Activity Planning

In addition to gathering information about the CYP's current baseline of activities, it can also be helpful to assess for any recent changes in engagement with activity. Curiosity regarding the impact of difficulties upon the range, nature, and frequency of activities can also be explored. This could include the identification of all the activities that the CYP used to do and is now avoiding, and activities they would like to commence. To support a stepped approach to introducing activity, it can be helpful to list activities in order of difficulty to help identify which activities would be easier to start with when planning the first activity. For example, Theo may find it easier to walk to the park and meet a friend than commit to going to a sports club every week. It can therefore be important to break an activity down into smaller steps to make it more manageable and achievable (see webpage – Handout 8: Being active part 2).

Step 3: Plan an Activity

The practitioner and Theo review the list of activities and choose the first activity to plan. Theo decides he would like to go swimming with his family, which links in with one of his goals. Carrying out a COM-B analysis can be helpful in problem-solving any barriers to achieving the activity (Michie et al., 2011). The COM-B framework suggests that three conditions: capability, opportunity, and motivation, are required to support behaviour change, and the practitioner can ask the young person questions to explore possible barriers to accessibility or engagement in the LICBT self-guided approach (Michie et al., 2011). For Theo, this involved the practitioner asking questions about doing this activity with his family to support him in getting to the swimming pool, assessing his motivation to do this with his family, and whether there would be an opportunity at a weekend to go swimming together. The activity was planned as an initial start point and felt to be a manageable commitment that could be a fun day out.

The first activity is a taster to see how the CYP feels when they start to engage in an activity. It is important to make the activity achievable so that the CYP is not too tired and tries to do too much too soon. Ideally this would support the development of a consistent level of activity across days which could then be built upon over time as more activity becomes possible.

The CYP uses an activity planner, beginning with the most possible activity (see webpage – Handout 9: Being active part 3). As the CYP moves through the intervention, and is able to gradually engage with activity, they may find that they have more energy. In this way they may be able to add in activities rated as being more challenging as things progress. It is important that the CYP is able to progress at their own pace, whilst the practitioner can monitor the potential for avoidance.

Step 4: Carry Out Activity to Practice Behaviour Change

In this step the CYP is supported to engage with their identified steps, and barriers may be explored and planned for.

Step 5: Record How It Went

The practitioner and CYP work together to review the record of activity, the nature of activity undertaken, what the CYP learned from doing the activity, and troubleshoot any issues that came up. A rating scale can be used to measure the level of enjoyment and sense of achievement to see how this relates to Theo's mood. Theo identified family swimming as his preferred activity as part of his home task and his family was engaged in planning the activity for the following weekend. On completing this, Theo reported back that he enjoyed the swimming session. He stated that initially he had felt a bit like he could not be bothered but that having the rest of his family there getting ready helped to motivate him to pack his things and be ready to go. Once he was there, he remembered how much he used to enjoy swimming and expressed a willingness to do this again. He reported that the whole family enjoyed the activity and set a goal to go once a month.

Step 6: Completing Further Activities and Troubleshooting

The CYP continues to use the planner to explore further activities which are reviewed collaboratively at each session, along with tracking ROMs, goals and problem-solving any issues.

Step 7: Ending and Relapse Prevention

Theo achieves his first and third goal. Both goals involved parental support, which in Theo's case, was key to increasing motivation and opportunity. At the end of treatment, Theo had made progress towards achieving his second goal. He chose to continue this goal beyond treatment as part of a future action plan with the aim of completing it. The practitioner talks through using the activity planner to support maintaining changes and encourages the CYP to review their wellbeing on a regular basis, with further support signposted if needed. Engagement with the support network around the CYP can support future planning and activity if acceptable to the CYP.

Key Points: Working with Activity

- Psychoeducation supports understanding of the intervention and how to make a change
- Exploring activities can help develop a list of possible future activity
- Planning activity in detail and seeking support network involvement can enhance the likelihood of its taking place
- Build activity slowly at the pace of the CYP
- Measuring achievement and enjoyment can support identification of the most helpful activities

Summary

This chapter has looked at how the evidence base can support LICBT lifestyle management interventions to help improve lifestyle areas such as sleep, exercise, and diet.

It has considered two case studies with CYP of different ages and across different lifestyle areas. This has highlighted how the practitioner may apply a Lifestyle Management intervention to support CYP who may be experiencing difficulties in these areas. Information about the specific difficulties experienced by each young person was gathered using LICBT materials such as a sleep diary and activity planner, which were reviewed on a weekly basis to help track patterns and explore behaviour change outcomes. Problem-solving techniques were used to help overcome barriers to engagement or the completion of home activities. In this way, the use of lifestyle management interventions has highlighted how a focus on behaviour change to break the vicious cycle of difficulties across lifestyle areas can result in improved patterns and routines that positively impact on mental health and wellbeing.

For further resources, and to access handout see https://cedar.exeter.ac.uk/resources/cyp/

References

Barnett, K., Mercer, S.W., Norbury, M., Watt., Wyke, S., & Guthrie, B. (2012). Epidemiology of multimorbidity and implications for health care, research, and medical education: A cross-sectional study. *The Lancet, 380*(9836), 37–43. doi: 10.1016/S0140-6736(12)60240-2.

Baum, K.T., Desai, A., Field, J., Miller, L.E., Rausch, J., & Beebe, D.W. (2014). Sleep restriction worsens mood and emotion regulation in adolescents. *The Journal of Child Psychology and Psychiatry, 55*(2), 180–190. doi: 10.1111/jcpp.12125.

Biddle, S.J.H., Ciaccioni, S., Thomas, G., & Vergeer, I. (2019). Physical activity and mental health in children and adolescents: An updated review of reviews and an analysis of causality. *Psychology of Sport and Exercise, 42*, 146–155. doi: 10.1016/j.psychsport.2018.08.011.

Bird, W. (2007). *Natural thinking.* Royal Society for the Protection of Birds. http://repositorio.minedu.gob.pe/handle/20.500.12799/3531

Cortese, S., Brown, T.E., Corkum, P., Gruber, R., O'Brien, L.M., Stein, M., Weiss, M., & Owens, J. (2013). Assessment and management of sleep problems in youths with Attention-Deficit/Hyperactivity Disorder. *Journal of the American Academy of Child and Adolescent Psychiatry, 52*(8), 784–796. doi: 10.1016/j.jaac.2013.06.001.

Cousins, J.C., Whalen, D.J., Dahl, R.E., Forbes, E.E., Olino, R., Ryan, N.D., & Silk, J.S. (2011). The bidirectional association between daytime affect and night-time sleep in youth with anxiety and depression. *Journal of Pediatric Psychology, 36*(9), 969–979. doi:10.1093/jpepsy/jsr036.

Crowley, S.J., Wolfson, A.R., Tarokh, L., & Carskadon, M.A. (2018). An update on adolescent sleep: New evidence informing the perfect storm model. *Journal of Adolescence, 67*, 55–65. doi: 10.1016/j.adolescence.2018.06.001.

Dahl, R.E., & Lewin, D.S. (2002). Pathways to adolescent health sleep regulation and behavior. *Journal of Adolescent Health, 31*(6), 175–184. doi:10.1016/S1054-139X(02)00506-2.

Department of Health and Social Care (2019). *Physical activity guidelines.* Retrieved September 7, 2021 from https://assets.publishing.service.gov.uk/government/uploads/system/uploads/attachment_data/file/832861/2-physical-activity-for-children-and-young-people-5-to-18-years.pdf

Department of Health and Social Care (2022). *Physical activity guidelines: Disabled children and disabled young people*. Retrieved August 31, 2022 from (https://www.gov.uk/government/publications/physical-activity-guidelines-disabled-children-and-disabled-young-people)

Elrod, M.G., & Hood, B.S. (2015). Sleep differences among children with autism spectrum disorders and typically developing peers: A meta-analysis. *Journal of Developmental and Behavioral Pediatrics, 36*, 166–177 doi:10.1097/DBP.0000000000000140.

Forbes, E.E., Bertocci, M.A., Gregory, A.M., Ryan, N.D., Axelson, M.D., Birmaher, B., & Dahl, R. (2008). Objective sleep in pediatric anxiety disorders and major depressive disorder. *Journal of the American Academy of Child and Adolescent Psychiatry, 47*(2), 148–155. doi: 10.1097/chi.0b013e31815cd9bc.

Great Ormond Street Hospital for Children (2020). Sleep hygiene in children and young people. https://www.gosh.nhs.uk/conditions-and-treatments/procedures-and-treatments/sleep-hygiene-children/

Gregory, A.M., & Sadeh, A. (2016). Annual research review: Sleep problems in childhood psychiatric disorders – a review of the latest science. *Journal of Child Psychology and Psychiatry, 57*, 296–317. doi:10.1111/jcpp.12469.

Khalid, S., Williams, C., & Reynolds, S. (2016). Is there an association between diet and depression in children and adolescents? A systematic review. *British Journal of Nutrition, 116*(12), 2097–2108. doi:10.1017/S0007114516004359.

Law, D., & Jacob, J. (2015). *Goals and goal based outcomes (GBOs): Some useful information* (3rd ed.). CAMHS Press. https://www.ucl.ac.uk/evidence-based-practice-unit/sites/evidence-based-practice-unit/files/pub_and_resources_resources_for_profs_goals_booklet.pdf.

McCormick, R. (2017). Does access to green space impact the mental well-being of children: A systematic review. *Journal of Pediatric Nursing, 37*, 3–7. doi:10.1016/j.pedn.2017.08.027.

Michie, S., van Stralen, M.M., & West, R (2011). The behaviour change wheel: A new method for characterising and designing behaviour change interventions. *Implementation Sci, 6,* 42. doi.org/10.1186/1748-5908-6-42.

Moss, S. (2012). *Natural childhood*. National Trust. https://www.outdoor-learning-research.org/Research/Research-Blog/ArtMID/560/ArticleID/24/Natural-Childhood-by-Stephen-Moss-2012-National-Trust-Report.

Naylor, C., Parsonage, M., McDaid, D., Knapp, M., Fossey, M., & Galea, A. (2012). *Long-term conditions and mental health: The cost of co-morbidities*. The King's Fund. Available at: http://eprints.lse.ac.uk/id/eprint/41873.

O'Neill, A., Quirk, S.E., Housden, S., Brennan, S.L., Williams, L.J., Pasco, J.A., Berk, M., & Jacka, F.N. (2014). Relationship between diet and mental health in children and adolescents: A systematic review. *American Journal of Public Health, 104*(10), e31–e42. doi: 10.2105/AJPH.2014.302110.

Orchard, F., Gregory, A., Gradisar, M., & Reynolds, S. (2020). Self-reported sleep patterns and quality amongst adolescents: Cross-sectional and prospective associations with anxiety and depression. *Journal of Child Psychology and Psychiatry, 61*(10), 1126–1137. doi:10.1111/jcpp.13288.

Padesky, C.A., & Mooney, K.A. (1990). Presenting the cognitive model to clients. *Cognitive Therapy Newsletter International, 6*, 13–14.

Pretty, J., Angus, C., Bain, M., Barton, J., Gladwell, V., Hine, R., Pilgrim, S., Sandercock, S., & Sellens, M. (2009). *Nature, childhood, health and life pathways*. Interdisciplinary Centre for Environment and Society Occasional Paper 2009-02. University of Essex, UK. www.essex.ac.uk/ces/esu/occ-papers.shtm.

Public Health England (2018). *The Eatwell guide*. https://assets.publishing.service.gov.uk/government/uploads/system/uploads/attachment_data/file/528193/Eatwell_guide_colour.pdf

Rodriguez-Ayllon, M., Cadenas-Sánchez, C., Estévez-López, F., Muñoz, N.E., Mora-Gonzalez, J., Migueles, J.H., Molina-García, P., Henriksson, H., Mena-Molina, A., Martínez-Vizcaíno, V., Catena, A., Löf, M., Erickson, K.I., Lubans, D.R., Ortega, F.B., & Esteban-Cornejo, I. (2019). Role of physical activity and sedentary behavior in the mental health of preschoolers, children and adolescents: A systematic review and meta-analysis. *Sports Medicine, 49*, 1383–1410. doi: 10.1007/s40279-019-01099-5.

Zahra, J., Ford, T., & Jodrell, D. (2014). Cross-sectional survey of daily junk food consumption, irregular eating, mental and physical health and parenting style of British secondary school children. *Child: Care, health and development, 40*(4), 481–491. doi: 10.1111/cch.12068.

Further resources

Activity guidelines:

Department of Health and Social Care (2019). *Physical activity guidelines.* https://assets. publishing.service.gov.uk/government/uploads/system/uploads/attachment_data/ file/832861/2-physical-activity-for-children-and-young-people-5-to-18-years.pdf.

Department of Health and Social Care (2022). *Physical activity guidelines: Disabled children and disabled young people.* (https://www.gov.uk/government/publications/physical-activity-guidelines-disabled-children-and-disabled-young-people).

Healthy Eating Tips

NHS live well, eat well pages: The Eatwell Guide - NHS (www.nhs.uk)

Public Health England (2018). The Eatwell Guide. https://assets.publishing.service.gov.uk/ government/uploads/system/uploads/attachment_data/file/528194/Eatwell_guide_ greyscale.pdf.

Sleep Tips

Sleep tips for children: https://www.nhsggc.org.uk/kids/life-skills/sleep/

Credits:

Sleep handouts adapted from Exeter University Wellbeing workbook: Get to bed and get some sleep! (Help yourself to improve your sleep). Authors: Jenny Cadman and Josie Bannon.

Exercise/activity worksheets adapted from Exeter University Wellbeing workbook: Busting the Blues: Getting Active – Help yourself to lift your mood. Author: Josie Bannon, Exeter University Wellbeing Services.

15

Behavioural Problems and Parenting

Mark Kime

Introduction

This chapter will focus on the use of a Low-Intensity Parenting intervention when working with parent(s)/carer(s) of a child who has been displaying mild to moderate behavioural difficulties. Within this chapter the key principles and activities will be explored and demonstrated. This will be applied to the case scenario of Elna, who was introduced within the assessment chapter. Exploration of some of the evidence base underpinning the approach will be identified and discussed. Step by step guidance is provided on the use of a parenting intervention workbook which contains psychoeducational information, collaborative activities and worksheets to support the delivery of this intervention. This is available to access as a free resource and can be found at: https://swcypiapt.com/resources/publications/

Brief parenting interventions have the potential to extend the reach and impact of parenting interventions and to steer children away from a trajectory of persistent behavioural problems (Tully & Hunt, 2016). There is now developing recognition that in order to extend the accessibility of parenting interventions a variety of more flexible 'low-intensity' interventions are required (Sanders & Kirby, 2010). Low-intensity interventions typically have a duration of eight sessions or less (Bradley et al., 2003). They may be individual or group interventions as well as self-directed interventions, where parents work through materials on their own with minimal or no therapist assistance. These can be offered as the first step as part of a stepped-care approach, with more intensive interventions offered to those who require more support (Haaga, 2000). The developing research into 'Low-Intensity' or 'Brief' parenting interventions identifies that these parenting interventions result in similar positive outcomes to more intensive therapist-led interventions (Tarver et al., 2004). Brief parenting interventions may be effective in reducing child externalising behaviours and dysfunctional parenting for parents seeking help for emerging problem behaviours in their young children across a range of settings and behaviours (Tully & Hunt, 2016).

The Low-Intensity Parenting Intervention Approach

This Low-Intensity guided self-help intervention rests upon the evidence base of social learning theory informed parenting interventions (Gardner & Leijten, 2017). Key components within the approach include psychoeducation, experiential learning activity and home practice activity. The intervention described here is supported by a workbook which has been developed to be used by practitioners in collaboration with parents and/or carers and is available on the accompanying website.

The intervention consists of six sessions, with each session providing a specific focus in order to cover key content. Though the sessions 'principles' are identified to support parent/carer understanding of behaviour. Reflection upon parental response to behaviour is explored, and opportunities are sought to implement positive and non-harmful approaches to supporting behaviour change in both parent behaviour and the behaviour of the child. Common factor skills are applied in the collaborative facilitation of the intervention and include active listening skills, warmth and empathy (Lambert & Barley, 2002). Recognising the parent/carer experience is an important element of the intervention, and alongside the information giving, can lead to the development of a shared understanding of the importance of the parent and child relationship (Irwin et al., 2007).

The intervention is delivered to parents/carers of a child for whom the assessment has identified mild to moderate behavioural difficulties. This should be guided by the content of information gathered during the LI assessment with particular attention paid to the Problem Statement, Child & Parental Goals for therapy, and routine outcome measures (ROMs) including the Parent reported Strength and Difficulties Questionnaire (SDQ-P; Goodman, 2001), the Parent reported Oppositional Defiance Disorder (ODD-P; Carter, 2014), the Brief Parental Efficacy Scale (BPSES; Selwyn et al., 2016) and Child Outcome Rating Scale (CORS; Anker et al., 2009). Case management supervision supports a decision on suitable treatment options for the child and parent. These are discussed collaboratively with the parent in a shared decision-making approach to the intervention applied.

The intervention workbook provides an overview of treatment and introduces two key principles. These are **the Reinforcement Principle**: Behaviour that is reinforced immediately is more likely to reoccur and **the Attention Principle:** Children's behaviour is often oriented to gaining attention from others, especially parents or carers. Additional psychoeducational content is included within the treatment overview. Concepts are provided to normalise the challenges that parents/carers may experience in relation to their own role in maintaining some behaviour difficulties.

The six sessions provide support in identifying less desired behaviours, and to reflectively explore the parent/carer's responses to these behaviours. The foundations of the intervention are found within the relational context of the parent and child experiences. Sessions increase opportunities for positive interactions to support and maintain the development of the relationship. The principle is to emphasise that behaviour communicates a need, and that young children desire attention from their care provider. A focus is given to supporting the importance of investing in the parent and child relationship.

The Theory behind the Intervention

The low-intensity cognitive behaviour parenting intervention has a broad theoretical base, which draws upon social learning theory. There is not scope within this chapter to explore this theory in full. Readers interested in learning more about theoretical underpinnings are directed towards exploring references provided. The work of Skinner (1985) and Bandura (1989) highlights the importance of observed behaviour acting as a model which the child will follow. Further components draw upon cognitive and attribution theories and the development of increasing parental self-esteem and self-confidence (Abramson et al., 1978; D'Zurilla & Nezu, 1982). Influence is drawn from the seminal work of Bowlby and others in exploring attachment and relationship theories (Bowlby, 1987; Bowlby, 1988; Grossmann et al., 2006).

Key Elements of the Low-Intensity Parenting Intervention

- Understanding a child's behaviour as a communication of need
- Exploring parental experiences of child behaviour through thoughts, feelings and behaviour
- Supporting the parent and child relationship though child directed play
- Using the power of positive praise to increase desired behaviours
- Using clear and calm communication to establish realistic expectations of child behaviour
- Using selective attention to support behaviour change

Each session provides the opportunity to discuss content and engage in activities. Through the use of different activities, the practitioner and parent(s)/carer(s) can rehearse key learning and skills, with feedback given to support development. The experience of rehearsal of skills can promote reflection upon ways of responding to the child within the context of a supportive therapeutic alliance. Here, the modelling process can be supportive of developing parental responses.

The 6-Session Protocol for LI CBT Parenting Intervention Using the Guided Self-Help Workbook

The intervention will be explored and applied to the case of Elna, who was introduced during the assessment chapter. Elna's mother, Katrina has received notification from school about some difficulties Elna has been experiencing in class. Elna has been refusing to do her classwork and has become disruptive when asked to complete tasks both independently and with peers. It is said Elna has been rude to the teaching and support staff and has started to leave the classroom. Elna has recently destroyed her own work and some displays of other children's work in the classroom. Katrina has also noticed similar behaviours at home and has recently found it difficult to know what to do. Katrina feels that the behaviour her daughter is displaying is having a negative impact on their relationship and feels sad.

Session 1 – Understanding Child Behaviour

Session 1 provides an overview of the parenting intervention. Psychoeducation is offered to explore the 'attention principle': that children desire attention from their caregiver. This leads into discussion of the 'reinforcement principle': that undesired behaviours can draw attention from the caregiver, and therefore become reinforced. Parents and caregivers are invited to share their thoughts and observations on these principles and consider how they may be relevant to their child's behaviour. Reflection upon the caregiver's own childhood experiences can also be helpful to support consideration of whether this provides an influence on their current ways of responding to the child.

This initial reflection explores an understanding of how **a child's behaviour communicates a need** from the caregiver, and that different patterns can emerge. Maslow's (1943) hierarchy of needs can be used as a framework to consider where the child's needs may lie. Therefore, needs for safety, belonging and self-esteem could be seen to contribute to the child's use of behaviour to communicate. Having established this lens around behaviour, the practitioner can use key skills of empathy and curiosity to explore the experience of the **child's** less desired behaviours and preferred behaviours (see Box 15.1). See accompanying website worksheet 15.1 for illustration of a worksheet used to identify these different types of behaviour to support a shared understanding.

Exploring Preferred Behaviours

Practitioner: So, I wonder if you could think about the things you would like to see more of from your daughter and the things which you would like to see less of. Let's start with those things which you would like to see more of from Elna. What are the things you see from Elna that help you know that you are feeling closer? What would you see from Elna if she was calm and feeling happy?

Katrina: Well, I love it when we can spend time together and we talk about things which we like. Sometimes we sit together and read and talk about our favourite books.

| Practitioner: | It sounds like that's a really important experience for you when you both have time together and can talk to each other? What else would you like to see more of from Elna? |

Once the nature of the child's behaviour is identified, the focus can move to exploring key preferred and less desired behaviours that the **parent/caregiver** can display (also worksheet 15.1). In this way an opportunity is developed to reflectively consider their experience of their own reactions. Exploration of any possible parental/caregiver maintaining factors can then be explored. This could include any coercive cycles (Lunkenheimer et al., 2016; Patterson et al., 1992; Ried & Patterson, 1989), where caregivers may offer a punitive response to behaviour such as shouting, threatening, rejecting, or expressing anger and physical aggression. These responses can provoke less desired behaviour from the young person, leading to further punitive responses from the parent. In this way a coercive cyclical process is maintained.

Alternatively, exploration of caregiver responses may also help to identify the common parenting experience of accidental reward cycles (Sanders & Turner, 2019). This involves a less desired behaviour being unintentionally rewarded. For example, a child who starts to communicate with less desired behaviours may be placated with food, which may act as a positive reinforcement for the behaviour, thereby making the behaviour more likely to be repeated.

Exploration of the caregiver's own experience is supported with the introduction of the 'Thoughts, Feelings, Behaviour cycle' (see Figure 15.1; White et al., 2003) which as a descriptive formulation diagram is familiar to the LI CBT practitioner. The relationship between these different domains is considered by asking the care-giver about a recent experience of less desired behaviour. The model is personalised to the caregiver's experience through identifying their cognitions, emotions and behaviours in the example found. It is essential that the practitioner offers empathy and an explicit non-judgemental approach in looking to understand the caregiver's experience. This may feel a difficult task for the caregiver for many reasons, so the supportive alliance becomes key.

A final activity in session 1 is the **'what'** about behaviours worksheet (see Figure 15.2). This draws upon functional analysis (Haynes & O'Brien, 1990) to support information gathering to understand the need a behaviour is seeking to meet. This means having a clear sense of **what** happened before a behaviour occurs, considering **what** the behaviour is seeking to communicate, **what** the response to the behaviour is, and **what** the outcome of this response is. This analysis can support understanding of the function of less desired behaviours. In other words: what is the behaviour able to achieve or seeking to achieve? From this approach awareness of patterns in behaviour may begin to emerge. For example, it may be that behaviours are triggered when a young person experiences physiological symptoms linked to feeling unsafe or distanced from caregivers. There may also be patterns in the response to behaviour, for example, the

Thoughts, Feelings and Behaviour Cycle

Let's explore the impact of child behaviour on your own thoughts feelings and behaviours.

Let's think of a recent experience where there were some difficult behaviours we had to manage. Let's use the form below to track our own responses to this experience.

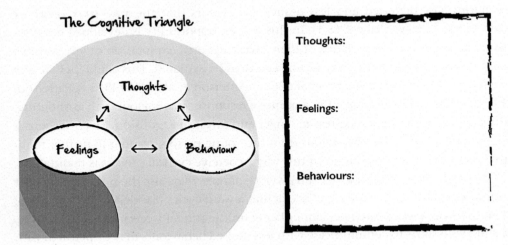

Figure 15.1 The Thoughts, Feelings and Behaviour Cycle

Source: CEDAR, 2021

withdrawal of caregiver demands when feeling anxious. The 'what' about behaviours sheet therefore explores the antecedents (what was happening before, who was around, what time of day), behaviours (what did the child say or do) and the consequences (what was said or done to help as a response) of that behaviour and its impact.

Importantly, there is also space for the parent to record their own thoughts, feelings, and behaviours in relation to the incident. This places the parent experience as a valuable asset in understanding the incident and validates the complexity of their individual experience. A clinical example transcript (clinical example 1) is provided on the accompanying resources website address at the end of this chapter.

Key Points from Session 1

- Behaviour is seen as a 'communication of need'
- Children desire attention from their caregiver, this can shape change
- Identify specific desired behaviours, and specific less desired behaviours
- Explore the parent/caregiver experience of their own thoughts, feelings, and behaviours in relation to difficult behaviours
- Explore the function of behaviour to communicate the child's needs.
- Home activity is set to track specific behaviour from the child

BEHAVIOURAL PROBLEMS AND PARENTING | 213

The 'What' about Behaviours
– Communication and Behaviour Record

Keep a note of behaviours using the 'What' about behaviours sheet(s).

What was happening before the problem behaviour occurred? Where did the problem behaviour happen? Who was / not around? What part of the day was it?	What did you see, hear from the problem behaviour? What was the problem behaviour communicating?	What did you do to help manage the problem behaviour? What did you say / not say? How did you communicate that the behaviour was a problem and not the child?	What were your thoughts and emotions after the problem? Intensity 1-5
			Thoughts: Emotions: Behaviour:

Figure 15.2 The 'What about behaviours' activity Session 1

Source: CEDAR, 2021

Session 2 – Connection before Correction

Sessions now begin with a review of activity from the previous session (see Figure 15.3). This provides the practitioner with the opportunity to model principles of the intervention, and to positively reinforce caregiver use of them. Key therapeutic skills for this will include active listening (Pavuluri & Smith, 1996), the use of empathy, validation of caregiver experience in undertaking planned activities (Feder & Diamond, 2016), curiosity, reframing, the use of positive descriptive labelled praise (Eames

Home Practice Feedback Review:

Completed HPF: Y / N:

What went well?

Any barriers / problem solving:

Figure 15.3 Home practice feedback review from the LI CBT parenting workbook

Source: CEDAR, 2021

et al., 2010) and problem solving. Exploring home practice can further examine the potential thought, feeling, behaviour cycle. This can reinforce the bidirectional relationship between these domains, as well as supporting reflective capacity and insight into their own experience during incidents of less desired behaviour. (See clinical example 2 on website for further illustration).

The second session supports the development of the parent and child relationship by promoting brief positive interactions. This is developed through the use of 'child directed play' (Webster-Stratton & Reid, 2010). Here, increased dedicated time for the caregiver and child to be together and immersed in a playful interaction is promoted. The psychoeducational content of this session relates to the importance of play in supporting social, emotional, and cognitive development. Practitioners should review and summarise the information provided in relation to this key topic and spend some time exploring the caregiver's perception of play, including both their experience of playing with their child and of play when they were a child. Strength in playing and any barriers to this can be explored, validated, or problem solved to increase caregiver awareness of the importance of child directed play.

Using Child Directed Play

Information is provided within the workbook (see website) which practitioners can review with caregivers to inform discussion of child directed play with the child. Guidance on conducting child directed play is included as the 'Do' and 'Try to' of play. Practitioners can be curious with caregivers in planning for these playful interactions and problem solve any barriers in relation to the caregiver implementing the process of child directed play. These interactions should be short, frequent, consistent and fun. Recommendations for implementing child directed play may include 10 minutes a day at a time when the caregiver can consistently maintain these interactions (Lorenzo & Bagner, 2022).

Experiential learning is a key element of the LI parenting intervention and there are opportunities for the practitioner to model the concepts of child directed play with the caregiver. This provides an opportunity for the caregiver to hear the use of descriptive commentary and experience the effect of positive attention during a playful interaction (Smith et al., 2015) and practice this principle before implementing this with their child (see website worksheet 15.2). Practitioners should normalise any unease in completing these rehearsal activities and model the specific factors skills, such as the use of positive descriptive praise, and problem solving to promote active engagement from the caregiver (see box 15.2).

Child Directed Play Commentary Practice

Practitioner: It would be great to give some of these ideas about child directed play a go together. It may help to get a sense of what this might feel like for Elna, and to see if this prompts any questions to help you give this a go at home with Elna. Could you choose a few of these toys I have brought, pick out a few and if you start playing with them, I'll use descriptive commentary whilst you play. Is that OK with you?

Katrina: Well, it feels a bit strange but OK I'll give it a try. I'll choose this goat, this action figure, and these cars. (Katrina begins to move the toys around and play with them.)

Practitioner: I can see that you have chosen the blue car and its driving away from the action figure. It's going very slowly. You look like you might be thinking about what to do next. Now the Goat has fallen over.

Katrina: He's asleep. The yellow car is coming to wake him up to see if he wants to go to the farmhouse to find the farmer.

Practitioner: You are making up a whole story about the toys, that's very creative of you. I can see that you are smiling as you are playing. You look happy and relaxed now. The goat is driving the yellow car and the blue car is following behind them, they are both speeding up and driving in big circles.

Katrina: I'm driving fast because the car is broken and has no brakes. The goat likes the speed but doesn't know the car is broken!

Practitioner: You are really getting into the story now and your ideas are so interesting. I like the way you are creating a story and enjoying the game so much. OK, Katrina, let's stop there. Can you tell me what you noticed about that short piece of play?

Experiential activities offer further opportunity for reflection with practitioner support, and could include the thought, feeling, behaviour cycle. Caregivers are supported to plan home practice of child directed play prior to the next session. The use of a handout prompts planning and recording of the experience of this (see website worksheet 15.3).

Key Points from Session 2

- Collaborative review of prior home activity.
- Practitioner models principles from the intervention, including the use of positive descriptive labelled praise for the parent/caregiver's efforts.
- Problem solving is applied to support the parent/caregiver to undertake home activities.
- Provide experiential learning to support parent/caregiver understanding and implementation of child led play.

Session 3 – The Power of Positive Praise.

The power of social rewards, such as positive attention, smiles, and affection can easily be overlooked. Caregivers may hold the belief that children should be able to behave appropriately without any specific recognition of their positive behaviours; with praise being reserved only to reinforce exceptional behaviours. By increasing parental awareness of the value of social rewards, there are myriad opportunities to reinforce all desirable behaviours. This can create a communication pattern which supports the development of clear expectations from the caregiver to the child as to what behaviours are more acceptable within the caregiver and child relationship.

Session 3 focuses upon the role of communication and positive reinforcement of desired behaviours. This relates to the underpinning attention principle – what we pay attention to we may see more of. By recognising the efforts and achievements of children, caregivers are able to reinforce these behaviours with their own attention. This is a free resource and is key to supporting behaviour change in children.

Psychoeducational content of this session focuses upon the effective use of 'positive labelled praise' (Bamford et al., 2018) to reinforce the development and maintenance of desirable behaviours. Where caregivers are able to notice and attend to behaviours which they would like to see repeated, this increases the likelihood of the child repeating these behaviours. Information is provided on the delivery and effective use of praise statements to support the underlying attention principle. Guidance is provided to support caregivers in how they can use specific and sincere praise statements to reinforce the desirable behaviours from the child (see website 'clinical example 3' for further illustration).

Experiential activities support the caregiver to practice the creation of a positive labelled praise statement about themselves. This will enable the parent to experience the impact of self-praise on their own thoughts, feelings and behaviour. The practitioner will also support the parent to consider the development of specific labelled praise statements for the identified target behaviours for their child (see website worksheet 15.4).

Key Points from Session 3

- Use positive labelled praise to support the development of self-esteem and motivation in children.
- Collaboratively explore ways of using positive praise.
- Model the use of positive labelled praise throughout the intervention.
- Aim for the parent/caregiver to understand how it feels to receive this specific attention to increase the likelihood of parents/caregivers implementing this principle.
- Home activity to support use.

Session 4 – Clear Calm Communication

Session 4 provides information on 'clear and calm communication' (Morawska et al., 2019), the development of family rules and making commands more effective. It is important to reinforce desirable behaviours with social and tangible rewards to support the development and maintenance of preferred behaviour. Caregivers are supported to be aware of habitual communication patterns within the parent-child relationship and to consider how these patterns impact both child behaviour and caregiver response.

Psychoeducational content explores the development of family rules to support the communication of expectations within the caregiver-child relationship. Having clear information on the expectations of the child's behaviour, via agreed rules, prompts the parent to role model these expectations, and to notice when the child's behaviour is in line with the agreed rules. This can then be responded to with social rewards to acknowledge and celebrate these behaviours.

Psychoeducational content considers changes in communication patterns with some helpful concepts for parents to consider when making requests of their child. This can increase the likelihood of the child complying with the caregiver's requests. Discussion with the caregiver explores their use of communication, and an activity supports identification and practice of using a positive command (see website 'clinical example 4' and worksheet 15.5 for further illustration). The use of social and tangible rewards is also considered, with some helpful information in relation to setting up reward systems with children to support the establishment and maintenance of desirable behaviours.

Key Points from Session 4

- Practitioner to be curious with the parent/caregiver about their experiences of communicating with the child by exploring the use of 'family rules.'
- Support consideration of developing rules for the family which are positively stated, inclusive, clear and creative.
- Consider ways to develop communication and explore how small changes in requests may increase the likelihood of the child responding differently.
- Workbook support to develop clear and calm communication.
- Use of social rewards to acknowledge when children respond to requests.

Sessions 5 and 6 – Limit Setting: Selective Attention, Logical Consequences, and Time-Out to Calm Down

The final two sessions in the intervention focus upon limit setting (Leijten et al., 2015; Webster-Stratton & Reid, 2018). There is a specific focus on self-regulation and co-regulation through the use of **selective attention** and **time-out to calm down**. Children's development includes seeking to test the boundaries laid down by their

218 | LOW-INTENSITY PRACTICE WITH CYP AND FAMILIES

caregivers. Caregivers looking to develop a more consistent approach to limit setting may experience the child testing these boundaries to see if caregivers are able to maintain boundaries in a consistent way. Children may seek a more familiar pattern of negative reinforcement, which may have been present within a prior approach.

The rationale for selective attention is straightforward. Children's behaviour is maintained by the attention it receives. By withdrawing attention from less desired behaviours and focusing positive attention on desirable behaviours, caregivers can build on the communication of the family agreements and expectations. Children are able to learn that they will receive the attention and connection that they require by repeating more desirable behaviours. Attempts to seek attention from undesirable behaviours will then naturally reduce over time.

The challenge for practitioners is to support caregivers to differentiate between withdrawing attention from the undesirable behaviour, and not from the child; and to support caregivers to be able to regulate their own emotional response to the child, who may be testing the consistency of the parents' boundaries. This is a significant and challenging concept. A focus of session 5 is therefore to support the parent to consider some 'calming thoughts' to support self-regulation and model this concept for their child.

Key Points from Session 5

- The 'Attention Principle' is revisited to explore the concept of using attention to reduce less desired behaviours.
- Explore any challenges in focusing on the withdrawal of attention from less desired behaviours.
- Consideration is given to managing the parent/caregiver's own responses to child behaviour.
- Use of calming thoughts to support self-regulation.
- Revisit the thoughts, feelings, and behaviours cycle to explore the impact of thoughts.

Natural and Logical Consequences and Time-Out to Calm Down

One of the most important factors of supporting a child with their emotions and behaviours is to respond in a consistent way. The concept of using natural and logical consequences and time-out to calm down are strategies to provide caregivers with a structured and non-harmful way of developing a consistent response to the child's behaviour. They can also support caregivers to feel more in control of their responses to complex and challenging experiences.

Natural and logical consequences are principles which support the child to learn from their mistakes and for caregivers to support children to learn independence and foster a sense of responsibility. Natural consequences are the natural results of decisions and choices which children make and are not imposed by parents or caregivers. For example, if Elna walks through a muddy puddle in her smart school shoes, the natural consequence is that she may get wet feet. A logical consequence is one imposed by the caregiver and should link to the behaviour as a negative consequence. For example, if Elna breaks a remote control by throwing it, the parent may suggest that she must complete chores to earn money to replace it. Practitioners will support caregivers to understand the principle of natural and logical consequences for the child's behaviour and consider how the caregiver may apply these principles in relation to the specific less desired behaviours (see website worksheet 15.6).

Time-Out to Calm Down

Children's emotional and social wellbeing is supported by loving and nurturing connections (Golding, 2008) clear communication, enriching interactions, clear expectations, and positive reinforcement (Vanschoonlandt et al., 2012). Time-out to calm down is a principle which offers a consistent and safe way for parents to model self-regulation, support their child to regulate their emotions, and provide non-harmful limits for less desired behaviour. Most parents/caregivers have tried varying approaches to discipline and may have individual reflections on their experiences of these. The practitioner provides information to support understanding and setting up time-out to calm down. This is used to manage more challenging behaviours and when children are not able to comply with requests made by the caregiver. A flow chart supports implementation of a time-out routine for caregivers to follow to promote a safe and non-harmful approach to responding consistently to a child's less desired behaviour (see Figure 15.4). See website 'clinical example 5' for further clinical illustration.

Key Points from Session 6

- Consideration of natural and logical consequences relating to child behaviour.
- Support parents/caregivers with non-harmful approaches to managing difficult behaviours.
- A consistent and calm approach to responding to difficult interactions.
- Use of Time-out to Calm Down as a response to less desired behaviours.

Summary

This chapter has highlighted the use of the workbook and steps involved in a LI parenting intervention for behaviour. Examples have been provided throughout with the case of Elna to support use. A focus is placed upon seeking to understand the communication

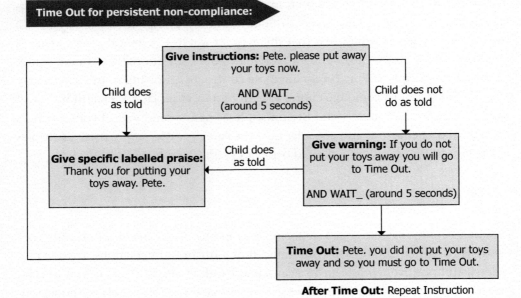

Figure 15.4 Example of time-out to calm down routine
Source: CEDAR, 2021

of need through behaviour, and to provide ways to promote positive interactions, praise these, and manage challenges. Understanding of the thoughts, feelings and behaviours cycle and experiential learning, support the application of the intervention and the parent-child relationship. Readers are encouraged to access the intervention workbook which includes additional information to support practitioners and parents/caregivers to explore further strategies including maintaining progress. This is free to access and can be found with other resources at: https://cedar.exeter.ac.uk/resources/cyp/

References

Abramson, L., Seligman, M., & Teasdale, J. (1978). Learned helplessness in humans: Critique and reformulation. *Journal of Abnormal Psychology, 87*(1), 49–74.

Anker, M.G., Duncan, B.L., & Sparks, J.A. (2009). Using client feedback to improve couple therapy outcomes: A randomized clinical trial in a naturalistic setting. *Journal of Consulting and Clinical Psychology, 77*(4), 693–704.

Bamford, A., Mackew, N., & Golawski, A. (2018). Coaching for parents: Empowering parents to create positive relationships with their children. In van Nieuwerburgh (Ed.), *Coaching in education* (pp. 133–152). Routledge.

Bandura, A. (1989). Regulation of cognitive processes through perceived self-efficacy. *Developmental Psychology, 25*(5), 729–735.

Bowlby, J. (1987). Defensive processes in the light of attachment theory.

Bowlby, J. (1988). *A secure base. Parent-child attachment and healthy human development*. Basic Books.

Bradley, S.J., Jadaa, D.A., Brody, J., Landy, S., Tallett, S.E., Watson, W., ... & Stephens, D. (2003). Brief psychoeducational parenting program: An evaluation and 1-year follow-up. *Journal of the American Academy of Child & Adolescent Psychiatry, 42*(10), 1171–1178.

Carter, M.J. (2014). Diagnostic and statistical manual of mental disorders. *Therapeutic Recreation Journal, 48*(3), 275–277.

D'Zurilla, T.J., & Nezu, A. (1982). Social problem solving in adults. In P.C. Kendall (Ed.), *Advances in cognitive–behavioral research and therapy* (pp. 201–274). Academic Press.

Eames, C., Daley, D., Hutchings, J., Whitaker, C.J., Bywater, T., Jones, K., & Hughes, J.C. (2010). The impact of group leaders' behaviour on parents' acquisition of key parenting skills during parent training. *Behaviour Research and Therapy, 48*(12), 1221–1226.

Feder, M.M., & Diamond, G.M. (2016). Parent-therapist alliance and parent attachment-promoting behaviour in attachment-based family therapy for suicidal and depressed adolescents. *Journal of Family Therapy, 38*(1), 82–101.

Gardner, F., & Leijten, P. (2017). Incredible years parenting interventions: Current effectiveness research and future directions. *Current Opinion in Psychology, 15*, 99–104.

Golding, K.S. (2008). *Nurturing attachments: Supporting children who are fostered or adopted*. Jessica Kingsley Publishers.

Goodman, R. (2001). Psychometric properties of the strengths and difficulties questionnaire. *Journal of the American Academy of Child and Adolescent Psychiatry, 40*(11), 1337–1345.

Grossmann, K.E., Grossmann, K., & Waters, E. (Eds.). (2006). *Attachment from infancy to adulthood: The major longitudinal studies*. Guilford Press.

Haaga, D.A. (2000). Introduction to the special section on stepped care models in psychotherapy. *Journal of Consulting and Clinical Psychology, 68*(4), 547.

Haynes, S.N., & O'Brien, W.H. (1990). Functional analysis in behavior therapy. *Clinical Psychology Review, 10*(6), 649–668.

Irwin, L.G., Siddiqi, A., & Hertzman, G. (2007). *Early child development: A powerful equalizer*. Human Early Learning Partnership

Lambert, M.J., & Barley, D.E. (2002). Research summary on the therapeutic relationship and psychotherapy outcome. In J.C. Norcross (Ed.), *Psychotherapy relationships that work: Therapist contributions and responsiveness of patients*. Oxford University Press.

Leijten, P., Dishion, T.J., Thomaes, S., Raaijmakers, M.A., Orobio de Castro, B., & Matthys, W. (2015). Bringing parenting interventions back to the future: How randomized microtrials may benefit parenting intervention efficacy. *Clinical Psychology: Science and Practice, 22*(1), 47–57.

Lorenzo, N.E., & Bagner, D.M. (2022). Impact of a behavioral parenting intervention in infancy on maternal emotion socialization. *Child Psychiatry and Human Development, 53*(3), 469–478.

Lunkenheimer, E., Lichtwarck-Aschoff, A., Hollenstein, T., Kemp, C.J., & Granic, I. (2016). Breaking down the coercive cycle: How parent and child risk factors influence real-time variability in parental responses to child misbehavior. *Parenting, 16*(4), 237–256.

Maslow, A.H. (1943). A theory of human motivation. *Psychological Review, 50*(4), 370–396.

Morawska, A., Dittman, C.K., & Rusby, J.C. (2019). Promoting self-regulation in young children: The role of parenting interventions. *Clinical Child and Family Psychology Review, 22*(1), 43–51.

Patterson, G.R., Reid, J.B., & Dishion, T.J. (1992). *Antisocial boys. A social interactional approach, Vol. 4*. Castalia Publishing Company.

Pavuluri, M., & Smith, M. (1996). Principles and practice of Cognitive Behaviour Therapy in working with parents of young children with behaviour disorder. *Australasian Journal of Early Childhood, 21*(2), 22–27.

Reid, J.B., & Patterson, G.R. (1989). The development of antisocial behaviour patterns in childhood and adolescence. *European Journal of Personality, 3*(2), 107–119.

Sanders, M.R., & Kirby, J.N. (2010). Parental programs for preventing behavioral and emotional problems in children. *Oxford guide to low intensity CBT interventions,* 399–406.

Sanders, M.R., & Turner, K.M. (2019). The triple P system: Parenting support for every family. In B.H. Fiese, M. Celano, K. Deater-Deckard, E.N. Jouriles, & M.A. Whisman (Eds.), *APA handbook of contemporary family psychology: Family therapy and training* (pp. 409–424). American Psychological Association.

Selwyn, J., Golding, K., Alper, J., Smith, B.G., & Hewitt, O. (2016). A quantitative and qualitative evaluation of the nurturing attachments group programme. *AdoptionPlus,* 42.

Skinner, B.F. (1985). Cognitive science and behaviourism. *British Journal of Psychology, 76*(3), 291–301.

Smith, E., Koerting, J., Latter, S., Knowles, M.M., McCann, D.C., Thompson, M., & Sonuga-Barke, E.J. (2015). Overcoming barriers to effective early parenting interventions for attention-deficit hyperactivity disorder (ADHD): Parent and practitioner views. *Child: Care, Health and Development, 41*(1), 93–102.

Tarver-Behring, S., & Spagna, M.E. (2004). Counseling with exceptional children. *Focus on Exceptional Children, 36*(8), 1–12.

Tully, L.A., & Hunt, C., (2016). Brief parenting interventions for children at risk of externalizing behavior problems: A systematic review. *Journal of Child and Family Studies, 25,* 705–719.

Vanschoonlandt, F., Vanderfaeillie, J., Van Holen, F., & De Maeyer, S. (2012). Development of an intervention for foster parents of young foster children with externalizing behavior: Theoretical basis and program description. *Clinical Child and Family Psychology Review, 15*(4), 330–344.

Webster-Stratton, C., & Reid, M.J. (2010). Parents, teachers, and therapists using child-directed play therapy and coaching skills to promote children's social and emotional competence and build positive relationships. In C.E. Schaefer (Ed.), *Play therapy for preschool children* (pp. 245–273). American Psychological Association.

Webster-Stratton, C., & Reid, M.J., (2018). The Incredible Years parents, teachers, and children training series: A multifaceted treatment approach for young children with conduct problems. In J.R. Weisz & A.E. Kazdin (Eds.), *Evidence-based psychotherapies for children and adolescents* (pp. 122–141). The Guilford Press.

White, C., McNally, D., & Cartwright-Hatton, S. (2003). Cognitively enhanced parent training. *Behavioural and Cognitive Psychotherapy, 31*(1), 99–102.

16

Brief Guided Parent-Delivered CBT for Child Anxiety

Chloe Chessell, Gemma Halliday, and Cathy Creswell

Introduction

This chapter focuses on using brief guided parent-delivered CBT (GPD-CBT) to treat child anxiety problems. The specific approach outlined ('Helping Your Child with Fears and Worries: A self-help guide for parents'; Creswell & Willetts, 2019) has been developed and evaluated for parents/carers (from here on 'parents') of pre-adolescent children aged five to twelve years. Here, we describe the underpinning theory and evidence base and illustrate how to conduct the intervention using two case scenarios, with example worksheets and troubleshooting tips.

Introduction to the Intervention

In GPD-CBT, parents are supported by a practitioner to work through a book or audiobook (e.g., Creswell & Willetts, 2019) to help them support their child to overcome anxiety problems. The practitioner works primarily with parents to develop their skills and confidence in managing their children's difficulties. The latest version of this intervention (Halldorsson et al., 2019) consists of six sessions delivered over an eight-week period, with a total practitioner contact time of four hours 40 minutes. Four sessions (approx. 60 minutes) are conducted face-to-face (or by video-call) and two sessions (approx. 20 minutes) by telephone. Although this intervention has been delivered in individual and group formats, we focus on the individual approach as this has been evaluated systematically.

Fundamental Principles

The content is broadly similar to other interventions for child anxiety in this book, with the key difference being the fundamental principle of working collaboratively with parents to empower them. Practitioners help parents to support their child in gaining exposure to feared stimuli, so opportunities are created for children to:

- learn new information about their fears
- build confidence in their ability to cope in feared situations
- build independence and autonomy

Core components include psychoeducation, identification of negative automatic thoughts/expectations, exposure, and problem solving. Practitioners support parents to individualise and apply these CBT techniques with their child by helping parents (a) rehearse key skills, (b) recognise their own skills and positive progress, and (c) problem solve challenges. Practice happens between sessions with home-based tasks being critical to bringing about change. For efficiency, parents read/listen to written materials before and between sessions and use worksheets to guide and record activities.

Theory behind the Intervention

Development and Maintenance of Child Anxiety

Child anxiety development is influenced by multiple interacting factors. Key interacting mechanisms include (a) an anxious predisposition, (b) restricted opportunities or negative life experiences, and/or (c) learning from others (for a comprehensive review see Murray et al., 2009; Creswell et al., 2015). For example, young children with an inhibited temperament are more likely to develop elevated anxiety in the context of certain parental behaviours (Hudson et al., 2019).

Anxiety in children is similarly *maintained* by multiple interacting factors (Cooper et al., 2009). Highly anxious children appear to respond to threat with a sense that (a) something bad will happen to them and/or others, and, particularly, (b) they won't be able to cope (e.g., Creswell & O'Connor, 2011; Waters et al., 2008); beliefs which are maintained by avoidance or other unhelpful coping. The responses of other people around the child may also inadvertently maintain the problem. Parental control has been most implicated (e.g., McLeod et al., 2007) on the basis that if parents excessively regulate children's behaviour and discourage independence then they are likely to (a) communicate that the world is dangerous and uncontrollable, and (b) prevent the child from developing competence and mastery, reinforcing avoidance.

However, it has been demonstrated that increased control is a normative response to child anxiety (e.g., Hudson et al., 2009), although it may then reinforce anxiety among children with a more anxious disposition (Thirlwall & Creswell, 2010). In other words, these are understandable and natural responses drawn out of parents and others by anxious children in attempts to help them. As such, a parent-led approach provides alternatives to responses that may inadvertently contribute to child anxiety maintenance, whilst improving efficiency by capitalising on parents' capacity to apply CBT strategies in their child's daily life.

Exposure

Exposure is considered the crucial ingredient for success in CBT with children (Peris et al., 2015; Plaisted et al., 2021; Whiteside et al., 2020). Recent experimental studies with adults suggest that 'learning by doing' and testing fears is more effective when negative expectations are violated by the exposure, i.e., exposure allows them to learn something new (e.g., Craske et al., 2008; Craske et al., 2014). Although it is currently unclear to what extent these findings generalise to children, in GPD-CBT we aim to optimise exposure by moving away from helping children to develop 'positive' or 'helpful' thoughts prior to exposure, as this may limit opportunities for expectancy violation and can risk feeling insensitive or coercive.

GPD-CBT focuses on helping children develop curiosity about possible outcomes in order to encourage approach to situations they avoid. We call this mental state 'have-a-go thinking' (Creswell & Willetts, 2019) and develop exposure plans around an analysis of **'what does the child need to learn'** to overcome their anxiety problem. This focus also moves away from a habituation-based approach, given findings (albeit with adults) that within-exposure fear reduction does not predict successful exposure outcomes (Craske et al., 2014). For similar reasons, and because of suggestions that treatment effects may be smaller for programmes that include relaxation (Whiteside et al., 2020), we do not include relaxation. Although there is some evidence (with adults) that conducting exposure in a graded way may not be the most effective approach (Craske et al., 2014), we deliberately take a gradual, step-by-step approach to allow children and parents to develop confidence through early positive experiences. Parents often, understandably, feel deskilled and disempowered by the time they access help and children may be less amenable to doing difficult things with their parents.

Evidence-Base for the Intervention

Although CBT for pre-adolescent child anxiety disorders is effective for many children (50 per cent recovery post-treatment; James et al., 2020), only a very small proportion who could benefit are able to access CBT (Reardon et al., 2020). Randomised controlled trials have shown that GPD-CBT is effective (Cobham, 2012; Rapee et al., 2006; Thirlwall et al., 2013), cost-effective compared to another brief intervention (solution-focused therapy) (Creswell et al., 2017), and acceptable to parents (Allard et al., 2022). Good outcomes have been achieved when GPD-CBT is delivered by novice practitioners who receive training and supervision (Thirlwall et al., 2013). For most children, treatment gains are maintained longer term, up to three to five years later (Brown et al., 2017). Good outcomes have still been achieved when parents themselves are highly anxious, with initial evidence suggesting GPD-CBT can still be offered without substantial adjustment (Hiller et al., 2016).

Some studies have not found clear differences between low-intensity GPD-CBT and more intensive approaches (Cobham, 2012). Pooled data across trials found no differences in treatment outcomes for GPD-CBT compared to individual child CBT for a primary diagnosis of generalised anxiety disorder, social anxiety disorder, or separation anxiety (McKinnon et al., 2018). However, outcomes were somewhat better from individual child CBT than GPD-CBT (and group CBT) for children with a specific phobia. This may reflect the benefits of practitioners working directly with children to tailor exposures in some circumstances, although good outcomes can still be achieved from GPD-CBT for phobias, and potentially more efficiently in terms of practitioner time.

Assessment

The key issue to confirm in a pre-treatment assessment is that anxiety is the child's primary presenting problem. Assessment should establish whether anxiety is disproportionate to the level of threat in the environment and that it is significantly interfering in the child's life. It is important to recognise that anxiety may be a proportionate response to environmental factors and in those cases would not be considered a 'disorder'; for example, is the child anxious about schoolwork because they have a specific learning disability that has not been addressed?

Whom Can I Offer GPD-CBT to?

GPD-CBT is a 'transdiagnostic' intervention, applying to a range of anxiety problems. There is not sufficient evidence to withhold offering it based on family or child clinical or demographic characteristics; for example, child age, higher symptom severity, and comorbid behavioural problems do not significantly predict outcomes (Thirlwall et al., 2017). In research trials it is the norm that children have co-occurring anxiety, mood, and/or behavioural problems (e.g., Leyfer et al., 2013). Therefore, if anxiety is the primary concern, then these should not necessarily be barriers. However, it is important to consider whether the symptoms of the co-occurring difficulty may make it difficult for the parent and/or child to engage with and use the strategies. If so, these may need to be addressed first. Anecdotally, GPD-CBT has been used successfully (with some adaptations) with parents of younger and older children aged two to 14 years (Cartwright-Hatton et al., 2011; Cobham, 2012), and with children with developmental delay or autism spectrum conditions, however, there is not a firm evidence base on which to make recommendations.

Intervention Overview

Session Structure

An overview of the content typically covered in each session is summarised in Table 16.1. Agreeing weekly contact encourages families to firmly prioritise practicing the intervention within busy lives.

Sessions adhere to the following structure, however, to ensure a collaborative approach, parents are always given the opportunity to contribute to the agenda at the start of the session:

- Agenda setting
- Routine outcome monitoring and brief update
- Review of home-based tasks
- Structured session activity
- Consideration of other issues parent adds to agenda
- Agree home-based tasks
- Brief review summarising main elements to ensure shared understanding

Communicating the Rationale

The central aim of GPD-CBT is to empower parents to feel confident in supporting their child. Understandably, parents may feel disempowered and demoralised by the time they reach help, so may want the practitioner to see their child. For successful engagement, it is crucial that parents understand the rationale and have an opportunity to express concerns, otherwise there is a risk of the parent concluding the practitioner thinks 'it's all their fault'. The assessment is a great starting point for this conversation, which continues into session one during psychoeducation.

Table 16.1 Table to show the overview of session content

Session	Format	Content
1	Face to face	Psychoeducation: anxiety maintenance and development 'SMART' goal setting
2	Face to face	Identifying anxious expectations and what the child needs to learn to overcome anxiety Promoting independence ('having a go')
3	Face to face	Testing fears (step-by-step plan)
4	Telephone/Videocall	Review
5	Face to face	Problem Solving
6	Telephone/Videocall	Review
1 month Follow-Up	Face to face	Review: discharge, monitor or step up

Source: Cathy Creswell, Monika Parkinson, Kerstin Thirlwall and Lucy Willetts. 'Parent-led CBT for Child Anxiety: helping parents help their kids'. Guildford Press, 2019. Reprinted with permission of Guilford Press.

LOW-INTENSITY PRACTICE WITH CYP AND FAMILIES

At the outset the practitioner can consider whether the parent is motivated, can attend regular sessions, and commit to the workload. It is important to share information (see Box 16.1) to address motivational issues and collaboratively and sensitively problem solve potential barriers (e.g., parental literacy or internet/device needs). Where two parents have different views on whether anxiety is a problem and/or what maintains or causes it, explore and acknowledge all viewpoints and emphasise that different views can be a hypotheses to be tested by giving the approach a good try.

Box 16.1 – Helpful Key Messages:

- Research has shown treatment to be just as effective when working with parents as when working with children.
- The same outcomes for children can be seen in fewer sessions.
- Parents know their children best and so are best placed to make changes.
- Many families tell us that they want to be able to manage their child's difficulties within the family and do not want their child to feel 'different' from missing school/ other activities to attend appointments.
- Parents can be more motivated than children to make changes as they are more likely to focus on long-term gain and to remember the strategies in future.
- Parents will be expected to read/listen before sessions, and to put their learning into practice with their child between sessions to be reviewed in session. We see the biggest changes when parents practise.

KEY TIP

The practitioner works **primarily with parents to help them develop skills and confidence** to help their child overcome anxiety problems, with parents working through a book/ audiobook. Assessment should identify whether **anxiety is the primary problem**. It is crucial parents are **on-board with the rationale** for the parent-led approach. GPD-CBT give parents **alternative ways of responding** to their anxious child to encourage them to test out fears and learn new information through exposure.

The Client Scenarios

Elna (eight years old) is experiencing worries about being separated from her mother Annika, which began six months after Annika was hospitalised with an illness. Despite Annika making a full recovery, Elna is worried about being away from her mother at bedtime and before school because she thinks that something bad will happen to herself or Annika. Understandably, these worries mean that Elna finds bedtime challenging and Annika is currently sleeping in Elna's bed with her most evenings. They both have a poor night's sleep and Elna struggles to concentrate at school, and Annika at work, the next day. Annika also spends prolonged periods of time in the car with Elna before school, reassuring her that nothing bad will happen, and Elna is often late going into school.

Theo (12 years old) started secondary school two months ago after attending a small primary school. Since starting Year 7, Theo is reluctant to talk to classmates he does not know and has found it difficult to ask the teacher questions in class when he does not understand. Theo says he feels sad because he recently fell out with his best friend. He thinks if he could make new friends, he would feel happier. Theo's mother, Florence, and stepdad, Steven, say that he has always been shy and has few friends. They think Theo is worried that his new peers will not like him and will laugh at him if he speaks up. They are keen to understand how to help Theo as his worries mean he is reluctant to join any school clubs, despite enjoying sport, and Florence worries he will struggle academically.

The Process of Conducting the Intervention

Below is a step-by-step guide on how to conduct this intervention using the client scenarios. Note – the handout numbers used below correspond to the handout numbers in the practitioner manual (Halldorsson et al., 2019). The worksheets identified here can be found on the accompanying website at: https://cedar.exeter.ac.uk/resources/cyp/

Session One (face-to-face): The practitioner explained the principles of CBT and explored Annika's views on the parent-led approach. The development of childhood anxiety was discussed, and Annika shared that she thought her illness had triggered Elna's worries, which made her feel guilty. First, the practitioner asked Annika to identify a recent situation/trigger for Elna's anxiety (see Figure 16.1).

Figure 16.1 HANDOUT 2, PART 1: Tigger or situation for Elna's anxiety

The practitioner then used open questions to help Annika to identify Elna's anxious expectations, physical responses, and behaviours, in response to this situation/trigger and explored how each of these factors keep Elna's anxiety going, using Handout 2, part 2 (see Figure 16.2).

The role that 'other people' (e.g., parents, teachers etc.) may inadvertently play in the maintenance of child anxiety was sensitively introduced and explored, using Handout 2, part 3 (see website Handout 2 part 3) and was set as a homework task (see Figure 16.3 for the completed example with Elna).

Three 'SMART' goals were identified which Annika was encouraged to discuss with Elna, including for Elna 'to be able to sleep in her bed, on her own, every night, for a

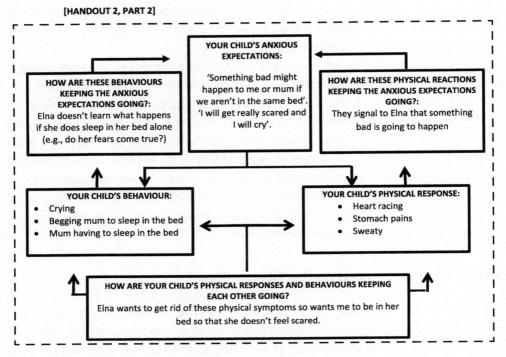

Figure 16.2 HANDOUT 2, PART 2: Elna's anxiety cycle

week', 'to be able to go straight into school when they arrive in the car, every morning, for two weeks' and 'to be able to go to a friend's house for a sleepover, once a month'.

Theo's maintenance cycle is identified on the website (Theo sheet 1, 2, 3 and 4). His 'SMART' goals were 'to ask a question in class, in front of his peers, twice a week, for two weeks' and 'to have a conversation with somebody different in his class, who he does not know, twice a week, for a month'. Given Theo's age, the practitioner emphasised the importance of Florence and Steven discussing these goals with Theo, to ensure he was on-board and motivated to work towards them. Florence and Steven were encouraged to make any changes/adaptations to the goals, as necessary, based on their discussions with Theo.

KEY TIP

It is important that parents do not feel blamed for their child's difficulties. We know that children's anxiety can provoke certain parental responses. Ensure you normalise parents' worries and concerns when discussing the development of childhood anxiety. When exploring the role of 'other people' in the maintenance of childhood anxiety, we purposely use the term 'other people' and keep this broad.

[Figure 16.3 HANDOUT 2, FULL VERSION: ELNA'S ANXIETY CYCLE]

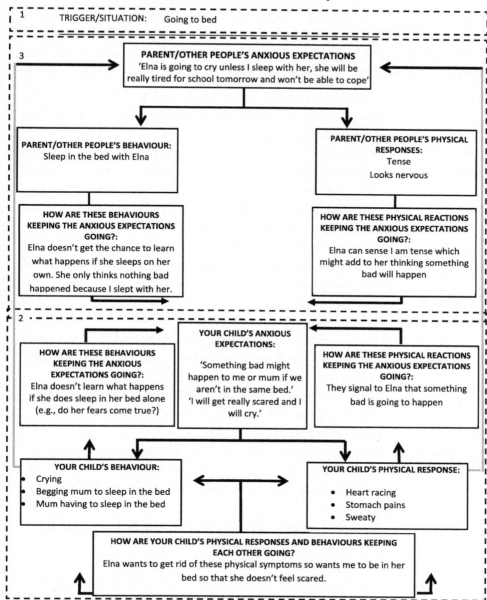

Figure 16.3 HANDOUT 2, FULL VERSION: ELNA'S ANXIETY CYCLE

Session Two (face-to-face): After reviewing the homework tasks, the practitioner explained this session would focus on helping Florence and Steven to identify Theo's anxious expectations in anxiety-provoking situations, so that they could identify what Theo needed to learn to overcome his anxiety and to achieve his goals. An in-session roleplay was

232 | LOW-INTENSITY PRACTICE WITH CYP AND FAMILIES

conducted with Florence and Steven, first, so that the practitioner could model key skills including asking open, curious questions, normalising, empathising with the child's experience, and checking understanding. Florence and Steven were then invited to have a go. The accompanying website contains illustration of this through 'Practice sheet 1 (Session 2, Theo)' and a transcript of the conversation with Theo's parents is given below:

[Practitioner]: Parents often find it helpful to have a practice at the key skills we have discussed, would you be happy for us to do this together now?

[Parents]: Um, [laughs], okay, we're a bit nervous but we can have a go!

[Practitioner]: That's okay, parents often find this nerve-wracking. To start with, I can pretend to be one of you, and one of you can pretend to be Theo, as you are the experts in Theo and how he might respond to these questions. We can then think about what might have worked well/not so well for Theo, before one/both of you can have a go at asking the questions. Does that sound okay?

[Parents]: Yes, that's okay

[Practitioner]: Okay, let's go into the roleplay now. Theo, I could see earlier that you were struggling to do your homework, is that right?

[Parent]: Yeah, I don't really understand it and I didn't want to ask the teacher for help.

[Practitioner]: It does look a bit tricky. I can see why you are finding it hard. Why was it that you didn't want to ask the teacher for help?

[Parent]: I don't know really.

[Practitioner]: Ah okay, was there anything that worried you about asking the teacher?

[Parent]: Um, there were lots of other people around, so I didn't really want to ask.

[Practitioner]: Hmm, and what is it about other people being around that made it difficult to ask the teacher?

[Parent]: I don't know, they might think I'm stupid or something.

[Practitioner]: That mustn't feel very nice Theo, if you are worried that people might think you are stupid. What do you think is the worst thing that might happen?

[Parent]: I guess that people will laugh at me and not want to be my friend.

[Practitioner]: Okay, so if you ask your teacher a question about the homework, you worry that people might think you are stupid and they might laugh at you or not want to be your friend, is that right?

BRIEF GUIDED PARENT-DELIVERED CBT FOR CHILD ANXIETY 233

Table 16.2 What does my child need to learn?

Goal	What does my child expect will happen?	What does my child need to learn?
For Theo to ask a question in class, in front of his peers, twice a week, for two weeks.	Theo thinks that other children will laugh at him and that he will get embarrassed. He thinks other children won't want to be his friend.	What happens if Theo asks a question in class? Will other children laugh at him? Will other children refuse to be his friend? If other children laugh/refuse to play with Theo, can he cope with this? Can he make other friends instead with children who he might enjoy spending time with?
For Theo to have a conversation with somebody different in his class, who he does not know, twice a week, for a month.	Theo thinks that if he tries to talk to someone new, they will ignore him and won't want to talk to him.	What happens if Theo tries to talk to someone new? Will they ignore him? If they don't want to talk to him, will this be as bad as Theo thinks? Can he cope in this situation and find someone else to talk to instead?

After completing the roleplay, the practitioner and parents considered what Theo's anxious expectations were for each goal, and what Theo needed to learn to achieve his goals (see Table 16.2). Florence and Steven were encouraged to use the questioning skills at home and add any further relevant information to the handout. Information on encouraging independence was discussed, and Florence and Steven were encouraged to identify possible rewards with Theo that could be drawn on in session three. Elna's anxious expectations and what she needed to learn to overcome her anxiety are shown on the accompanying website ('Practice sheet 2 What does my child need to learn – Elna).

KEY TIP

Parents often feel nervous or might be initially hesitant to do a roleplay with you. Approach this with a positive, non-judgemental, and normalising stance to encourage parents to 'have a go'.

Session Three (face-to-face): Annika identified the 'ultimate goal' that she and Elna wanted to work towards was for Elna 'to be able to sleep in her bed, on her own, every night, for a week'. This goal was broken down into smaller steps so that Elna could build confidence in testing her fears (and to make it easier for Annika to help her), specifically focusing on creating opportunities for Elna to learn new information about her fears and her ability to cope in her feared situation at bedtime. Annika rated how anxiety-provoking Elna would find each step from 0 (no anxiety) to 10 (very anxiety-provoking), and the steps were ordered from least to most anxiety-provoking. Each step was paired with an appropriate reward (see Figure 16.4 'Step-by-step plan - Elna) and Annika was encouraged to check the order of the steps and the rewards with Elna at home. Annika agreed to have a go at the first step with Elna this week, remembering to ask Elna before she tried the step what she thought would happen, and then to review afterwards what Elna learned from doing this step and to reward Elna if she managed to achieve this.

Step-by-step plan - Elna

PREDICTION	ULTIMATE GOAL For Elna to sleep in her own bed alone, for a week	ULTIMATE REWARD TO GO TO THE CINEMA
PREDICTION	**STEP 5** For Elna to sleep in her own bed alone, for one night	REWARD TO GET A FAVOURITE MAGAZINE
PREDICTION	**STEP 4** For Elna to go to sleep in her own bed, whilst mum is sat downstairs	REWARD TO PICK A FILM TO WATCH WITH MUM
PREDICTION	**STEP 3** For Elna to sleep in her own bed, whilst mum waits outside of her bedroom for her to fall asleep	REWARD HAVE A FRIEND OVER ON THE WEEKEND
PREDICTION	**STEP 2** For Elna to sleep in her own bed, whilst mum sits in the room and waits for her to fall asleep	REWARD TRIP TO THE SWEET SHOP ON THE WAY HOME FROM SCHOOL
PREDICTION SOMETHING BAD MIGHT HAPPEN TO ME OR MUM IF MUM DOESN'T SLEEP IN THE BED WITH ME	**STEP 1** For Elna to sleep in her own bed, whilst mum sleeps on the floor in her bedroom	REWARD BAKING CAKES ON THE WEEKEND

Figure 16.4   HANDOUT 8: ELNA'S STEP-BY-STEP PLAN

Theo's step-by-step plan is shown online ('step by step plan – Theo'). As Theo's plan would take place at school, the practitioner explored with Florence and Steven how they might discuss this plan with Theo's teacher, and encourage Theo to join in with this, to ensure there were adequate opportunities for Theo to have a go at these steps.

Parents were also encouraged to look out for natural opportunities for their children to learn new information about their fears and their ability to cope. For example, if Annika needed to pop into a shop on the way home from school, this could mean seeing if Elna could stay in the car on her own for a minute. Parents were encouraged to ask their child beforehand what they think would happen, encourage them to have a go, and then review afterwards what they learned from doing this, and to reward them for their efforts.

KEY TIP

It's important to encourage parents to discuss with their child what they think will happen before they try each step on their step-by-step plan, and then to ask their child afterwards what happened when they did the step, and what they learned from this. This will help children to maximise their learning from new information. This information is also key to see whether the step-by-step plan needs to be adapted moving forwards, for example, if Elna told her mother that the first step was only okay because she had her favourite teddy bear with her, the next step might be to encourage Elna to have a go at this step without her teddy.

Session Four (Telephone/Video call): Florence and Theo had not made any changes to their step-by-step plan, and Theo had completed the first step three times. Steven said that Theo was initially reluctant to 'have a go', however, he was motivated by the rewards to complete the step. Theo predicted that if he asked a pre-prepared question in class other children would laugh at him. He learned that, although he was nervous, nobody laughed. He was rewarded by some extra time playing computer games and was happy to have a go at the next step.

Session Five (face-to-face): Elna had learned she was able to go to sleep whilst Annika stood outside her bedroom door but was scared about what would happen if her mother was downstairs. Annika felt confident to continue using the step-by-step plan to help Elna to learn new information about her fears and her ability to sleep whilst Annika was downstairs. Annika had not been able to read the 'problem-solving' chapter of the book and agreed it would be helpful to review this after the session. The rationale for problem solving was explained and Annika was asked to identify a problem she had faced during the treatment so that the practitioner could illustrate the stages of problem solving (see website 'Problem Solving – Elna'). Annika was encouraged to use problem solving with Elna, focusing on allowing Elna to come up with her own suggestions on how to solve problems and choosing what she thought would be the best solution to implement.

KEY TIP

Sometimes, parents might not have completed the relevant homework task. In this instance discuss with the parent if there were any barriers to homework completion and normalise this challenge. Collaboratively explore possible solutions, make concrete plans to address them, and emphasise the importance of completing homework tasks so that parents and their child can get the maximum benefit. Praise the parent for any homework tasks they have been able to complete and explore what makes that possible.

Session Six (Telephone/Video call): Theo had been able to ask a spontaneous question in class, in front of a small group of peers. He'd learned that no one had laughed at him and the 'butterflies' in his stomach tended to go away. Florence and Steven had also looked out for natural opportunities for Theo to test his fears and had encouraged Theo to ask a shop assistant where they could find an ingredient to make his sister a birthday cake. Florence and Steven reflected on the techniques that had been most helpful during the treatment and what to continue working on now that treatment had finished; this can be supported by listing these (see website 'Reducing my child's anxiety – Theo', and 'Things for my child and me to work on').

Review

Parents are the key agent for change in this intervention, so it is essential that parents feel **valued** and **empowered** to help their child to overcome their anxiety difficulties. Practitioners can achieve this by **listening** to concerns and ensuring parents feel heard, **normalising** common parental experiences, providing **opportunities** for parents to practise key skills, **collaboratively trouble-shooting** challenges, and **recognising** positive changes the child experienced are the result of the parent's hard work.

Summary

GPD CBT has been illustrated as an evidence-based approach to transdiagnostic anxiety difficulties in pre-adolescent children. Clear applicability to low-intensity practice is seen in the demonstration of intervention steps with Elna and Theo. Here, psycho-education, exploring anxious thoughts, use of exposure, and problem solving can empower parents to support their child and facilitate positive outcomes over the long term. Further information on the intervention can be found within the work of Creswell and Willetts (2019) and Halldorsson et al. (2019). Supporting materials identified within this chapter can be found on the CEDAR website at: https://cedar. exeter.ac.uk/resources/cyp/

References

Allard, C., Thirlwall, K., Cooper, P., Brown, A., O'Brien, D., & Creswell, C. (2022). Parents' perspectives on guided parent-delivered cognitive behavioural therapy for childhood anxiety disorders: A qualitative study. *Journal of Emotional and Behavioral Disorders, 30*(3), 235–244.

Brown, A., Creswell, C., Barker, C., Butler, S., Cooper, P., Hobbs, C., & Thirlwall, K. (2017). Guided parent-delivered cognitive behaviour therapy for children with anxiety disorders: Outcomes at 3- to 5-year follow-up. *British Journal of Clinical Psychology, 56*(2), 149–159.

Cartwright-Hatton, S., McNally, D., Field, A.P., Rust, S., Laskey, B., Dixon, C., Gallagher, B., Harrington, R., Miller, C., Pemberton, K., Symes, W., White, C., & Woodham, A. (2011). A new parenting-based group intervention for young anxious children: Results of a randomized controlled trial. *Journal of the American Academy of Child and Adolescent Psychiatry, 50*(3), 242–251.

Cobham, V.E. (2012). Do anxiety-disordered children need to come into the clinic for efficacious treatment? *Journal of Consulting and Clinical Psychology, 80*(3), 465–476.

Craske, M.G., Kircanski, K., Zelikowsky, M., Mystkowski, J., Chowdhury, N., & Baker, A. (2008). Optimizing inhibitory learning during exposure therapy. *Behaviour Research and Therapy, 46*(1), 5–27.

Craske, M.G., Treanor, M., Conway, C.C., Zbozinek, T., & Ervliet, B. (2014). Maximizing exposure therapy: An inhibitory learning approach. *Behaviour Research and Therapy, 58*, 10–23.

Creswell, C., Cruddace, S., Gerry, S., Gitau, R., McIntosh, E., Mollison, J., Murray, L., Shafran, R., Stein, A., Violato, M., Voysey, M., Willetts, L., Williams, N., Yu, L-M., & Cooper, P.J. (2015). Treatment of childhood anxiety disorder in the context of maternal anxiety disorder: A randomised controlled trial and economic analysis. *Health Technology Assessment, 19*(38), 1–184.

Creswell, C., & O'Connor, T.G. (2011). Interpretation bias and anxiety in childhood: Stability, specificity and longitudinal associations. *Behavioural and Cognitive Psychotherapy, 39*(2), 191–204.

Creswell, C., Parkinson, M., Thirlwall, K., & Willetts, L. (2019). *Parent-led CBT for child anxiety: Helping parents help their kids.* Guilford Press.

Creswell, C., Violato, M., Fairbanks, H., White, E., Parkinson, M., Abitabile, G., Leidi, A., & Cooper, P.J. (2017). Clinical outcomes and cost-effectiveness of brief guided parent-delivered cognitive behavioural therapy and solution-focused brief therapy for treatment of childhood anxiety disorders: A randomised controlled trial. *The Lancet Psychiatry, 4*(7), 529–539.

Creswell, C., & Willetts, L. (2019). *Helping your child with fears and worries: A self-help guide for parents* (2nd ed.). Robinson.

Halldorsson, B., Elliott, L., Chessell, C., Willetts, L., & Creswell, C. (2019). *Helping your child with fears and worries: A self-help guide for parents treatment manual for therapists.* (Unpublished).

Hiller, R.M., Apetroaia, A., Clarke, K., Hughes, Z., Orchard, F., Parkinson, M., & Creswell, C. (2016), The effect of targeting tolerance of children's negative emotions among anxious parents of children with anxiety disorders: A pilot randomised controlled trial. *Journal of Anxiety Disorders, 42*, 52–59.

Hudson, J.L., Doyle, A.M., & Gar, N. (2009). Child and maternal influence on parenting behavior in clinically anxious children. *Journal of Clinical Child and Adolescent Psychology, 38*(2), 256–262.

Hudson, J.L., Murayama, K., Meteyard, L., Morris, T., & Dodd, H. (2019). Early childhood predictors of anxiety in early adolescence. *Journal of Abnormal Child Psychology, 47*, 1121–1133.

James, A.C., Reardon, T., Soler, A., James, G., & Creswell, C. (2020). Cognitive behavioural therapy for anxiety disorders in children and adolescents. *Cochrane Database of Systematic Reviews, 11*, CD013162.

Leyfer, O., Gallo, K.P., Cooper-Vince, C., & Pincus, D.B. (2013). Patterns and predictors of comorbidity of DSM-IV anxiety disorders in a clinical sample of children and Adolescents. *Journal of Anxiety Disorders, 27*(3), 306–311.

McLeod, B.D., Wood, J.J., & Weisz, J.R. (2007). Examining the association between parenting and childhood anxiety: A meta-analysis. *Clinical Psychology Review, 27*(2), 155–172.

McKinnon, A., Keers, R., Coleman, J.R., Lester, K.J., Roberts, S., Arendt, K., Bögels, S.M., Cooper, P., Creswell, C., Hartman, C.A., Fjermestad, K.W., In-Albon, T., Lavallee, K., Lyneham, H.J., Smith, P., Meiser-Stedman, R., Nauta, M.H., Rapee, R.M., Rey, Y., … Hudson, J.L. (2018).

The impact of treatment delivery format on response to cognitive behaviour therapy for preadolescent children with anxiety disorders. *Journal of Child Psychology and Psychiatry*, *59*(7), 763–772.

Murray, L., Creswell, C., & Cooper, P. J. (2009). The development of anxiety disorders in childhood: An integrative review. *Psychological Medicine*, *39*(9), 1413–1423.

Peris, T.S., Compton, S.N., Kendall, P.C., Birmaher, B., Sherrill, J., March, J., Gosch, E., Ginsburg, G., Rynn, M., McCracken, J.T., Keeton, C.P., Sakolsky, D., Suveg, C., Aschenbrand, S., Almirall, D., Iyengar, S., Walkup, J.T., Albano, A.M., & Piacentini, J. (2015). Trajectories of change in youth anxiety during cognitive-behavior therapy. *Journal of Consulting and Clinical Psychology*, *83*(2), 239–252.

Plaisted, H., Waite, P., Gordon, K., & Creswell, C. (2021). Optimising exposure for children and adolescents with anxiety, OCD and PTSD: A systematic review. *Clinical Child and Family Psychology Review*, *24*(2), 1–22.

Rapee, R.M., Abbott, M.J., & Lyneham, H.J. (2006). Bibliotherapy for children with anxiety disorders using written materials for parents: A randomized controlled trial. *Journal of Consulting and Clinical Psychology*, *74*(3), 436–444.

Reardon, T., Harvey, K., & Creswell, C. (2020). Seeking and accessing professional support for child anxiety in a community sample. *European Child and Adolescent Psychiatry*, *29*, 649–664.

Thirlwall, K., & Creswell, C. (2010). The impact of maternal control on children's anxious cognitions, behaviours and affect: *An experimental study. Behaviour Research and Therapy*, *48*(10), 1041–1046.

Thirlwall, K., Cooper, P., & Creswell, C. (2017). Guided parent-delivered cognitive behavioral therapy for childhood anxiety: Predictors of treatment response. *Journal of Anxiety Disorders*, *45*, 43–48.

Thirlwall, K., Cooper, P.J., Karalus, J., Voysey, M., Willetts, L., & Creswell, C. (2013). Treatment of child anxiety disorders via guided parent-delivered cognitive–behavioural therapy: Randomised controlled trial. *The British Journal of Psychiatry*, *203*(6), 436–444.

Thirlwall, K., & Creswell, C. (2010). The impact of maternal control on children's anxious cognitions, behaviours and affect: An experimental study. *Behaviour Research and Therapy*, *48*(10), 1041–1046.

Waters, A.M., Wharton, T.A., Zimmer-Gembeck, M.J., & Craske, M.G. (2008). Threat-based cognitive biases in anxious children: Comparison with non-anxious children before and after cognitive behavioural treatment. *Behaviour Research and Therapy*, *46*(3), 358–374.

Whiteside, S.P., Sim, L.A., Morrow, A.S., Farah, W.H., Hilliker, D.R., Murad, M.H., & Wang, Z. (2020). A meta-analysis to guide the enhancement of CBT for childhood anxiety: Exposure over anxiety management. *Clinical Child and Family Psychology Review*, *23*(1), 102–121.

Conflict of Interest

Cathy Creswell receives royalties from the sale of the 'Helping Your Child with Fears and Worries' book. Copies of this book may be freely available from books-on-prescription and local libraries.

Part 4
Professional Issues and Service Implications

17

Service Implementation and Evaluation

Jonathan Parker and Hollie Gay

Introduction

It is recognised that the journey of research informed, evidence-based healthcare approaches into real-world clinical practice (Beidas & Kendall, 2010) can be protracted and problematic (Harvey & Kitson, 2015). Implementation science literature indicates that it can take upwards of 15 years for even a small percentage of recommended evidence-based treatments to be implemented into routine healthcare delivery (Allen et al., 2018). As a result, within any healthcare development initiative it is essential to consider the factors that may support a successful transition of evidence-based taught theory into effective real-world practice. This chapter will consider these factors, providing an overview of the context and background to implementation and examining several key considerations specifically related to the deployment of low-intensity practice. It will review the principles and practicalities associated with successful implementation and present a real-world case study of how a low-intensity workforce has been embedded within a community-based service provider. Latterly, the foundational function of evaluation will be discussed, reviewing the importance of developing a clear and consistent understanding of outcomes and the central role this has in the ongoing design, development and delivery of a low-intensity provision for children, young people and families.

Service Implementation

Background and Context

At inception, healthcare initiatives can be vulnerable to placing an emphasis on the *what* to the detriment of the *how*. Although it is clearly critical to give appropriate attention to developing and teaching evidence-based practice approaches, a disproportionate focus on content can lead to a gap between the care that is intended to be provided, underpinned by best practice and research, and the care that is actually transitioned into practice (Allen et al., 2018). Successful and sustainable implementation is difficult (Proctor et al., 2009), and it is important to acknowledge that many children and young people's mental health services share the challenges of operating within and across a demanding, complex and multifaceted health and social care system. In his book *Better* (2007), Atul Gawande reflects on these real-world complexities within the healthcare profession and the often disorganised and vexing systems in which it operates. These assertions hint at the challenges that face organisations and leaders as they grapple with both the implementation of workforce initiatives and organisational development in a broader sense. Organisations will be composed of a range of professionals that will include individuals and teams with a strong sense of purpose and advocacy for their professional group. Although this stance is understandable and often appropriate, it can contribute to discord when engaging with clinical and/or operational change. Alongside this, a wrestling for strategic positioning within and between organisations may occur, which can impact on cultural and operational stability. These factors can lead to creating a difficult, unpredictable, and at times chaotic context for implementation. However, despite often challenging conditions and complex operational structures, workforce and training initiatives can provide fresh opportunity to evaluate and reconsider delivery models, care pathways and the wider clinical architecture of mental health service provision. Such opportunity should be embraced and approached thoughtfully with a clear implementation roadmap that carefully considers fundamental strategic and operational factors and includes the collaborative engagement with a diverse range of participants.

Principles and Practicalities of Implementing Low-Intensity Practice

The introduction of a new, evidenced-based, low-intensity provision presents several unique and critical considerations when planning its implementation. From the outset, it is important for a service to identify an individual, or individuals, who can have delegated ownership over the development and implementation of the new provision. Effective leadership has been shown to play a central role in the success of healthcare implementation (Aarons et al., 2015) and, for those commissioned with this responsibility, it will be critical to consolidate a core understanding of low-intensity practice principles. Equipped with this foundational knowledge, the service lead may want to develop a communication strategy (Metz & Bartley, 2012) to enable information about the low-intensity offer to be clearly disseminated within their own service, to partner agencies and other regional organisations as well as to those who may wish to access support themselves. It is important for the service to deploy and convey the low-intensity offer in a manner that is compatible and consistent with low-intensity practice principles. It should embrace the early intervention remit of a focused but flexible type of intervention, with both the function and frequency of delivery reflecting this. The underlying aim of this initial process is to increase awareness and access to evidence-based psychological therapies for children, young people and parents/carers whilst ensuring delivery and communications strategies are inclusive and can be adapted to accommodate diversity.

At this stage, it can be helpful to engage and collaborate with a diverse range of participants, or stakeholders, that can help communicate and develop the offer. Care and time should be taken to ensure that the collaboration is authentic and empowering to all participants. Such an approach can drive and direct implementation and enable shared ownership which can subsequently facilitate awareness, advocacy and early adoption for the role (Fixsen et al., 2005). The initiation and facilitation of regional steering groups can provide a platform to review and develop the principles of effective low-intensity delivery and can support decisions on how and where the provision is most helpfully located to support access by young people and families. Good communication between agencies can provide a platform for effective referral and triage processes, step-up and step-down support as well as developing and maintaining a shared understanding of the wider local offer as it evolves. In addition, consistent local and regional engagement can support the low-intensity provision to adapt to changes in need within the locality as well as support the development and innovation in low-intensity delivery through sharing of good practice.

Supporting the Developing Workforce

It is likely that the commencement of a new low-intensity provision will originate from the deployment of practitioners undertaking a clinical training programme. In this context, ensuring effective and consistent support for the needs of the developing practitioner aids not only the individual trainee, but the wider service implementation requirements. Following the initial training period, it is the expectation that a trainee low-intensity practitioner will begin clinical practice in a graduated manner and start to deliver interventions face to face, by phone, and online. An incremental approach assists the transitioning of theory into practice, enabling engagement with the range of guidance, supervision and academic requirements in support of developing their low-intensity assessment and intervention competencies. It is essential for the service to prioritise consistent and high-quality clinical supervision for the low-intensity practitioner; both before and after qualification. This provision provides the bedrock from which the practitioner can develop and refine their competencies whilst supporting a consistent framework for low-intensity case management which is central to enabling appropriate delivery flexibility whilst maintaining fidelity to the low-intensity model.

Operational Support

An area that may be considered mundane but is of central importance to the successful implementation of low-intensity practice, is the operational environment. Poorly

SERVICE IMPLEMENTATION AND EVALUATION | 243

Table 17.1 Example Implementation Checklist

Access	Referrals
✔ Public information and awareness ✔ Accessibility of locations/hubs ✔ Remote and online delivery offer ✔ Self-referral pathway ✔ Early intervention 'Drop-in' for support opportunities ✔ Themed workshops/group work e.g., psychoeducation	✔ Clear referral guidelines to support appropriate and timely access ✔ Referral and triage management ✔ Step-up and step-down processes ✔ Updated directory of local, universal, and associated services for supported signposting, liaison, and onwards support provision

Operational Processes	Management and Supervision
✔ Delegated leadership and clear decision-making processes ✔ Administrative support ✔ Outcome data collection, tracking and reporting ✔ Case management recording	✔ Weekly case management supervision ✔ Fortnightly clinical skills supervision ✔ Monthly line management ✔ Robust and clear risk management and safeguarding procedures

planned or managed operational support can hinder development and delivery of any clinical role but can be particularly detrimental to low-intensity practice due to the likely high-volume caseloads and requirement to deliver support in a flexible and responsive manner. Consequently, clear lines of communication and decision making are critical with practitioners supported by a management, operational and administrative infrastructure that enables them to conduct their clinical practice unhindered. In practice this can mean access to, and understanding of IT, case-management software, clinical resources, policies, and procedures as well as the range of logistical and administrative resources required to deliver, monitor, and manage their clinical practice. Table 17.1 provides an example checklist of operational and organisational considerations when implementing a low-intensity provision.

Case Study

Community Based Service in the South West of England

What were the main hopes and aims when developing a low-intensity offer?

Our main hopes and aims were to deliver support to young people who were not meeting specialist referral criteria to access support by creating a workforce that could and would intervene before difficulties escalated into requiring more high-intensity or specialist care. We wanted to broaden the offer to CYP and provide an opportunity in a space and place and at a time that suits them – to offer something that was different to what typically existed and provide a new and fresh way of engaging young people and families. It also was hoped that the LI role would offer training and employment opportunities for highly skilled youth workers who might not otherwise get the chance to train in evidence-based interventions.

What were the main challenges of implementing the new role?

Establishing a referral pathway was challenging, particularly in support of getting appropriate referrals for the low-intensity pathway. Initially this new pathway was seen as accepting any type of mental health referral, and it was a real but important challenge to hold to the low-intensity, early intervention remit. Finding appropriate and accessible local community venues and hubs has also been difficult at times. The expectations on the practitioners have been problematic at points, particularly in respect to what they should be able to do. When the low-intensity role has not been suitable to support a young person, this can lead to criticism from parents, carers or referrers and subsequent demands for specialist care – which has been difficult to manage with limited resources. Finally, the low-intensity role has increased our working with and across partner services, which although often beneficial has also raised the challenge of how different providers view and manage risk.

What have been the most helpful factors in establishing the low-intensity offer?

The low-intensity role was introduced to us as a service with a good local reputation and it has been helpful to have a strong relationship with local partners, commissioners, education settings and community services. Alongside this, it has been helpful to have a strong working relationship with the training provider and collaborative engagement with other services developing this offer. When operating in a system with specialist, clinical provision it has been helpful to be a more community based offer and be closer to the localities in which we have deployed this role. We have been led by the 'where and how'; the service user has wanted this role to be implemented through our strong participation values. This has enabled the role to be implemented in a way that has been directly influenced and shaped by the young people who use our service. To support the early intervention remit, it has been really helpful that we have set up support hubs across the region to act as drop-ins to encourage access to support before they reach a stage of formal referral or specialist need.

Ongoing Service Development

Following initial implementation, the sustainability and development of the low-intensity provision will be an important area of focus. When working collaboratively with local and regional partners, there should be regular discussion and review of accessibility, referral management processes and operational support structures. A natural pitfall of service development and collaboration between organisations can be the dominance of inherent bias or slanted viewpoints dependent on individual experience or professional grouping (Dobler et al., 2019). To help mitigate this, good quality data should be at the centre of any ongoing review and service development process, informing discussion and underpinning decision making. However, the usefulness of data will be cognisant to the quality of the operational infrastructure available to practitioners, managers and administrators. Every effort should be made to facilitate effective data and outcome collection as rigorous and continual evaluation of service provision is integral to the implementation and expansion and of the low-intensity workforce (Ludlow et al., 2020). In addition, role sustainability is reliant on data transparency (Clark et al., 2018) and validates the low-intensity workforces' objectives: increasing mental health access for children and young people, reducing waiting times for evidence-based interventions, and evidencing impact through routine outcome monitoring.

Evaluation

Background and Context

Despite several initiatives advocating the use of routine outcome monitoring (ROM) as a core principle of service delivery, the children and young people's mental health system in England has experienced systemic challenges in effectively administering, collecting, analysing and reporting a robust level of data, particularly in relation to outcomes (Wolpert et al., 2014). Organisational infrastructure, practitioner resistance and/or ambiguity as well as inconsistent acceptance within localities has negatively impacted on data quality (Wolpert & Rutter, 2018). Furthermore, strong differences of opinion can occur regarding the suitability and application of measurement tools (Smith et al., 2013).

However, it is widely acknowledged that demonstrating the provision of quality care is an obligation for any healthcare provider (Svirydzenka et al., 2017) (Svirydzenka, Ronzoni, & Dogra, 2017) with an expectation that services will routinely measure the quality of care provided (NHSE, 2015). Routine data collection is recognised as an important component of this process contributing to the transparency and accountability of healthcare service provision (NHSE, 2015) and providing important information regarding effectiveness, safety and quality to staff, service users and the wider public (Smith et al., 2013).

Supporting and Developing Outcome Informed Practice

Proactive and collaborative engagement should be a central focus for teams wanting to support and promote the effective use of outcome measures within service; aiming to facilitate a shared understanding of the benefit of the effective use of ROM, feedback tools and clinical questionnaires. As illustrated in Table 17.2, there are numerous compelling illustrations within the literature demonstrating the value of using routine data collection in-service. These examples highlight that outcome monitoring not only enhances the individual experience of accessing support, but also produces evidence of impact, an essential element in commissioning ongoing services.

Table 17.2 Benefits of Routine Outcome Monitoring

Benefits of Using Routine Outcome Monitoring
✔ Session-by-session monitoring and feedback of outcomes (for example, symptoms, functioning and therapeutic alliance) is an evidence-based intervention of itself (Edbrooke-Childs, Gondek, Deighton, Fonagy, & Wolpert, 2016). As such, it is an essential component of good clinical practice (Department of Health, 2011).
✔ Enhances communication between service users and practitioners, providing a way to monitor the impact of treatment, and to help inform subsequent treatment plans especially for non-responders (Carlier et al., 2012).
✔ Shared decision making between patient and practitioner can be enhanced using routine data collection (Law & Wolpert, 2014).
✔ Routine data collection can be used to inform supervision (Wolpert & Law, 2014) (Richards, Chellingsworth, Hope, Turpin, & Whyte, 2010) and is an essential component of CWP case management supervision.
✔ Session-by-session outcome measurement is associated with increased treatment effectiveness (Gondek, Edbrooke-Childs, Fink, Deighton, & Wolpert, 2016).
✔ Session-by-session data correlates to increased data-completeness (Clark, D., 2011).
✔ Children, young people, and families support the application of routine data collection (Badham, 2011).
✔ The collection of routine service and clinical data can be used to inform improvements in service development (Flemming, Jones, Bradley, & Wolpert, 2016).
✔ Routine data collection is essential for ongoing service commissioning; with objective outcome measurement being crucial to secure future funding for all health services (Law & Wolpert, 2014).

Teams can obtain valuable feedback through the collection of routine outcome monitoring. Feedback from outcomes becomes cyclical, resulting in improved clinical practice. Data collection can improve service provision, giving a voice to the children and young people accessing support. Furthermore, feedback can ensure the views of children, young people and families are respected and actioned. Routine data collection represents an invaluable tool for teams to monitor the effectiveness of service delivery and should be viewed as an essential resource to improve mental health support for children and young people.

Case Study

Future in Mind (Department of Health, 2015) published by the UK government was aimed at transforming children and young people's mental health provision in England by promoting early intervention and increasing access to support. The guidance led to an enhancement of the low-intensity workforce through the creation of the Children and Young People's Wellbeing Practitioner (CWP) programme. Higher Education Institutes from each region were tasked with evidencing the impact of the CWP initiative. Given the historically low-quality outcome reporting in children's mental health services, it was important that as a new provision, CWP outcomes were transparent and accountable to children, young people and families accessing support.

Partner services within the South West of England were actively engaged with to establish their existing infrastructure, processes and guidelines for the routine use and collection of assessment and outcome information. It was recognised that across partner services, there would be a significant disparity between individual organisations' readiness to achieve successful routine outcome measure (ROM) collection and processing. Communicating and maintaining a minimum data standard for services from the beginning was essential. Support, challenge and guidance was given both across and within services to implement operational solutions in support of achieving robust ROM collections and administration processes. This included orientation and engagement with patient management record systems, data recording processes, related training as well as ongoing support and follow up from the specifically recruited research and evaluation team. Consequently, significant progress was made with the application and recording of outcome and feedback data. Data sharing agreements were drawn up between participating services and the University based evaluation team enabling quarterly service evaluation reports to be shared with each provider. This facilitated the provision of local service feedback loops, impact analysis, service development considerations and contribution towards the implementation, development and sustainability of the CWP role. Through this focused, consistent, and collaborative implementation and evaluation process, the CWP role has established itself across the region as a new and effective psychological profession which has demonstrated reliable positive outcomes for children, young people and families accessing support.

Figure 17.1 summarises the impact and benefits of collaborative evaluation and an ongoing commitment to high quality data collection from CWP services across the South West of England. Findings from the evaluation, conducted by CEDAR at the University of Exeter, align with low-intensity workforce ambitions to reduce waiting times, improve outcomes, and increase access to children's mental health support at a stage of early intervention. The evaluation has demonstrated that young people presenting with mild-moderate difficulties demonstrate over 50% reliable improvement on self-reported measures of anxiety and depression. This data continues to support the ongoing implementation, development, and expansion of the workforce to deliver evidence-based low-intensity interventions.

Summary

This chapter has provided an outline of the key functions of implementation and evaluation when establishing and delivering low-intensity practice for children, young people and families. The core components of implementation, including operational and clinical considerations have been presented, highlighting the importance of preparing the ground within an organisation to support the successful founding of low-intensity practice. Finally, the fundamental principles of outcome monitoring and evaluation are reviewed, highlighting how these processes support and inform not only good clinical practice but also ongoing service development and sustainable embedding of the low-intensity workforce.

LOW-INTENSITY PRACTICE WITH CYP AND FAMILIES

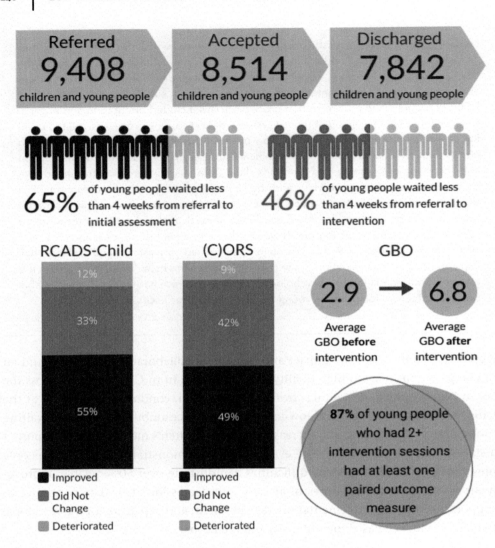

Figure 17.1 Regional CWP Evaluation Summary (2017–2021)

References

Aarons, G.A., Ehrhart, M.G., Farahnak, L.R., & Hurlburt, M.S. (2015). Leadership and organizational change for implementation (LOCI): a randomized mixed method pilot study of a leadership and organization development intervention for evidence-based practice implementation. *Implementation Science*, 10(1), 1–12.

Allen, P., Jacob, R.R., Lakshman, M., Best, L.A., Bass, K., & Brownson, R.C. (2018). Lessons learned in promoting evidence-based public health: Perspectives from managers in state public health departments. *Journal of Community Health*, 43(5), 856–863. https://doi-org.uoelibrary.idm.oclc.org/10.1007/s10900-018-0494-0

Badham, B. (2011). *Talking about Talking Therapies: Thinking and planning about how best to make good and accessible talking therapies available to children and young people*. Young Minds, London.

SERVICE IMPLEMENTATION AND EVALUATION | 249

Beidas, R.S., & Kendall, P.C. (2010). Training therapists in evidence-based practice: A critical review of studies from a systems-contextual perspective. *Clinical Psychology: Science and Practice, 17*(1), 1–30. https://doi-org.uoelibrary.idm.oclc.org/10.1111/j.1468-2850.2009.01187.x

Carlier, I.V.E., Meuldijk, D., Van Vliet, I.M., Van Fenema, E., Van der Wee, N.J.A., & Zitman, F.G. (2012). Routine outcome monitoring and feedback on physical or mental health status: Evidence and theory. *Journal of Evaluation in Clinical Practice, 18*, 104–110.

Clark, D.M., Canvin, L., Green, J., Layard, R., Pilling, S., & Janecka, M. (2018). Transparency about the outcomes of mental health services (IAPT approach): An analysis of public data. *The Lancet, 391*(10121), 679–686. https://doi-org.uoelibrary.idm.oclc.org/10.1016/S0140-6736(17)32133-5

Clark, D.M. (2011). Implementing NICE guidelines for the psychological treatment of depression and anxiety disorders: The IAPT experience. *International Review of Psychiatry, 23*, 318–327.

Dobler, C.C., Morrow, A.S., & Kamath, C.C. (2019). Clinicians' cognitive biases: A potential barrier to implementation of evidence-based clinical practice. *BMJ Evidence-Based Medicine, 24*(4), 137–140. https://doi-org.uoelibrary.idm.oclc.org/10.1136/bmjebm-2018-111074

Department of Health. (2011). *Talking therapies: A four-year plan of action*. London: Personal Social Services Research Unit.

Department of Health. (2015). *Future in mind: Promoting, protecting and improving our children and young people's mental health and wellbeing (NHS England Publication Gateway Ref. No 02939)*. National Health Service England. https://assets.publishingservice.gov.uk/government/uploads/system/uploads/attachment_data/file/414024/Childrens_Mental_Health.pdf

Edbrooke-Childs, J.H., Gondek, D., Deighton, J., Fonagy, P., & Wolpert, M. (2016). When is sessional monitoring more likely in child and adolescent mental health services?. *Administration and Policy in Mental Health and Mental Health Services Research, 43*, 316–324.

Fleming, I., Jones, M., Bradley, J., & Wolpert, M. (2016). Learning from a learning collaboration: The CORC approach to combining research, evaluation and practice in child mental health. *Administration and Policy in Mental Health and Mental Health Services Research, 43*, 297–301.

Fixsen, D., Naoom, S., Blase, K., Friedman, R., & Wallace, F. (2005). *Implementation research: A synthesis of the literature*. University of South Florida, Louis de la Parte Florida Mental Health Institute, National Implementation Research Network.

Gawande, A. (2007). *Better: A surgeon's notes on performance*. Profile Books Ltd.

Gondek, D., Edbrooke-Childs, J., Fink, E., Deighton, J., & Wolpert, M. (2016). Routine outcome monitoring and treatment effectiveness, treatment efficiency, and collaborative practice: A systematic review. *Administration and Policy in Mental Health and Mental Health Services Research, 43*, 325–343.

Harvey, G., & Kitson, A. (2015). Translating evidence into healthcare policy and practice: Single versus multi-faceted implementation strategies – Is there a simple answer to a complex question? *International Journal of Health Policy and Management, 4*(3), 123–126. https://doi-org.uoelibrary.idm.oclc.org/10.15171/ijhpm.2015.54

Law, D., & Wolpert, M. (Eds.). (2014). *Guide to Using Outcomes and Feedback Tools With Children, Young People and Families* (2 ed.). London: CAMHS Press.

Ludlow, C., Hurn, R., & Lansdell, S. (2020). A current review of the children and young people's improving access to psychological therapies (CYP IAPT) program: Perspectives on developing an accessible workforce. *Adolescent Health, Medicine and Therapeutics, 11*, 21–28.

Metz, A., & Bartley, L. (2012). Active implementation frameworks for program success: How to use implementation science to improve outcomes for children. *Zero to Three Journal, 34*(4), 11–18.

NHS England. (2015). *Delivering the five year forward view for mental health: Developing quality and outcomes measures*. https://www.england.nhs.uk/mentalhealth/wp-content/uploads/sites/29/2016/02/mh-quality-outcome.pdf

Proctor, E.K., Landsverk, J., Aarons, G., Chambers, D., Glisson, C., & Mittman, B. (2009). Implementation research in mental health services: An emerging science with conceptual, methodological, and training challenges. *Administration and Policy In Mental Health*, *36*(1), 24–34.

Richards, D., Chellingsworth, M., Hope, R., Turpin, G., & Whtye, M. (2010). *National programme supervisor materials to support the delivery of training for psychological wellbeing practitioners delivering low intensity interventions*. Rethink, London.

Smith, E.E., Warner, J., Johnston, M., Atwood, K., Hall, R., Mah, J.K., Maxwell, C., Fortin, C.M., Lowerison, M., Kapral, M.K., Noonan, V.K., Pfister, T., Mackean, G., Casselman, L., Pringsheim, T., Jette, N., & Korngut, L. (2013). Neurological registry data collection methods and configuration. *The Canadian Journal of Neurological Sciences*, *40*(4 Suppl 2), S27–S31. https://doi-org.uoelibrary.idm.oclc.org/10.1017/s0317167100017133

Svirydzenka, N., Ronzoni, P., & Dogra, N. (2017). Meaning and barriers to quality care service provision in child and adolescent mental health services: Quality study of stakeholder perspectives. *BMC Health Services Research*, *17*(151). https://doi.org/10.1186/s12913-017-2080-z

Wolpert, M., Deighton, J., de De Francesco, D., Martin, P., Fonagy, P., & Ford, T. (2014). From "reckless" to "mindful" in the use of outcome data to inform service-level performance management: Perspectives from child mental health. *BMJ Quality and Safety*, *23*(4), 272–276. https://doi-org.uoelibrary.idm.oclc.org/10.1136/bmjqs-2013-002557

Wolpert, M., & Rutter, H. (2018). Using flawed, uncertain, proximate and sparse (FUPS) data in the context of complexity: Learning from the case of child mental health. *BMC Medicine*, *16*(1), 1–11. https://doi-org.uoelibrary.idm.oclc.org/10.1186/s12916-018-1079-6

18

Supervision of Low-Intensity Practice with Children and Young People

Kirsty Roberts and Jonathan Parker

Introduction

Competent and consistent supervision is a fundamental component of safe and effective psychological practice (Milne & Watkins, 2014). This chapter aims to develop an understanding of the purpose and requirements of supervision of low-intensity practice within children and young people's services; mapping the format of the two main approaches that exist within the low-intensity role. Beginning with an overview of case management supervision (CMS), the suggested frequency, category options and format will be presented. Following this, the second approach of clinical skills supervision (CSS) will be appraised, providing an overview of the frequency, format and purpose of this space; with consideration given to the dynamics within the group setting and how contracting contrasts with CMS.

The chapter will also consider the key role that practitioners play in the effective use of supervision. Guidance will be given on how to effectively prepare for CMS sessions to help ensure it is timely and facilitates effective and safe practice. Preparation for CSS will be discussed including the formulation of appropriate and helpful supervision questions, how to maximise the effective use of the group space and what tools can be used within supervision to enhance clinical practice. In addition, some of the practicalities of how supervision is delivered within a children and young people service provision will be reviewed; discussing barriers and facilitators to good practice that may exist within the operational context and considering how, within a service setting, to safely manage presenting issues or difficulties that may not fit within the low-intensity remit.

Background

Milne (2017) defines supervision as a formal provision by approved (e.g., professionally registered) supervisors, who manage, develop, support and evaluate the work of their colleagues. Milne and Watkins (2014) propose that the supervisor is a distinctive and essential professional role within psychological clinical practice. Furthermore, supervision supports the CYP mental health principle of accountability (NHS England, 2014) and can contribute to the provision of safer CYP mental health care (Hayes et al., 2015). Across the spectrum of therapeutic modalities, the process of supervision can differ significantly and be subject to variation in frequency and function depending on clinical and professional requirements. Within LI cognitive behavioural therapy there is a recognised framework offering clear guidance to the anticipated supervisory format. It is expected that this approach facilitates a consistency of quality irrespective of the service context whilst also benefiting both practitioner and supervisor in supporting a shared understanding and expectation of supervision practice.

Despite having a distinct identity and format, LI supervision does have several similarities with other types of supervision, particularly in relation to the three widely recognised supervision objectives, the formative, normative and restorative functions for the supervisee. Inskipp and Proctor (1993) describe that the formative function supports the maintenance and development of competency and capability of the supervisee whilst the normative aspect ensures quality control through a gatekeeping function of supervision, with its strong evaluative components (Milne, 2017). Finally, the restorative elements relate to the emotional processing experienced by the practitioner in relation to their caseload as well as wider wellbeing awareness and support of the supervisee to, for example, reduce risk of burnout. Bennett-Levy et al. (2010) expand on this further by linking Turpin and Wheeler's (2011) five purposes of supervision to LI supervision:

- Fidelity to the evidence-base
- Case management
- Clinical governance
- Skills development
- Worker support

In England, the benefits of the specific framework of low-intensity CBT supervision have been observed within the adult Psychological Wellbeing Practitioners (PWPs) workforce. For example, Branson et al. (2018) demonstrated that the more competent the therapist, the better outcomes were for those receiving LI CBT. The practitioner's competencies (Richards, 2011) used within the study included the effective use of case management supervision; specifically, the practitioners' preparation and prioritisation of cases for discussion in supervision (Branson et al., 2018). This signifies the central role of supervision within low-intensity practice and the beneficial impact that good utilisation of supervision can have. The word *utilisation* is deliberately used here rather than *receiving*; both formats of low-intensity supervision expect significant

SUPERVISION OF LOW-INTENSITY PRACTICE WITH CHILDREN AND YOUNG PEOPLE | 253

preparation. Rather than it being something passive, low-intensity supervision is a two-way process requiring active participation on the part of the practitioner.

In comparison to other psychological approaches, LI practice and supervision are characterised by a more structured approach to delivery and Milne (2016) highlights several benefits of having a more manualised approach to supervision within low-intensity CBT. These include the enabling of operational definition to support standardisation across service contexts and, relatedly, the consistent implementation and application of supervision, which can allow for more reliable research and service evaluation to take place. Expectations are clear for all parties, with a focus on fidelity and competency sitting centrally within the LI CBT supervision approach.

Contracting

Contracting within LI CBT supervision, which may also be referred to as a learning agreement, is the requirement for a clear, comprehensive and agreed supervision contract within CBT (Corrie & Lane, 2015). Contracting early is recommended as standard for CMS and CSS to clearly define a shared understanding of the expectations and responsibilities from both supervisor and supervisee. Within the contract, there will also be a guidance on the required steps that should be taken in the event of a breakdown in the agreed arrangements and / or supervisory relationship. Corrie & Lane (2015) explain that within the normative function of supervision, the supervisor is ethically compelled to evaluate practitioner performance and constructive feedback learning areas, ensuring practitioners are working safely and to their organisational policies and professional framework. Having this inclusion of a pre-agreement, in the event of a relationship breakdown, can open the discussion to managing expectations of ongoing feedback and the obligations on the supervisor to gate-keep these elements. These contracts typically include those outlined in Table 18.1, tailored to the specific supervision format.

Case Management Supervision

CMS should be undertaken consistently, with 60 minutes per week assigned to a full-time low-intensity practitioner, adjusted accordingly for part-time members of staff, for example a minimum of 30 mins per week (Turpin & Wheeler, 2011). CMS has a set structure within LI CBT practice with four main elements to a CMS session:

- Supporting the organisation of the supervisee's caseload
- Monitoring information giving and identifying issues
- Discussion of cases
- Shared decision making

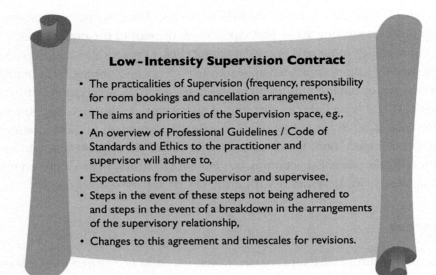

Figure 18.1 Typical Inclusions within a Low-Intensity Supervision Contract

Within the first element, *supporting the organisation of caseload*, the supervisor supports the presentation of the number of cases on the practitioner's current caseload, with the appropriate organisation of the cases for supervision using the CMS categories. Bennett-Levy et al. (2010) explain that the preparation and process of CMS can often be a high-volume undertaking and is a skill that needs refining to be successful. The supervisor typically facilitates a discussion regarding the manageability of the practitioner's current caseload, and where necessary, considers potential for burnout. The supervisor should scaffold the process appropriately from an early session to enable the practitioner to use the proforma correctly and to help ensure all selected cases are discussed within the allocated time. It may be useful for this aspect of supervision to practise in CSS or with peers to fine tune the presentation of cases succinctly as this may present a challenge for the developing practitioner.

The second and third elements to CMS are intertwined in *monitoring information giving and identifying issues* and the *discussion of cases*. Throughout the cases reviewed, the supervisor should ensure that the appropriate information is given by the practitioner for all cases presented, with this process supported by the correct use of the proforma. The specific context of the child, young person and family should be reviewed with both protective and vulnerability factors discussed. Across the caseload, risk or safeguarding concerns should be consistently monitored and reviewed along with any ethical or professional issues. The supervisor should aim to empower the practitioner to work with minimal drift and present the CMS information succinctly and accurately throughout the supervision hour, signposting if this is a clinical skills deficit, and to use this space appropriately. *Shared decision making* would come into play at the discussion of each individual case. The supervisor should facilitate collaborative discussion and review to support shared decision making, encouraging regularly summarising an understanding of the discussions with a clear action plan formulated for each case. This element also encompasses the expectation for the supervisor to sensitively identify any potential skills deficits and signpost these as supervision questions for CSS to protect the process of CMS and its relatively high-volume nature. It is important to note that due to the structured approach of CMS, it is possible there may be limited capacity for restoration for the practitioner, so consideration should be given as to how this important function will best be incorporated. In addition, practitioners and supervisors may enquire where an appropriate place is to review an ending of a case or where celebrations of success might fit within the supervisory process. It may be suitable to discuss celebrations in either line management as a performance topic or to reflect on positives and learning within clinical skills supervision. Service-related or operational issues should be discussed within line management supervision rather than in these spaces.

Leading on from these elements of CMS, there is a specific proforma (Table 18.1) that is expected to be used to streamline the process for both parties. It would be expected that the practitioner and supervisor have a shared view of this form, whether a printed version each or electronically shared, to support the processing of the information. Preparation is a key skill within low-intensity working, and the practitioner would usually set aside time to prepare these forms in advance and support the streamlining of the supervision experience.

Table 18.1 Information for Cases Required in Case Management Supervision

Presented for all Cases

Age
Gender
Main problem statement
Risk
Contextual informational – Previous episodes/past treatment and current life situation
Trauma/abuse (current/historical)
School
Impact – family, wider social environment
Routine Outcome Measures

Additional Information for 4 Weekly Review, Risk, High Scores or Further Support

Reason for supervision
Intervention summary so far
Client engagement
Client response to treatment
Action plan

Additional Information for DNA (Optional)

Reason for supervision
Summary of progress before non-contact
Number and methods of contacts attempted-
Contact plan/next steps

A key component of LI CMS, and one that is highlighted within in Table 18.1, is the regular review of routine outcome measures (ROMs). A typical range of measures might include, for example, the Revised Children's Anxiety and Depression Scale (RCADS) (Chorpita et al., 2000), the Outcome Rating Scale (ORS) (Miller et al., 2003) and the Goal Based Outcomes (GBO) tool. It is important for both the practitioner and supervisor to have a good understanding of the clinical purpose and scoring process of each ROM that is used. For example, the reporting of the RCADS within this section may prove problematic if only the 'RAW' scores are used and reported, as these would need to be adjusted according to the CYP's age and gender. Practitioners should, instead, report on the significance of these scores from the scoring programme (low, medium or high), or report on the data range of scores based on the contextual information from the scoring programme. However, within CMS, effective collaborative engagement with ROM to help inform case discussion, track progress and monitor effectiveness is a key component of good quality clinical supervision.

Clinical Skills Supervision

The specific format of clinical skills supervision may vary depending on the service context and supervisor preferences for the group. Typically, there are two main variations with the first modality identifying and developing a specific theme(s) and deciding as a group the main area(s) of focus, perhaps drawn from what has arisen during the week. This is normally suitable for slightly larger groups and is modelled from adult PWP working, with groups of no more than 12 (Turpin & Wheeler, 2011). The supervisor may facilitate this approach by summarising the range of topics supervisees would like to discuss and asking the group to prioritise the order in which these are covered. This process of assignment requires skill and a degree of diplomacy from the supervisor and will be important to support an experience of equitability over the course of the group's continuation. The other variation of CSS would be as a smaller group of four practitioners, which is designed to take at least two hours, with half an hour per trainee (Richards, 2011). The total time spent in the group is usually counted towards this supervisee's accumulative supervision time and falls in line with guidance recommending at least 1 hour per fortnight of CSS (Turpin & Wheeler, 2011). The latter format is more typical within a children and young person's service setting due to the additional complexities and developmental considerations that would typically need to be discussed, reviewed and developed. As part of the preparation process, practitioners would be expected to identify and bring to CSS a short recording of their topic to accompany a clinical skills question. Milne (2016) suggests that the use of video clips in CSS allows for more detailed illustrations, and although of particular value during the LI practitioner's training stage, should be something that continues post qualification as standard to ensure best practice approaches are developed and upheld.

With the group format of CSS, each supervisee could have four roles within a group supervision context (Proctor & Inskipp, 2018). First, as a supervisee; acting efficiently, with good preparation and presenting topics in a succinct and engaging way for colleagues. The second role may be as a practitioner, identifying individual personal and professional needs, and communicating how the group could be a helpful learning source. The third role may be as a group member; being aware of time spent discussing a topic and becoming conscious of thoughts, feelings, and communications which help or hinder the group's progress. Lastly, the supervisee's role might be as a co-supervisor and paying close attention to other group members' presentations and being prepared to mutually support and challenge each other through clear feedback and responses. Practitioners may experience all these roles within clinical skills supervision.

Formulating a Supervision Question

Typical supervisee questions may be either learning questions, such as 'how could I...?', a feedback question: 'Was this element okay....?' or information questions, such as 'Who, what, why, when....?'. It is helpful for supervisees to be aware of the type of question they are asking and what they are hoping the response will give them. Roscoe et al. (2022) describe the clinical supervision question as a 'front wheel' supervision task, highlighting the importance of guiding the session and setting agenda items, goals and a focus. Furthermore, a helpful and well-prepared supervision question clarifies the specific issues to be addressed, enables reflection, builds skills and knowledge whilst also supporting adherence to the 5-minute guideline with discussions remaining focused. To further enhance the CSS space, the Declarative-Procedural-Reflective (DPR) model (Bennett-Levy, 2006) is a helpful model for practitioners when presenting or supporting others with their clinical skills questions. This supports the group to explore whether the issue is rooted in a skills deficit with a gap in either their knowledge (in which case research could be done to ensure evidence-based practice is adhered to), procedural skills which need practising (with the benefit of role plays often being felt within this group space as a good feedback method), or an area that requires individual reflection to occur.

Proctor and Inskipp (2018) outline how group supervision settings may give rise to the forming, storming, norming, performing and adjourning stages, first illustrated by Tuckman (1965). Within a supervision group this may mean that there is an over reliance on the supervisor's opinion to begin with (forming), moving into the storming stage which can be prolonged within some groups. This then moves into the norming stage where the group feels more settled and a better quality of skills development may occur, leading into performing and adjourning when the group is going to end or alter its make-up. The supervisor should be aware of the processes' that are happening over the course of the group's development and, if appropriate, may choose to facilitate a reflection on this as a group.

Supervision within the Service and Workforce Context

Within the service context, supporting the operational and clinical needs of the CYP low-intensity role is critical. It is essential to develop an awareness of its main purpose and function within and across organisational boundaries, requiring support and advocacy from colleagues and across senior clinical and leadership structures. It is important to note that the LI practitioner workforce may be composed of individuals undertaking training and with lower levels of experience, and without such advocacy the role may struggle to establish itself. Consistent and supportive supervision is a key component of this process and is a central function in the establishment of the role and the ongoing safe and effective practice of the low-intensity practitioner. The specific format of low-intensity supervision, as outlined within this chapter, may differ from the typical supervisory approaches within the service context. It is important for the structures of the low-intensity approach to supervision to be implemented and upheld, both during a training programme and following practitioner qualification. The supervision format underpins the function and clinical architecture of the low-intensity practitioner role and represents a crucial component in sustaining good quality, safe and consistent support for children, young people and families accessing services. In addition, appropriately delivered low-intensity supervision can support, advocate and protect the early intervention pathway that the low-intensity practitioner would typically operate within. This is a critical consideration, as without an aspect of supervisory gatekeeping and clinical advocacy, the role can lose identity and fidelity; quickly being at risk of dilution and being subsumed into a poorly defined or generic offer.

Sitting within the aspiration to deliver consistent and high quality low-intensity supervision are several important practical steps that a service should consider when planning the development of a low-intensity pathway. First, supervision should be clearly mapped within the practitioner and supervisor workplans, allocating time for preparation and administration. In addition, priority should be given to the logistics of delivery including appropriate room allocation and/or access to required technology for online or remote supervision purposes. Practitioners should have ongoing access to recording equipment and up-to-date consent processes to facilitate the bringing of clinical practice recordings as part of CSS. It is also important to define the mechanisms for triage, signposting and onwards referral to support both supervisors and practitioners in managing their caseload with the appropriate information and direction if individuals are considered unsuitable for low-intensity support. Finally, the identification and/or recruitment of a specialist low-intensity supervisor is critical with formal low-intensity supervision training highly recommended. Identifying appropriately qualified or experienced low-intensity supervisors may be problematic, particularly if the role or pathway constitutes a new development within an organisation or represents a wider workforce initiative. However, every effort should be made to problem solve difficulties that may arise in this area to support the appropriate supervisory infrastructure that is so critical to the form and function of the low-intensity role.

Summary

This chapter has overviewed the purpose and requirements of low-intensity supervision within CYP services; covering the primary areas in relation to CMS and CSS. The importance of practitioner preparation and their active involvement in CMS has been discussed, and the format of CMS with the presentation of cases to help standardise this space and to maximise time. Similarly, how to maximise CSS to enhance clinical practice has been discussed, with barriers and facilitators to good practice considered, alongside information on working within a service setting. This chapter emphasises the importance of promoting fidelity to low-intensity working as a supervisor, and how to support practitioners with the variety of issues that may be experienced.

For further resources, please visit the CEDAR website at: https://cedar.exeter.ac.uk/resources/cyp/

References

Bennett-Levy, J. (2006). Therapist skills: A cognitive model of their acquisition and refinement. *Behavioural and Cognitive Psychotherapy*, *34*(1), 57–78.

Bennett-Levy, J., Farrand, P., Christensen, H., & Griffiths, K. (Eds.). (2010). *Oxford guide to low intensity CBT interventions*. Oxford University Press.

Branson, A., Myles, P., Mahdi, M., & Shafran, R. (2018). The relationship between competence and patient outcome with low-intensity cognitive behavioural interventions. *Behavioural and Cognitive Psychotherapy*, *46*(1), 101–114.

Chorpita, B.F., Yim, L.F., Moffitt, C.E., Umemoto, L.A., & Francis, S.E. (2000). Assessment of symptoms of DSM-IV anxiety and depression in children: A Revised Child Anxiety and Depression Scale. *Behaviour Research and Therapy*, *28*(4), 712–728.

Corrie, S., & Lane, D.A. (2015). *CBT supervision*. Sage.

Hayes, D., Fleming, I., & Wolpert, M. (2015). Developing safe care in mental health for children and young people: Drawing on UK experience for solutions to an under-recognised problem. *Current Treatment Options in Pediatrics*, *1*(4), 309–319.

Inskipp, F., & Proctor, B., (1993). The art, craft and tasks of counselling supervision. Part 1: Making the most of supervision. Cascade Publications.

Miller, S., Barry, D., & Brown, J. (2003). The outcome rating scale: A preliminary study of the reliability, validity, and feasibility of a brief visual analog measure. *Journal of Brief Therapy*, *2*(2), 91–100.

Milne, D.L. (2016). Guiding CBT supervision: How well do manuals and guidelines fulfil their promise? *The Cognitive Behaviour Therapist, 9,* E1. doi:10.1017/S1754470X15000720

Milne, D.L. (2017). Evidence-based CBT supervision: Principles and practice. John Wiley and Sons.

Milne, D.L., & Watkins, C.E., Jr. (2014). Defining and understanding clinical supervision: A functional approach. In C.E. Watkins, Jr. & D.L. Milne (Eds.), *The Wiley international handbook of clinical supervision* (pp. 3–19). Wiley-Blackwell. https://doi.org/10.1002/9781118846360.ch1

NHS England. (2014). *IAPT principles in child & adolescent mental health services, values and standards*. "Delivering With and Delivering Well". Retrieved 2 October 2021 from: www.england.nhs.uk/wp-content/uploads/2014/12/delvr-with-delvrng-well.pdf

Proctor, B., & Inskipp, F. (2018). Training for group supervision. In *Supervisor training* (pp. 157–171). Routledge.

Richards, D. (2011). Reach out: National programme supervisor materials to support the delivery of training for psychological wellbeing practitioners delivering low intensity interventions. Rethink.

Roscoe, J., Taylor, J., Harrington, R., & Wilbraham, S. (2022). CBT supervision behind closed doors: Supervisor and supervisee reflections on their expectations and use of clinical supervision. *Counselling and Psychotherapy Research, 22*(4).

Tuckman, B.W. (1965). Developmental sequence in small groups. *Psychological Bulletin, 63*(6), 384–399. https://doi.org/10.1037/h0022100

Turpin, G., & Wheeler, S. (2011). *IAPT supervision guidance*. Department of Health.

19

Adaptations to Working with Children and Young People with Neurodiversity

Lealah Hewitt-Johns

Introduction

Given the high prevalence of Autistic children and young people (CYP) in mental health services, this chapter outlines the case for Low-Intensity (LI) practitioners to be able to adapt their practice for neurodiversity. It advocates for a focus on building strong therapeutic relationships through understanding Autistic traits that impact on traditional interventions and techniques. It outlines core adaptations and reasonable adjustments for LI practice for Autistic CYP, concluding that values-based adaptations work well to deliver creative, flexible and importantly effective interventions.

Definitions

Neurodiversity is a broad term that means all brains are different. Some use the term neuro-divergent to convey that a CYP's brain and ways of thinking might be atypical, or different to neuro-typical brains.

Prevalence rates for neurodiversity conditions such as Autism are 1 per cent (Brugha et al., 2011) meaning one in every 100 CYP has Autism. Debate amongst diagnosticians however indicates this number may be higher (Brugha et al., 2011), as our gold-standard assessment tools and diagnostic manuals are tailored for masculine presentations of Autism, leaving women and girls frequently under-diagnosed (Gould & Ashton-Smith, 2011).

ICD-11, the diagnostic manual used in the UK states that Autism is characterised by persistent difficulties in the ability to initiate and sustain reciprocal social interaction and social communication, and by a range of restricted, repetitive, and inflexible patterns of behaviour and interests. Onset is expected prior to age five, although sometimes it is not until social demands exceed capacity that difficulties become apparent (World Health Organisation, 2021).

The Case for Low-Intensity Work

Prevalence rates of 1 per cent are significant which make mandates for all health and social care staff to have adequate training in Autism key (Department of Health & Social Care, 2019). However, mental health services for CYP see an overrepresentation of young people with Autism, with 1 in 10 young people using CAMHS with a diagnosis of Autism (Wistow & Barnes, 2009). CYP with Autism often have poor experiences of mental health services, citing difficulties with service access, lack of appropriately adapted intervention, and poor levels of staff knowledge about Autism (Read & Schofield, 2010). These experiences often serve to compound difficulties for CYP and their families, create mistrust of services, and perpetuate the myth that Autistic CYP's mental health needs do not respond well to therapeutic offers (Read & Schofield, 2010).

On the contrary, evidence suggests that when practitioners have good knowledge of Autism, and interventions are well adapted, outcomes for Autistic CYP are good (Cooper et al., 2018). NICE guidance (National Institute for Health and Care Excellence, 2021) states that Autistic CYP who have the verbal and cognitive ability to engage in CBT should be offered therapy that is adjusted to their needs. NICE advocates for adjustments that include emotion recognition training, greater use of written and visual information and structured worksheets, a more cognitively concrete and structured approach, simplified cognitive activities such as multiple choice worksheets, involving a parent or carer in sessions, offering regular breaks to support attention maintenance, and engaging the CYP's special interests in therapy.

As such, LI practice for CYP, which often includes brief, focussed, structured sessions, delivered by practitioners trained in involving parents and carers, whilst utilising the creative skills necessary to work with CYP can be a highly appropriate part of an intervention. Autistic characteristics such as difficulties with rigidity, inflexible thinking, and a preference for structure and an ordered, logical process, lend themselves well to CBT approaches (Spain & Happe, 2020), which place emphasis on systematic evidence gathering to challenge cognitive rigidity from anxiety or depression (Kennerley et al., 2016).

Engagement

As LI-CBT approaches lend themselves well to Autistic thinking, and much of the literature around cognitive processes in Autism focusses on systemising and logical preferences (Baron-Cohen et al., 2009), it is easy to overlook the need for careful engagement with CYP with Autism. Well-adapted interventions can have excellent outcomes but are useless if the CYP never makes it into the therapy room.

It is important not to pathologise a lack of reasonable adjustments or adaptations made to the CYP's home, education or work environment when considering whether to offer therapy for presentations of low mood and anxiety. LI practitioners can be well placed however to offer psycho-education, adapted for Autism about anxiety or low mood that supports the CYP and their network to appropriately introduce tools to reduce anxiety, like visual timetables, social stories, sensory ladders, or emotional states scales. Setting homework for CYP and their parents around implementing such tools and tracking their impact in sessions can be a helpful way of supporting CYP's systems to be accountable in supporting reduction of mental health symptoms.

One of the core challenges Autistic CYP face is difficulties imagining situations beyond their own experience (Lind et al., 2014). This means that any new environments, or processes, even if they may be fairly predictable to neuro-typical CYP, will likely feel daunting. It can be helpful for practitioners to walk themselves through the process of arriving at therapy from receiving an appointment letter and telephoning in multiple choice opt-in processes, to car parks, buzzing into the building and navigating receptionists and waiting areas. Clear, concrete steps of the process, what to expect and how to navigate it, supported with photographs can make the impossible seem possible, and support CYP through the door. It also serves to build trust in the practitioner, as it demonstrates that a neurodiverse mind has been considered in operational procedures.

Some Autistic CYP can find attending therapy challenging, given the nature of discussions. It is therefore sometimes important that intervention sessions are motivating and carry sufficient reward, beyond the motivation of symptom reduction. For some this can be some extra time to engage in games or other fun activities with their practitioner, or time to discuss a special interest. Autistic CYP are often socially isolated, and rarely in positions of power or influence. Space and time to talk about their special interest or enjoy social time with someone that has unconditional positive regard for them outside of their family circle are rare and therefore can be hugely motivating.

Reasonable Adjustments

The Equality Act (2010) makes it a legal requirement that health services are as easy to access for disabled people, as those without disabilities. Services are obligated to make reasonable adjustments to their processes, procedures and environments to support such access.

Core Adaptations

The following core adaptations are recommended for working with CYP with neuro-diversity.

Say As You Do and Do As You Say – Self-Narration

It is well known that social stories, comic strip conversations, and other visual methods that help communicate social rules and upcoming scenarios are helpful for Autistic CYP (Bondy & Frost, 2011; Gray, 1998; 2021) as they support navigating the unknown and provide clear expectations and structure for new experiences. Autistic CYP often struggle to make inferences based on the information they have (Bodner et al., 2015), which means they can misinterpret their practitioner's actions or thought processes frequently. Explaining aloud simple things like 'I'm jotting down what you are saying so I don't forget,' can be helpful to stop assumptions like 'you must be doodling because I'm boring you' or saying, 'I'm going to take a moment to think about what you just said,' rather than sit in silence.

Sensory Room Adaptations

There are many available guides on how to make a space 'Autism friendly' (National Autistic Society, 2022), most of which highlight the value of softer lighting, calming blue and green toned colour palettes, freedom from clutter, and the availability of fidget items. Whilst such changes are of course recommended, they are not always possible to implement in busy clinics with little resource. Strip lighting is notoriously difficult and can feel like strobe lighting to some Autistic people (Grandin, 2009), so turning off bright lights can be helpful. Consider the noise in the therapy room, understanding that many Autistic people can struggle to filter out background auditory information from their practitioner's voice (Rotschafer, 2021). Autistic brains tend to regard each piece of information as being as salient as the next, and do not tend to focus in on faces and voices in the same way that pro-social neurotypical brains do (Behrmann et al., 2006). Don't take it personally but you aren't likely to be the most important thing in the room to an Autistic brain, so it will cause the Autistic person additional strain to focus on you if there are other unnecessary auditory or visual distractions. Support them by minimising background noise by closing windows, choosing the room furthest from busy corridors or playgrounds.

Consider the setup of the room and make this part of your contracting with your client. Chairs facing opposite each other is rarely comfortable for CYP with Autism, who do not rely on non-verbal communication as heavily to interact as neurotypical people. Many CYP report that the additional strain of having to make eye contact, look at faces, and try to interpret others' expressions can be hugely fatiguing (Trevisan et al., 2017). Supporting your CYP to move the room about in a way that works for them can make an enormous difference to their engagement in sessions, and how exhausting they find them. Additionally, giving people explicit permission to move in the space can be especially important. Unwritten social rules are rarely implicitly understood (Grandin et al., 2017), so being explicit that your CYP can re-arrange, move, and stim (a self- stimulatory repetitive movement or behaviour) freely during your sessions is important.

If you cannot make any changes, let your CYP know. It can be hugely validating to have your needs understood and acknowledged, even if they cannot be met.

Additional Time

Common reasonable adjustments include more sessions, longer sessions, or shorter sessions, based on the person's needs. Many Autistic people have difficulties with processing speed and can take longer to hear, process, formulate and respond to questions (Haigh et al., 2018). I often give the rule of thumb of 15 seconds that practitioners should wait after asking a question before expecting a response. It is a common feature of Autistic conversations to have longer pauses, which often contributes to the sense of poor social reciprocity (Haigh et al., 2018). Subsequently, it is important that reasonable adjustments are made to session length to accommodate this difference. Practitioners are also advised to get more comfortable with silence, it is often only uncomfortable for the neuro-typical person, and can be vital in giving the neurodiverse person time to respond meaningfully.

Chunking Sessions

Owing to the difficulties with processing speed above, it can therefore be helpful to focus a block of sessions on one area of difficulty, to slow the pace of the intervention enough to allow thorough processing and retention. This may mean that goals need to be broken down into smaller chunks again. It may take one full session to do psycho-education around CBT approaches, rather than the first 10 minutes for example, so the initial 'block' of sessions may need to focus on psycho-education of condition, orientation to model/approach, and building rapport, rather than expecting these topics to be covered in the first couple of sessions. If someone was presenting with social anxiety, associated with PE lessons, and getting on the school bus, it might be helpful to tackle this one element at a time, so a block of sessions on understanding social anxiety, a block of sessions focussed on PE lessons, a block of sessions on the school bus. The work remains low-intensity, but will, quite appropriately, take longer to work through.

Psycho-education and Emotional Literacy

Psycho-education is often a hugely important part of any psychological intervention; however, this is especially so for neurodiverse CYP who may be more likely to struggle to normalise their experiences, have fewer social opportunities to validate their experiences, and have a tendency for black and white thinking (Cooper et al., 2018). Shared understanding over key terms, particularly in LI-CBT, is essential, as idiosyncratic understanding of what 'panic' is for example, could mean the wrong intervention is offered, when the focus should be more on generalised or social anxiety.

It is common for practitioners to assume shared knowledge around basic feelings, and how they might link or escalate, particularly for older CYP who are articulate and without intellectual disability. Psycho-education around emotional literacy must not be overlooked however as many young people with Autism struggle with identifying, articulating, and managing responses to both their own and others' emotional states (Mazefsky & White, 2014). It can therefore be a helpful standalone LI intervention for neurodiverse CYP. The principles of labelling emotions, creating idiosyncratic ladders to support understanding of moving up and down emotional states such as in The Incredible Five Point Scale (Dunn & Curtis, 2021) are excellent starting points for learning about emotions and finding ways to manage them.

Session Records

Processing and memory difficulties, combined with difficulties in inference and transferability of knowledge and application from one setting to another (Bodner et al., 2015), mean that even powerful therapeutic sessions can be difficult for Autistic CYP to remember afterwards, which can hamper progress as more time is needed for recap and learning at each new session. Agreeing a simple method of recapping the key headlines from the session and doing this routinely before the session ends can therefore be transformative. For some this is writing together in a special notebook, log, or phone note that the CYP takes home, or it could be recording a voice note, drawing a brief mind map, or cue card. Asking the CYP to describe the 'headlines' in their own words is also a great opportunity to check their understanding and correct any misconceptions.

Getting Out of the Therapy Room

Difficulties with transferring learning from one setting to another are common amongst Autistic CYP (Bodner et al., 2015), which means that great learning can happen in the therapy room, but often it stays there. Working with neurodiverse CYP presents a brilliant opportunity to get outside the therapy room, particularly for evidence gathering, and behavioural experiments and activation. If you create social stories, or visual resources to support storying new learning, take the resource out in public and use it in practice to trial it. It cements real world application, ensures sessions are memorable and keeps challenging steps fun.

Offer Multiple Choices

Open questions can be particularly difficult for Autistic CYP due to initiation difficulties common to Autistic CYP (Cooper et al., 2018); often open questions such as 'how have you been?' can lead to silence and uncertainty about how to answer such a question. To the neurodiverse brain there may be too many possibilities.

'When someone asks me how I've been, I don't know what they mean. Have I been good? Have I been unwell? Have I done what they asked me to do last session? Have I been feeling despair? How have I been at school, and do they mean at lunch or in that maths lesson with the teacher I hate? Do they mean how I've been at home? Like when was I at home? What did I do there? Do they want to know what I watched on TV? Do they want to know HOW I've been doing things, or WHAT I am feeling now? It's been a week since our last session so I could answer that question in approximately a million ways! It's hard to say all that without sounding like you are trying to be awkward so I would probably just shrug.'

Instead, it is helpful to use more concrete, closed questions, often with multiple choices. Practitioners can worry that this limits the young person's responses or can be too leading, but most young people report that being offered choices helps orientate them to the nature of the question and starts them off. Try to ensure you explicitly give permission for the CYP to correct you or say something completely different too.

Keep It Visual

Fortunately, working with neurotypical CYP already requires creative, engaging and visual approaches that often utilise flip charts, white boards, pens and paper and lots of drawing out of ideas, concepts, and mapping thought processes. These skills provide excellent foundations for working with neurodiverse CYP. Where neurodiverse CYP may need additional drawing out is when they are being asked to think hypothetically, or to imagine novel or new situations or scenarios, a common feature in LI-CBT. If practitioners are asking for different thoughts, or generating lots of different possible thoughts from strangers – practitioners should really emphasise the visual elements of this – redraw the scene each time rather than using multiple thought bubbles, use post-it pads stuck on your head, draw out and make 'negative thinking' or 'positive thinking' hats that you try on to emphasise your meaning and keep what is a cognitively challenging exercise playful and engaging.

If following an agenda, try using post-it pads to write this together, and remove and discard when each element is done. It supports collaboration and shared responsibility as well as making it easier for the neurodiverse mind to gauge time and have a sense of control in an unfamiliar situation.

Include Parents or Carers

Whilst it is of course vital to respect CYP's wish for privacy and independence in their health care, it can sometimes be important and valuable to include parents in low-intensity interventions. Not only can this provide excellent opportunities for psycho-education and modelling, it can also support parents' understanding of, and ability to, disrupt maintaining factors (Hudson et al., 2017). Parents of neurodiverse CYP are often their children's best translators, and can support practitioners in better understanding likely triggers and unusual contextual factors such as sensory needs that can 'trip up' the therapeutic relationship if unknown (Rilveria, 2022).

Including Neurodiversity in the Descriptive Formulation

Not all neurodiverse CYP will have formal diagnoses, and of those that do, not all will be aware of their diagnoses depending on age, understanding and parental decisions. It is important to understand how much the CYP knows and understands about their condition, as this will influence how you frame discussions around their needs. Although it is important to differentiate between mental health conditions and neurodiversity, co-morbid presentations mean the issues become entwined and it is therefore essential to ensure that descriptive formulations include neurodiversity in whatever way is relevant. In relation to CBT formulations, it is worth the practitioner asking themselves questions such as:

- Is the thinking more concrete/black and white because of Autism?
- Are sensory differences impacting on how the CYP notices and responds to physical sensations associated with anxiety? Hypo or hypersensitivity to different senses, including interoception (the perception of sensations within the body such as temperature, pain, heartbeat, breath and hunger) can be different in neurodiverse CYP (Marco et al., 2011), which can mean they struggle to identify physical sensations as expected, which in turn can impact on thoughts and subsequent actions associated with them. Practitioners may therefore need to be creative in exploring other ways to identify physical manifestations of anxiety.
- Are Autistic difficulties with change and transition exacerbating anxiety about new situations? There may be some good intervention around managing anxiety around change and newness, but this could additionally be supported by visual methods such as visual timetables, change cards, or social stories in a two-pronged attack.
- Is a lack of knowledge about social rules and absence of appropriate social scripts causing social anxiety? Often social anxiety is accompanied by fears of not knowing what to say or how to say it; Autistic individuals often have

additional difficulties with knowing what to say and how to say it without the presence of anxiety. Opportunities to understand and learn typical scripts can mediate these difficulties enough to work with the underlying anxiety.

In many of these examples it is often about addressing the 'Autistic' element at play in the descriptive formulation first, which leaves space to explore the mental health issues that are left. It is hugely important to validate that life is harder by virtue of being Autistic, not because Autistic brains are impaired or less desirable, but because society is not set up for neurodiverse brains, so there are extra barriers in the way. Practitioners have to support individuals to remove as many barriers as possible, by looking at the world (and the problems brought to the therapy space) through an Autistic lens and tackling them together, before addressing the more common mental health difficulties.

Including Autism or neurodiversity in descriptive formulations also has the potential for longer-term benefits. If we see therapeutic experiences, even at the LI level, as ways of understanding our experiences and ourselves better – it follows that supporting a CYP to understand their Autism, and therefore themselves better will help them in future endeavours.

Managing Endings

Relationships, even professional ones are often hard won for Autistic people, which coupled with a tendency to struggle to manage change can make endings hard (Kim, 2011). Having their Autism well understood, embraced, and even celebrated outside of the family circle can be a special but rare experience for CYP, and endings may come with fears about not being understood again, or where to take conversations about feelings and emotions. It is not uncommon, particularly for CYP with neurodiversity and intellectual disability, to have little opportunities to talk about 'sad, mad or bad' feelings (Arthur, 2003), with an overemphasis on leisure time and being happy (Brown, 1994; MacDonald, 2015). Practitioners can support endings for Autistic CYP by being clear from the outset about session blocks, counting down each session explicitly and visually as you go. It is also helpful to support the CYP and whomever is in their network to agree and timetable in regular time to practise skills learned, or 'talk time' for emotions. Scheduling time to talk can be a powerful permission giving exercise for both the CYP and their supporters alike.

Summary

Whilst the core adaptations discussed above are helpful additions to LI CYP practice when working with neurodiversity, it is likely that these are not radically different or new skills being used, simply existing skills applied in different ways. They also represent an application of values in practice, that focus around placing the CYP, however their brains are wired, at the centre of our thinking. If we get things right for neurodiverse CYP, we often get them right for lots of other CYP who will benefit from finding services and their practitioners more adaptable, creative, and flexible.

References

Arthur, A.R. (2003). The emotional lives of people with learning disability. *British Journal of Learning Disabilities, 31*(1), 25–30. https://doi.org/10.1046/j.1468-3156.2003.00193.x

Baron-Cohen, S., Ashwin, E., Ashwin, C., Tavassoli, T., & Chakrabarti, B. (2009). Talent in autism: Hyper-systemizing, hyper-attention to detail and sensory hypersensitivity. *Philosophical Transactions of the Royal Society, 364*(1522), 1377–1383. https://doi.org/10.1098%2Frstb.2008.0337

Behrmann, M., Thomas, C., & Humphreys, K. (2006). Seeing it differently: Visual processing. *Trends in Cognitive Sciences, 10*(6), 258–264. https://doi.org/10.1016/j.tics.2006.05.001

Bodner, K.E., Engelhardt, C.R., Minshew, N.J., & Williams, D.L. (2015). Making inferences: Comprehension of physical causality, intentionality, and emotions in discourse by high-functioning older children, adolescents, and adults with autism. *Journal of Autism and Developmental Disorders, 45*(9), 2721–2733. https://doi.org/10.1007/s10803-015-2436-3

Bondy, A., & Frost, L. (2011). A picture's worth: PECS and other visual communication strategies in autism (2nd ed.). Woodbine House.

Brown, H. (1994). What price theory if you cannot afford the bus fare: Normalization and leisure services for people with learning disabilities. *Health and Social Care in the Community, 2*(3), 153–159. https://doi.org/10.1111/j.1365-2524.1994.tb00160.x

Brugha, T.S., McManus, S., Bankart, J., Scott, F., Purdon, S., Smith, J., Bebbington, P., Jenkins, R., & Meltzer, G.C. (2011). Epidemiology of autism spectrum disorders in adults in the community in England. *Archives of General Psychiatry, 68*(5), 459–465. https://doi.org/10.1001/archgenpsychiatry.2011.38

Cooper, K., Loades, M.E., & Russell, A.J. (2018). Adapting psychological therapies for autism – Therapist experience, skills and confidence. *Research in Autism Spectrum Disorders, 45*, 43–50. https://doi.org/10.1016/j.rasd.2017.11.002

Department of Health & Social Care. (2019). *Learning disability and autism; a consultation*. Crown.

Dunn, B.K., & Curtis, M. (2021). The incredible 5-point scale: Assisting students in understanding social interactions and managing their emotional responses. Kari Dunn.

Gould, J., & Ashton-Smith, J. (2011). Missed diagnosis or misdiagnosis? Girls and women on the autism spectrum. *Good Autism Practice, 8*, 34–41.

Grandin, T. (2009). *Thinking in pictures*. Bloomsbury Publishing.

Grandin, T., Barron, S., & Zysk, V. (2017). Unwritten rules of social relationships: Decoding social mysteries through the unique perspectives of autism. Future Horizons Inc.

Gray, C. (1998). Social stories and comic strip conversations with students with asperger syndrome and high-functioning autism. In E.M. Schopler (Ed.), *Asperger syndrome or high-functioning autism? Current issues in autism* (pp. 167–198). Springer.

Gray, C. (2021). *Social stories*. Routledge.

Haigh, S.M., Walsh, J.A., Mazefsky, C.A., Minshew, N.J., & Eask, S.M. (2018). Processing speed is impaired in adults with autism spectrum disorder and relates to social communication abilities. *Journal of Autism and Developmental Disorders*, 48(8), 2653–2662. https://doi.org/10.1007%2Fs10803-018-3515-z

Hudson, M., Dallos, R., & McKenzie, R. (2017). Systemic-attachment formulation for families of children with autism. *Advances in Autism*, 3(3), 142–153. https://doi.org/10.1108/AIA-02-2017-0005

Kennerley, H., Kirk, J., & Westbrook, D. (2016). An introduction to cognitive behavior therapy: Skills and applications. Sage.

Kim, J. (2011). The trauma of parting: Endings of music therapy with children with autism spectrum disorders. *Nordic Journal of Music Therapy*, 23(3), 263–281. https://doi.org/10.1080/08098131.2013.854269

Lind, S.E., Williams, D.M., Bowler, D.M., & Peel, A. (2014). Episodic memory and episodic future thinking impairments in high-functioning autism spectrum disorder: An underlying difficulty with scene construction or self-projection? *Neuropsychology*, 28(1), 55–67. https://doi.org/10.1037/neu0000005

MacDonald, D. (2015). Creative ways of talking: A narrative literature review concerning emotional support for adults with mild or moderate learning difficulties. *British Journal of Learning Disabilities*, 44(3), 233–239. https://doi.org/10.1111/bld.12143

Marco, E.J., Hinkley, L.B., Hill, S.S., & Nagarajan, S.S. (2011). Sensory processing in autism: A review of neurophysiologic findings. *Pediatric Research*, 69(5), 48–54. https://doi.org/10.1203/pdr.0b013e3182130c54

Mazefsky, C.A., & White, S.W. (2014). Emotion regulation: Concepts and practice in autism spectrum disorder. *Child and Adolescent Psychiatric Clinics of North America*, 23(1), 15–24. https://doi.org/10.1016/j.chc.2013.07.002

National Autistic Society. (2022). *Accessible environments*. https://dy55nndrxke1w.cloudfront.net/file/24/UQOocJfUQAI68NWUQXM_UQPonhF/Accessible_environments_0822.pdf

National Institute for Health and Care Excellence. (2021). *Autism spectrum disorder in under 19s: Support and management* [Clinical Guideline170]. www.nice.org.uk/guidance/cg170

Read, N., & Schofield, A. (2010). Autism: Are mental health services failing children and parents? *Journal of Family Health Care*, 20(4), 120–124.

Rilveria, J.R. (2022). Understanding the secondary system of therapeutic alliance in autism interventions from the perspectives of parents and caregivers. *International Journal of Child Care and Education Policy*, 16(1), 1–24. https://doi.org/10.1186/s40723-021-00094-6

Rotschafer, S.E. (2021). Auditory discrimination in autism spectrum disorder. *Frontiers in Neuroscience*, 15, 1–13. https://doi.org/10.3389/fnins.2021.651209

Spain, D., & Happe, F. (2020). How to optimise cognitive behaviour therapy (CBT) for people with autism spectrum disorders (ASD): A delphi study. *Journal of Rational Emotive and Cognitive-Behavior Therapy*, 38, 184–208. https://doi.org/10.1007/s10942-019-00335-1

Trevisan, D.A., Roberts, N., Lin, C., & Birmingham, E. (2017). How do adults and teens with self-declared autism spectrum disorder experience eye contact? A qualitative analysis of first-hand accounts. *Public Library of Science*, 12(11), 1–22. https://doi.org/10.1371/journal.pone.0188446

Wistow, R., & Barnes, D. (2009). A profile of child and adolescent mental health services in England 2007/8: Findings from children's services mapping. Department of Health, Department of Children Schools and Families.

World Health Organisation. (2021). *International classification of diseases*, Eleventh Revision. WHO.

20

Inclusive Practice

Indiana Montaque

Introduction

This chapter will introduce the foundations of inclusive practice in LI-CBT, with some exploration of the ways practitioners can uphold this. This topic is broad and rich, and as such, this chapter alone will be unable to address every facet of inclusive practice and specific adaptations for groups and communities. Instead, the discussions aim to acknowledge the fundamentals of inclusive practice, with an emphasis on the need to sensitively and meaningfully gather information from CYP about their values and identity. It is hoped that these underpinnings can be used by practitioners to make individualised, considered adaptations to support their clients. As there are several minoritised groups who face additional barriers when accessing support (Beck & Naz, 2019), the discussions will acknowledge the responsibility practitioners hold in providing equitable support for CYP who may have been disadvantaged or under-served. Although this is a standalone chapter, the emphasis is on encouraging inclusive practice that is woven throughout the CYP's journey with services, from pre-assessment to after discharge.

This chapter's purpose is to:

- Introduce the key principles of inclusive practice for *all* CYP in LI-CBT.
- Begin to consider the journey within services that deliver low-intensity practice through the lens of inclusivity.
- Give recognition to the need to consider adaptations to LI-CBT to enable working in an inclusive manner.
- Acknowledge further professional development and wider practice issues that are relevant to the context of inclusive working within low-intensity practice.

The Importance of Inclusive Practice in LI-CBT

The principles of LI-CBT rest on working in a collaborative, inclusive manner, to provide evidence-based support at a time that prevents difficulties escalating (Papworth et al., 2013). Inclusive practice can be defined as the approaches that ensure all individuals and communities are included in the service and its provisions, and that practice promotes their diversity with respect and dignity. This is a key clinical skill, and practitioners should

INCLUSIVE PRACTICE | 273

hold in mind that continual development and reflection will enhance inclusive practice approaches throughout training and beyond. This centres on the need to authentically value the diversity of *all* CYP and that practice should be free from approaches that have the potential to perpetuate harmful biases and stereotypes, which can prevent minoritised groups from accessing support in the first instance (Memon et al., 2016).

It is important that inclusive practice is used as a lens in which to view the entire service provision. Through this lens, it can be seen that many minoritised groups face several barriers throughout the journey to wellbeing. Inclusive practice is concerned with acknowledging this on an individual level and advocating for service change at a systems level.

Foundations of Inclusive Practice in LI-CBT

Some core values that make up the foundations of inclusive practice could include equity, curiosity and respect. With these values in mind, focusing on specific areas of 'diversity' based on CYP identity has the potential to negate the individuality in experiences and needs when supporting CYP through LI-CBT. 'Diversity' implies there are default identities and that working in an inclusive manner is only reserved for those who do not fit these defaults. This risks using unhelpful biases and stereotypes to assume an understanding of identity, which may not be true (Lago, 2011). By regarding inclusive practice as a competency that is relevant to *all* CYP, this prevents the lens being activated only when faced with 'difference'.

Despite the need to consider inclusivity for all CYP, it is important to acknowledge that there are communities that may not find mental health support inclusive, and adaptations may be needed to support equity of service. As a foundation of inclusive practice, low-intensity practitioners may wish to use Burnham's (2013) Social GGR-RAAACCEEESSS or the ADDRESSING framework (Hays, 2001) to curiously explore areas of identity. These include, but are not limited to:

- Age
- Religion
- Ethnicity
- Sexuality and Sexual Identity
- Religion
- (Dis)ability

Exploring these areas of identity should be standard for all CYP accessing support from Low-Intensity services, and an intersectional approach will allow multiple, overlapping areas of identity to be explored to prevent defining CYP by a single identity in isolation. Alongside this, practitioners should commit to their own self-practice/self-reflection through exploring their own identity and culture (Laireiter, 2003) as this will interact with the client's sense of identity. Knowledge of one's personal and professional self is important for exploring concepts such as culture, values and diversity with clients.

As part of delivering equitable services, practitioners' awareness of the specific sub-groups of identity that may be underrepresented in referrals to primary care services is a core foundation of inclusive practice. The context in which services exist should be considered to facilitate equity as discrimination, harassment and abuse may be present for minoritised communities (Lawton et al., 2021) which low-intensity prac-titioners will be required to explore.

With these foundations in mind, the next sections will explore how inclusive practice can be upheld within the context of low-intensity practice; to move from recognition to action.

Pre-assessment Considerations

Before a referral has been accepted into the service where a low-intensity practitioner is based, the lens of inclusive practice can be used to ensure equitable, accessible ser-vices for all who need mental health support. Structural inequalities exist that make it difficult for some individuals and communities to access support (Grant et al., 2012). In the UK context, the notion of the 'hard-to-reach' emerged following the recogni-tion that some families would be 'easier' to engage in statutory services than others. These groups often include, people from racially minoritised backgrounds, people from the LGBTQ+ community, Gypsy, Roma, Traveller communities and those from lower income backgrounds (Osgood et al., 2013). These communities often have a multitude of reasons why they cannot, or have no desire to, access the care that other groups do. Therefore, it is the responsibility of services to address this, through out-reach work and integration with these communities to support service equity.

In LI-CBT services, there are groups who are disproportionately underrepresented in referrals (Lawton et al., 2021), which implies that the lens of inclusive practice should be used to consider how to engage these communities. The low-intensity workforce can address this in a number of ways:

- Working towards a diverse workforce (Hakim et al., 2019) which will support people from minoritised groups meeting practitioners who may be able to reso-nate with some of their experiences.
- Exploration of values and ways in which these communities define help and support. This could come in the form of outreach work within these communities and sharing information in local hubs.
- Evaluation of service policies to ensure services are supportive of these groups and the difficulties they may face when accessing support.

INCLUSIVE PRACTICE | 275

- Multi-agency working with specialist support services and communities. This could include young carer organisations, gender identity and sexuality services, religious groups and organisations, or parenting support groups. Practitioners should see their support as embedded in the communities that their clients exist within and ensure outreach work collaborates with these networks.
- Consistently collecting and evaluating demographic and accessibility information as part of the referral process.

These suggestions are not exhaustive; there will be variances in the ways inclusive practice can be considered before the CYP steps into the therapeutic space based on the service location. Pre-assessment consideration works to break barriers that prevent access to services for those from minoritised groups, before they get into the therapy room (Beck & Naz, 2019).

Assessment

The assessment session can be a pivotal opportunity to set the tone of inclusive practice for the low-intensity intervention support to follow. Depending on the client's needs, adaptations may have been required before the session started, such as wheelchair/mobility access, car parking, larger rooms, and more breaks. Where possible, adaptations should be set up before the CYP arrives at the service.

Accurate and thorough assessment of the CYP's presenting difficulty should be done alongside equally thorough exploration of their identity, culture and values. Practitioners report feeling apprehensive asking about some areas of identity, including race and gender identity, out of fear that they will come across as insensitive or discriminatory; however, CYP value practitioners acknowledging aspects of identity in a curious and considered way and this enhances outcomes (Beck, 2016). To ensure that this sensitive information is gathered and discussed meaningfully, practitioners should ask these questions as standard to all CYP and communicate that the purpose of gathering this information is to provide a more supportive, appropriate service. The demographic information form should be used as a tool to funnel for further information from a curious stance. Making space to discuss this information in the assessment session ensures its collection is meaningful to the service and to the CYP's presenting difficulty, as different cultures and communities discuss and describe wellbeing differently (Hakim et al., 2019).

Combining an inclusive approach with creativity supports gathering this information in a developmentally appropriate way. In keeping with the LI-CBT model, using body maps can be a helpful way to gather information about Autonomic, Behavioural, Cognitive and Emotional (ABCE) experiences, as well as considering the identity of the young person and what they value. Family sculpts can be an interactive

LOW-INTENSITY PRACTICE WITH CYP AND FAMILIES

tool to gain a sense of the system, cultures and practices that are important. Areas of identity can be asked in an indirect manner to invite the CYP's language and description as a priority to ensure a shared understanding (Rathod & Kingdon, 2009), with the funnelling technique used to ensure that further information is gathered. Some potential indirect questions may include:

- Tell me about your relationships at school/college?
- How do you spend your weekend/free time?
- What is important to you and your family that keeps you well?
- Tell me about your school/college work?

These questions allow information to be gathered about identity from an open perspective. To balance problem-saturated assessment sessions, inclusive practice values exploring areas of strength and resilience, as these often lie in the young person's wider system, culture and practices. Open questions allow the CYP to describe their strengths and difficulties in language that is fitting with their community and values and ensure assessments are free from unhelpful assumptions and stereotypes. It is also imperative that underrepresented and minoritised groups' strengths are championed, which can be achieved by asking about these in the context of their identity (Craig et al., 2013).

Routine Outcome Measures (ROMs) should be considered in relation to inclusive practice. To support the accessible use of ROMs, they may require translation by a professional associated with the service. There may not be a direct translation for particular words and phrases in some languages, which emphasises the need to have a discussion around the individual questions and their scores. Having visual images to aid the ROMs may facilitate a shared understanding and is an appropriate adaptation to consider to the needs of many communities.

The problem statement has the potential to be adapted using pictures and images to enable an inclusive approach for CYP who require information in a different format. Collaborating on culturally considered goals is a cornerstone of inclusive practice (Arthur & Collins, 2010; Craig et al., 2013). As the goals form the direction of the intervention support, it is important that these reflect the CYP's values, and that they are in keeping with their individual identity.

Overall, there is more than sufficient flexibility within the assessment structure to ensure all CYP have the space to discuss their identity and values in the context of strengths and difficulties. This will not only inform the intervention support to follow but will uphold the individuality of support for all CYP.

Intervention

To continue inclusive practice into the low-intensity intervention offered, the information gathered at first contact can be meaningfully applied within the sessions.

INCLUSIVE PRACTICE | 277

Part of instilling power for marginalised groups comes in the form of support that is considered of their individual needs, which enhances the need to gather the information prior to the chosen intervention support.

For some groups and communities, there may be a 'culture clash' between their personal values and beliefs and the underpinnings of LI-CBT approaches. For example, for some groups and communities, healing is important from a collective perspective, which may not feel reflected in the individualised sessions in LI-CBT. To adapt appropriately for this, inviting family members into sessions and referrals to in-school groups may be a suitable adaptation. Some interventions, for example Cognitive Restructuring, if used incorrectly might imply that beliefs that are rooted in religious or cultural practices need to be challenged (Abudabbeh & Hays, 2006). This is where checking in with the CYP is imperative, to ensure pathologising or challenging of religious beliefs does not occur.

It is possible to uphold both the core skills of LI-CBT and adapting for cultural values. Practitioners will be required to hold in mind both the evidence-based intervention and the needs of the CYP, which can be achieved through collaborative working (Miranda et al., 2005). Clinical skills and case management supervision can be utilised to ensure advice is sought on suitability of adaptations (Iwamasa et al., 2006) and working within LI-CBT guidelines. Some examples of appropriate, inclusive adaptations are:

- Exploring values to embed these into CYP goals and rewards in Coping Cat.
- Designing experiments to test prediction considering accessibility to ensure the CYP can engage in the intervention.
- Creating an adapted version of the 'Worry Monster' to suit the CYP's interests.
- Offering alternative approaches to the 'Thought Diary' in Cognitive Restructuring in the form of apps, audio journaling, diaries and planners.
- Using a Brief Behavioural Activation (BA) values worksheet to explore a breadth of values.

As well as these general suggestions, more specific adaptations may be required, which is particularly important when working alongside CYP with a disability. Home tasks may come in the form of written information and worksheets, which may be inaccessible for several groups of CYP and practitioners should explore alternative approaches, such as digitalising support through apps and emailing resources. Digital formats enable screen-readers, spell-check and other accessibility tools to be used, which makes worksheets more accessible. This will not only support CYPs to complete homework tasks but will ensure reduced confidence or self-esteem is not a barrier to these tasks.

Adaptations should be organised prior to intervention support starting, which reinforces the need to gather this information at assessment. Carer-focused approaches (Behavioural Interventions and Parent-Led CBT for Anxiety) rely heavily on reading

LOW-INTENSITY PRACTICE WITH CYP AND FAMILIES

the content ahead of the session, which should be discussed with inclusivity at the forefront. Alternative approaches to written material can be offered to ensure equity of support, which might include translation of materials, the option of audio delivery or allowing extra time in session to discuss the content.

To conclude this section, key practice considerations can be drawn from Craig et al.'s (2013) work with sexual minority youths. Their adaptations to CBT for this client group indicated that a preferred adaptation to the intervention came in the form of acknowledging the unique struggles and strengths that this group face and possess. This indicates that appreciating CYPs' identity and strengths as part of their mental health support conveys a powerful message and can be an intervention in itself.

Inclusive Practice beyond Intervention Endings

Inclusive practice requires a continuous feedback loop of evaluation and monitoring, to ensure development of services and meaningful adjustments to service provision. This is especially important when working alongside minoritised groups, as these communities face additional barriers when accessing services. Inclusive approaches with groups who have unfairly been deemed 'hard-to-reach' goes beyond discharge from services. In order for services to progress and widen, structural barriers that minoritised groups and communities face to be addressed, low-intensity practitioners have a responsibility to continue developing services in a way that centres CYPs' voice (Whitehead & Barnard, 2013).

Outreach and evaluation projects should include, and ideally be led by, CYP who have been through the service to improve access and outcomes (Kada, 2019; Beck & Naz, 2019). Outreach work is especially important for those whom services have historically underserved, to support active inclusion of these communities. Participation groups help to create communities of support that continue wellbeing after discharge from services. Authentic participation groups will be:

- Service-user led
- Evaluated and adjusted through feedback
- Serving a purpose and function that is both reflective and development focused
- Mutually beneficial
- Reimbursing service users for their contribution

As part of routine monitoring of low-intensity services, the Experience of Service Questionnaire (ESQ) completed by CYP should be utilised to explore feedback at the point of discharge, which should be used to facilitate service level change (Flott et al., 2017). A positive experience of service should also be viewed as vitally important to recovery and ongoing wellbeing. The premise of early intervention services

INCLUSIVE PRACTICE | 279

may mean that CYP do not need to use services again, however, a positive experience of service could increase the likelihood of applying skills and techniques from support if they experience lapses and the likelihood of them re-engaging with services should this be required (Hamilton et al., 2011). A positive experience may be shared with peers and within their communities, which will break down stigma and could have a more pervasive impact within communities (Hamilton et al., 2011).

Summary

This chapter has introduced inclusive practice specific to the LI-CBT workforce and the importance of using this lens for all CYP. The discussions have outlined that there is an inequity of services for some individuals in minoritised groups and that service equity should always be the aim when working inclusively.

Inclusive practice is not an end point or a goal in LI-CBT but is an ongoing loop of development and learning. It should be viewed as a need rather than an option, to continue upholding ethical working guidelines and the principles of LI-CBT. The discussions of inclusive practice cannot be separated from the historical inequity of services that continue to underserve minoritised groups accessing primary care and early intervention support. Low-intensity practitioners are in an exciting and important position to support inclusive practice in the therapeutic space and advocate for structural service change at a systems level. Both are required to be truly inclusive in practice and approaches.

References

Abudabbeh, N., & Hays, P.A. (2006). Cognitive-behavioral therapy with people of Arab heritage. In P.A. Hays & G.Y. Iwamasa (Eds.), *Culturally responsive cognitive-behavioral therapy: Assessment, practice, and supervision* (pp. 141–159). American Psychological Association. https://doi.org/10.1037/11433-006

Arthur, N., & Collins, S. (Eds.). (2010). *Culture-infused counselling* (2nd ed.). Counselling Concepts.

Beck, A. (2016). Transcultural cognitive behaviour therapy for anxiety and depression: A practical guide. Routledge.

Beck, A., & Naz, S. (2019). The need for service change and community outreach work to support trans-cultural cognitive behaviour therapy with black and minority ethnic communities. *The Cognitive Behaviour Therapist, 12*, E1. https://doi.org/10.1017/S1754470X18000016

Burnham, J. (2013). Developments in social GGRRAAACCEEESSS: Visible-invisible, voiced-unvoiced. In I. Krause (Ed.), *Cultural reflexivity*. Routledge.

Craig, S.L., Austin, A., & Alessi, E. (2013). Gay affirmative cognitive behavioral therapy for sexual minority youth: A clinical adaptation. *Clinical Social Work Journal, 41*, 258–266. https://doi.org/10.1007/s10615-012-0427-9

David, E.J.R., & Derthick, A.O. (2014). What is internalized oppression, and so what? In E.J.R. David (Ed.), *Internalized oppression: The psychology of marginalized groups* (pp. 1–30). Springer Publishing Company.

Flott, K.M., Graham, C., Darzi, A., & Mayer, E. (2017). Can we use patient-reported feedback to drive change? The challenges of using patient-reported feedback and how they might be addressed. *BMJ Quality & Safety, 26*, 502–507. https://doi.org/10.1136/bmjqs-2016-005223

Grant, K., McMeekin, E., Jamieson, R., Fairfull, A., Miller, C., & White, J. (2012). Individual therapy attrition rates in a low-intensity service: A comparison of cognitive behavioural and person-centred therapies and the impact of deprivation. *Behavioural and Cognitive Psychotherapy, 40*, 245–249.https://doi.org/10.1017/S1352465811000476

Hakim, N., Thompson, A., & Coleman-Oluwabusola, G. (2019). An evaluation of the transition from BAME community mental health worker to IAPT low intensity psychological wellbeing practitioner. *The Cognitive Behaviour Therapist, 12*, E15. https://doi.org/10.1017/S1754470X18000296

Hamilton, S., Hicks, A., Sayers, R., Faulkner, A., Larsen, J., Patterson, S., & Pinfold, V. (2011). A user-focused evaluation of IAPT services in London. *Report for Commissioning Support for London*. www.rethink.org/resources/a/a-user-focused-evaluation-of-iapt-services-in-london

Hays, P.A. (2001). Addressing cultural complexities in practice: A framework for clinicians and counselors. American Psychological Association.

Iwamasa, G.Y., Pai, S.M., & Sorocco, K.H. (2006). Multicultural cognitive-behavioral therapy supervision. In P.A. Hays & G.Y. Iwamasa (Eds.), *Culturally responsive cognitive-behavioral therapy: Assessment, practice, and supervision* (pp. 267–281). American Psychological Association. https://doi.org/10.1037/11433-012

Kada, R. (2019). Cultural adaptations of CBT for the British Jewish Orthodox community. *The Cognitive Behaviour Therapist, 12*, E4. doi:10.1017/S1754470X18000120

Lago, C. (2011). The handbook of transcultural counselling and psychotherapy. McGraw-Hill Education.

Laireiter, A.R., & Willutzki, U. (2003). Self-reflection and self-practice in training of cognitive behaviour therapy: An overview. *Clinical Psychology & Psychotherapy: An International Journal of Theory & Practice, 10*(1), 19–30.

Lawton, L., McRae, M., & Gordon, L. (2021). Frontline yet at the back of the queue – improving access and adaptations to CBT for Black African and Caribbean communities. *The Cognitive Behaviour Therapist, 14*, E30. doi:10.1017/S1754470X21000271

Memon, A., Taylor, K., Mohebati, L.M., Sundin, J., Cooper, M., Scanlon, T., & de Visser, R. (2016). Perceived barriers to accessing mental health services among black and minority ethnic (BME) communities: A qualitative study in Southeast England. *BMJ Open, 6*, E012337. https://doi.org/10.1136/bmjopen-2016-012337

Miranda, J., Bernal, G., Lau, A., Kohn, L., Hwang, W.C., & LaFromboise, T. (2005). State of the science on psychosocial interventions for ethnic minorities. *Annual Review of Clinical Psychology, 1*, 113–142. https://doi.org/10.1146/annurev.clinpsy.1.102803.143822

Osgood, J., Albon, D., Allen, K., & Hollingworth, S. (2013). 'Hard to reach' or nomadic resistance? Families 'choosing' not to participate in early childhood services. *Global Studies of Childhood, 3*, 208–220. https://doi.org/10.2304/gsch.2013.3.3.208

Papworth, M., Marrinan, T., Martin, B., Keegan, D., & Chaddock, A. (2013). *Low intensity cognitive behaviour therapy: A practitioner's guide*. Sage Publications Ltd.

Rathod, S., & Kingdon, D. (2009). Cognitive behaviour therapy across cultures. *Psychiatry, 8*, 370–371. doi:10.1016/j.mppsy.2009.06.011

Whitehead, G., & Barnard, A. (2013). Developing inclusive environments in mental health provision for people with disabilities. *The Journal of Mental Health Training, Education and Practice, 8*, 103–111. https://doi.org/10.1108/JMHTEP-07-2012-0021

21

Developing Meta-Competencies in Low-Intensity Practice

Sadie Williams, Susanna Payne, Carolyn Edwards and Jessica Richardson

Introduction

In this chapter we present a definition of competencies and meta-competencies in relation to low-intensity clinical practice with children and young people (LI-CYP). We consider the value of supporting the deliberate development and nurturing of meta-competencies for LI practitioners and their supervisors and managers, for the benefit of the CYP and families they serve. In the absence of an extensive evidence-base regarding the development of clinical meta-competency in LI practitioners, we present a pragmatic guide, building on the Roth and Pilling (2007) framework of clinical competency in CBT practice, and reflections on developing practice from previous LI-CYP practitioners in training.

Definitions

For the purposes of this chapter, we define *competencies* as the skills that are necessary to deliver evidence-based low-intensity interventions. These can be thought of as procedural methods including non-therapy-specific factors, as well as model-specific skills and strategies (e.g., Roth & Pilling, 2007). We define *meta-competencies* as over-arching, higher-order competencies, which practitioners need to evaluate and guide the effectiveness of their work and generalise their skills-set within the limits of their competence. Meta-competencies develop with experience, and increased opportunity to reflect critically on practice with supervision and independently. Bogo et al. (2014) note that competence in a given area requires the ability to develop and implement both procedural and meta-competencies. The purpose of this chapter is to consider ways in which a LI-CYP practitioner can develop meta-competencies in the years post-qualification.

The Need and Impact of Meta-Competence within Low-Intensity Practice

'Riding a bike without the stabilisers...' (Qualified CWP)

Every year, increasing numbers of practitioners around the country qualify in Low-Intensity Practice with Children and Young People (LI-CYP) training. Newly qualified practitioners go on to positions within the NHS, local authority, and charity sectors, where they will consolidate their skills and practice with increasing autonomy. LI-CYP practitioners typically train intensively for one year, regardless of previous experience, and so training is largely focused on developing the essential, clearly defined assessment and intervention competencies. In order for LI-CYP practitioners to develop and thrive after qualifying, their supervisors, managers and trainers need to consider how to nurture their trainees' ability to manage their own competence, i.e., to develop meta-competencies in self-awareness, self-reflection and self-evaluation. It is through these skills that they can become more effective, autonomous and accountable low-intensity practitioners.

Stress, Burnout and Role Clarity

The real prospect of stress and burnout is a compelling reason to focus on meta-competencies, especially given that there may be a higher risk for newly qualified practitioners, and LI-CYP practitioners in general, due to higher caseloads and limited training (e.g., Thwaites et al., 2015). Job stress is a real problem for the health sector in general. In one meta-analysis that included 9,409 health professionals in 62 studies, burnout was present in a significant minority, with prevalence rates of 40 per cent for emotional exhaustion, 22 per cent for depersonalisation and 19 per cent for low levels of personal accomplishment (O'Connor et al., 2018). In this paper, among other determinants, the authors pulled out *'role clarity'*, '*a sense of professional autonomy'* and *'regular supervision'* as protective factors.

Developing meta-competencies around therapeutic practice is likely to increase role clarity and professional autonomy, and there are clear benefits to developing specific meta-competencies around emotional well-being both during and after training. Noticing early warning signs of emotional exhaustion and depersonalisation, and responding to these, requires a skilled awareness and skilled action that can be supported in low-intensity supervision.

Self-Practice–Self-Reflection

Although research into formal and manualised practice specifically designed to increase meta-competencies in LI practitioners is rare, there is rich qualitative informal information from previous LI practitioners in training. Furthermore, Bennett-Levy and colleagues' work (e.g., Chigwedere et al., 2021) on self-practice and self-reflection will be of value to supervisors and employers when considering what support to provide for qualified LI practitioners to support the development of meta-competencies. This approach can build on the pilot research by Thwaites et al. (2015) in low-intensity practitioners. This showed that a focus on developing self-practice (using cognitive behavioural therapy on the self) and self-reflection (reflecting on that experience) increased the sense of skill and change intervention behaviours in seven Psychological Well-being Practitioners (PWPs). This was especially the case when working with more complicated clients (although initially some had felt de-skilled by the practices).

In the Absence of an Evidence Base: A Pragmatic Approach

The new LI-CYP workforce is a vitally important resource, and practitioners committing to these roles need to be supported and nurtured in their development. While the evidence base for developing meta-competencies is limited, the authors intend to present a 'practical guide', drawing on the meta-competency CBT framework of Roth and Pilling (2007). This was developed through consultation with expert reference groups, and with our own consultation with experienced local practitioners, trainers and supervisors. Our purpose is to begin a discussion intended to more clearly define what meta-competencies *are* in LI-CYP practice, and how we might notice and develop them in our different roles.

Roth and Pilling (2007) describe meta-competencies for both generic and specific CBT practice:

Generic meta-competencies refer to:

- 'The capacity to implement models flexibly in a coherent manner'
- 'A capacity to adapt intervention in response to client feedback' and
- 'Capacity to use and respond to humour'

Meta-competencies specific to cognitive behaviour therapy (CBT), and CBT-informed approaches, refer to:

- 'The capacity to implement CBT practice in a manner that is consonant with its underlying philosophy'
- 'Capacity to formulate and apply CBT models to the individual client'
- 'Capacity to select and apply the most appropriate CBT intervention method'
- 'Capacity to structure sessions and maintain appropriate pacing'
- 'Capacity to manage obstacles in carrying out CBT'

Translating Meta-Competencies into Low-Intensity Clinical Practice

Generic Meta-Competencies: Flexibility, Adaptation, Humour

The capacity to use clinical judgement when implementing intervention models or 'Flexibility within fidelity' (Kendall, 2022) is a key concept for the developing practitioner, where the practitioner becomes increasingly able to be responsive to the young person's needs while retaining the effective components of the intervention. Owen and Hilsenroth (2014) have demonstrated that practitioner flexibility is associated with treatment adherence. This sounds simple but is potentially one of the most challenging skills for a low-intensity practitioner to develop. They are likely feeling enthusiastic with their recent up-to-date training and newly acquired skills, making it a difficult time to feel fenced in by limits of their own competence.

A supervisor observing this meta-competency develop would note the practitioner being aware when they are working 'on' or 'off' model and why; knowing the evidence base and its limitations; appreciating when it's appropriate to stray from an agenda, and when not; when it's right to use creativity, and when not.

Central to this skill is asking for feedback. A supervisor observing this meta-competency develop in a newly qualified practitioner would expect to see the practitioner routinely asking for formal and informal feedback from their clients and *responding* to this by changing aspects of their procedural competencies. For example, if the young person says they haven't been able to talk about all they wanted to (e.g., Session Rating Scale, Duncan et al., 2003), altering the agenda to make space for this. Feedback would need to be considered alongside progress on the routine outcome measures, and supervisors can support newly qualified practitioners to continue to develop their skills using this information to guide treatment decisions (e.g., Lambert & Harmon, 2018).

The use of humour in therapy has been debated (Rothenberg, 2020). However, if used appropriately, it can enable the exploration of thoughts and feelings with genuine compassion between practitioner and client (Dziegielewski, 2003). The use of humour is a skill that develops over time and is linked to flexibility and skill in the practitioner that can increase engagement and normalise a situation (Zur Institute, n.d.).

Specific Meta-Competencies

Descriptive Formulation

As there is skill in choosing the 'right' evidence-based intervention for a family, and sticking to it, there is a meta-competency in identifying which descriptive formulation best suits the assessment material and how to share this with the young person and/or their family. In some cases, a descriptive formulation containing developmental factors is helpful, and in some just the 'here and now' maintenance cycle.

A further meta-competency is being able to think about the assessment material from multiple sources and work out whether a generic or specific formulation is most helpful to developing the shared understanding of the presenting problem. Roth and Pilling advise the formulation should not be simplified in order to offer a reduced intervention. Therefore, it is important that the young person is signposted to a different team, or tier, if the formulation suggests more complexity than can be reasonably addressed by an early intervention approach.

Treatment Decisions

The descriptive formulation provides the direction of treatment by addressing maintaining factors highlighted by the evidence base. For example, in a case where low-moderate depression is indicated, research indicates behavioural activation will be useful (Martin & Oliver, 2019). In agreement with the young person, this intervention will be delivered in weekly sessions of approximately 45 minutes. From this moment, the procedural competencies of therapy begin to be enhanced by developing meta-competencies. Key areas of meta-competence in this area are: (1) routine gathering of reliable and valid information that indicates progress, (2) responding to this information by accessing supervision and the wider team regarding case management decisions. The ability to access parts of the larger system to address maintaining factors outside the control of the young person is also central to developing a meta-competency in this area.

Session Structure and Pacing

Pacing is crucial for the young person's engagement in low-intensity practice and relies on empathy, validation and good time keeping. Meta-competency in this area involves noticing where there is a problem with agenda keeping and pacing, and bringing these to supervision to reflect on how to improve practice. A supervisor observing the emergence of this meta-competency would expect to see a practitioner becoming more skilled at the ability to organise a collaborative session agenda and pace accordingly, depending on what the young person brings. Supervisors can nurture this by asking questions about the session's agenda and pacing, and offering practical solutions for time management.

Managing Obstacles

Recognising that the sessions do not seem to be running as smoothly as expected and an awareness to bring these cases to supervision for discussion is another important meta-competency. There are numerous articles on managing obstacles in sessions. For example, the American Psychological Association (Monitor, 2019) as part of their continuing education series note that the therapeutic relationship is important and that skills around recognising and managing ruptures are key to 'therapeutic growth'.

Eliciting feedback, pacing, collaboration, empathy and managing endings well are all core competencies that can be utilised to manage obstacles. In practice the LI-CYP practitioner may be able to notice subtle shifts in verbal or non-verbal cues. For example, notice with the young person what is happening in the session e.g., 'I notice that you looked uncomfortable when I asked you about x'. The ability to recognise obstacles is key to the developing and improving practitioner. Obstacles can be reduced with careful consideration in supervision and with peers.

Emerging Skills and Meta-Competencies

In addition to Roth and Pilling's meta-competencies, there are other potential skills and competencies which may be considered over-arching meta-competencies for the developing LI-CYP workforce that will be discussed here.

Caseloads and Decision Making

The post-qualified practitioners were able to reflect on the change in caseload since qualifying. There is an expectation that qualified low-intensity practitioners can hold many more cases and demonstrate a higher and constant turnover of cases. In practical terms, this means that the qualified practitioner needs to apply skills related to good assessment and formulation to make decisions about the suitability of cases before proceeding with the intervention. Managing a caseload with the associated liaison with the young person's network is a meta-competence, which develops over the course and post training and is constantly monitored by the LI-CYP practitioner and their line manager and/or supervisor to ensure the smooth running of the service. While this is often supervised practice, it is a skill that develops over time and autonomous and safe decision making is a key meta-competence.

The current and trained practitioners in the conversations below are discussing developing how these skills have developed post-qualification.

What Has Changed since Leaving Training?

Jasmine	I'm managing a more complex caseload that seems bigger than when I was training. I have to case manage, plan care and care co-ordinate. I've had to learn to be flexible.
Lucas	I've had to learn about the organisational structure, meetings and linking in with other services around case management.
Paul	I've had to be firm with myself about discharging cases when the work is complete. The main difference is that I'm now responsible for my caseload. I need to work autonomously and make decisions in a way I didn't before.
Dionne	I contribute more in team meetings and feel more visible. The team include me in decisions about case allocations.

Reflection on Training Needs – Insight of Personal Development Needs

The qualified LI-CYP practitioners in the conversation below speak about being proactive in identifying continuing professional development needs. There is no 'end point' to learning. Continuing to maintain and develop competence and confidence in skills could reasonably be expected to be important predictors of job satisfaction. Further, promoting professional autonomy is one of the key interventions to prevent burnout (O'Connor et al., 2018). Identifying further training needs can be considered as part of supervision.

What Support Have You Had in Your Qualified Roles?

Paul   My supervisor has helped me with my increased responsibilities.

Jasmine   I've spoken to the qualified practitioner network.

Dionne   I have a personal professional development plan and identified areas for further training.

Lucas   I work in an established team, so I can discuss formulations with my peers, and work out if the intervention is on the right track. I value supervision as a space to think about case progression.

Working with Neurodiversity

Practitioners and their supervisors have consistently reported that a significant number of young people referred for the low-intensity service have additional neuro-developmental needs. LI-CYP practitioners often question their skills in this area and may need additional training. As discussed in Chapter 19, work needs to be even more flexible, and the practitioner may need to specifically adapt interventions to meet the needs of the young people and families they are working with. As with all clients, receiving feedback is essential as is an acute awareness of when humour could be misunderstood and should be avoided. Although the same CBT-based protocols can be used, individual formulations to include the young person's needs are vital, and sessions benefit from being shorter, clearly structured, more concrete with visual aids and perhaps at a slower pace (e.g., NICE, 2021). With good enough supervision in place, practitioners can adapt and develop these additional required meta-competencies to meet the needs of those referred within the low-intensity threshold.

Inclusive Practice

There is a clear need for all mental health practitioners to develop meta-competency in inclusive practice and making sure what they are providing is accessible for all in the communities they serve. As discussed in Chapter 20, LI-CYP practitioners should develop a sound knowledge of whether their clients are representative of the community they serve, and a curiosity if this is not the case. They are well placed to think of pragmatic ideas to increase access, if not necessarily the ability to effect change from their position within the system. It is of key importance that LI-CYP practitioners are able to develop skills in recognising and escalating concerns about accessibility and inclusion to supervisors and managers, and these are specific skills that can be developed as meta-competencies, including the flexibility and adaptation of the intervention to the young person.

Liaison and Networking

As the LI-CYP practitioner moves onto qualified status, the responsibilities around case management often increase. Work may involve liaison with other professionals involved in the young person's care, such as requested attendance at school or safeguarding meetings and/or making referrals to alternative teams and services. It is useful to consider whether the meetings are statutory and to discuss in supervision, or with the wider team, the appropriateness of attending meetings and clear expectations of the LI-CYP practitioner's role within these.

Use of Supervision and Reflections on Practice

We have referred to supervision throughout the chapter and its key part in supporting and developing LI-CYP practitioners' development of meta-competencies post-qualification and beyond. As discussed in Chapter 18, good supervision serves a number of functions including supporting the well-being of the now qualified practitioner ('restorative'), supporting the maintenance and improved competence of the practitioners ('formative') and case management to monitor the throughput of cases and quality control to ensure that interventions match and are effective for young people being seen ('normative'), (Milne, 2009). Supervision is a two-way process and being prepared for supervision with what is needed from the supervisor may also be viewed as a meta-competency.

'Riding a bike without the stabilisers' requires becoming a reflective practitioner, learning from experience about what has worked in the past and working with new challenges that have not been encountered before. Reflecting on practice individually, in supervision and with colleagues is important to continuing safe and effective working; and self-awareness will be one of the ways in which meta-competencies will develop.

Summary

Key take-home messages from newly qualified LI-CYP practitioners include:

- 'Being qualified does not mean that you stop learning – it is a transition, and any practitioner role involves lifelong learning.'
- 'Learning to use supervision effectively will increase your autonomy, effectiveness and efficiency.'
- 'Think through personal development plans with your supervisor and consider reflective practice opportunities.'
- 'Meta-competencies continue to develop throughout the practitioner's time in a qualified role.'
- 'It is vital to know the limits of competence and when to ask for help for you and for the young people you are working with.'
- 'The work is multi-layered and challenging, and taking care of yourself is part of being an effective practitioner.'

Acknowledgements

Student names are anonymised. With thanks to the students on the KCL CWP PG certificate training 2021 for their views shared at the CWP shared Learning Event Dec 2021.

References

American Psychological Association. (2019). *Monitor on psychology.* www.apa.org/education-career/ce/therapeutic-relationships.pdf

Bogo, M., Rawlings, M., Katz, E., & Logie, C. (2014). *Using simulation in assessment and teaching.* CSWE Press.

Duncan, B., Miller, S., Sparks, J., Claud, D., Reynolds, L., Brown, J., & Johnson, L. (2003). The session rating scale: Preliminary psychometric properties of a 'working' alliance measure. *Journal of Brief Therapy, 3*(1), 3–12.

Chigwedere, C., Bennett-Levy, J., Fitzmaurice, B., & Donohoe, G. (2020). Personal practice in counselling and CBT trainees: The self-perceived impact of personal therapy and self-practice/self-reflection on personal and professional development. *Cognitive Behaviour Therapy, 50*(5), 422–438. https://10.1080/16506073.2020.1846608

Dziegielewski, S. (2003). Humor. *International Journal of Mental Health, 32*(3), 74–90. https://doi.org/10.1080/00207411.2003.11449592

Kendall, P. (2022). Flexibility within fidelity: Breathing life into a psychological treatment manual. Oxford University Press.

Lambert, M., & Harmon, K. (2018). The merits of implementing routine outcome monitoring in clinical practice. *Clinical Psychology: Science and Practice, 25*(4). https://doi.org/10.1111/cpsp.12268

Martin, F., & Oliver, T. (2019). Behavioral activation for children and adolescents: A systematic review of progress and promise. *European Child and Adolescent Psychiatry*, *28*(4), 427–441. https://doi.org/10.1007%2Fs00787-018-1126-z

Milne, D. (2009). *Evidence-based clinical supervision: Principles and practice*. British Psychological Society Wiley.

National Institute for Health and Care Excellence. (2021). *Autism spectrum disorder in under 19s: Support and management* [Clinical Guideline170]. https://www.nice.org.uk/guidance/cg170

O'Connor, K., Muller Neff, D., & Pitman, S. (2018). Burnout in mental health professionals: A systematic review and meta-analysis of prevalence and determinants. *European Psychiatry*, *53*, 74–99. https://doi.org/10.1016/j.eurpsy.2018.06.003

Owen, J., & Hilsenroth, M.J. (2014). Treatment adherence: The importance of therapist flexibility in relation to therapy outcomes. *Journal of Counseling Psychology*, *61*(2), 280–288. https://doi.org/10.1037/a0035753

Roth, A., & Pilling, S. (2007). The competences required to deliver effective cognitive and behavioural therapy for people with depression and with anxiety disorders. Department of Health. https://www.ucl.ac.uk/clinical-psychology//CORE/CBT_Competences/CBT_Competence_List.pdf

Rothenberg, A. (2020). The beneficial use of humor in psychotherapy. A therapist's careful use of humorous interpretations can facilitate changes. *Psychology Today*. www.psychologytoday.com/gb/blog/creative-explorations/202002/the-beneficial-use-humor-in-psychotherapy

Thwaites, R., Cairns, L., Bennett-Levy, J., Johnston, L., Lowrie, R., Robinson, A., Turner, M., Haarhoff, B., & Perry, H. (2015). Developing metacompetence in low intensity Cognitive-Behavioural Therapy (CBT) interventions: Evaluating a self-practice/self-reflection programme for experienced low intensity CBT practitioners. *Australian Psychologist*, *50*(5), 311–321. https://doi.org/10.1111/ap.12151

Zur Institute (n.d.). *Humour in therapy*. Zur institute. https://www.zurinstitute.com/clinical-updates/humor-in-therapy/

Index

Note: Page numbers followed by "*f*" indicate figure and "*t*" indicate table in the text.

ABC chart, 61*t*
access, 3–4
ACE-I ratings, 110
activity
    log, 110–111
    planning, 201–202
    steps to planning, 201–202
adaptations, 81–92, 160, 261–270, 284
Adolescent Depression, 70
adverse childhood experiences (ACEs),
    55–56, 63
aggressive behaviour, 56
American Psychological Association, 285
analogies, 90
anxiety, 71, 117, 118, 122*f*, 130, 156, 163,
    164, 166, 175, 263
    baseline measures of, 178–182
    child, 223–236
    cycle, 230, 231
    disorders, 127, 163
    habituation, 123*f*
    interventions, 71, 165
    normalise, 166–168
    physical symptoms of, 165
    scales, 124
    tigger/situation, 229
assessment, 20, 30–50, 93
    COM-B model, 48–49, 49*f*

descriptive formulation, 39*f*
FIDO questions, 41
Four W questions, 41
funnelling, 38–40
impact, 41
information, 44
information gathering, 38
interpersonal skills, 37–38
LICBT, 34
normalising, 98
probable diagnosis, 47–48
problem statement, 45
process, 74, 107–108
risk, 44, 99–100
Routine Outcome Measures (ROMs),
    42–43*t*, 42–44
specialist, 53
triggers, 41
attention principle, 208
Autonomic, Behavioural, Cognitive and
    Emotional (ABCE), 275
autonomic bodily sensations, 84–85

balanced alternative, 140–141
Bandura, A., 175, 209
Barrio, C.A., 60
Beck, A.T., 175
Beck, Judith, 180

behaviour, 86
  change, 202
  changing, 197
  cycle, 212
  practice behaviour change, 197
  relationship between thinking, feeling and, 178–182
  understanding child behaviour, 210–213
behavioural activation (BA), 67, 77, 106, 192
behavioural change, 191
behavioural difficulties, 72
behavioural experiments (BEs), 71, 144–160
  adaptation of, 148–149
  benefits of, 145–146
  clinical use of, 149–150
  evidence, 146–148
  low-intensity (LI) practice, 145
  maintaining factors, 146
  make predictions, 155–158
  orientation to, 150–160
  predictions, 144
  stages of, 149f
  steps of, 145, 150t
  therapeutic model, 151f
  thoughts, 144
behavioural problems, 207–220
behavioural theory, 104, 116
beneficial effects, 192
Bennett-Levy, J., 146, 252, 254, 283
Bennett, S.D., 67
Better (2007), 241
Blenkiron, P., 90
body maps, 84, 85f
Bogo, M., 281
Bower, P., 99
Branson, A., 252
Brent, D.A., 57
Brief Behavioural Activation (Brief BA), 104–116
  assessment process, 107–108
  cycle, 105f
  end of, 115
  evidence base, 106
  identifying values, 111–112
  learning theory, 104–105
  rationale, 109
  'review and repeat' cycle, 113
  Routine Outcome Measures (ROMs), 114
  treatment goals, 107

Brief Coping Cat (BCC), 164
  process, 166–172
  reprise, 162–163
  trouble shooting, 171
Brief Parental Efficacy Scale, 208
burnout, 282

capability, 202
capability, opportunity, motivation and behaviour model (COM-B model), 48–49, 49f, 76, 101, 127
case management supervision (CMS), 251, 253–256
central point of access (CPA), 24
Child and Adolescent Mental Health, 5
child and adolescent mental health services (CAMHS), 5, 8, 36
child anxiety, 223–236
Child Behaviour Checklist (CBCL), 176
child directed play, 214
Child Outcome Rating Scale (CORS), 208
Child Outcomes Research Consortium (CORC), 42
children
  low-intensity practice, 8
  psychological practitioners, 8
  understanding child behaviour, 210
children and young people (CYP), 2, 3, 30, 35, 81, 127, 162, 175, 191
  child and young person engagement, 127
  cognitive level of, 125–126
  core adaptations, 263–268
  engagement, 262–263
  ethical considerations, 126
  low-intensity practice, 81–92
  low-intensity workforce, 9–10
  managing endings, 269
  mental health policies, 10
  mental health services, 6, 67
  with neurodiversity, 261–270
  participation, 18
  political context, 4–6
Children and Young People's Improved Access to Psychological Therapies (CYP-IAPT) programme, 5
Children's Wellbeing Practitioners (CWPs), 8–9, 68
(CEDAR), 148
Choo, C., 148
Chu, B.C., 106

clinical skills, 97
clinical skills supervision (CSS), 251, 253, 256–257
cognitive-behavioural approach, 164
cognitive-behavioural therapy (CBT), 14, 81, 118, 130, 131, 147, 164, 283
    behavioural experiments, 152
    computer game, 175–189
cognitive distortions, 163
cognitive maturity, 130
cognitive restructuring (CR), 130–142, 185–187
    assessment process, 132–141
    balanced alternative, 140–141
    evidence for, 138–140
    with thoughts, 130–132
cognitive symptoms, 85–86
collaboration, 95–96
collaborative practice, 17
communication, 217
    behaviour, 96
    non-verbal, 264
Community Based Service (South West of England), 243–244
competencies, 281
computerised CBT (CCBT), 67, 73
confidentiality, 34–35, 94
consent, 35, 93–94
context, 2–10
conversation cards, 83
Cooney, P., 176
Coping Cat, 85, 164
core beliefs, 187–188
Corrie, S., 253
creativity, 81–92
Creswell, C., 236
Crib sheet, 83f

Declarative-Procedural-Reflective (DPR) model, 97, 257
delivery methods, 70
demonstrating empathy, 95
Department for Education, 61
depression, 112, 192
    behavioural theory of, 116
    intervention, 70
    symptoms of, 108
    thought, 146
    trap, 109
descriptive formulation, 83

diet, 194
difficulties
    memory, 266
    processing, 266
disorder, 163–164
diversity, 273
Donaldson, M., 131, 175
Dunn, J., 175
dysfunctional negative self-statements, 165

Early Values Assessment (EVA), 73
Education Mental Health Practitioners (EMHPs), 8–9, 68
effective service user engagement, 18
efficacy, 67
emoji faces, 84
emotions, 165
    impact, 130
    negative, 108
    symptoms, 84
empathy, 95
engagement, 54–55, 82–83, 91
Equality Act (2010), 263
ethical frameworks, 23
evaluation, 245–247
    background, 245
    context, 245
    outcome informed practice, 245–247
evidence, 37, 138–140
evidence-based interventions, 66
evidence-based practice, 15–16, 16f
evidence-based psychological therapies, 242
Experience of Service Questionnaire (ESQ), 278
exposure, 71, 225
Exposure and Habituation (EH), 117–127
    empirical evidence, 118–119
    exposure activities, 121–124
    exposure exercises, 125f, 126
    formulation diagram, 120f
    hierarchy, 121, 121f
    intervention process, 119–125
    low-intensity, 117
    plan exposures, 124–125
    problem statement, 119
    treatment goals, 119–125
    troubleshooting, 125–127
    without distraction, 124
exposure therapy, 118

fear, 163
  hierarchy, 169–171
  ladder, 121*f*
  realistic, 171
FEAR plan, 165, 166, 172
  A-step, 165, 169
  E-step, 165, 168–169
  F-step, 165, 168–169
  R-step, 165, 169
feelings, 84, 178–182, 212
feelings faces
  drawing, 84
  masks with, 84
FINDIE, 60*t*, 63
Five Year Forward View (FYFV), 4, 17
Flavell, J.H., 131
flexibility, 284
Four W questions, 41
Freeman, J. B., 148
Frequency, Intensity, Duration and Onset
  (FIDO), 41
Friedberg, R.D., 87, 90, 131
funnelling, 38–40, 97–98
Future in Mind, 20

game, 83
  world, 176
game structure, 177
  level one, 178–182
  level two, 182–185
  level three, 182–185
  level four, 185–187
  level five, 187–188
  level six, 188
  level seven, 188–189
  level structure, 177
Garland, A., 38
gathering information, 83, 86
generalized anxiety disorder, 163
Gilbody, S., 99
gNATs
  cognitive restructuring, 185–187
  core beliefs, 187–188
  gallery, 183
  hunting, 187–188
  swatting, 185–188
  trapping, 182–185
Goal Based Outcomes (GBO), 46, 199, 256

goals, 100–101
  setting, 46–47
  track goal progress, 199
Gosch, E., 168
Green Paper for Transforming Children and
  Young People's Mental Health, 5
guided parent-delivered CBT (GPD-CBT),
  223–236

habituation, 71, 123, 127, 225
Halldorsson, B., 236
head-heart split, 146
Health and Social Care Committee, 6
Health Education England, 8
Health Select Committee, 6
healthy life plan, 188–189
Hedtke, K.A., 85
hierarchy, 121, 167
Hilsenroth, M.J., 284
hives, 187
  beliefs, 187–188
  splatting, 188
hopelessness, 56
humour, 284
hypersensitivity, 268

ice breaker, 82
identifying values, 111–112
IIPAP (ideation, intent, plans, actions, and
  protectives), 63
Improving Access to Psychological Therapies
  (IAPT), 72
inclusive practice, 272–279, 287–288
  assessment, 275–276
  foundations of, 273–274
  importance of, 272–273
  intervention, 276–279
  in LI-CBT, 272–274
  low-intensity intervention, 276
  pre-assessment, 274–275
Incredible Five Point Scale, 266
information gathering, 31, 38, 91, 97–100
  funnelling, 97–98
  risk assessments, 99–100
  Routine Outcome Measures (ROMs),
    98–99
information giving, 31, 45–48
Inskipp, F., 252, 257

INDEX | 295

interpersonal skills, 37–38, 101
intervention, 223
    agenda, 227
    anxiety, 71
    assessment, 226
    attention principle, 208
    client scenarios, 228–229
    depression, 70
    evidence-based low-intensity
      interventions, 281
    evidence-base for, 225–226
    exposure, 225
    low-intensity interventions, 207
    low-intensity parenting, 208–209
    map, 68, 69f
    overview, 227
    plan, 74–77
    process, 119–125
    process of conducting, 229–236
    reinforcement principle, 208
    self-directed interventions, 207
    step-by-step plan, 234
    theory behind, 164–166, 209, 224–225

Jacobson, N.S., 70

Kendall, P.C., 85, 168
Khanna, M., 168
Killick, S., 90
Kitchen, C.E., 106
Kiyimba, N., 59
Kuyken, W., 147

Lambert, M.J., 43
Lane, D.A., 253
Law, D., 99
Leahy, L.R., 138
learning theory, 104–105, 116
Lee, R., 147
LGBTQ+ community, 274
Liaison, 288
LI Cognitive Behavioural Therapy (LICBT),
    30, 37, 193, 200
    assessment, 34
    model, 275
lifestyle management (LM), 73–74, 191
lifestyle management intervention, 191–204
    diet, 194
    overview, 191–192

    physical activity, 192–193
    sleep, 193–194
LI practitioners, 23–24
LLTF-YP, 73
logical consequences, 217–219
low-intensity (LI), 175, 261
    approach, 132
    assessment, 49
    behavioural interventions, 72
    evidence base, 66–67
    interventions, 68
    parenting, 207
    practitioner, 68, 74, 77, 85
    practitioners, 278, 279, 283
    risk assessment, 53–54
    service, 287
    supervision, 253
    supervision contract, 254
    support, 259
    work, 262
low-intensity assessment, 30–50, 96
    challenges in, 97–101
    information gathering, 31
    information giving, 31
    shared decision making, 31
    structure of, 32f, 34
    vignettes, 31–33
low-intensity cognitive behaviour therapy
    (LICBT), 191–192
    funnelling, 97–98
    risk assessments, 99–100
    Routine Outcome Measures (ROMs), 98–99
low-intensity interventions, 131, 207
    computerised or online CBT (CCBT), 72
    lifestyle management, 73–74
    map, 69f
low-intensity practice, 8, 236, 251–259, 272
    background, 251–253
    case management supervision, 253–256
    clinical skills supervision, 256–257
    contracting, 253
    low-intensity supervision contract, 254
    meta-competencies, 281–289
    practicalities of, 241–242
    principles of, 241–242
    supervision question, 257–258
    workforce context, 258–259
Low-Intensity Practice with Children and
    Young People (LI-CYP), 282

MacMillian, D., 147
management, 53–56
Maslow, A.H., 210
McCashin, D., 176
McCauley, E., 106
McClure, J.M., 131
McGillivray, L., 36
mental health, 38
  ambitions, 4–6
  issues, 2–3
  relationship between physical and, 192
  services, 4
Mental Health Support Teams (MHSTs), 6, 9
meta-analysis, 282
meta-competence
  impact of, 282
  need of, 282
  self-practice–self-reflection, 282–283
meta-competencies, 281
  emerging skills and, 286
  generic, 284
  specific, 284–286
metaphor, 89–91
Milne, D.L., 251, 253, 256
mindfulness, 182
Minds, Young, 55–56
model effective coping, 165
mood
  baseline measures of, 178–182
  low, 175, 192, 263
Mooney, K., 38
motivation, 202
multiple targets, 172

National Institute for Health and Care
  Excellence (NICE), 55
natural consequences, 218–219
Negative Automatic Thoughts (NATs), 70,
  176, 182–185
negative emotions, 108
negative reinforcement, 104–105
networking, 288
neurodiversity, 131, 261–270, 287
NHS, 4, 5
non-anxious CYP, 164
non-therapy-specific factors, 281
non-verbal communication, 264
non-verbal skills, 94–95
normalisation, 101
normalize anxiety, 166–168

obstacles, 285–286
Office for National Statistics (ONS), 2
operant conditioning, 104
opportunity, 202
O'Reilly, M., 58
outcome informed practice, 16–17
Outcome Rating Scale (ORS), 256
Owen, J., 284

pacing, 285
Padesky, C.A., 38
parental psychopathology, 56
parenting, 207–220
  impact of, 207
  low-intensity parenting, 207, 208–209
Parent-Led Cognitive Behavioural Therapy
  (PL-CBT), 67, 71–72
parent reported oppositional defiance
  disorder (ODD-P), 208
parent reported strength and difficulties
  questionnaire (SDQ-P), 208
parents/caregivers, 96, 126, 211
Pass, L., 106
Pesky gNATs, 175–189
  game structure, 177
  game world, 176
  theory, 175–176
Pesky-Gnats, 67
physical activity, 192–193
physical health, 192
Piaget, J., 130, 175
Pilling, S., 281, 283, 285, 286
Podell, J., 168
positive reinforcement, 104
post-qualified practitioners, 286
power, 216
practice, 19–20
  access, 20–21
  assessment, 20–21
  case closure, 22
  case management, 22
  ethical frameworks, 23
  interventions, 22
  liaison work, 21–22
  LI practice, 253
  professional practice, 23
  referral, 20–21
  reflections on, 288
  service considerations, 23–24
  signposting, 21–22

INDEX | 297

pragmatic approach, 283
predictions, 155–158
preventative family support programmes, 19
prevention
    ending, 199, 203
    relapse, 199, 203
probable diagnosis, 47–48, 100–101
problem-solving, 235
    skills, 165
    techniques, 204
problem statement, 45, 100–101, 107, 119
    template, 46
    Theo's, 45
Proctor, B., 252, 257
professional practice, 23
psychoeducation, 132–134, 165, 196–197,
    200–201, 210, 224, 265–266
psychological clinical practice, 252
psychological practitioners, 8
psychological professions workforce, 6–7
Psychological Professions Workforce Plan for
    England, 7
psychological treatment, 108
Psychological Wellbeing Practitioners
    (PWPs), 252, 283

qualified low-intensity practitioners, 286

realistic fears, 171
record
    five-part thought, 140
    thought, 134–137
referrals, 3–4
    suitability, 21t
reflections, 288
Rego, A.S., 138
reinforcement, 104
    principle, 208, 210
relaxation, 182
Report the Select Committee, 7
Revised Children's Anxiety and
    Depression Rating Scale
    (RCADS), 75, 98–99, 107, 115,
    118, 148, 178, 200, 256
    depression, 114
    scale, 179
rewarding, 125
risk, 35
    assessments, 99–100
    management, 62–63

risk assessment, 44, 53–63
    areas, 58t
    core components of, 57–61
    factors, 56
    factors influencing, 55–57
    incremental approach, 59
    initial, 57
    in intervention sessions, 57
    risk from others, 54
    risk to others, 54
    risk to self, 54, 62
    scope of, 60
    suicide, 56
    tools, 55
    types of, 54
role clarity, 282
Roscoe, J., 257
Roth, A., 281, 283, 285, 286
routine outcome measures (ROMs), 16,
    42–43t, 42–44, 50, 75–76, 98–99, 114,
    137, 199, 208, 245, 256, 276
Ryan, A., 175

safety plan, 62
scaffolding, 131, 137, 141
school refusal, 172
Schulte, D., 147
screen-based activities, 192
selective attention, 217–219
self-directed interventions, 207
self-evaluation, 165
self-help, 70
self-practice, 283
Self-practice, self-reflection (SP-SR), 97
self-reflection, 283
separation anxiety disorder, 163
service implementation, 240–248
    background, 240–241
    checklist, 243
    context, 240–241
    developing workforce, 242
    operational support, 242–243
    service development, 244–245
service user involvement, 17–18
Session Rating Scale (SRS), 50
shared decision making, 31, 45–47, 76–77,
    100–101
SilverCloud, 73
Sim, L.A., 118
Skinner, B.F., 209

sleep, 193–194
    diary, 197–199
SMART goals, 46, 50
social anxiety, 122, 265
    disorder, 99, 163
Social Learning Theory, 175
Stallard, P., 85, 90
STIC task, 171
stories, 87–89
stress, 282
success, 125
supervision, 253
    case management supervision, 253–256
    LI CBT, 253
    purposes of, 252
    within service, 258–259
    supervision question, 257–258
    use of, 288
    workforce context, 258–259
sustainability, 244

tasks, 169–171
    STIC, 171
Theo, 138
    descriptive formulation diagram, 133
    problem statement, 45
    RCADS, 75f
therapeutic alliance, 37, 93–97
therapeutic model, 151f
therapeutic work, 90
thermometer, 90
thoughts, 212
three-part thought record, 134, 135
Thwaites, R., 283
time-management skills, 34
time-out to calm down, 217–220
Transforming Children and Young People's
    Mental Health: A Green Paper, 9
transparency, 35
treatment goals, 119–125
troubleshooting, 113–114, 171, 199, 203

Tuckman, B.W., 257
Turpin, G., 252

understanding thoughts, 85–86
Unhelpful Hive Belief, 188

Vallance, A.K., 36
values, 14–19
    collaborative practice, 17
    evidence-based practice, 15–16, 16f
    outcome informed practice, 16–17
    participation, 17–18
    service user involvement, 17–18
    working with families and systems,
        18–19
vignettes, 31–33
Vygotsky, L.S., 131, 175

Wang, Z., 118
Watkins, C.E., Jr., 251
Wellman, H.M., 131
Westbrook, D., 134
Wheeler, S., 252
Whiteside, S.P.H., 118
'whole system-based' approach, 4
widening treatment gap, 3–4
Williams, C., 38
Wilt, L.H., 90
Wolpert, D., 99
Worthern, V.E., 43
worthlessness, 56

young people
    low-intensity practice, 8
    psychological practitioners, 8
Children and Young People's Wellbeing
    Practitioner (CWP), 246
    evaluation summary, 248
young person-led metaphor, 89

Zone of Proximal Development, 175